RAF Bomber Command Profiles

90 Squadron

RAF Bomber Command Profiles

90 Squadron

Chris Ward with Shannon Taylor

www.aviationbooks.org

This edition first published 2024 by Aviation Books Ltd., 25 Cromwell Street, Merthyr Tydfil, CF47 8RY.

Copyright 2024 © Chris Ward.

The right of Chris Ward to be identified as Author of this work is asserted by him in accordance with the Copyright, Designs and Patents Act 1988.

The original Operational Record Book of 90 Squadron RAF and the Bomber Command Night Raid Reports are Crown Copyright and stored in microfiche and digital format by the National Archives. Material is reproduced under Open Licence v. 3.0.

All rights reserved. No part of this publication may be reproduced, stored in a retrieval system, transmitted in any form or by any means, electronic, mechanical, or photocopied, recorded or otherwise, without the written permission of the copyright owners.

This squadron profile has been researched, compiled and written by its author, who has made every effort to ensure the accuracy of the information contained in it. The author will not be liable for any damages caused, or alleged to be caused, by any information contained in this book. E. & O.E.

Every effort is made to trace the copyright holders of photographs and we apologise in advance for any unintentional omissions. These and other errors brought to our attention will be corrected in subsequent editions of this Profile.

Cover design: Topics - The Creative Partnership www.topicsdesign.co.uk

Photos and captions: Clare Bennett

A CIP catalogue reference for this book is available from the British Library.

ISBN 9781915335418

Also by Chris Ward from Bomber Command Books:

Casualty of War: Letters Home from Flight Lieutenant Bill Astell DFC

Dambuster Deering: The Life and Death of an Unsung Hero

Dambusters : The Complete WWII History of 617 Squadron
(with Andy Lee and Andreas Wachtel)

Other RAF Bomber Command Profiles:

IX Squadron
10 Squadron (with Ian MacMillan)
35 (Madras Presidency) Squadron
44 (Rhodesia) Squadron
49 Squadron
50 Squadron
57 Squadron
75(NZ) Squadron (with Chris Newey)
83 Squadron
101 Squadron
102 (Ceylon) Squadron
103 Squadron (with David Fell)
106 Squadron (with Herman Bijlard)
115 Squadron
138 Squadron (with Piotr Hodyra)
207 Squadron (with Raymond Glynne-Owen)
300 Squadron (with Grzegorz Korcz)
301, 304 and 305 Squadrons (with Grzegorz Korcz)
405 (Vancouver) Squadron RCAF
408 (Goose) Squadron RCAF
455, 458, 462,464 Squadrons RAAF
460 Squadron RAAF
467 Squadron RAAF
514 Squadron (with Simon Hepworth)
619 Squadron

Table of Contents

Introduction 9
May 1941 12
June 1941 14
July 1941 16
August 1941 20
September 1941 23
1942 27
January 1943 32
February 1943 37
March 1943 44
April 1943 52
May 1943 59
June 1943 65
July 1943 73
August 1943 104
September 1943 113
October 1943 120
November 1943 125
December 1943 131
January 1944 136
February 1944 142
March 1944 147
April 1944 154
May 1944 162
June 1944 196
July 1944 203
August 1944 210
September 1944 219
October 1944 225
November 1944 234

December 1944	240
January 1945	248
February 1945	254
March 1945	261
April 1945	270
Farnborough and the Ju88.	275
A Miscellany of 90 Squadron Photographs	277
Roll of Honour	284
Stations	301
Commanding Officers	301
Aircraft	301
Operational Record	302
Aircraft Histories	303

Introduction

RAF Bomber Command Squadron Profiles first appeared in the late nineties and proved to be very popular with enthusiasts of RAF Bomber Command during the Second World War. They became a useful research tool, particularly for those whose family members had served and were no longer around. The original purpose was to provide a point of reference for all of the gallant men and women who had fought the war, either in the air, or on the ground in a support capacity, and for whom no written history of their unit or station existed. I wanted to provide them with something they could hold up, point to and say, "this was my unit, this is what I did in the war". Many veterans were reticent to talk about their time on bombers, partly because of modesty, but perhaps mostly because the majority of those with whom they came into contact had no notion of what it was to be a "Bomber Boy", to face the prospect of death every time they took to the air, whether during training or on operations. Only those who shared the experience really understood what it was to go to war in bombers, which is why reunions were so important. As they approached the end of their lives, many veterans began to speak openly for the first time about their life in wartime Bomber Command, and most were hurt by the callous treatment they received at the hands of successive governments with regard to the lack of recognition of their contribution to victory. It is sad that this recognition in the form of a national memorial and the granting of a campaign medal came too late for the majority. Now this inspirational, noble generation, the like of which will probably never grace this earth again, has all but departed from us, and the world will be a poorer place as a result.

RAF Bomber Command Squadron Profiles are back. The basic format remains, but, where needed, additional information has been provided. Squadron Profiles do not claim to be comprehensive histories, but rather detailed overviews of the activities of the squadron. There is insufficient space to mention as many names as one would like, but all aircraft losses are accompanied by the name of the pilot. Fundamentally, the narrative section is an account of Bomber Command's war from the perspective of the bomber group under which the individual squadron served, and the deeds of the squadron are interwoven into this story. Information has been drawn from official records, such as group, squadron and station ORBs, and from the many, like me, amateur enthusiasts, who dedicate much of their time to researching individual units, and become unrivalled authorities on them. I am grateful for their generous contributions, and their names will appear in the appropriate Profiles. The statistics quoted in this series are taken from The Bomber Command War Diaries, that indispensable tome written by Martin Middlebrook and Chris Everitt, and I am indebted to Martin for his kind permission to use them.

Finally, let me apologize in advance for the inevitable errors, for no matter how hard I and other authors try to write "nothing but the truth", there is no such thing as a definitive account of history, and there will always be room for disagreement and debate. Official records are notoriously unreliable tools, and yet we have little choice but to put our faith in them. It is not my intention to misrepresent any person or Bomber Command unit, and I ask my readers to understand the enormity of the task I have undertaken. It is relatively easy to become an authority on single units or even a bomber group, but I chose to write about them all, idiot that I am, which means 128 squadrons serving operationally in Bomber Command at some time between the 3rd of September 1939 and the 8th of May 1945. I am dealing with eight bomber groups, in which some 120,000 airmen served, and I am juggling around 28,000 aircraft serial numbers, code letters and details of provenance and fate. I ask not for your sympathy, it was, after all, my choice, but rather your understanding if you should find something with which you disagree. My thanks to you, my readers, for making the original series of RAF Bomber Command Squadron Profiles so popular, and I hope you receive this new incarnation equally enthusiastically.

I am indebted to Shannon Taylor, who provided many photographs and whose passion for 90 Squadron is unrivalled. My thanks are due, as always, to my gang members, Andreas Wachtel, photo editor, Clare Bennett, Steve Smith and Greg Korcz for their unstinting support, without which my Profiles would be the poorer. Finally, my appreciation to my publisher, Simon Hepworth of Aviation Books Ltd, formerly Mention the War Publications, for his belief in my work, untiring efforts to promote it, and for the stress I put him through to bring my books to publication.

Chris Ward. Skegness, Lincolnshire. July 2024.

Dedication

This history of 90 Squadron is dedicated to the memory of P/O Alexander "Sandy" Powell and his crew as representatives of all those men and women who served with the squadron in the air and on the ground and on the RAF stations it inhabited during WWII.

P/O A C Powell Pilot
Sgt J Firth Flight Engineer
Sgt R C Hunter RCAF Navigator
F/O W Picton Bomb-Aimer
Sgt N Wilman Wireless Operator
Sgt R J T Dack Mid-upper Gunner
Sgt L Grice Rear Gunner

Narrative history

First formed on the 8th of October 1917, 90 Squadron was originally a fighter unit, which never achieved operational status before being disbanded on the 3rd of August 1918. Eleven days later it reformed in the home defence role, but was never brought into action, and was disbanded again on the 13th of June 1919. Resurrected in March 1937, the squadron received Blenheims in May, and fulfilled a training role, which eventually saw it absorbed into 17 OTU on the 4th of April 1940.

As preparations were put in hand to reform 90 Squadron in 2 Group, it had already been decided that it was to be given the task of introducing the Boeing B17C to RAF service under the designation Fortress I. Twenty of the type had been gifted to the RAF, and despite strong representations from the USAAC that the B17C, already in their view obsolete, should be restricted to a training role to familiarize crews for the B17E, which was now in production, the RAF had other plans. It intended to employ the aircraft as a high-altitude daylight bomber, hoping to exploit its speed and height capability to evade enemy fighters. The first two examples of the type, AN521 and AN534, were flown over from Gander, Newfoundland, on Easter Monday, the 14th of April 1941, and landed at 06.11 at Ayr after a record-breaking crossing of the Atlantic in eight hours and twenty-six minutes. The former was captained by Major Walshe of the USAAC, who, later in the day, flew it down to Watton to demonstrate it to RAF onlookers, before delivering it to the designated maintenance unit at Burtonwood in Cheshire, where it joined AN534 for conversion to RAF standard. AN521 was then delivered by Major Walshe to the 2 Group station at Watton in Norfolk on the 30th.

May 1941

The plan was to recruit fit, young, experienced airmen with an upper age limit of twenty-four, who were thought to be best able to cope with the rigours of high-altitude flying. They would come from across the Command and be required to take and pass an oxygen test at Farnborough, which simulated flying for four hours at 35,000 feet. Major Walshe took P/O Roake for a dual instruction flight on the 3rd and again on the 4th, and the building of the squadron continued with the arrival from Marham on the 5th of P/O Robertson, who was accompanied by four other airmen from 3 Group's 115 Squadron. They were joined on the 6th by F/O Hawley from 51 Squadron, P/O Boast from 35 Squadron and two airmen from other 4 Group units, and by four more from the same source on the 7th. It was also on the 7th that 90 Squadron was officially reformed at Watton under the command of Wing Commander (W/C) J Macdougall DFC, who was posted in from his command of 101 Squadron at Oakington. Major Walshe flew AN521 to Burtonwood on this day with F/O Hawley and P/Os Robertson and Boast as passengers, and all returned later in AN534, which thus became the first of the twenty Fortress Is to be taken on charge. F/L Bennett DFC arrived from 5 Group's 50 Squadron on the 8th, the day on which W/C Macdougall began his conversion to the B17 under the instruction of Major Walshe, carrying out a fifteen-minute exercise in the morning and another of seventy-five minutes duration in the afternoon. On the morning of the 9th the commanding officer met the crews, to which had now been added P/O Mathieson from 207 Squadron and three other airmen from 5 Group and delivered a lecture on the squadron's future role. Major Walshe then addressed them on the limitations of the aircraft, and in the afternoon talked also about the engines and their management, before he and W/C Macdougall completed a forty-five-minute local flight.

The squadron spent the 10th trying to equip its office accommodation, which was bereft of anything of use. Ground personnel had to be borrowed from 21 and 82 Squadrons, but at least an adjutant had been assigned in the form of F/O Armstrong, and an engineering officer, P/O Boswell. Major Walshe and W/C Macdougall carried out circuits and landings at Great Massingham on this day to ascertain its suitability for Fortress operations, and flew to Burtonwood in AN534 on the 11th, with F/L Bennett and P/O Hawley on board. While W/C Macdougall and F/L Bennett flew to Boscombe Down later in AN534 to learn of bombing trials, Major Walshe and P/O Hawley returned to Watton in AN529, which thus became the second B17 to be taken on charge. Aircrew continued to trickle in, and among those arriving on this day was F/O Barnes DFM from 101 Squadron, who would be appointed gunnery leader. It was decided at group level on the 12th that operations would be conducted from Watton's satellite airfield at Bodney, and both aircraft were flown there that afternoon, only to find that the runway undulated excessively and was unsuitable for the B17. W/C Macdougall travelled to 2 Group HQ at Huntingdon to deliver the bad news, and while he was absent from Watton, Captain Connally, Lieutenant Bradley and Sgt Covington of the USAAC arrived from Boscombe Down to join the squadron.

The decision was taken at group to move squadron operations to Great Massingham, a satellite of West Raynham situated further north in the county of Norfolk, while the crews took up residence at West Raynham, some five miles east-north-east. Despite this, the 13th was spent carrying out circuits and landings at Bodney under the instruction of Major Walshe and Capt Connally. Major Walshe and F/L Bennett flew a B17 from Bodney to Watton on the 14th for an inspection by the 2 Group Air-Officer-Commanding (A-O-C), Air-Vice-Marshal (AVM) Stevenson, who was accompanied by W/C Elworthy, who had just relinquished his command of 82 Squadron to take up duties as an air-staff officer at 2 Group HQ. Following a brief circuit, both expressed themselves to be impressed by the aircraft. During the course of the day, Bomber Command Armaments Inspector, W/C MacDonald, carried out an examination of the B17s, while that evening, a Mr Franklyn Joseph arrived at Watton by car accompanied by a Dr Cawood. The former had flown over from the United States in a Liberator on the 14th of April to advise on the Sperry bomb-sight, on which he was an acknowledged authority. By the end of the day, the squadron's goods and chattels had been packed and prepared for the move, and early on the morning of the 15th, transports arrived from West Raynham to begin the process of moving the squadron lock, stock and barrel to its new home, while the B17s were flown over to Great Massingham. At about this time, the previously-mentioned P/O Roake, having failed the oxygen test at Farnborough, was posted with his crew to the Hampden-equipped 144 Squadron at North Luffenham in the county of Rutland. Shortly after taking-off for an operation on the 7th of September, they crashed at Stamford, and all lost their lives. Having fulfilled their obligations to the move, W/C Macdougall, F/O Skelton and F/O Barnes flew down to Farnborough to subject themselves to the oxygen test, which presumably, they passed.

S/L Robson was posted to the squadron from Benson on the 16th as the Medical Officer, having particular experience in complaints associated with operating at high altitude. Thereafter, whenever weather conditions allowed, conversion training took place under the tutelage of Major Walshe, Capt Connally and Lt Bradley, and lectures familiarised the crews with their new aircraft and the management of its systems. Meanwhile, an inspection of the runway at Great Massingham had suggested a requirement to monitor its condition on a monthly basis, to ensure that it remained serviceable. On the 23rd, HM King George VI held a review of RAF aircraft at Abingdon and was accompanied by the Queen and princesses Elizabeth and Margaret. Also present were Air Marshal Sir Richard Peirse, the Commander-in-Chief (C-in-C) of Bomber Command, and the A-O-C of 6 Group, which at that time was a training group and should not to be confused with the RCAF 6 Group formed on New Year's Day 1943. The aircraft lined up for inspection were a Halifax, a Stirling, a Manchester, a Merlin-powered Wellington, a Maryland, and even a Lancaster, which was in the earliest stages of development, and finally a Fortress I. The royal party spent fifteen minutes at the Fortress, and expressed a great interest in it, before being treated to a fly-past by all of the types on show, both at cruising speed and at full throttle. The Fortress then proceeded directly to Great Massingham, where, earlier in the day, S/L McLaren had arrived from 19 O.T.U at Bicester as flight commander designate.

P/O Wayman and his crew of two were posted in from 21 Squadron at Watton on the 24th and were immediately drafted in as members of S/L McLaren's B17 crew. Three more aircraft, AN521, AN523 and AN527, were flown in on the 25th and taken on charge, and the crews of W/C Macdougall, F/L Bennett and F/O Hawley were cleared for solo flying without an instructor on the 26th, with S/L McLaren and crew still under training. With doubts about the long-term serviceability of Great Massingham in mind, W/C Macdougall and crew carried out an inspection from the air of Polebrook on the 27th, one of the new airfields commissioned by the RAF to be built by George Wimpey and Co in 1940 and 1941 in the Northamptonshire and Huntingdonshire region. Situated south-west of Peterborough, it lay at the extreme western end of 2 Group territory, in an area that would be taken over by the American 8th Air Force in the following year. Crucially, it benefitted from having concrete runways, which as aircraft became heavier in design and bomb-carrying capacity was essential, as was its all-year-round serviceability, in contrast to the tendency of grass airfields to become waterlogged in winter and spring weather conditions.

June 1941

Three further B17s were collected from Burtonwood on the evening of the 3rd, but only one was able to land at Great Massingham because of the presence of very low cloud. F/L Bennett and F/O Hawley spent the night at Coningsby and Sutton Bridge respectively, which no doubt caused a surge of interest on the ground. On the 4th, W/C Macdougall and crew took a Fortress on an altitude test and reached 38,000 feet in a very creditable forty minutes, while still achieving five hundred feet per minute. The purpose of the flight was to test wireless equipment, intercommunications and oxygen and pass on the findings to group signals personnel and representatives of the Royal Aircraft Establishment at Farnborough, who were currently on station. However, using imperfect equipment, the crew began to feel the effects of the extreme altitude, and a conference held at the RAE to discuss the test was attended by W/C Macdougall. Intensive training would occupy the ensuing days, while on the 6th, a review of new aircraft types was carried out at West Raynham attended by the Prime Minister, Winston Churchill, the Lord Privy Seal and future Prime Minister, Clement Atlee, the Secretary of State for War, Chief-of-the-Air-Staff, Sir Charles Portal, the C-in-C bomber Command, the A-O-C 2 Group and a selection of other service dignitaries including General Royce of the USAAC. The aircraft on display were a Fortress I, a Halifax, a Stirling, a Manchester and a Wellington II, with the Lancaster conspicuous this time by its absence. A fly-past followed the inspection, with Major Walshe and Capt Connally at the controls of the B17. The party took lunch in the officers' mess with the station commander and 90 Squadron officers and departed at 16.00.

Over the next two weeks, further height, bombing and firing tests were carried out revealing some of the problems which would dog the aircraft in the months ahead. The principal problems encountered were engine oil leaks, frozen superchargers and guns freezing solid, but it was also proving difficult to get to grips with the oxygen system and a number of accidents occurred, although none resulting in serious consequences. Armament was poor, and when the side gun ports were open the temperature plunged to a very uncomfortable point at somewhere around minus fifty degrees. The aircraft could carry only American bombs and was restricted to a paltry load of between 2,300 and 4,000 lbs, a weight easily carried by the RAF's twin-engine fleet of Hampdens, Whitley's and Wellingtons. On the 22nd, F/O Hawley took off at 14.30 in AN522 for a training flight, and at 18.00 a message was received from RAF Catterick that a Fortress had crashed ten miles to the north with just a single survivor, F/L Steward AFC, a medical officer from Farnborough. He was able to report that the aircraft had entered ice-bearing storm clouds at 33,000 feet over Yorkshire and had collected large amounts of ice on its flying surfaces, while hail stones the size of golf balls had penetrated the fuselage through the open gun ports. The pilot appeared to lose control, upon which the aircraft entered a spin and dived vertically, until a wing was torn off at 25,000 feet and the fuselage broke in two. The G forces and lack of oxygen prevented the occupants in the forward section from abandoning the stricken Fortress, but the rear section, where F/L Steward was stationed, fell at a slower rate, and he was able to jump clear at around 12,000 feet and land safely by parachute. Among the seven fatalities were Lt Bradley of the USAAC, who was part of the team converting the RAF crews, and S/L Robson, the medical officer.

The decision was finally taken to move the squadron to Polebrook, and W/C Macdougall flew over on the 26th to carry out an inspection. The advance party of 90 Squadron travelled by road to Polebrook on the 27th, while F/L Bennett and F/O Boast flew up to Dishforth to attend the funeral of F/O Hawley. The main move took place on the 28th by road and rail, and the rear party concluded the transfer on the 29th, the B17s having been ferried over a few at a time during the three-day period of the move. F/L Bennett was posted to 50 Squadron at Lindholme on the 30th to take up flight commander duties, and responsibility for maintaining the squadron's operations record book (ORB) was handed to P/O Wayman.

July 1941

AN528 had arrived on squadron charge on the 29th of June and had experienced engine problems, which the ground crew worked on throughout the day of the 3rd. While being given its final ground test at 23.00, a fire broke out which could not be contained, and the aircraft burned out. With the squadron's first operation looming, intensive training continued with bombing practice on the 4th at the Ashton range, situated on Polebrook's doorstep a mile or so to the north-west. Bombing practice took place again on the 5th, along with further high-altitude tests, this time with the new station Medical Officer, S/L Bright, involved. The formerly troublesome oxygen system seemed to work well and there were no instances of guns freezing at heights above 30,000 feet. Similar activities occupied the 6th and following an early start for P/O Mathieson and crew on the 7th, when carrying out another bombing practice, the remainder of the day was spent in preparation for the squadron's maiden operation planned for the following day.

Although operating in 2 Group, 90 Squadron was something of a cuckoo with nothing in common with the other members of the host nest. 2 Group itself did not fit comfortably into Bomber Command, which had been forced by serious losses in 1939 to conclude that daylight forays over enemy territory were not viable and had become a largely nocturnal operational organism. 2 Group, in contrast, which began the war with ten operational squadrons, flirted with night operations as required to make up the numbers in 1940, but was intrinsically a daylight force, flying light, twin-engine Blenheim IVs in low-level anti-shipping sweeps and attacks on aerodromes, factories and communications targets mostly in the occupied countries. They engaged also in "circus" and "ramrod" operations, in which they acted as bait to bring the Luftwaffe into a battle of attrition with RAF Spitfires. In circus operations the targets were of secondary importance to the engagement with the Luftwaffe, while the targets for ramrod operations were of primary importance and the engagement with the enemy a planned bi-product. This meant that the high-level role of 90 Squadron in four-engine heavy bombers was anomalous to the group's other activities and one wonders why it found a home in 2 Group at all.

The period into which 90 squadron was shoehorned saw Bomber Command at its lowest ebb and under scrutiny by civil servant David Bensusan-Butt, a member of the War Cabinet Secretariat on the staff of Lord Cherwell (Professor Lindemann), Winston Churchill's chief scientific advisor. He had been commissioned by Cherwell to produce a report on the effectiveness of bomber operations and would study those conducted by night during June and July, when the major Ruhr cities and nearby Cologne shared the spotlight with the north-western port cities of Hamburg and Bremen, with occasional attempts to hit the German cruisers sheltering in Brest. It was a time of failure caused largely by a lack of navigational and bombing aids and a policy of hitting multiple targets simultaneously in pinprick attacks.

At Polebrook, AN519, AN526 and AN529 were made ready during the morning of the 8th, and each was loaded with four 1,100-pounders to be delivered across the target in a single stick. The crews of W/C Macdougall, S/L McLaren and P/O Mathieson attended briefing at 13.00 hours and learned that the Kriegsmarinewerft U-Boot construction yards at Wilhelmshaven were to be the aiming-point, and that they were to fly out in open formation, climbing to 27,000 feet for the attack, before climbing again on the way home to 32,000 feet. They took off at 15.00, with W/C Macdougall and crew in AN526, S/L McLaren and crew in AN519 and P/O Mathieson and crew in AN529, and formed up as they set course while climbing to operational altitude. As they passed through 18,000 feet, W/C Macdougall's astrodome froze over, and this would render fire-control impossible. S/L McLaren's aircraft began to exhibit engine problems in the form of oil leaking from the breather valves on all four power-plants as they reached 20,000 feet and it was spurting out by the time they attained 27,000 feet, leaving an inch-thick frozen deposit on the tailplane and the B17 refusing to climb any higher. The gunners reported a severe vibration, and with the oil pressure falling away rapidly, S/L McLaren opted to bomb a last resort target, which was found on the Frisian island of Norderney, although the bombs failed to hit the town. Shortly after turning back, when still at 27,000 feet, the aircraft began to vibrate so violently that it broke the wireless operator's key, and it would continue for fourteen minutes while S/L McLaren shed height, losing twelve thousand feet in the first four minutes. At 4,000 feet the ice broke away and the vibration ceased, allowing a safe return to base.

Meanwhile, W/C Macdougall and P/O Mathieson had reached the target and dropped their bombs across it from 28,000 and 30,000 feet respectively at 16.50 and 17.00, the latter observing the first of his bombs to fall to the west of the Bauhafen aiming-point and the others at 150-yard intervals to the south-east. W/C Macdougall observed the bursts on the target of two of his bombs, but realised that the remaining two had hung up and made a second unsuccessful pass. He attempted to release them over the East Frisians on the way home, but they resolutely refused to drop and would have to be brought home. Shortly afterwards, two BF109s were spotted forty miles north of the island of Terschelling at 30,000 feet, two thousand feet below the B17s. They climbed and approached to within six hundred yards on the starboard beam, before one of them appeared to fall into an involuntary spin and was last seen some six hundred feet below still out of control. The second enemy aircraft broke away to follow the first one down and no fire was exchanged. Both B17s arrived home safely, where it was discovered that the electrical failure of their cameras had resulted in the absence of a visual record of the squadron's maiden operation.

A new Air Ministry directive issued on the 9th signalled an end to the maritime diversion, which had been in force since March, as it was now assessed that the enemy's transportation system and the morale of its civilian population represented the weakest points, and that Peirse should direct his main effort in these directions. A new list of targets was drawn up that included all of the main railway centres ringing the industrial Ruhr, the destruction of which would inhibit the import of raw materials and the export of finished products. Railways were relatively precise targets, and were to be attacked during the moon period, while on moonless nights, the Rhine cities of Cologne, Düsseldorf and Duisburg would be easier to locate for "area" attacks. During periods of less favourable weather conditions, Peirse was to launch operations against more distant objectives in northern, eastern and southern Germany, while still making the occasional concession to the U-Boot campaign and continuing to divert a proportion of the Command's resources to the ongoing situation of the enemy "fleet in being" at Brest.

Flight testing and crew training continued for the ensuing two weeks as attempts were made to iron out the teething problems associated with the Fortress I, and new recruits arrived to bolster squadron strength. P/O Stokes and P/O Hart were Blenheim pilots who were posted in from XV and 101 Squadrons respectively on the 12th, and there were commissions for pilots MacDonald and Sturmey a few days later. Operational crews were put on stand-by on the 15th and 16th, but no orders were confirmed, while the experienced Hampden and Manchester pilot, F/O Dave Romans DFC, arrived from 207 Squadron at Waddington on the 19th. On the 21st, W/C Macdougall spent twenty minutes at 38,000 feet in AN530, during which time the oxygen system worked satisfactorily, although some ice formed on the masks. Four new crews were completely or partially formed from among the available personnel, with P/Os Sturmey, Taylor and Stokes and Sgt Brown as first pilots and captains, and respectively, P/Os Franks, Hart and MacDonald and Sgt Hindshaw as second pilots. The Taylor, Stokes and Brown crews were, as yet, lacking gunners, and another pilot, P/O Tuckwell, was posted in from 4 Group's Halifax-equipped 76 Squadron on the 22nd.

An operation to Berlin by three aircraft was planned for the 23rd, with Kiel as an alternative target, and the same three crews attended briefing at 06.30 to learn of the details. F/L Mathieson and crew would retain AN529, while W/C Macdougall and S/L McLaren and their crews were given AN530 and AN523 respectively and departed Polebrook during a five-minute slot either side of 09.00, before setting course for the Danish coast. Before reaching an area of clear sky over the North Sea, they would have to climb through storm-laden ten-tenths cumulus cloud with tops at 20,000 feet, a frequent meteorological feature that acted as a gatekeeper protecting north-western Germany. S/L McLaren was unable to maintain altitude and remain in the formation and turned back when at 23,000 feet and some sixty miles from the coast of southern Jutland. The remaining two pressed on across Jutland for fifty-eight miles at 32,000 feet, until the formation of condensation trails advertised their presence and W/C Macdougall abandoned the operation.

That night, thirty Whitleys were sent to attack the dry dock at La Pallice, the deep-water port located west of La Rochelle on the Biscay coast between St-Nazaire to the north and Bordeaux to the south. It was home to the 3rd U-Boot Flotilla that was feeding wolfpacks into the Atlantic to savage Allied convoys bringing vital supplies to Britain. However, the objective for this operation was the cruiser Scharnhorst, which had slipped away from Brest unnoticed and was feared to be about to break out into the Atlantic for a campaign of surface raiding. A most complex plan under the codename Operation Sunrise had been developed during the preceding week to target Scharnhorst and Gneisenau at Brest in daylight on the 24th, but the discovery that Scharnhorst had slipped away and was now at berth at La Pallice, some two hundred miles further south, demanded a last-minute alteration. It was decided to send the 4 Group Halifax element to attend to her, while the original plan went ahead at Brest.

This called for three Fortress 1s of 90 Squadron to open proceedings at 30,000 feet to draw up the enemy fighters, while eighteen 5 Group Hampdens acted as further bait at a less extreme altitude under the umbrella of a Spitfire escort, somewhat in the manner of a 2 Group "circus" operation to allow the RAF fighters to get amongst the BF109s, BF110s and FW190s. This was intended to leave the way clear for the seventy-nine Wellingtons, twenty-four from 1 Group, thirty-six representing 3 Group and nineteen Mk IIs of 4 Group, to sneak in and attack the objectives unescorted. The Wellingtons flew to forward bases, while the crews of W/C Macdougall, S/L McLaren and F/L Mathieson departed Polebrook between 11.20 and 11.30 with a time on target of 14.00 and arrived to find clear skies and good visibility. The Macdougall and McLaren crews delivered four 1,100-pounders each from 30,000 feet and the

Mathieson crew from 32,000 feet between 14.06 and 14.10 and observed bursts on the torpedo station along the western side of the Quay at Rade Abri and on the outer corner of the dry dock. Two single-engine enemy fighters were seen at a distance at 14.15 and three BF109s climbed steeply towards the trio but made no contact before disappearing from sight. Flak was observed to burst a thousand feet below and behind, but the operation for the Fortresses was largely uneventful and concluded with safe landings between 15.30 and 15.45.

It was a different experience for the Wellington crews, however, who on approaching the French coast discovered that the flak and fighter opposition was going to be much more intense than had been expected, with many engagements took place between fighters and bombers. Ten of the Wellingtons and two Hampdens were brought down, in exchange for which were claimed a number of unconfirmed hits on Gneisenau. Meanwhile to the south, Scharnhorst suffered more severely at La Pallice, while inflicting heavy casualties on the attacking Halifaxes, all of which were damaged by flak and five shot down, and she was forced to return to Brest to take advantage of the superior repair facilities on offer.

The crews of F/L Mathieson and Sgt Wood attended briefing at Polebrook at 04.30 on the 26th to learn of their part in an operation against a railway junction in Hamburg with Bremen or the port of Emden as the alternatives. Sgt Wood was to be crew captain for the first time with P/O Stokes as second pilot, and the two B17s took off together at 07.30, each carrying four 1,100-pounders. They headed for landfall on the enemy coast via the Dutch Frisians but were confronted by the "gatekeeper", the towering, thunder-filled cloud formation extending to 30,000 feet and beyond, which persuaded Sgt Wood and crew to turn back when some thirty miles short of Vlieland. They returned the bombs to the dump, while F/L Mathieson and crew managed to push through the conditions and bombed Emden from 32,000 feet, observing bursts in the north-western built-up area. On the way home, both port engines began to falter, and an emergency landing was carried out at Horsham-St-Faith.

W/C Macdougall was posted out on this day to be succeeded by the experienced former commanding officer of 21 Squadron, W/C Webster. His war had begun in the rank of flying officer with 15 Squadron, with which he initially served in France as part of the Advanced Air Striking Force (AASF) flying Fairey Battles. After the squadron had been withdrawn to the UK and transferred to 2 Group in December 1939, he continued his operational career on Blenheims. He had been in the thick of the air battles during the fall of the Low Countries and France in May and June 1940, by which time he had risen to the rank of squadron leader and flight commander, eventually taking over command of 21 Squadron on the failure to return of his predecessor.

F/L Mathieson and crew returned to Horsham-St-Faith to collect AN530 on the 27th, and P/O Sturmey and crew carried out a height test on a flight between Catterick and Prestwick and achieved 38,000 feet. They made a further altitude climb during the morning of the 28th, and F/Sgt Brooks and crew took off in AN534 for a similar test at 17.00, only to encounter severe turbulence, which led to the loss of a wing and a crash near Wilbarston, some four miles to the west of Corby in Northamptonshire, in which there were no survivors from among the six occupants.

During the course of the month the squadron conducted four operations and dispatched eleven sorties for the loss of two B17s and one crew.

August 1941

As a result of the unique altitude capabilities of the Fortress I and its lack of suitability to engage in 2 Group operations generally, 90 Squadron would plough a lonely furrow, operating independently of the rest of the bomber force. On the 2nd, the crews of P/O Sturmey and the newly promoted S/L Mathieson were briefed for high altitude attacks on the Baltic coast port of Kiel, the importance of which was based on the three shipbuilding yards, Deutsche Werke, Krupp-Germania Werft and Howaldtswerke, which were predominantly producing U-Boots. They departed Polebrook at 13.38 and 13.41 respectively at the same time as another B17C took off on a training sortie. P/O Sturmey mistakenly formated on the training aircraft and by the time the mistake was realised, he was unable to catch up with S/L Mathieson and returned to base. S/L Mathieson and crew, meanwhile, continued on to reach the target at 33,000 feet and delivered four 1,100-pounders at 17.35, observing columns of smoke rising from a point some two hundred yards south of Kiel Fjord, and returned safely to report no flak or fighter opposition. P/O Sturmey and crew departed Polebrook for the second time at 17.15 bound for the port of Emden, located on the western side of the Niedersachsen headland that forms Germany's north-western frontier with Holland. Cloud developed to eight-tenths over the Frisian Islands, threatening total cover in the target area, and it was decided to bomb the Frisian Island of Borkum as an alternative, releasing the four 1,100-pounders from 32,000 feet without observing the outcome. When homebound some twenty miles north-west of Texel at 22,000 feet, two BF109s engaged the B17C, scoring some hits and inflicting minor damage, but the attacks were not pressed home and a burst of return fire that hit the engine of one assailant was sufficient to discourage a further attack.

There was an early start for the crews of S/L Mathieson and P/O Sturmey on the 6th as they departed Polebrook at 06.38 and 06.40 in AN529 and AN523 respectively bound for Brest to attack Scharnhorst and Gneisenau. They climbed steadily as they made their way south and S/L Mathieson and crew had reached 33,000 feet as they began the bombing run, only to find that ice accretion on the bomb sight prevented an accurate attack and the bombs were jettisoned "live" over the general area, detonating in the sea in the Rade Abri to the south-east of Laninon. The Sturmey crew attacked from 32,000 feet and watched their bombs also fall harmlessly into the Rade Abri. No fighters were encountered, which was fortunate as the twin upper and two lower guns in AN529 froze up and could not be made serviceable.

A special daylight operation was planned by 2 Group on the 12th to target the Knapsack and Quadrath power stations near Cologne with fifty-four Blenheims. The intention was to persuade the Luftwaffe to withdraw fighter resources from the eastern front to protect vital German assets and thus assist Russian forces, which had suffered heavy defeats following the opening of Operation Barbarossa in June. Diversionary operations involving other Blenheims and Hampdens at locations in France were to take place under Spitfire escorts, but the Cologne area was beyond range and the main event would be unescorted. 90 Squadron briefed the crews of P/Os Sturmey, Taylor and Wayman and Sgt Wood for high-level attacks on Cologne, De Kooy aerodrome and Emden and dispatched them from Polebrook between 09.00 and 10.03, each carrying the standard load of four 1,100-pounders. Sgt Wood and crew were heading south over Oxfordshire and were climbing through 14,000 feet when forced to turn back because of an issue with the port-inner engine, while P/O Sturmey and crew were heading almost due east with the shortest trip ahead of them, the hour-long crossing of the North Sea to De Kooy aerodrome located on the eastern side of the peninsula south of Den Helder. They had reached 32,000 feet by the time that they ran across the aiming point to release their payload, but cloud prevented them from observing the outcome. They faced no opposition and landed at base after a round trip of two hours and twenty-five minutes. P/O Wayman and crew had been assigned to an undisclosed target in Cologne but were unable to locate it through cloud from 34,000 feet and selected a built-up area some three thousand yards to the north-east. One bomb fell away, and its impact was not observed, while the remaining three hung up and were released late. P/O Taylor and crew attacked Emden from 33,000 feet on e.t.a. in the face of cloud cover, observing nothing of the outcome, and were the last to land, at 13.50, after three hours and forty-seven minutes aloft.

Meanwhile, the main event in the Cologne area was claimed as a success but proved to be expensive, costing Bomber Command twelve Blenheims and Fighter Command six Spitfires in return for ten Luftwaffe fighters destroyed or probably destroyed.

The same four 90 Squadron crews were on duty again on the 16th, when Brest and Düsseldorf were the destinations respectively for P/Os Sturmey and Wayman and P/O Taylor and Sgt Wood, and it was the former pair who departed Polebrook first at 09.03 briefed to locate the heavily camouflaged Scharnhorst and Gneisenau at their berth. What would prove to be an eleven-month-long saga had begun at the end of March, when the two vessels had arrived at Brest to take shelter, where they would be joined on occasions by the Hipper Class cruiser Prinz Eugen, Bismarck's consort during the Battle of the Denmark Straits in May, which had resulted in the shocking loss of HMS Hood and eventually Bismarck. The British press decided to have fun with the initials of the German cruisers and dubbed them as Salmon & Gluckstein, in a comic reference to Britain's largest tobacconist, established in 1873 by a German Jewish émigré and his English partner. Until their breakout from Brest in February 1942, the vessels would be a thorn in the flesh of Bomber Command and a major distraction as the Admiralty, paranoid about their presence as "a fleet in being", pressed for them to be attacked at every opportunity.

P/O Wayman and crew attacked from 35,000 feet and were denied by cloud from observing the outcome, but faced only slight, inaccurate flak and returned safely after a sortie lasting three hours and fifty-two minutes. P/O Sturmey and crew arrived on target a little later at 32,000 feet and further to the west, by which time the Luftwaffe had alerted fighters, and they appeared on the scene shortly after the bombs had been released. According to the survivors, two Heinkel 113s and five BF109s attacked in what must have been the highest interception ever, but as Heinkel 113s were a propaganda myth, we must assume that they were FW190s. AN523's upper rearward-firing gun was unserviceable and early during the engagement the three gunners were killed, and another member of the crew wounded. The Fortress sustained extensive damage and unable to climb to evade his assailants, P/O Sturmey began to descend while taking evasive action and was at 6,000 feet by the time the enemy broke away with the English coast in sight. He attempted to land the crippled Fortress at Roborough near Plymouth, but overshot and crashed, fortunately without further casualties, but the aircraft was consumed by fire. This operation demonstrated that extreme altitude did not afford the expected protection from fighters, and it probably came as something of a shock that the one attribute setting it apart from other bombers was ineffective.

On the 18th, the Butt Report on the Command's operational effectiveness was released, and it sent shock waves reverberating around the War Cabinet and the Air Ministry. Having taken into account around four thousand bombing photos produced during night operations in June and July, it concluded that only a fraction of bombs had fallen within miles of their intended targets, and the poorest performances had been over the Ruhr. It was a massive blow to morale and demonstrated that thus far the efforts of the crews had been almost totally ineffective in reducing Germany's capacity to wage war. The claims of the crews were shown to be wildly optimistic, as were those of the Command, and Sir Richard Peirse's tenure as Commander-in-Chief would forever be blighted by the report's conclusions. In addition, the report provided ammunition for those seeking the dissolution of an independent bomber force, principally the Admiralty, which was calling for the redistribution of bombers to combat the U-Boot menace in the Atlantic, while others pointed to reversals in the Middle East as a pressing need.

An early start on the 19th saw the crews of P/O Wayman and Sgt Wood depart Polebrook at 05.42 and 05.44 bound for undisclosed targets in the Ruhr city of Düsseldorf, and both had reached 35,000 feet and were a few miles off Walcheren Island at the mouth of the Scheldt when frozen guns and the formation of condensation trails from 25,000 feet persuaded them to turn back and bring their bombs home. Two days later, the crews of Sgt Wood, S/L Mathieson and P/O Wayman took off between 06.45 and 06.55 bound for the same destination and encountered similar conditions and frozen guns that compelled Sgt Wood and crew to abandon their sortie at 30,000 feet before even reaching the midpoint of the North Sea crossing, while S/L Mathieson and crew abandoned theirs on arrival over Walcheren at 35,000 feet. P/O Wayman and crew penetrated some twenty miles inland to reach the Dordrecht area of Holland at 36,000 feet, before the superchargers failed on both inner engines and the bombs were dumped in the sea on the way home.

A further attempt to reach Düsseldorf on the 29th proved to be another frustrating and disappointing experience, as first Sgt Wood and crew were unable to take off at 06.20 because of an engine issue, while P/O Wayman and crew did get away at the same time and progressed as far as the Scheldt estuary at 33,000 feet, only to be thwarted by cloud, condensation trails and engine issues. Finally, on the 31st, Sgt Wood and crew managed to reach their assigned target of Bremen in AN518 after departing Polebrook at 14.53 as one of three crews assigned to individual targets. It was not a trouble-free sortie, however, as the bombs hung up initially and had to be jettisoned "live" from 31,000 feet, their detonation masked by cloud. The newly promoted F/O Wayman and crew had taken off at 14.51 bound for Kiel and were heavily engaged by flak when at 32,000 feet over Heligoland, shortly after which, engine issues persuaded them to curtail their sortie and head for Den Helder as an alternative target. On arrival they encountered cloud and brought their load, consisting on this occasion of just two 1,100-pounders, back to base. S/L Mathieson and crew had been last to take off, at 14.54, and were bound for Hamburg, employing Heligoland as a pinpoint before turning south for the bombing run. At 30,000 feet an issue developed affecting the port-outer engine and it was decided to bomb Heligoland as a last resort target. A square search failed to locate it and the four 1,100-

pounders were eventually dropped towards the Frisian Island of Spiekeroog but missed and fell into the sea.

During the course of the month the squadron carried out ten operations, four of them by single aircraft, and dispatched eighteen sorties for the loss of a single Fortress and three crew members.

September 1941

September's operational account opened for 90 Squadron on the 2nd with the briefing of the crews of S/L Mathieson, P/O Sturmey and Sgt Wood for the next round of high-level attacks on individual targets, respectively Bremen and Hamburg in north-western Germany and Duisburg on the western edge of the Ruhr. Sgt Wood and crew departed Polebrook first at 13.30 and progressed as far as Newbury in Berkshire before the intercom failed and brought a premature end to their sortie. The Mathieson and Sturmey crews took off at 14.00 and 14.05, the former with Mr Vose of the Sperry Bombsight Company flying as bomb-aimer, and they headed out over the Norfolk coast to begin the North Sea crossing. The Sturmey crew flew parallel to the Frisian Islands with the intention of pinpointing on Heligoland and encountered ten-tenths cloud at between 25,000 and 30,000 feet, which boded ill for their chances of seeing the target, and when condensation trails began to form as they approached Heligoland, they decided to turn back and return the four 1,100-pounders to the bomb dump. Meanwhile, S/L Mathieson and crew had made landfall over the Dutch coast and reached Bremen under largely clear skies to deliver their payload from 30,000 feet, observing one bomb to burst within the town area and three outside. Heavy flak followed them from the target to the coast, but no fighters were evident, and they returned safely to base after five hours in the air.

During the morning of the 4th, the crews of F/O Romans, P/O Sturmey and Sgt Wood were briefed for their sorties, while out on their dispersal pans AN533, AN532 and AN518 were being loaded with four 1,100-pounders each, the first two-mentioned for use against the northern city of Hannover and the last-mentioned, Hamburg. Sgt Wood and crew took off at 14.10 bound for the latter in the same aircraft that had let them down two days earlier, and this time they had progressed some fifty miles out over the North Sea before the same fault occurred to end their interest in proceedings. The crews of P/O Sturmey and F/O Romans departed Polebrook at 14.10 and 14.20 respectively bound for Hannover, a city that was a major contributor to the German war effort and home among others to the Accumulatoren-Fabrik A G, manufacturers of lead acid batteries for U-Boots and torpedoes, the Continental tyre and rubber factory at Limmer, the Deurag-Nerag synthetic oil refinery at Misburg, the VLW (Volkswagen) metalworks, and the Maschinenfabrik Niedersachsen Hannover and Hanomag factories, which were producing guns and tracked vehicles. P/O Sturmey and crew were at 30,000 feet some sixty miles short of Heligoland when the port-outer engine failed and left them with no choice but to jettison the bombs and turn for home. The engine provided the power for the bomb doors, which had to be hand-cranked to the closed position. There were no condensation trails on this occasion, but in the distance, two enemy fighters could be seen trailing the other Fortress. Frustratingly, as P/O Sturmey descended through 20,000 feet, the port-outer engine came back to life. The stalkers had been spotted and F/O Romans climbed away at 1,500 feet per minute to leave them behind, but at 31,000 feet condensation trails formed and it was decided to seek an alternative target. They headed south and bombed the docks at Rotterdam, well out of reach of the heavy flak that sought to bring them down and landed safely after three hours and fifteen minutes aloft.

On the 5th, four aircraft plus a reserve were made ready to send north to a forward base at Kinloss in the Moray region of north-western Scotland for an operation on the 6th against the surface raider, Admiral Scheer, currently at anchor in Oslo harbour. During the early thirties, Hitler had sanctioned the construction of three so-called "pocket battleships" to circumvent the restrictions imposed after the Great War under the Treaty of Versailles. The Deutschland class Graf Spee, Admiral Scheer and Deutschland, later renamed Lützow, were fast cruisers with heavy armament, and even before the outbreak of war, had been sent roaming the oceans in preparation for the signal to begin attacking merchant vessels. After a highly successful tour in the Atlantic between the African and south American coasts, the Graf Spee was cornered in Montivideo harbour during the Battle of the River Plate in December 1939 and in the midst of world-wide publicity, was scuttled a few miles outside of the port. The crews of S/L Mathieson, F/O Romans, P/O Sturmey and Sgt Wood headed north with S/L McLaren in command of the reserve aircraft, which was carrying maintenance personnel and spares. They departed Kinloss at 08.00 and Sgt Wood's run of ill-luck continued with the failure of the turbo on the starboard-inner engine when at 15,000 feet some fifty miles into the outward flight. The others reached the target but failed to identify the vessel, and all bombed the docks area from around 30,000 feet without observing the results, before returning to Kinloss after up to five-and-three-quarter-hours in the air.

They remained in Scotland awaiting another opportunity and the arrival of more American bombs by road from Polebrook, and it was 09.15 on the 8th when the crews of F/O Romans, P/O Sturmey and Sgt Wood took to the air, ten minutes ahead of that of S/L Mathieson. What followed was a disaster for the squadron, beginning when AN525 was attacked by fighters at 25,000 feet, and despite shooting one down, crashed in mountainous country at 11.27 with no survivors from the crew of F/O Romans DFC, an officer who had served with distinction on Hampdens with 5 Group's 44 Squadron in 1940 and on Manchesters with 207 Squadron in 1941. AN533 also fell victim to BF109s and disappeared without trace, presumably in the sea, with the crew of S/L Mathieson. Sgt Wood and crew abandoned their sortie at 11.30 and jettisoned the bomb load in the mountains, before climbing to 34,000 feet to evade the fighters, and it was at that inopportune moment that an oxygen system failure left various crew members in dire straits. Sgt Wood had no choice but to reduce height and they were passing through 24,000 feet when a fighter attacked from close range, injuring both gunners, one of them fatally. With one engine dead and the others hit, Sgt Wood began the long journey back to Kinloss, where AN535 was crash-landed without further casualties. P/O Sturmey and crew abandoned their sortie when at 27,500 feet some eighty miles short of Oslo on encountering ten-tenths cloud that stretched out ahead of them to beyond the target area, and on return to Kinloss reported observing the end of the Romans crew. On the 9th, the crews of P/O Sturmey and Sgt Wood searched some three thousand square miles of the North Sea and a number of Whitleys were dispatched also, but no sign of S/L Mathieson and his crew was sighted, and their loss would be keenly felt by the squadron and Polebrook communities.

The crews of S/L McLaren and P/O Sturmey returned to Polebrook on the 10th with ground crew and equipment, while Sgt Wood and crew took the train. Fighter affiliation exercises and conferences followed in an attempt to find a strategy to combat the vulnerability of the Fortress to fighter attack, but the frequent technical failures and the guarantee of condensation trails to advertise their presence over enemy territory challenged the entire point of their existence as high-level daylight bombers. On the 15th, F/O Wayman and crew were briefed for a high-altitude attack on Cologne and departed Polebrook at 13.05, reaching 32,000 feet over the North Sea and announcing their position to the enemy with their vapour trails. At the Dutch coast the condensation trails of enemy fighters were seen turning towards the Fortress, and it was decided to abandon the sortie and return to base with their two 2,000-pounders. P/O Sturmey and crew took off at 13.10 on the 16th for another attempt to reach Cologne, but an issue with the port-inner engine, illness of a crew member and the sight of enemy vapour trails in the distance persuaded them to turn back when thirty miles short of the Dutch coast. The target was switched to the port of Emden on the 20th, for which P/O Sturmey and crew departed Polebrook at 12.55 and made it all the way without condensation trails forming. The target was attacked with four 1,100-pounders from 32,000 feet and two columns of smoke were evidence that something combustible had been hit.

On the 21st, P/O Sturmey and crew were made available to a film crew from Warner Bros Film Studios for ground and air shots of aircraft and crew for inclusion in the film "Flying-Fortress". On the 24th, F/L McLaren attended an investiture at Buckingham Palace to receive his DFC from the hand of HM King George VI. Emden was posted again as the target on the 25th, for which P/O Sturmey and crew took off at 12.00, unaware that they were conducting the final sortie in the B17C's short RAF operational career. On this occasion heavy vapour trails did form at 27,000 feet and persisted, and the sortie was abandoned fifty miles short of the Dutch coast. On the way home the bottom gunner's electrically-heated flying suit caught fire and had to be removed. No further operations were attempted, and although the squadron remained intact as a functional unit and conducted fighter affiliation exercises and training for another five months, it was clear that operations with the Fortress in winter were not feasible.

During the course of the month the squadron operated on eight occasions, dispatching eighteen sorties for the loss of two Fortresses and crews and an additional gunner.

In October, a detachment of four aircraft was sent to the Middle East, where it became absorbed into 220 Squadron, and from that point until disbandment on the 12th of February 1942, the home echelon entered into a period of limbo, continuing to fly the Fortress non-operationally along with Blenheims. For Sir Richard Peirse, September and October had been a time of frustration, brought about largely by unfavourable weather conditions, and with the damning Butt Report still fresh in the mind, he was desperate to strike a telling blow at a target in Germany. Conditions over the targets had been persistently unfavourable, and a number of operations had been subject to a recall while the crews were outbound over the North Sea. Even when conditions had allowed sight of the ground, results were disappointing, and aircraft and crews continued to be frittered away for little return. It was perhaps this situation which prompted a major night of operations to be planned for the night of the 7/8th of November, the main event of which was an intended assault on Berlin by a force of over two hundred aircraft. Doubts about the weather led to an objection from the 5 Group A-O-C, and he was allowed to withdraw his element and send it instead to Cologne. The night's order of battle ultimately saw 169 aircraft take off for Berlin, while seventy-five Hampdens and Manchesters from 5 Group headed for Cologne, and fifty-three Wellingtons and two Stirlings from 1 and 3 Groups set off for Mannheim. Together with those involved in the night's extensive minor operations, the total number of sorties despatched was a new record of 392.

Sadly, this massive effort was not rewarded with success as fewer than half of the Berlin contingent reached the outskirts of the city to bomb, and damage was restricted to fourteen houses destroyed and an equal number damaged, along with an item or two of an industrial or municipal nature. In return for this, twenty-one aircraft were lost, and although there were no casualties among the Cologne force, it too had failed dismally, and managed to destroy only two houses. No bombs at all fell on Mannheim, but seven Wellingtons failed to return home, and when these were added to the nine aircraft missing from the minor operations, the total stood at thirty-seven, more than twice the previous highest for a single night. This was the final straw for the War Cabinet, and Peirse was summoned to an uncomfortable meeting at Chequers with Churchill to make his explanations. On the 13th, he was ordered to restrict further activity, while the future of Bomber Command was considered at the highest level.

The remainder of November was very low key, and apart from two raids on Hamburg and one each on Emden and Düsseldorf, operations consisted mainly of small-scale attacks on ports in Germany and the occupied countries. 90 Squadron could only watch from the sidelines, while continuing a programme of training flights in Fortresses, and the main excitement came with the return of the Warner Bros film crew on the 4th accompanied by the celebrated actor, Richard Greene, a "heartthrob", who was playing a lead role in the movie Flying Fortress. Although highly successful in his film career, he would become best known in the 1950s for portraying Robin Hood in a television series of more than 140 episodes. While at Polebrook, Greene was actually serving with the 27th Lancers, having obtained a release from Fox, his film studio, in order to enlist and had earned a commission. Filming occupied a number of days, while training went on around and on the 15th W/C Webster went on leave pending his imminent posting to 2 Group HQ, leaving S/L James Swain in command. On the 21st S/L Swain was confirmed as the new commanding officer and was promoted to acting wing commander rank accordingly. Sadly, W/C Webster would lose his life on the 1st of March 1944 while test-flying a Fairey Firefly.

The main fare during December was Brest, where the Scharnhorst and Gneisenau and occasionally Prinz Eugen continued to shelter and no fewer than thirteen operations were directed at the port and its lodgers by small numbers of aircraft, and this situation would continue into the coming year. 1941 had been a bad year for the Command, with few advances made on the performances of 1940, and most disappointingly, the three aircraft types, the Stirling, Halifax and Manchester, introduced to operations in the early part of the year, had all failed to meet expectations and each had undergone long periods of grounding while essential modifications were carried out. The Butt Report had been just the official label applied to the results of what had perhaps been unrealistic expectations on the part of the policy makers and Peirse had done his utmost to fulfil the demands placed upon him by his masters. The crews also had done their best with the equipment available at the time, but their best simply was not good enough in the face of an as yet, all-conquering enemy.

1942

AM Sir Richard Peirse left his post as C-in-C Bomber Command on the 8th of January to be succeeded temporarily by AVM Baldwin, the A-O-C 3 Group. In February, Peirse would take up a new appointment as C-in-C Allied Air Forces in India and South-East Asia, but the sense that he had been "sacked" from Bomber Command would linger, and perhaps unjustly tarnish his legacy.

The long-running saga at Brest was finally resolved in February following the final attack on the port and its German cruiser guests by eighteen Wellingtons of 1 Group on the evening of the 11th. As the sound of RAF engines receded into the eastern cloud-filled skies, Vice-Admiral Otto Cilliax, the Brest Group commander, whose flag was on Scharnhorst, put Operation Cerberus into action at 21.14, Scharnhorst, Gneisenau and Prinz Eugen slipping anchor, before heading into the English Channel under an escort of destroyers and E-Boats. It was an audacious bid for freedom, covered by bad weather, widespread jamming and meticulously planned support by the Kriegsmarine and the Luftwaffe, all of which had been rehearsed extensively during January. The planning, and a little good fortune, allowed the fleet to make undetected progress until spotted off Le Touquet by two Spitfires piloted by G/C Victor Beamish, the commanding officer of Kenley, and W/C Finlay Boyd, both of whom maintained radio silence and did not report their find until landing at 10.42 on the morning of the 12th.

The British authorities had prepared a plan in advance for precisely this eventuality under the Codename, Operation Fuller, and once the enemy fleet was spotted in the late morning, frantic efforts were made to deploy Bomber and Coastal Command and Fleet Air Arm aircraft, and it was after 13.00 before the first sorties took off in an attempt to intercept the enemy fleet off the Belgian and later the Dutch coasts. Some aircraft made contact in the most challenging weather conditions of squalls and low cloud with a base at 300 feet and carried out attacks while under fire from shipborne flak and Luftwaffe fighters. They were part of the largest commitment of aircraft by daylight in the war to date, amounting to 242 sorties, but the Germans had expertly timed their break-out to exploit the weather conditions and there had been little chance of a successful outcome for the British forces. Operation Fuller cost Bomber Command fifteen aircraft, 5 Group alone posting missing nine Hampdens and crews, all lost in the North Sea, six of them without trace, and they could be added to all of those sacrificed to this endeavour over the past eleven months.

The enemy fleet made good its escape into open sea, although its own trials and tribulations were not yet over. Scharnhorst struck a mine in the late afternoon and began to fall back, and at 19.55, a magnetic mine detonated close enough to Gneisenau, when off Terschelling, to open a small hole in the starboard side, and temporarily slow her progress also. Later still, at 21.34, when passing through the same stretch of water, Scharnhorst hit another mine which stopped both engines and damaged steering and fire control. The vessel got under way again at 22.23 using its starboard engines and making twelve knots, while carrying an additional one thousand tons of seawater. The day's activities were not yet over for 5 Group, and the crews of fourteen Hampdens and nine Manchesters were briefed to lay mines in the Nectarine gardens off the Frisians through which the enemy fleet would have to pass to reach safety.

Gneisenau and Prinz Eugen arrived at the Elbe Estuary at 07.00 on the 13th, and tied up at Brunsbüttel North Locks at 09.30, while Scharnhorst arrived at Wilhelmshaven at 10.00 with three months-worth of damage to repair. The mines had been laid almost certainly by 5 Group Hampdens over the preceding nights and demonstrated the remarkable effectiveness of this war-long campaign. The "Channel Dash" as it came to be known was a huge embarrassment to the government and the nation, but if nothing else, this annoying itch had been scratched for the last time and the Command could now focus its energies on the strategic targets to which it was better suited.

The 12th was also the day on which 90 Squadron was disbanded for the fourth time in its history and would spend the next ten months on the shelf awaiting yet another resurrection. W/C Swain and most of the aircrew were posted to 1653 Conversion Unit pending reassignment, while a number were posted to the newly reforming 159 and 160 Squadrons, which were about to be posted to the Middle East and later India operating B24 Liberators. W/C Swain would be appointed to command 1 Group's 100 Squadron at Grimsby (Waltham) on the 26th of December 1942 and lose his life during an operation to Stettin on the night of the 20/21st of April 1943.

Many changes would take place during the squadron's time on the shelf as a number only. Two days after its disbandment, a new Air Ministry directive was handed down, which reaffirmed the assault on the morale of the enemy's civilian population, particularly its workers, and authorised the blatant area bombing of Germany's urban centres. This had, of course, been going on for a considerable time, but the new directive swept away the pretence that crews were aiming for specific industrial and military targets within the cities being bombed. Waiting in the wings, and, in fact, at this very moment, four days into his voyage from the United States in the armed merchantman, Alcantara, was a new leader, a man well-known to 5 Group, who not only would pursue this policy with a will, but also possessed the self-belief, arrogance and stubbornness to fight his corner against all-comers on behalf of his beleaguered Bomber Command. On the 22nd, ACM Sir Arthur Harris was appointed as the new Commander-in-Chief, and over the ensuing weeks, he would set about the gargantuan task of turning Bomber Command into a war-winning weapon. He arrived at the helm with firm ideas already in place about how to win the war by bombing alone. He recognized the need to overwhelm the enemy's defences by pushing the maximum number of aircraft across an aiming point in the shortest possible time. This would signal the birth of the bomber stream, and an end to the former practice, whereby crews determined for themselves the details of their sortie. He also knew that urban areas are destroyed most efficiently by fire rather than blast, and it would not be long before the bomb loads carried by his aircraft reflected this thinking.

After settling in for the remainder of February, and continuing the relatively small-scale operations against Wilhelmshaven and Kiel, where the cruisers Scharnhorst and Gneisenau were under repair, he changed the face of bombing by despatching the largest force yet to a single target, 235 aircraft, to attack the Renault lorry works at Billancourt in Paris on the 3rd of March. The operation set a pattern for the future, in being conducted in three waves, led by experienced crews, and with extensive use of flares to provide illumination. The attack was an outstanding success for the loss of just one aircraft, although it was somewhat ironic, that Harris, as a champion of area bombing, should gain his first major victory by way of a precision raid. This was followed by dismal failures at Essen, despite the fact that the new Gee navigation device was now fitted to the leading aircraft, and the Ruhr would continue to be elusive until well into the following year. The first major success for the area bombing policy came at the Baltic city port of Lübeck at the end of March, when 30% of its built-up area was destroyed by fire. This was followed up in a four-raid series at Rostock, also on the Baltic coast, on consecutive nights towards the end of April, when 60% of the main town area was reduced to ruins. The masterpiece came at the end of May, when Operation Millennium was born out of the need to protect the Command's interests at a time when critics were still calling for bomber aircraft to be diverted to other causes.

When he became commander-in-chief, Harris had asked for four thousand bombers with which to win the war, and although there was never a chance of getting them, he needed to ensure that those earmarked for him were not spirited away to what he considered to be less deserving causes. He needed a major victory, and perhaps a dose of symbolism with which to make his point, and this could only be satisfied by the commitment of a thousand aircraft in one night against an important German city, for which Hamburg had been pencilled in. Harris did not have a thousand front-line aircraft, and he would have to lean upon other Commands, principally Coastal, to achieve the magic figure. Support was initially forthcoming from this direction in a letter on the 22nd, which pledged a sizeable contribution of aircraft, but this changed following an intervention by the Admiralty. Undaunted, Harris, or more likely his able deputy, AM Sir Robert Saundby, scraped together every airframe capable of controlled flight, or something resembling it, and pulled in the screened crews from their instructional duties. Come the day, not only would the figure be achieved, but it would also be comfortably surpassed. The weather almost scuppered Harris's plans but relented at the last minute to let the operation go ahead with Cologne, not Hamburg, as the target. 1047 aircraft took off for the now familiar three wave attack, some of the older training hacks lifted more by the enthusiasm of their crews than by the power of their engines. The operation was, by any standards, an outstanding success, which destroyed over 3,300 buildings, although this was gained for a new record loss of forty-one aircraft. Two nights later, Harris launched the Thousand Force against Essen, and scattered bombs all over the Ruhr, few if any landing within the intended target. The third thousand bomber raid took place at Bremen on the 25/26th of June, and while falling well short of the Cologne triumph, it far surpassed the debacle of Essen, and Harris had by now made his point. The Lancaster, the "shining sword" in Harris's armoury, had begun operations in March, and 5 Group was now fully converted, while 1 Group would shortly begin that process.

A new era began for the Command on the 15th of August, when the Path Finder Force was formed. Harris was opposed in principle to the idea of an elite target finding and marking force, a view shared by all but one of his Group commanders, but he was overruled by higher authority, and in typical fashion, then gave it his unstinting support. The new force was formed under the leadership of the then Group Captain Don Bennett, who was undoubtedly among the most highly qualified airmen in the world. After a career as an airline pilot and Master Navigator, he was entrusted with the job of setting up the Atlantic Air Bridge, to ferry much needed aircraft from America. On joining bomber Command in 1941, he was given command of 4 Group's 77 Squadron, before moving on to 10 Squadron and Halifaxes in early 1942. He demonstrated his determination and resourcefulness by returning to the squadron within a month of being shot down over Norway when attacking the Tirpitz in April. His appointment by Harris as the Pathfinder leader was both controversial and inspired, but he would go on to mould a highly professional and dedicated force. After an ignominious start to what would become an illustrious career, the Path Finder Force began to get to grips with its demanding role in September, when an unprecedented series of highly effective raids was delivered on Germany's towns and cities. If any period could be said to represent the turning point in Bomber Command's long and painful road to becoming a war-winning weapon, then these first two weeks in September was it. The last three months of the year were dominated by a campaign against Italian cities in support of Operation Torch, the landings in North Africa, during which General Montgomery would achieve a stunning victory over Rommel at El Alamein and push the Afrika Korps out of the war. This, then, was the situation into which 90 Squadron was reborn, and the coming year would provide it with ample opportunity to play a valuable part in the proceedings.

It was actually while the Battle of El Alamein was approaching its climax that 90 Squadron's fifth incarnation began on the 7th of November 1942, when it reformed in temporary lodgings at Bottesford, a 5 Group station located on the Leicestershire/Lincolnshire border. On the same day 467 Squadron RAAF was also formed and would join 90 Squadron at Bottesford on the 23rd, however, their destinies lay in different groups, 467 Squadron in 5 Group with which it would operate the Lancaster, while 90 Squadron's future lay in 3 Group, at the time equipped almost exclusively with the Short Stirling. The first entry in the 90 Squadron Operations Record Book (ORB) occurs on the 1st of December, completely ignoring events in January, which leaves us uncertain as to during which month various events occurred. It is necessary, therefore, to rely on other sources, principally the book "On the Wings of the Morning" by Vincent Holyoak, an excellent history of RAF Bottesford. W/C J C Claydon arrived from 1501 BAT Flight to assume command, having served previously, it is believed, on Wellingtons with 101 Squadron, but much of the process of forming the squadron fell on the shoulders of the adjutant, F/L George Rawley, who in turn relied heavily upon the NCO responsible for discipline, F/Sgt George Gee. It was common practice during the formation of a new squadron for unscrupulous squadron commanders to off-load undesirable characters, and the two Georges personally interviewed all incoming ground staff to weed them out. It must be assumed that A Flight commander, S/L Giles, arrived on posting on the 8th of November, not December as recorded in the ORB, having recently returned from India, and S/L Alexander presumably took up his post as B Flight commander at around the same time. It was a hectic period of activity, but if time remained after work was done, the favourite watering holes were the Ram Jam Inn off the A1 or the Hole in the Wall in Nottingham.

The first four Stirlings, W7510, W7575, W7623 and W7627 were delivered by Air Transport Auxiliary pilots on the 16th and 17th, and one of them was flown in by the well-known aviation pioneer, Jim Mollinson, whose even more famous wife, Amy Johnson, had been lost ferrying a Wellington for the ATA during the previous year. BF409 followed on the 18th, BF410 on the 26th and R9256, BF414, and BF415 on the 28th, and when BK644 landed on the 1st of December in the hands of an ATA pilot, it was immediately involved in an accident after taxiing onto the perimeter track and colliding with a moving roller that had been abandoned by its panicked civilian driver. Aircraft and crews continued to arrive and working up was sufficiently advanced to put eight aircraft into the air for a "Bullseye" exercise, a night cross-country, on the 11th, led by S/L Alexander. They began to depart Bottesford at 18.30 and matters proceeded smoothly until F/Sgt Henderson radioed that an engine had cut out at 5,000 feet, and he returned to

Bottesford to carry out a perfect landing. The meteorological section then confessed that all of their weather predictions were wrong and that severe icing conditions would prevail, prompting the dispatch of a recall signal that resulted in three landing at base and four at other airfields.

3 Group had been hinting at a possible move to Ridgewell on the 1st of January, a recently built station located midway between Cambridge to the north-west and Colchester to the south-east as a satellite of Stradishall. On the 16th W/C Claydon, the adjutant, the engineering officer and the discipline NCO paid the station a visit and expressed themselves delighted with what they found. The Stirling's main problem on the ground was the weakness of its undercarriage, which frequently collapsed after a heavy landing or during a swing on take-off and many aircraft were written off to this malaise. Tragically, it brought about the death of the experienced ground crew member, F/Sgt McGavin, who was alerted on the 18th of December to a buckling undercarriage leg on "Q", believed to be R9271, and was in the process of shoring it up when it collapsed on him and crushed him to death. He was almost certainly killed instantly, but as lifting equipment had to be accessed from elsewhere, it took time to release his body, by which time all hope was gone.

By this time, the crews had been allotted to their flights, A Flight consisting of the crews of S/L Giles, F/L Knowles, P/Os Brydon, Fowler, Hartney, Morgan, O'Connell and Scott, F/Sgts Freeman and Wood and Sgts King and Routen, while B Flight contained the crews of S/L Alexander, F/O Parton, P/Os Everiss, Lacey, Ross, Sayers and White, F/Sgts Henderson, Macdougall, Wilson and Young and Sgts Miles and Pugh. F/L Bowen was appointed navigation officer, and F/L Stowe DFM, P/O Jenkins and F/L Ewing were appointed respectively as bombing, signals and gunnery leaders.

Elsewhere, a major raid on Duisburg on the 20th masked a small-scale operation of great significance for the future of bombing, which was being carried out by six Mosquitos of the Path Finder Force's 109 Squadron against a power station in the Dutch town of Lutterade. The target was of no consequence, but was believed to be free of craters, so that the fall of the bombs delivered employing the Oboe blind bombing device could be plotted and calibrated to establish the device's margin of error. Unfortunately, three of the Mosquitos suffered Oboe failure and went on to bomb Duisburg instead, leaving W/C Hal Bufton and two other crews to deliver the bombs. What they hadn't bargained for was a whole carpet of bomb craters left over from the attack on Aachen, seventeen miles away, in October, and it proved impossible to identify those aimed by Oboe. It was a temporary setback, and further trials would take place before the end of the year, and come the spring, Oboe would be ready to unleash with devastating results against the Ruhr.

On the 29th, ten 90 Squadron Stirlings departed Bottesford with the intention of landing at their new home, where F/Sgt Freeman and crew in BK625 were the first to arrive and crashed on landing, ending up wrecked in a ditch, happily without crew casualties. The remaining aircraft turned round and headed back to Bottesford for the night, while the squadron's ground personnel marched to the railway station and arrived at their final destination just as a heavy snowstorm was beginning. A delicious hot meal greeted them, after which they explored their new surroundings and were well satisfied with what they found. The Stirlings and aircrew arrived on the following day and an inspection of the workshops, offices and accommodation resulted in unanimous approval. The squadron's first dance was held in the NAAFI on New Year's Eve and went with a swing.

It had not been an outstanding year for 3 Group, which had been depleted by four of its leading squadrons during the second half of 1942, 7 Squadron to the Path Finder Force as a founder member, 101 Squadron to 1 Group and 9 and 57 Squadrons to 5 Group, the last three-mentioned all Wellington units scheduled for conversion to the Stirling. Stirling production was slow and losses on operations and in landing accidents high, and it was no secret that ACM Harris disliked the type because of its lack of development potential and inability because of the design of its segmented bomb bay to carry bombs larger than 2,000lbs. 90 Squadron would be joining XV, 75(NZ), 149, 214 and 218 Squadrons as operators of the type, while 115 Squadron continued on Wellingtons pending its imminent conversion to the Mk II Lancaster.

The Halifax also had become unpopular and distrusted by its crews after a spate of unexplained fatal crashes, and the type had actually been withdrawn from operations for a number of weeks in the late summer of 1942 to provide crews with intense training in an effort to restore confidence in the type. The cause of the accidents was traced to rudder lock and the "Christmas tree" effect, the addition of extra equipment in the form of exhaust shrouds, non-aerodynamic turrets and a rough paint finish to prevent reflection, all of which added around 5,000lbs of weight and drag with no increase in power to compensate. The rudder lock was cured by the removal of the triangular fin in favour of a large square design, but the Mk II Halifax would remain unpopular until the advent of the Hercules-powered Mk III late in 1943. Given the opportunity, Harris would have shelved the Stirlings and Halifaxes and have a fully Lancaster-equipped bomber force, and the posting of the three squadrons from 3 Group, thus preventing their conversion to Stirlings, was a move to restrict the proliferation of the type.

January 1943

The first act of the New Year took place a minute into the 1st of January with the official formation of the Canadian 6 Group, which would operate from the former 4 Group stations in northern Yorkshire and County Durham. The Oboe trials programme would dominate the first two weeks of the year as seven small-scale attacks on Essen and one on Duisburg were mounted, although these would involve only Lancasters of 1 and 5 Groups and the Mosquitos of 109 Squadron. For the first time, the cloud cover and ever-present blanket of industrial haze should have no bearing on the outcome of the raid as reliance on e.t.a., DR and Gee was cast aside in favour of Oboe, at least that is, at targets within the device's range. Until the advent of mobile transmitter stations late in the war, Oboe would be restricted by the curvature of the earth and the altitude at which Mosquitos could fly to pick up the radar pulse, but this meant that the entire Ruhr lay within range of Harris's bombers. That said, the success of a raid would still rely on the ability of the Path Finders to back up the initial Oboe markers and maintain a supply of target indicators (TIs) on the aiming-point. In the midst of this on the 8th, the Path Finder Force was granted group status as 8 Group, and duly took ownership of the 3 Group stations upon which it had lodged since its formation in August. For the purpose of this book the terms Path Finder and 8 Group are interchangeable.

90 Squadron had declared itself operational from the 1st and able to offer four Stirlings and crews, should they be required, but snowstorms swept the country to restrict opportunities during the first week and it would be a week before the squadron finally returned to the war. New crews, and indeed squadrons, would be eased gently into operations where possible, often being assigned to ports in the occupied countries or to mining operations, and it was the latter that was chosen for 90 Squadron's debut on the 8th. The very first mining operation of the war had been conducted by 5 Group on the night of the 13/14th of April 1940, in what represented the initial tentative steps in a new departure for Bomber Command operations, which would prove to be hugely successful and by war's end would have sunk or damaged more enemy vessels than the Royal Navy. The laying of parachute mines by air was given the code-name "gardening" and the entire enemy-held coastline from the Pyrenees in the south-west to the Baltic port of Königsberg in the north-east, and even the northern Italian coast, was divided into gardens, each with a horticultural or marine biological name. The process of delivery was known as planting and the mines were referred to as vegetables, and 5 Group was soon joined by other groups to help create a spiders' web of mines in chains across all of the sea-lanes employed by the enemy.

On the 8th, 3 Group sent instructions to Downham Market, Mildenhall, Oakington, Stradishall and Ridgewell to prepare between them sixteen Stirlings for mining duties at locations between the central Frisians and the Baltic. At the Ridgewell briefing the crews of F/Sgts Wilson and Wood were assigned to the Nectarine II garden and those of P/O Sayers and F/Sgt Macdougall to Jasmine, with S/L Alexander flying as second pilot in the Sayers crew. The Nectarine region encompassed the entire Frisian island chain and was divided into three gardens, Nectarine I from Texel to the eastern tip of Ameland, Nectarine II, from east of Ameland to Memmert, and Nectarine III, Juist to Wangerooge. The Jasmine garden was in the Baltic, off the port of Warnemünde, where the docks were the site of U-Boot crew training, and also supplied German forces on the Russian front, but equally important was the nearby Heinkel aircraft factory. F/Sgt Wood's sortie was cancelled, leaving the others to depart Ridgewell for the first time in anger between 17.35 and 18.00, F/Sgt Wilson and crew arriving at their destination first to encounter nine-tenths cloud, which forced them to rely on a Gee-fix to establish their approximate position. The vegetables were released from 1,000 feet at 19.30, before a safe return was completed with a landing at Stradishall at 21.58. Meanwhile, at the same time some five hundred miles to the east, P/O Sayers and crew were delivering three 1,500lb mines on a westerly heading from 4,500 feet, following in the wake of F/Sgt Macdougall and crew, who had passed this way thirty-eight minutes earlier. The latter had dropped their mines on a north-westerly heading from 3,000 feet into an approximate position based on dead-reckoning (DR) in the face of unfavourable weather conditions and landed at Leuchars in Scotland after a round trip of eight hours and twenty minutes. It was not a night in which 3 Group distinguished itself after seven aircraft failed to take off and five others returned early, which meant that three of the four successful sorties were carried out by 90 Squadron crews.

On the 12th 3 Group detailed fifteen Stirlings for mining operations at a number of locations off the Biscay coast, the most distant of them, the Deodar garden located in the Gironde estuary some five hundred miles away from Ridgewell, assigned to five Stirlings from 90 Squadron. The mighty Gironde estuary narrows as it leads inland towards the south-east, before dividing to become the Garonne River to the west and the Dordogne to the east. Its banks and islands were home to a number of important oil production and storage sites at Pauillac, Blaye, Bec-d'Ambes and at Bassens in Bordeaux itself, and the region was a frequent destination for gardening activities. Bordeaux, a gateway to the Atlantic, was vitally important to the enemy as a base for U-Boots, which meant that it was heavily defended along the entire length of the waterway. The crews of the recently commissioned P/O Henderson, F/L Knowles, Sgt Pugh and F/Sgt Wilson took off in that order between 23.38 and 23.53, leaving the crew of F/Sgt Young behind after they were prevented from taking off by an obstruction on the runway. Sgt Pugh and crew dropped out twenty miles south of Abingdon after losing their starboard-outer engine, while the others headed out over the Channel to make landfall on the Brittany coast in the region of St-Malo. F/L Knowles and crew were eight miles north-east of Brest when an electrical issue ended their sortie, leaving the Henderson and Wilson crews to complete the next three hundred miles to their destination. The visibility beneath the eight-tenths cloud was not ideal, but the Henderson crew delivered their four vegetables from 1,500 feet at 03.48 on a westerly heading, and the parachutes were observed to deploy. The Wilson crew pinpointed first on Lake Hourtin, located between the estuary and the Atlantic, and flew over the drop zone before turning on a reciprocal course to release their stores from 1,000 feet at 04.33. When they landed at base, they had been airborne for nine hours and three minutes, while the Henderson crew had lobbed in at Exeter short of fuel after seven hours and forty-two minutes aloft.

A new Air Ministry directive was issued on the 14th, which authorised the area bombing of the French ports with concrete bunkers and support facilities for U-Boots, and a target list was drawn up accordingly, headed by Lorient and including St-Nazaire, Brest and La Pallice. Between February 1941 and January 1942, the Germans had built three giant concrete structures K1, K2 and K3 on the southernmost point of Lorient's Keroman peninsula, which were capable of housing and servicing thirty U-Boots and providing accommodation for their crews. They were impregnable to the bombs available to Bomber Command at the time, and the purpose of this new campaign, therefore, was to render the town and port uninhabitable and block or sever all road and rail communications to them, while mining took care of access by sea. The first of the series of nine attacks on the port over the ensuing four weeks took place that very night at the hands of a force of 122 aircraft, of which twenty Stirlings were provided by 3 and 8 Groups, and despite accurate marking by the Path Finder element, the main force bombing was scattered and destroyed a modest 120 buildings.

90 Squadron was not involved in the above and instead continued its more gentle introduction to operations with a return by five crews with NCO pilots to the Deodar garden. The crews of Sgt Spain, F/Sgt Young, F/Sgt Wilson, Sgt Tabor and F/Sgt Macdougall departed Ridgewell in that order between 17.07 and 17.15 and lost the services of the Young and Macdougall crews to engine issues within the first two hours. The others reached the target area to find four-tenths cloud with a base at 2,000 feet and a bright moon above, and two of them were subjected to machine gun fire from Cap Ferrat and light flak from Pointe-de-la-Coubre after pinpointing on the coast. They planted between them ten vegetables from 700 to 900 feet between 21.25 and 21.38, the Tabor crew having to bring two home after they hung up.

Twenty-four hours later, a force of 157 aircraft was assembled for round two at Lorient, and this time 90 Squadron was invited to take part in what would be its first bombing operation, as part of a 3 Group initial contribution of twenty-nine Stirlings and ten Wellingtons. Seven

Stirlings were made ready at Ridgewell, but four would be withdrawn along with seven other aircraft from the group, leaving a total of forty Stirlings representing 3 and 8 Groups. The crews of F/Sgts Wilson and Macdougall and F/L Knowles took off in that order between 17.28 and 17.33, only to lose the Wilson crew to an engine issue when passing to the west of the Channel Islands. The remaining two reached the target area to find three to seven-tenths cloud and bright moonlight and delivered their 1,000-pounders and incendiaries from 9,000 and 10,000 feet at 20.30 and 20.31 in what was a vast improvement on the previous night's modest results. Post-raid reconnaissance and local sources assessed that eight hundred houses had been destroyed, but as most of the inhabitants had left the town, the casualties were relatively light.

3 Group was not involved in operations on the 16th and 17th against Berlin, which were predominantly Lancaster affairs and failed to produce the hoped-for outcomes. The broadcaster Richard Dimbleby famously accompanied W/C Guy Gibson in a 106 Squadron Lancaster on the first occasion and a recording of his impressions was released over the airwaves to millions of radio listeners.

3 Group would operate alone on the 18th, when sending twenty-two Stirlings and seven Wellingtons to lay mines in the Nectarine I and II gardens in the southern and central Frisian island chain. 90 Squadron briefed the crews of Sgts Spain and Tabor, W/C Claydon, P/O Brydon and Sgt Pugh and sent them on their way from Ridgewell in that order between 17.12 and 17.33 bound for Nectarine I. Sgt Tabor was experiencing engine issues as he and his crew approached Terschelling and released their four mines early based on a Gee-fix and DR on a northerly heading at 18.56 from 900 feet, observing the fourth mine to detonate on impact. The other crews benefitted from favourable conditions with bright moonlight and delivered their mines from 850 to 3,000 feet between 19.09 and 19.31 after pinpointing on Ameland and drawing fire from flak ships anchored to the west and east of Terschelling.

The target area for a large mining effort involving seventy aircraft on the 21st was again the Frisian chain, for which 3 Group provided ten Stirlings from 90 and 214 (Federated Malay States) Squadrons. The crews of W/C Claydon, P/O White and Sgt Pugh departed Ridgewell between 17.03 and 17.25, each with a second pilot on board, S/L Giles performing that function in the crew of the commanding officer. They were bound for the Nectarine II garden and arrived in the target area to find three-tenths cloud below 500 feet with bright moonlight to aid the process of pinpointing on a suitable starting point for the timed run to the release point. A hang-up caused Sgt Pugh and crew to drop their mines in a salvo from 2,000 feet at 19.18 while off Schiermonnikoog and under fire from flak ships, to which the rear gunner responded with three two-second bursts. The others pinpointed on Rottumerplaat and the sandbank of Simonszand to the west, after which the White crew delivered their vegetables from 1,950 feet at 19.04 and the Claydon crew from 1,000 feet at 19.15.

The third attack of the series on Lorient was posted on the 23rd, for which 121 aircraft were made ready, including twenty-eight Stirlings of 3 Group, while Ridgewell remained inactive. The operation was claimed as a success and was followed up by the fourth raid on the 26th, for which a force of 157 aircraft was assembled, 3 Group represented by a dozen Wellingtons of 115 Squadron, while the Stirlings remained on the ground.

The main operation on the 27th was directed at the Ruhr city of Düsseldorf, for which a force of 162 Lancasters, Halifaxes and Mosquitos was assembled, while fifty-four other aircraft were assigned to mining duties. 3 Group contributed seventeen Stirlings and six Wellingtons to four gardens, off the Biscay coast at La Rochelle (Cinnamon) and further south in the Gironde estuary (Deodar), the Kadet Channel between Denmark's Lolland Island and Warnemünde on Germany's Mecklenburg Bay coast (Sweet Pea) and the west Frisians (Nectarine I). *(As the Frisian chain runs nominally from south-west to north-east, the terms western and southern are interchangeable as are northern and eastern.)* The six 90 Squadron participants departed Ridgewell between 17.00 and 17.07 bound for the Deodar garden with S/L Giles the senior pilot on duty, whereupon F/Sgt Young and crew immediately lost their Gee and DR compass. They continued on to the French coast, at which point the P4 compass also failed and they dumped three mines "safe" in the sea between the Island of Ushant and the mainland north-west of Brest before heading home. The others reached the target area to encounter less than ideal conditions, Sgt Spain and crew running into thick fog which persuaded them to jettison their load from 700 feet, while P/O Sayers and crew stumbled around for thirty minutes in ten-tenths cloud down to 500 feet without Gee to assist them, before abandoning the sortie and taking the vegetables home. F/Sgt Macdougall and crew also fell foul of the cloud and poor visibility and released their mines on estimated position at 21.42, observing one to explode on impact. S/L Giles and crew complained of dark conditions and stayed above the cloud to release their stores from 4,000 feet at 21.31, while Sgt Miles and crew ventured down through the murk to drop theirs from 1,000 feet at 21.55.

Other squadrons from other groups completed the month's operations, including the above-mentioned attack on Düsseldorf, where Mosquito-borne Oboe ground markers were employed for the first time as a reference for the Path Finder heavy brigade and were designed to burst and cascade just above the ground. The presence of a thin layer of cloud over the target, which pre-Oboe would have rendered the attack a lottery, had no detrimental effect and the bombing was concentrated in southern districts, where a significant amount of damage resulted. The fifth raid on Lorient took place on the 29th and was followed twenty-four hours later by a 1, 5 and 8 Group attack on Hamburg, which lay beyond the range of Oboe and called upon the first deployment in Path Finder Halifaxes and Stirlings of the ground-mapping H2S radar. In time, particularly with the introduction of an updated device at the end of the year, H2S would become a highly effective tool and standard equipment in frontline aircraft, but it would take time for the operators to learn how to interpret the jumble of images on their cathode-ray tubes and bombing was scattered on this occasion.

On the 29th, P/O Henderson RNZAF and his crew had been posted to 75(NZ) Squadron to continue the war among their own countrymen. During the course of the month the squadron took part in seven operations and dispatched twenty-nine sorties without loss.

February 1943

The new month was a time of honing and refining for Bomber Command in preparation for the launching of a major campaign a month hence. February opened with the posting of the Rhineland capital Cologne as the target for an experimental raid on the 2nd, during which two marking methods were to be employed to further explore target marking techniques at a target situated just to the south of the Ruhr and well within range of Oboe. The plan called for the initial marking to be carried out by Oboe Mosquitos of 109 Squadron, followed by H2S-equipped Stirlings and Halifaxes from 7 and 35 (Madras Presidency) Squadrons, all with red TIs, and for the Path Finder Lancaster element to back up with green TIs. A force of 159 heavy aircraft included a Path Finder contribution of twenty-six Lancasters, Halifaxes and Stirlings with two 109 Squadron Mosquitos but no contribution from 3 Group. It is interesting to note that the 3 Group ORB was still recording Path Finder numbers as if it were still part of the group. In the event, the experiment was not successful, and bombing was scattered across the city, causing no significant damage.

A force of 263 aircraft was assembled on the 3rd to send against Hamburg, this number including a contribution from 3 Group of twenty-seven Stirlings and three Wellingtons, seven of the former representing 90 Squadron. The sight of numerous bomb trolleys loaded with small bomb cases (SBCs) of 4lb and 4lb "X" incendiaries had created excitement among the crews at Ridgewell, as they pondered the prospect of taking part in a bombing operation rather than the dull, usually uneventful almost routine nature of mining duties. Each aircraft received a bomb load of 1,860 standard 4lb incendiaries and 120 of the type "X" before taking off between 18.05 and 18.55 with P/Os Brydon and White the senior pilots on duty. They set course for the North Sea on a night of heavy cloud with icing conditions, having been told at briefing to turn back if the conditions proved to be too challenging. Twenty-two 3 Group crews took advantage of the get-out-of-jail-free card in the face of the towering storm-laded cumulonimbus cloud form a barrier over the North Sea, and on this night extended beyond 22,000 feet. P/O White and crew lost their starboard-inner engine and jettisoned their load, leaving the others to cross the Dutch coast near Rotterdam, and Sgt Tabor and crew were some five miles south-east of Dordrecht when they turned back and jettisoned their load after failing to climb out of icing conditions. P/O Brydon and crew had been the last to take off, delayed for twenty minutes by mechanical issues, and having used up an excessive amount of fuel trying to climb and catch up with a troublesome starboard-outer engine, they sought out an alternative target and unloaded the contents of their bomb bay on the town of Hoya, twenty miles south-east of Bremen. The others followed the briefed track, which approached the target from the south, passing to the east of the designated alternative target of Bremen. The plan called for the Path Finder heavy brigade to open the attack with red skymarker flares with green stars at 21.00, but the conditions intervened, and the operation did not proceed as intended.

North-western Germany was found to be covered by ten-tenths cloud with tops at 10,000 to 12,000 feet and positions over Hamburg had to be established by the Path Finder crews blindly on H2S. In the event, they were unable to provide more than a few scattered skymarkers for the main force crews, among which were those of Sgts Pugh and Spain and F/Sgt Wilson, who delivered their attacks from 8,000 to 13,000 feet between 20.55 and 21.14. Sgt Pugh's navigator was wounded in the hand and shoulder by flak splinters, but after a short rest was able to resume his duties. Absent from debriefing was the eight-man crew captained by the experienced F/Sgt Macdougall, who was undertaking his twenty-seventh sortie. Flying as rear gunner was P/O Parton, a member of W/C Claydon's crew, who had volunteered to stand in for the regular occupant of the rear turret who had reported sick. There were no survivors after BF415 was shot down by a night-fighter to crash some ten miles south-west of Utrecht in central Holland, and the presence of this crew would be missed by the squadron and Ridgewell communities.

Turin was posted as the main target on the following day and a force of 188 aircraft assembled, of which thirty-three Stirlings and three Wellingtons were provided by 3 Group. While this operation was in progress, 128 other aircraft, mostly Wellingtons, were to continue the assault on Lorient. Located in the Piedmont region of northern Italy, Turin was an industrial powerhouse and home to Fiat's Lingotto and Mirafiori car plants, the Lancia motor works, the Arsenale army munitions factory, the RIV submachine gun factory, the Nebioli foundry and plants belonging to the American Westinghouse company. The 90 Squadron crews of S/L Giles, F/L Knowles and Sgts Miles and Spain attended briefing, while out on the dispersal pans each of their Stirlings was being loaded with two 1,000-pounders, 592 x 4lb and 38 x 4lb "X" incendiaries. They departed Ridgewell between 18.06 and 18.15 and lost the services of F/L Knowles and crew to a starboard-inner engine issue as they approached the French coast between Fecamp and Dieppe. S/L Giles and crew reached the Bourges area of central France before admitting defeat in the face of a failing starboard-inner engine, which would prevent them from gaining the altitude necessary to traverse the Alps. The two remaining crews flew the length of eastern France over heavy cloud and were able to make the necessary height to clear the Alps, guided by route markers dropped over Lake Bourget in the foothills on the French side. On the Italian side they found clear skies and excellent visibility and had red marker flares in their bomb sights as they delivered their loads from 12,000 feet at 21.35 and 21.43. They observed the development of large fires, including a particularly extensive one in the city centre as they retreated, and their reports were corroborated by returning Path Finder crews, who had identified ground features in the form of the marshalling yards and sports stadium and had witnessed many bomb detonations in the city centre.

On the 5th, the crews of Sgt Scholey and F/Sgts Wood and King departed Ridgewell in that order between 17.59 and 18.17 bound for the Nectarine I garden as part of a nineteen-strong 3 Group effort, each of the 90 Squadron Stirlings carrying six B200 mines, none of which would reach their assigned drop zones. They flew out in ten-tenths cloud from the English coast to the garden around the southern Frisians and lost the services of F/Sgt King and crew to a starboard-inner engine issue before they even crossed the coast at Cromer. Sgt Scholey and crew lost the use of their Gee and found themselves in ten-tenths low cloud with a base, they believed, as low as 1,000 feet by the time that they reached the midpoint of the North Sea, and acting upon orders not to attempt to pinpoint from below 2,500 feet, they turned back. BK644 disappeared without trace with the eight-man crew captained by F/Sgt Wood, and it is believed that they may have gone down close to Cromer in the same general area as the other failure to return, a 75(NZ) Squadron aircraft.

The squadron made ready six Stirlings on the 7th as part of a 3 Group contingent of fifty-five of the type for the seventh raid on Lorient scheduled for that night. It was to be a large-scale operation in two phases involving 323 aircraft, for which the phase I crews of P/O Sayers and

F/Sgt Young departed Ridgewell at 17.46 and 17.59 respectively, to be followed into the air between 18.52 and 19.05 by the phase II crews of P/Os White, Scott and Bryden and F/L Knowles. Each crew was sitting on either two 1,000-pounders and 1,269 x 4lb and 81 x 4lb "X" type incendiaries or 1,692 and 108 incendiaries respectively, and for a change there were no early returns to reduce the squadron's impact. They exploited the clear conditions and concentrated Path Finder marking to deliver an outstandingly destructive attack, the Sayers and Young crews dropping their loads from 10,000 and 14,000 feet at 20.29 and 20.32 and the second phase crews from 9,500 to 10,800 feet between 21.33 and 21.49. The town was seen to be well ablaze with smoke rising to 8,000 feet as the bombers retreated, and all from Ridgewell returned safely to make their reports.

Minor operations occupied the ensuing nights, and 3 Group was not involved when other elements of the Command carried out a raid on the shipbuilding port of Wilhelmshaven on the night of the 11/12th, conducted through complete cloud cover and employing H2S-guided skymarking, the least accurate of all marking methods. An enormous explosion lit up the clouds with a glow that lingered for ten minutes, and it was discovered later that it came from the naval ammunition dump at Mariensiel in the south of the town. The eruption devastated an area of 120 acres and caused major destruction in the town and dockyard.

It was not until the 13th that the next operation was posted on 3 Group stations, and that was for a return to Lorient that night for what would prove to be the penultimate raid of the series and the heaviest of the war on this target. A force of 466 aircraft was made ready, which included sixty-four 3 Group Stirlings, nine of them belonging to 90 Squadron. They again took off in two shifts, eight between 17.42 and 18.06 with W/C Claydon and S/L Giles the senior pilots on duty and Sgt Routen and crew bringing up the rear at 18.44. Each crew had four 1,000-pounders and 900 x 4lb incendiaries beneath their feet as they climbed out over the station, and it was at this point that F/Sgt Young and crew abandoned their sortie when all air pressure-dependent instruments failed. The others pushed on to the target, which they found under bright moonlight from clear skies with good visibility. The plan called for a number of Path Finder aircraft to station themselves over the Ile-de-Groix, an island situated some five miles off the mouth of the estuary leading to the port and illuminate it continuously as a navigation pinpoint. They arrived at 20.30 and under perfect conditions of clear skies and bright moonlight, delivered three white and one red flare from 14,000 feet, and ten minutes later, ten white flares and four green TIs, which fell to the north-west of the aiming-point. The other Path Finder crews followed up over Lorient itself with flares, green TIs and 1,000 pounders in a number of passes from 11,000 to 14,000 feet between 20.35 and 20.56, paving the way for the main force element to carry out their attacks. The 90 Squadron crews delivered their payloads from 9,000 to 11,000 feet between 20.37 and 21.33, contributing to the first non-1,000 operation to drop a thousand tons of bombs on a single target. At debriefings across the Command, crews reported massive fires right across the town and the port area.

Two operations were mounted on the following night, the larger by 243 Halifaxes, Wellingtons and Stirlings against Cologne, while 142 Lancasters of 1, 5 and 8 Groups targeted Milan. 3 Group offered fifty-three Stirlings for the Rhineland capital, eight of them made ready by 90 Squadron and loaded with three 1,000-pounders and 4lb incendiaries before departing Ridgewell between 18.31 and 19.03 with S/L Giles the senior pilot on duty. He and his crew were forced to turn back after losing their intercom early on and they were joined on the ground within minutes by the crew of F/Sgt King, whose R9306 resolutely refused to climb beyond 7,500 feet. The others flew out in broken cloud, which built up from the Scheldt estuary and was at ten-tenths with tops at around 7,000 feet by the time that the Path Finders arrived in the target area to establish their positions by H2S and the evidence of the accurate flak penetrating the cloud tops. They opened the attack bang on schedule at 20.15 with red flares with green stars and 1,000 pounders, which the main force bomb-aimers had in their sights as they let their high explosives and incendiaries go, those from 90 Squadron from 10,000 to 14,000 feet between 20.20 and 20.28. The cloud prevented an assessment of the results, and the intensity of the flak dissuaded crews from hanging around, but they observed some evidence of burgeoning fires that gave hope of a successful raid. Local sources confirmed only limited success in western districts, the failure to achieve better results, perhaps in part, caused by a bunch of red flares with green stars observed to fall ten miles to the north. Nine aircraft failed to return, three of each type, and among them was BF438, which disappeared without trace with the crew of Sgt Tabor RNZAF.

Preparations were put in hand on the 16th for the final attack on Lorient, to be delivered that night by an initial force of 377 aircraft, of which 3 Group contributed forty-one Stirlings and six Wellingtons, the latter belonging to 115 Squadron, the group's only operator of the type until its impending conversion to the Mk II Lancaster. At the same time, thirty-two aircraft would be taking advantage of the distraction to conduct mining sorties at other locations off the Biscay coast. The plan at Lorient called for two Halifaxes and four Lancasters of 8 Group to drop sticks of flares across the town, before the remaining Path Finders delivered red TIs onto the aiming-point and maintained the illumination as required. W/C Claydon was the senior pilot on duty as six crews attended the Ridgewell briefing for the main event, while out on the dispersals each of their aircraft was being loaded with four 1,000-pounders and nine hundred assorted 4lb incendiaries. Three additional Stirlings to be occupied by the crews of F/O Scott, P/O Fowlie and Sgt Scholey each received a load of three 1,500lb mines for delivery to the Elderberry garden located off the resort town of Biarritz, some fifteen miles from the frontier with Spain.

They took off together between 18.55 and 19.16, the latter time that of Sgt Pugh and crew, who lifted off six minutes after the deadline time and lost a further eleven minutes while still over England. They were a few miles north of the Dorset coast when it became clear that they could not reach the target within the allotted window and abandoned their sortie. The Path Finder spearhead arrived in the target area to find widely-dispersed low cloud and excellent conditions and the initial illuminator crews opened the attack with thirty-two white flares from 14,000 feet a minute ahead of schedule at 20.44. The main force crews were able to identify the river and its bridges and braved an intense searchlight and flak response in the early stages until it became overwhelmed. The Ridgewell crews carried out their attacks from 8,000 to 12,000 feet between 20.55 and 21.08 and as they retreated towards the north observed a massive explosion at 21.20 that sent a huge column of smoke into the air. As few buildings remained standing in Lorient, this final attack had been predominantly an incendiary affair, and the glow from the fires remained visible on the horizon for fifty miles into the return flight. As R9306 arrived back over Dorset, both starboard engines failed, and at 2,500 feet the order was issued to abandon the Stirling to its fate. According to the squadron ORB, only the RAF flight engineer had time to comply and landed safely, while the RAF rear and mid-upper gunners survived the crash at 23.05 on Bold Barrow Hill to the west of Blandford Forum, the latter with severe injuries. The pilot, F/O Brydon RCAF and the other three crewmen, all members of the RCAF, lost their lives.

As this tragedy was playing out, six hundred miles to the south the mining trio had arrived at their destination to find up to seven-tenths cloud with a base at around 4,000 feet and began their search for a pinpoint from which to carry out a timed run to the release point. F/O Scott and crew identified the mouth of the river at Bayonne and dropped their mines from 3,000 feet at 22.59, while Sgt Scholey and crew found themselves off the illuminated seafront at the Spanish resort of San Sebastian and retraced their steps northwards to plant their vegetables under moonlight from 1,200 feet at 23.18. This left P/O Fowlie and crew to complete their sortie from 4,000 feet at 23.50, before beginning the long trek home and landing at Exeter with precious little fuel in the tanks after almost ten hours aloft.

During the course of the nine raids on Lorient, 1,967 sorties had been sent against the port, which was now a deserted ruin with little other than the impervious K1, K2 and K3 U-Boot structures still standing.

The only heavy aircraft active on the following night belonged to 3 Group, and a dozen Stirlings from 90 and 214 (Federated Malay States) Squadrons were assigned to mining duties, again off the southern Biscay coast between the Gironde estuary and Bayonne. The crews of F/L Knowles, P/O White and F/Sgt Wilson were handed the Elderberry garden as their destination, while those of F/Sgt Young and Sgts Miles and Routen were assigned to Deodar, more than a hundred miles to the north in the Gironde estuary. They departed Ridgewell together between 18.02 and 18.31 and immediately lost the services of F/L Knowles and crew after the undercarriage motor burned out and left the wheels suspended. The others headed for the south coast and the Channel crossing, and the Routen crew had reached a position some ten miles north-east of Brest when their port-outer engine failed and ended their interest in proceedings. P/O White and crew reported nine-tenths cloud with a base at 2,500 feet and pinpointed on Cape Higuer before planting their vegetables from 2,000 feet at 22.05. The Wilson crew reported only three-tenths cloud and pinpointed on the mouth of the river at Bayonne before releasing their three mines from 860 feet at 22.34. Further south bright moonlight assisted the search for a pinpoint, which was found at Lake Hourtin, and the mines were delivered from 800 feet at 22.19 and 22.30. The presence of the Miles crew attracted flak fire from the lakeside and minor damage was caused to the rear turret, the occupant of which responded with well-aimed bursts that silenced three batteries.

The main operation on the night of the 18/19th was the first of a series of three against Wilhelmshaven and involved 195 aircraft, although none from 3 Group, which instead continued supporting gardening operations off south-western France. The outcome of the main event was a disappointment after much of the bombing fell in open country to the west of the town, and it was a larger force of 338 aircraft which was assembled for the second attack, which would be supported this time by forty-one Stirlings and four Wellingtons of 3 Group. 90 Squadron made ready eight Stirlings, seven Mk Is and one recently-acquired Mk III, loading some with eight 1,000-pounders and others with SBCs of 4lb or 30lb incendiaries, and all departed Ridgewell between 17.40 and 18.10, the latter time that of F/Sgt King whose take-off had been delayed. Sgt Routen and crew turned back while still over Norfolk after discovering an oil leak in the port-inner engine, leaving the others to head out over Cromer with F/Sgt King attempting with difficulty to attain and maintain the required speed to reach the target in time. They had reached the midpoint of the North Sea crossing when the rear gunner reported that his turret had become unserviceable, and the sortie was abandoned. The others pressed on to find the Path Finders dropping preliminary green warning flares by H2S, before skymarking the release point and ground marking the aiming-point with red TIs. The port was covered by a thin layer of ten-tenths low cloud and was further protected by a smoke screen, which prevented any from determining what was happening on the ground, although the TIs were visible. The 90 Squadron participants carried out their attacks from 9,000 to 13,000 feet between 20.00 and 20.11 and four returned home to attend debriefing, at which some reported the glow of fires spreading quickly through the town. In fact, the Path Finder marking had led to the bombing of an area of open country north of the town, and this would be put down later to the use of out-of-date maps. Absent from the debriefing ritual were the crews of F/L Knowles in R9276 and Sgt Scholey in BK627, the former lost without trace, presumably in the North Sea, and the latter definitely so, the remains of the flight engineer, Sgt Fisher, coming ashore in April for burial on the Island of Sylt.

Bad weather kept the Command on the ground over the ensuing days, and the time was filled with lectures, drills and sporting activity. The last of the three raids on Wilhelmshaven was mounted on the night of the 24/25th in the absence of 3 Group in what was another inconclusive operation, after which the port would be left in peace until October 1944.

Five 90 Squadron crews were called to briefing on the 25th to learn that their destination was to be Nuremberg in southern Germany, the scene of massive Nazi rallies during Hitler's rise to power in the thirties. A force of 337 aircraft was drawn from 1, 3, 4, 5 and 8 Groups, 3 Group represented by forty-four Stirlings, the crews of which attended briefings to learn that the plan called for all Path Finder aircraft to drop a yellow TI as a route marker, and for the H2S-equipped Halifaxes and Stirlings to release a white TI each fifteen miles from the target. These were then to deliver a red TI onto the aiming-point, which the remaining Path Finder Halifaxes and Lancasters would back up with greens. The main force Stirlings' petrol tanks were filled to the top and we know that of the five 90 Squadron participants, two received bomb loads of five 1,000-pounders, while another would carry seventeen SBCs each containing eight 30lb incendiaries and a fourth thirteen SBCs, twelve containing ninety 4lb incendiaries and one seventy of the type X variety. They took off over an extended period between 19.48 and 20.39 with S/L Giles the senior pilot on duty, and after battling their way through a bank of towering ice-bearing cloud over south-eastern England, crossed the Channel and or North Sea to make landfall over north-eastern France and maintained a course parallel with the Franco-Belgian frontier to enter Germany south of Luxembourg. The route markers were dropped over Speyer on the western bank of the Rhine south of Mainz, by which time the Path Finder element had already fallen behind schedule by some margin on what was a dark night with clear skies and no moon. Thick haze in the target area blotted out ground detail, but the leading Path Finder crews established their positions by H2S and dropped red TIs and 1,000 pounders at 23.16, sixteen minutes after the attack had been due to begin. The TIs fell around eight hundred yards from aiming-point C and were backed up by greens from other aircraft. The late arrival of the

Path Finders forced the main force crews to orbit, and many bombed on the first markers, with the result that the main weight of the attack fell into northern and western districts. The 90 Squadron crew delivered their respective loads from 11,000 to 12,500 feet between 23.28 and 23.51 and four returned to report what appeared to be a moderately effective raid, which was confirmed by local reports of damage to three hundred buildings. These sources also revealed that bombs had fallen onto other communities and open country up to seven miles to the north of the city. Nine aircraft failed to return, and among them was BF410, which crashed homebound near Rastatt, close to the frontier with France north of Strasbourg and only the rear gunner survived from the eight-man crew of Sgt Miles to fall into enemy hands.

Cologne was selected for its third raid of the month that night and a force of 427 aircraft was assembled from all heavy groups, 3 Group detailing forty Stirlings and three Wellingtons, six of the former belonging to 90 Squadron. At least two received a bomb load of eight 1,000 pounders and the others up to twenty SBCs of 4lb incendiaries before departing Ridgewell between 18.58 and 19.06 with F/O Scott the senior pilot on duty. The bomber stream made its way to the target via Southwold to make landfall between the Scheldt estuary and the Hague, and it was when seven miles north-east of the Dutch capital that W7575 was attacked by a BF110, which raked the starboard flank with cannon and machine-gun fire inflicting severe damage. The contents of the bomb bay were jettisoned once the North Sea was regained, and Sgt Pugh and crew nursed the wounded Stirling back to base and reported that return fire had damaged their assailant. Meanwhile, the crews of the heavy brigade were unaware that three of the four Oboe Mosquitos had dropped out with technical problems leaving just one to mark the target with a red TI. The skies over Cologne were clear, but haze and smoke impaired the vertical visibility and most main force crews were drawn to the target area by red and green TIs and the burst of incendiaries. The 90 Squadron crews performed as briefed from 11,000 to 14,000 feet between 21.15 and 21.21 and observed many explosions and fires, the glow from which remained visible to some for a hundred miles into the return flight. A post-raid analysis revealed fires in the city centre and decoys to the west of the city, and bombing photos showed fire tracks and smoke that suggested an effective raid. Some Path Finder bombing photos depicted open countryside between eight thousand and six thousand yards west of the aiming-point and an assessment confirmed that a large proportion of the effort had fallen to the south-west of the city, with perhaps only a quarter landing in the built-up area, where it inflicted much damage upon housing, minor industry and public buildings. However, with Oboe about to be unleashed on all targets within its range, the picture would soon change and the ratio of successful to unsuccessful operations would swing decisively in the Command's favour.

While the main raid went ahead at Cologne, other aircraft were sent mining in the Nectarine gardens off the Frisians, and among them were two representing 90 Squadron containing the crews of F/O Fowlie and F/Sgt Cheek. They had departed Ridgewell at 18.35 and 18.38 respectively bound for Nectarine I, and on reaching the target area encountered sea mist which severely restricted visibility. Pinpoints were made on Ameland and six vegetables each were delivered into the allotted positions from 1,500 feet at 20.27 and 1,200 feet at 20.48.

The night of the 27/28th was devoted to mining operations from the Frisians to south-western France, for which 3 Group detailed twenty-two Stirlings from Mildenhall and Downham Market, while 90 Squadron remained at home.

Having effectively wiped the town of Lorient from the map, the Command now turned its attention upon St-Nazaire in accordance with the January directive and assembled a force of 437 aircraft on the 28th. 3 Group detailed fifty-three Stirlings and four Wellingtons, nine of the former from 90 Squadron, and crews learned at briefing that three Oboe Mosquitos would be operating to mark singly with green TIs at ten-minute intervals, which the Path Finder Halifaxes and Lancasters would back up with greens also. The 90 Squadron element departed Ridgewell between 18.00 and 18.23 with W/C Claydon the senior pilot on duty and three crews sitting on seven 1,000-pounders each, while the others had all-incendiary loads beneath their feet. The main force arrived in the target area in clear skies but only fair visibility because of haze, those in the rear-guard drawn on for the final forty miles by the fires already burning fiercely. Those from Ridgewell delivered their payloads into the target area from 10,000 to 12,000 feet between 21.12 and 21.27, adding to the extensive damage inflicted upon the town and port area, and a local report suggested that 60% of the town had been destroyed in this one raid. Five aircraft failed to return, and the single missing Stirling was the Squadron's R9349, which exploded in the air while outbound and came down near Avranches on the Normandy coast, with fatal consequences for Sgt Spain RNZAF and all but two of his crew, who fell into enemy hands.

It had been a busy and bruising month for the squadron, characterized to some extent by serviceability problems, particularly with engines and fourteen operations had produced eighty-two sorties for the loss of eight Stirlings, seven complete crews and four members of another.

March 1943

Harris was about to embark on the first major campaign of the year, and the first of the war for which the Command was adequately equipped and truly prepared. Since joining the Path Finder Force in the previous August, 109 Squadron had been carrying out magnificent work under W/C Hal Bufton, preparing the Oboe blind-bombing device for operational use and marrying it to the Mosquito. The endeavours were about to bear fruit in spectacular fashion and would finally negate the Ruhr's protective cloak of industrial haze, but first the crews had two major operations to negotiate, beginning with Berlin on the night of the 1/2nd. A force of 302 aircraft was assembled made up of 156 Lancasters, eighty-six Halifaxes and sixty Stirlings, with 3 Group responsible for thirty-eight of the Stirlings, seven of them, including two of the new Mk III variant, belonging to 90 Squadron. The crews learned at briefing that six Path Finder Halifaxes and ten Stirlings equipped with H2S were to drop a "landmark" yellow TI each at Butzow, situated some eighty miles north of Berlin, which were to be backed up by seven Halifaxes and sixteen Lancasters. The "special" (H2S-equipped) aircraft were then to release red warning flares twelve miles short of the target followed by red TIs on the aiming-point at the time-on-target of 22.00, which the seven Halifaxes and sixteen Lancasters would back-up with green TIs. As always, the plan was based on a forecast of favourable conditions, in the absence of which, skymarkers would substitute for TIs.

The 90 Squadron element departed Ridgewell between 18.17 and 18.54 with S/L Giles the senior pilot on duty, he and his crew and that of F/O Scott in the Mk IIIs carrying four 1,000-pounders each supplemented with incendiaries, while the Mk Is had all-incendiary loads in their bomb bays. Both Mk IIIs were soon in trouble and had to turn back, S/L Giles and crew with a technical malfunction affecting the operation of the guns and F/O Scott and crew because of a severe oil leak in the starboard-outer engine, The remaining five crews pressed on to cross the Schleswig-Holstein peninsula and approach Berlin from the Baltic and find on arrival clear, starlit skies and good visibility, which enabled them to identify ground detail and drop their bombs on the Path Finder red and green TIs from 10,000 to 15,400 feet between 22.03 and 22.28. Sgt Pugh's bomb-aimer was unable to extract the firing switch from its safety housing, and in his efforts to do so accidentally released the contents of the bomb bay some five to eight miles short of the TIs.

This operation would highlight the flaws in the early version of the H2S device when seeking an aiming-point over a massive urban sprawl like Berlin. It would take experience and great skill on the part of the H2S navigators to interpret the jumble of indistinct images on their screens, and on this night, the marking fell predominantly over the south-western districts, well short of the planned city centre aiming point. It was clear that the marking had been scattered over a wide area, with a particular concentration over the southern half of the city, despite which, some returning crews claimed exultantly that the concentrated bombing had eclipsed even the thousand bomber raid on Cologne, with the glow of fires visible from Bremen, some two hundred miles away. A post-raid analysis based on bombing photos revealed the attack to have been spread over an area of a hundred square miles, but because of the increasing bomb tonnages now being carried, more damage had been inflicted upon the city than on any previous raid. 875 buildings, mostly houses, were destroyed and twenty factories seriously damaged, along with railway workshops in the Tempelhof district. Seventeen aircraft failed to return, four of them Stirlings, and it is interesting to analyse the percentage loss rate of each type on this night, as it would be an accurate indicator of their future fortunes. The statistics revealed the loss rate of Lancasters to be 4.5%, and those of the Halifaxes and Stirlings to be 7%.

Germany's second city, Hamburg, was posted as the target for the night of the 3/4th and a force of 417 aircraft assembled, which included forty-two Stirlings and four Wellingtons of 3 Group. Five 90 Squadron Stirlings were made ready, one loaded with seven 1,000-pounders and the others with either 4lb or 30lb incendiaries before departing Ridgewell between 18.03 and 18.19 with S/L Giles the senior pilot on duty. They headed out above ten-tenths cloud, but otherwise excellent weather conditions, which would hold firm for the entire operation and provide clear skies over Hamburg. P/O Fowlie and crew were almost two hours out when they discovered that they had strayed twenty miles off track and were so far behind schedule that they could not reach the target in time. The seven 1,000-pounders were added to the thousands of tons of iron already lying at the bottom of the North Sea, while the four remaining Ridgewell crews arrived at the target to find fairly good visibility, with some haze, and the wide River Elbe providing strong H2S returns for the Path Finder navigators. Despite that, some misinterpreted what they saw on their screens and a batch of red and green TIs was released well to the west of the planned aiming-point and onto the town of Wedel, situated on the northern bank of the Elbe thirteen miles downstream of Hamburg city centre. To the crews high above, everything appeared normal, with cones of searchlights and intense light and heavy flak, and many bombed on the Path Finder markers assuming them to be accurate. Meanwhile, other Path Finders had identified and marked the intended aiming point, and main force crews had bombed the central area encompassing the Hamburg-America landing stage, the Blohm & Voss shipyards, the Binnen-Alster Lake and the main railway station, those from 90 Squadron from 11,000 to

15,000 feet between 21.10 and 21.25. On return they reported an apparently successful raid, which left a pall of rising black smoke and a hundred fires to be dealt with before the city's Feurwehr could go to the aid of their neighbour.

The decks were now cleared for the opening of the Ruhr offensive, which, over the ensuing months, would change the face of bombing and provide for the enemy an indication of the evolving power of the Command. This was a momentous occasion, a culmination of all that had gone before during three and a half years of Bomber Command operations. The backs-to-the-wall desperation of 1940, the tentative almost token offensives of 1941, the treading water and gradual metamorphosis under Harris in 1942, when failures still far outnumbered successes, had all been leading to this night, from which point would begin the calculated and systematic dismantling of Germany's industrial and population centres. The only shining light during these dark years had been the quality and spirit of the aircrews, and this had never faltered.

To the residents of bomber stations from County Durham to Cambridgeshire, the 5th of March probably felt no different from any other day on which a major operation was posted. By its end, however, Germany's industrial heartland had lost its invulnerability to Bomber Command attacks, and notice had been served, that the Ruhr Valley was to be taken apart piece-by-piece. The campaign was to begin at Harris's nemesis, Essen, the home of the giant Krupp empire, which had thus far escaped serious damage despite being targeted on many occasions over the past twelve months. The name Krupp conjures up a vision of a massive factory, but this is far from what actually existed. The Krupp organisation had been the largest manufacturer of weapons in Europe since before the Great War and had a hand in all aspects of German war production from tanks to artillery and ship and U-Boot construction and was given a controlling share in all major heavy engineering companies in Germany and the occupied countries. It also built manufacturing sites in other parts of Germany, many situated close to concentration camps and employed vast numbers of forced workers in all of its factories. Once known as "Die Waffenschmiede des Reichs", the weapons-forge of the realm, its manufacturing sites in Essen included among others the Friedrich Krupp steelworks, the Friedrich Krupp locomotive and general engineering works, six coal mines and ten coke-oven plants, the Altenberg zinc works, the Presswerk plastics factory and the Goldschmidt non-ferrous metals smelting plant, all situated either within or close to the four Borbeck districts in a segment radiating out from near the city centre to the Rhine-Herne Canal on the north-western boundary on the banks of the Emscher River. The steel and engineering works alone employed in the region of eighty thousand workers and the company's sites covered an area of more than two thousand acres, of which three hundred acres were occupied by factories and workshops. All of that required massive rail and canal access in the form of marshalling yards and its own harbour, and energy was provided by at least four nearby power stations.

A force of 442 aircraft was assembled, which included a contribution from 3 Group of fifty-four Stirlings and four 115 Squadron Hercules-powered Lancasters. The 90 Squadron crews for this momentous occasion were those of B Flight deputy commander, F/L Sayers in BF462, F/O Scott in W7627, P/O White in BF407, P/O Fowlie in R9271, F/Sgt Wilson in BK665, F/Sgt Cheek in BF414 and Sgt Pugh in EF334. The main force element was to bomb in three waves, Halifaxes first, followed by Wellingtons and Stirlings with Lancasters bringing up the rear. Six Path Finder Halifax and fifteen Lancaster crews had been briefed to drop a warning yellow TI each when fifteen miles from the target, before backing up the Mosquitos' red TIs on the aiming-point with greens, and the force was to adopt the southern route to the central Ruhr, making landfall over the Scheldt estuary.

The 90 Squadron element departed Ridgewell between 19.00 and 19.16, two of them carrying two 2,000 and four 1,000-pounders each and the others all-incendiary loads, and two of the latter ended up in the North Sea after Sgt Pugh and F/Sgt Cheek experienced engine issues that restricted performance. They were just two of eleven 3 Group early returns in an unusually high number of fifty-six "boomerangs" from the force as a whole, representing 13% of the force. Critically, among them were three of the eight 109 Squadron Mosquitos, whose markers would provide the initial reference for their colleagues in the heavy Path Finder aircraft. The spearhead of the bomber stream arrived in the target area to be greeted by a thin layer of stratocumulus between 16,000 and 18,000 feet, which blotted out ground detail but allowed the red TIs on the aiming point to be visible. This was the game-changer, the fact that a "blind" attack was reliant entirely upon electronics and made irrelevant the need to identify ground detail. Three 90 Squadron crews are known to have bombed from 10,000 to 15,300 feet at 21.10 and shortly thereafter and the overwhelming impression was of a concentrated attack, which left many fires burning and a glow in the sky reported by some to be visible from the North Sea homebound. Some crews reported a terrific explosion at 21.18, which lit up the sky, and a pall of smoke hanging above the dull, red centre of the resulting conflagration. Twenty-four crews reported attacking alternative targets, and together with the early returns, this reduced the numbers attacking the primary target to 362 aircraft. Fourteen aircraft failed to return, and among them was 90 Squadron's R9271, which crashed on farmland somewhere near Mönchengladbach, killing P/O Fowlie and two of his crew and delivering the four survivors into enemy hands. Post-raid reconnaissance revealed the destruction of 3,018 houses in 160 acres of devastation, and fifty-three buildings had been hit within the giant Krupp complex. This stunning victory elicited a message of congratulations from the C-in-C, which was received on all participating stations on the following day.

A week would elapse before the next operation to a Ruhr target, and in the meantime Harris switched his focus to three important industrial cities in southern Germany, beginning with Nuremberg on the night of the 8/9th. Such operations were beyond the range of Oboe, and thus, success would rely upon the skill of the H2S operators to accurately interpret what they were seeing on their cathode-ray tubes. A force of 335 aircraft included fifty-four 3 Group Stirlings from Downham market, Mildenhall, Oakington and Stradishall, while Ridgewell remained inactive. The marking and bombing spread along a ten-mile-long corridor, which resulted in half of the bomb loads falling outside of the city, but returning crews described many fires and one large explosion emanating from the centre of the target seen from a hundred miles into the return journey. Post-raid analysis and local sources confirmed that six hundred buildings had been destroyed and fourteen hundred others damaged, including a number of important war-industry factories. The operation cost a modest eight aircraft, but half of these were Stirlings

On the following day preparations were put in hand to return to southern Germany to attack the city of Munich, situated deep in the Bavarian mountains of south-eastern Germany, a round-trip of more than 1,200 miles. A force of 264 aircraft was assembled, which included thirty-one 3 Group Stirlings from the same stations that had supported the previous operation, but again none representing 90 Squadron, which would be active elsewhere as part of a 3 Group contribution of a dozen Stirlings with freshman crews to a mining effort involving sixty-two aircraft. The crew of P/O Elliott was assigned to the Deodar garden in the Gironde estuary, while those of Sgt Peryer, F/Sgt Cheek and P/O Birdsall had even further to travel to reach their destination, the Silverthorn IV garden in the Kattegat region of the Baltic to the south of Anholt Island. They departed Ridgewell between 19.27 and 19.33, the Elliott crew to head south and the others east, and it was just after reaching the midpoint of the North Sea crossing that the Peryer crew turned back with an engine issue and swung off the runway on landing at 23.00, collapsing the undercarriage and writing off BF449. P/O Elliott and crew landed at 01.23, claiming to have reached the Deodar area only to encounter an impenetrable haze extending below 1,000 feet, which prevented any chance of establishing a pinpoint. However, after only five hours and fifty minutes aloft, on what was normally a seven-hour minimum round-trip, the likelihood is that the sortie was abandoned well before the target area was reached. Meanwhile, the crews of F/Sgt Cheek and P/O Birdsall pinpointed on Anholt Island and delivered their three mines each through sea mist under starlit skies from 1,000 feet at 22.29 and 22.52 respectively.

A post-raid analysis of the Munich operation concluded that a strong wind had pushed the attack into the western half of the city, where 291 buildings had been destroyed and 660 severely damaged. The aero-engine assembly shop at the B.M.W factory was put out of action for six weeks, and many other industrial concerns also lost vital production. Numerous other industrial premises were also hit, as were military, retail, public and cultural buildings, and this was achieved for the loss of eight aircraft, of which just one was a Stirling.

The trio of operations to destinations in southern Germany concluded with the highly industrial city of Stuttgart, for which the force of 314 aircraft assembled on the 11th included forty-three Stirlings from the same four 3 Group stations. 90 Squadron briefed the freshman crews of P/Os Birdsall and Elliott and Sgts Platt and Wheeler for mining duties in the Nectarine I garden off the western Frisians and dispatched them from Ridgewell between 19.01 and 19.08. They flew out under clear skies with good visibility that enabled them to identify the Islands of Ameland and Terschelling and establish pinpoints from which to conduct a timed run, and each delivered six B200 mines into the allotted locations from 900 to 2,000 feet between 20.59 and 21.19. Meanwhile, the main event at Stuttgart had not proceeded according to plan after the main force had been delayed by wrongly forecast winds and arrived as the TIs were burning out, which left the way clear for dummy TIs and a decoy site to lure away many bomb loads. It emerged later that most of the effort had been wasted in open country, but that the south-western suburbs of Vaihingen and Kaltental had been hit and 118 buildings, mostly houses, destroyed in what was a disappointing outcome costing eleven aircraft, two of them Stirlings.

A week after the spectacular success of the opening round of the Ruhr offensive at Essen, the same city was selected to host round two and a force of 457 aircraft made ready on the 12th, of which forty Stirlings and four Lancasters were provided by 3 Group, 90 Squadron responsible for nine of the former. Briefings revealed that the force was to adopt the northern route to the Ruhr, and sixteen Path Finders were to ground-mark the town of Dorsten with white TIs as a track guide. With a time-on-target for the Path Finders of 21.15, they would then back up the Mosquito-borne Oboe red TIs with greens to provide the main force crews with a solid aiming point. Before those involved in the main event departed Ridgewell, the freshman crews of Sgt

Gedak and the newly-commissioned P/O Platt continued their apprenticeships when taking off at 19.00 and 19.02 respectively bound for the Nectarine I garden. They were followed into the air between 19.32 and 20.09 by the bombing element with S/L Giles the senior pilot on duty, three of the Stirlings carrying a 2,000-pounder and four 1,000-pounders and the others all-incendiary loads. The gardeners arrived at their destination to find good visibility below 2,500 feet and were able to establish pinpoints, from which they proceeded to the drop zone on a more-or-less northerly heading at an indicated air speed of 180 to 190 m.p.h, and delivered their six mines each according to brief at roughly ten-second intervals, before returning home safely from uneventful sorties within three-and-a-half hours.

There were no early returns among the Ridgewell bombing brigade, and all arrived in the target area under clear skies to find the visibility compromised to an extent by haze and smoke, with intense searchlight and flak activity making it an uncomfortable place to spend time. As was the case a week earlier, and for all future attacks on Ruhr targets, visibility was no longer a consideration, as Oboe allowed the Path Finders to mark an area within the Krupp complex. The 90 Squadron crews attacked from 10,000 to 14,000 feet between 21.28 and 21.42 and observed large fires that lit up the entire area, and a number of explosions were reported to have emanated from the munitions plant. Post-raid reconnaissance showed that the bombing had centred on the Krupp-dominated area of the city, where 30% more damage was inflicted than a week earlier and a further five hundred houses were also destroyed. The loss of twenty-three aircraft reminded the crews that success at the Ruhr would not be gained cheaply, but there were no empty dispersal pans at Ridgewell.

On the 13th, S/L May arrived from 1657 Conversion Unit to assume command of the newly-forming C Flight, but in the event, he would be installed as B Flight commander and S/L Alexander would take over C Flight. The ensuing nine days saw operations posted for Berlin, Augsburg and St-Nazaire, but all were cancelled, and while persistent fog restricted training, F/O Overton and crew, who had arrived on posting from 1657 Conversion Unit just two days earlier, took advantage of a window of opportunity to get into the air on the 18th. W7627 developed a swing during the take-off run and was written off after colliding with BK693, which was undergoing repair on its dispersal pan. Sadly, a member of ground crew, LAC Innes, was fatally injured and a Court of Investigation would be convened eight days hence to enquire into the matter. BK693 and the Overton crew would be returned to service, only for the unfortunate pilot to be involved in another accident three weeks hence.

It was the 22nd before a briefing took place for an operation that actually went ahead, when the town of St-Nazaire and its U-Boot and port facilities were selected for attention in compliance with the January directive. Out on the dispersals on 3 Group stations, fifty-nine Stirlings and seven Lancasters were being made ready as part of an overall force of 357 aircraft, and among them were seven 90 Squadron Stirlings, which departed Ridgewell between 18.55 and 19.16 with W/C Claydon the senior pilot on duty. The crews were glad to be going to war again after the long lay-off, such periods of operational inactivity always a source of irritation and boredom, and they were frustrated when deteriorating weather conditions over the 3 Group region persuaded group to send a recall signal at 21.00, just as its aircraft were passing to the west of the Channel Islands having covered two-thirds of the outward leg. Eight 3 Group crews either failed to pick up the signal or chose to ignore it, leaving the others, including all from

Ridgewell, to turn back and jettison their bomb loads. Sgt Routen decided to land with the bombs on board and was on final approach at 22.58 when both starboard engines cut, forcing him to dump the contents of the bomb bay from 50 feet four miles west of the station. The engines picked up again and a safe landing was carried out eleven minutes later.

When Duisburg was posted as the target for round three of the Ruhr offensive on the 26th, 3 Group was called upon to provide only seven Lancasters of 115 Squadron to the overall force of 455 aircraft. In the event, technical problems with the Oboe element probably saved Duisburg from the full impact, and, in fact, only superficial damage resulted from a highly scattered attack. On the following day, Harris called for a maximum effort by the four-engine types and 396 Lancasters, Halifaxes and Stirlings answered the call for an attack on the "Big City", Berlin. 3 Group contributed sixty-six Stirlings and six Lancasters, and at briefings the Path Finder crews were told of their part in the plan, which required eleven Stirlings and eight Halifaxes to drop green route marker flares and yellow warning flares by H2S, before marking the aiming-point with red TIs for two Stirlings, five Halifaxes and twenty-one Lancasters to back up with green TIs. In the event of cloud blotting out the ground, skymarking would be employed. Three of 90 Squadron's ten Stirlings received a bomb load of two 2,000 and two 500-pounders each, while the rest carried all-incendiary loads as they departed Ridgewell between 19.30 and 19.48 with W/C Claydon and S/L Giles the senior pilots on duty.

The route took them into enemy territory between the Frisian Islands of Texel and Vlieland, and then on a course a little north of Hannover to a point to the south-west of the capital for the run-in to the intended city-centre aiming-point. P/O Wilson and crew were heading north over The Wash and were some five miles south of Skegness when forced to shut down the starboard-inner engine because of an oil leak and fire and turn back. S/L Giles and crew had reached enemy territory and were thirty miles south of Emden when they, too, experienced starboard engine issues, which ended their interest in proceedings. P/O Elliott and crew penetrated even further into Germany and were twenty miles north-west of Braunschweig (Brunswick) when severe icing conditions rendered BK626 almost uncontrollable and shedding height to 8,000 feet by the time that the sortie was abandoned. The above were among eleven 3 Group early returns, and whether or not F/Sgt Young and crew were included in that statistic is unclear, as they released their load over Brandenburg, some thirty miles west of Berlin city centre, the activity over which could be seen in the distance. The reason for the premature release was flak damage, sustained at 13,500 feet at 22.44, which left a one-foot-wide hole in the starboard mainplane. The others pressed on to approach the capital from the south-west, the Path Finders reliant upon H2S and establishing two areas of marking, both well short, which the main force crews had little choice but to aim for. There was the usual discrepancy in the reported cloud state of zero to nine-tenths as the main force crews carried out their attacks, those from 90 Squadron from 10,000 to 13,000 feet between 22.53 and 23.12, before returning to report moderate flak, extensive searchlight activity and many fires within the city. The truth was, that the nearest bombs to the city centre were plotted five miles short, and the creep-back resulted in most falling between seven and seventeen miles along the line of approach. According to local sources, 25% of the bombs were "duds", and if true, this was another reason behind the lack of serious damage, but at least the losses were modest at nine aircraft.

A force of 323 aircraft was assembled for a return to St-Nazaire on the 28th, for which 3 Group provided thirty-one Stirlings, four of them at Ridgewell, where the crews of W/C Claydon and P/O Elliott were joined at briefing by the freshman crews of P/Os Crew and Beldin. Each was sitting on an all-incendiary bomb load as they took off between 19.30 and 19.51 and set course for the Dorset coast and the Channel crossing to make landfall on the Brittany coast between Paimpol and Lannion. P/O Crew and crew were passing to the west of the Channel Islands when the rear turret became unserviceable and the bombs were jettisoned, leaving the others to press on to reach the target area under clear, starlit skies and deliver their attacks onto red and green TIs from 10,500 to 12,000 feet between 22.16 and 22.17. Bomb bursts and fires were reported, and the operation appeared to achieve its aims.

The month's final operation was posted on the 29th, when the red tape on the briefing-room wall maps ended again at Berlin. A force of 329 aircraft was made ready, of which sixty Stirlings and eight Lancasters were detailed by 3 Group, while a main force of 149 Wellingtons continued the Ruhr campaign at Bochum. The plan for the main event required all Path Finder aircraft to drop yellow route markers at predetermined points, and the marker crews to illuminate the Müggelsee, to the south-east of Berlin, with sticks of white flares and bundles of green flares with red stars by H2S. They were then to carrying out a DR run to the aiming-point to deliver red TIs, and the backers-up were to follow a similar procedure. Seven 90 Squadron crews were briefed, while out on the dispersals the three participating Mk III Stirlings each received a bomb load of two 2,000-pounders, while the Mk Is had all-incendiary loads in their bomb bays as they departed Ridgewell between 21.16 and 21.40 with S/L Giles the senior pilot on duty. The route to Berlin on this night would take the bomber stream further north than two nights earlier, to cross southern Jutland, but bad weather in the form of heavy ice-bearing cloud and static electricity extending from the North Sea to the Baltic forced many crews to turn for home, among them a massive seventeen from 3 Group and an alarming twenty-four from 4 Group. P/O Wilson and crew were some ninety miles out over the North Sea when starboard-outer engine failure brought an end to their sortie, while a few miles further on, F/Sgt Cheek and crew were prevented by severe icing conditions from climbing beyond 8,300 feet, and when the rear gunner reported that his turret Perspex had been cracked by ice, they too abandoned their sortie. Later, Sgt Routen and crew were over southern Jutland in ice-bearing cloud and struggling to gain height, at which point they dumped part of the bomb load and managed to attain 16,500 feet. However, they still had two thousand feet of cloud above them, and in trying to maintain height had consumed too much fuel to allow them to reach Berlin, forcing upon them the decision to dump the rest of the bomb load a few miles short of Aabenraa on the Baltic coast and turn back.

Those pressing on through the front to reach the "Big City" found good visibility that enabled them to identify the Müggelsee to the south-east as a reference point from which to run in on the aiming-point. Inaccurately forecast winds may have contributed to the Path Finders marking an area some six miles to the south of the planned aiming point, and the main force arrived late, by which time some of the markers had burned themselves out. The main force crews bombed in the face of a heavy searchlight and flak defence, the 90 Squadron element from 8,000 to 14,000 feet between 00.55 and 01.04 and set off home in the belief that the fires they had left behind, the glow from which was still visible from 150 miles away, indicated that an effective attack had been delivered. In fact, most of the bombing had been wasted in open country to the south-east of the city, and an accurate figure for damage was not forthcoming, although 148 houses were believed to have been destroyed in the suburbs at a cost to the Command of twenty-one aircraft.

During the course of the month, the squadron carried out eleven operations and dispatched sixty-six sorties for the loss of two Stirling and one crew and a member of ground crew.

April 1943

The establishment of a C Flight increased the squadron's strength on paper to twenty-four aircraft IE (immediate equipment) plus 3 IR (in reserve), and with the improved serviceability of the Stirling and the efficiency of the ground crews, it was expected that this would enable the squadron to achieve a consistently high sortie rate. The squadron actually had thirty crews available, sixteen of which were allotted to A Flight under S/L Giles, eight to B Flight under S/L May and six to C Flight under S/L Alexander.

The final operations under the January directive were posted on the 2nd and featured St-Nazaire and Lorient, for which forces of fifty-five and forty-seven aircraft were assembled, 3 Group providing a 115 Squadron Lancaster for each and five Stirlings from XV Squadron for the former and five from 90 Squadron for the latter. The Ridgewell contingent took off between 20.30 and 20.44 with S/L May the senior pilot on duty for the first time, three carrying eight 1,000-pounders, while one had six 1,000 and two 500-pounders in the bomb bay. S/L May and his crew were forced to turn back early after the failure of their port-inner engine, leaving the others to find the target basking under clear, starlit skies and easily identifiable visually, and with the aiming point marked by red TIs. They delivered their attacks from 9,000 to 11,500 feet between 23.13 and 23.23, and on return, the freshman crew of P/O Cross admitted dropping their load "safe" after the fusing switches were accidentally left in the off position.

The only 3 Group presence in a force of 348 Lancasters, Halifaxes and Oboe Mosquitos bound for Essen on the 3rd was an element of nine Mk II Lancasters provided by 115 Squadron, on what was the first raid to employ more than two hundred Lancasters. Clear skies and accurate sky and ground marking led to concentrated bombing in which 635 buildings were destroyed and more than five hundred seriously damaged.

Orders were sent out across 3 Group stations on the 4th to prepare between them seventy-six Stirlings and eleven Lancasters as part of an overall force of 577 aircraft to target the shipbuilding port of Kiel. This represented the largest non-1,000 force of front-line aircraft thus far in the war and the news of it at briefing would have engendered excitement among the crews taking part. Twelve 90 Squadron crews listened intently to the details of the plan, while out on the dispersals seven Mk III and five Mk I Stirlings were being given all-incendiary bomb loads. The plan of attack called for a time-on-target of 23.00 and for yellow TIs to be dropped by the Path Finders as route markers, before the H2S marker crews in ten Stirlings and six Halifaxes illuminated the aiming-point with flares and marked it with red TIs. Two Stirlings, five Halifaxes and fifteen Lancasters were to back up with green TIs, leaving two of each type to bomb with the main force. The Ridgewell contingent took off between 20.09 and 20.44 with S/Ls Giles and May the senior pilots on duty and set course for the western coast of Schleswig-

Holstein, joining up with the bomber stream on the way. Nine 3 Group aircraft turned back early, but none from the 90 Squadron element, and they encountered ten-tenths cloud from the midpoint of the North Sea at 3° East, which would persist for the remainder of the operation, topping out over the target at 8,000 feet. The marker element arrived on time, but the failure of H2S equipment reduced the numbers and the red and green TIs could be seen only dimly through the clouds. It seems likely that strong winds caused the skymarkers to drift, and this along with decoy fire sites conspired to draw the main weight of the attack away from the town. The 90 Squadron crews carried out their attacks from 10,000 to 14,800 feet between 23.12 and 23.25 and all returned safely, sadly unable to offer an assessment of the raid, other than to report the glow of fires beneath the cloud. Local reports confirm that damage was light and restricted to the destruction of eleven houses, which was a massive disappointment in view of the effort expended, and the only consolation for the Command was the relatively modest loss of twelve aircraft, a little over 2% of the force.

Later, on the 5th, and while landing BF409 on three engines after a training flight, F/O Overton was forced to take avoiding action when an airman ran across his path, and this caused the Stirling to stall and crash heavily, happily though, without injury to the occupants. The Stirling would never fly again, while F/O Overton, who had just survived his second crash within a month, would shortly be posted for the first of two spells with 218 Squadron, sandwiching a period with 623 Squadron, and would rise to the rank of squadron leader. S/L Alexander attended an investiture at Buckingham Palace on this day and received the Air Force Cross from the hand of His Majesty King George VI in recognition of his many years of excellent service training bomber pilots.

The night of the 6/7th was devoted to mining operations off the Biscay coast for which forty-seven aircraft were detailed, 3 Group contributing a dozen Stirlings for the Deodar garden in the Gironde estuary. The 90 Squadron freshman crews of F/L Prioleau and Sgt Coombs departed Ridgewell at 21.11 and 21.30 respectively, each carrying four mines of various types. The Coombs crew delivered theirs into the briefed location from 1,200 feet at 23.50 after pinpointing on Pointe de la Coubre and the Prioleau crew followed suit from 1,400 feet at 00.21 at the end of a timed run from Point de Grave.

The Ruhr offensive continued at Duisburg on the night of the 8/9th, for which a force of 392 aircraft was made ready, forty-four of them representing 3 Group. Crews learned at briefing that ten Oboe Mosquitos would provide the initial marking, backed up by the Path Finder heavy brigade consisting of four Stirlings, twenty Lancasters and eight Halifaxes. 90 Squadron loaded five of its Mk IIIs with a 2,000-pounder, one or two 500-pounders and incendiaries and sent them on their way from Ridgewell between 21.35 and 21.43 with S/Ls Giles and May the senior pilots on duty. Time-on-target was set for 23.15, before which the ten Oboe Mosquitos were to drop red warning flares and then greens with red stars and green TIs over the aiming-point. If the weather conditions permitted, one Stirling, seven Halifaxes and fourteen Lancasters would back up with red TIs, while the remaining 8 Group aircraft supported the main force. P/O Platt and crew turned back with an engine issue within the hour, while the rest of the bomber stream had to climb through ten-tenths ice-bearing cloud and electrical storms over the North Sea and reach 12,000 feet before breaking into clear air, a task that proved impossible for fifteen of the 3 Group Stirlings. The cloud over Duisburg extended to 20,500 feet, and for whatever reason,

Oboe failed to provide the main force crews with anything more than the hint of red and green TIs. The 90 Squadron crews carried out their attacks from 11,000 to 16,500 feet between 23.26 and 23.36, before returning with nothing of use to pass on at debriefing. Local sources confirmed a widely scattered raid, which hit at least fifteen other Ruhr locations and destroyed just forty buildings in Duisburg at a cost to the Command of nineteen aircraft.

A 5 Group main force of 104 Lancasters and five Oboe Mosquitos returned to Duisburg on the following night to find similar weather conditions and Oboe again failed to facilitate a successful assault, resulting in a disappointing raid that managed to destroy just fifty houses in return for the loss of eight Lancasters or 7.7% of the force. The city would continue to enjoy a relatively charmed life for another five weeks.

Frankfurt was posted as the destination on the 10th for a force of 502 aircraft, of which the 144 Wellingtons would represent the most populous type, demonstrating that this trusty old warhorse still had an important part to play in Bomber Command operations. The plan was standard for a target beyond the range of Oboe and required eleven Path Finder Stirlings and six Halifaxes to drop yellow TIs as route markers by H2S, followed by preliminary warning flares, all of which were to be backed up by two Stirlings, ten Halifaxes and seventeen Lancasters. Cloud conditions permitting, the aiming-point was then to be marked by red TIs on H2S, and if not, by green flares with red stars and a white flare, with appropriate backing up with green TIs or coloured flares. 3 Group contributed ninety aircraft, 90 Squadron represented by a record fifteen, made up of eight Mk IIIs and seven Mk Is, which were loaded with either three 2,000-pounders and a single 1,000-pounder or SBCs of incendiaries before departing Ridgewell between 00.01 and 00.37 with S/L Giles the senior pilot on duty. They set course for Hythe on the Kent coast and after thirty minutes, F/Sgt Cheek became one of nine 3 Group early returns after both inner engines overheated.

The bomber stream adopted the usual course to south-central Germany, following the line of the Franco/Belgian frontier to cross into Germany on an east-north-easterly heading north of Saarbrücken. The H2S marker crews arrived in the target area to be confronted by ten-tenths cloud with tops at between 8,000 and 12,000 feet but found that their red TIs were visible and opted not to sky mark. This was fine in the early stages, until it became impossible to distinguish the genuine TIs from decoys among the incendiaries and searchlights, and the backers up experienced great difficulty in establishing an aiming-point. Largely ineffective heavy and light flak was operating in concert with searchlights as the 90 Squadron participants carried out their attacks from 10,000 to 15,000 feet between 02.47 and 03.06. BF471 arrived over the Kent coast on fumes and crash-landed at 07.04 a mile or so south of Manston airfield never to fly again, but P/O Pugh and crew walked away, the rear gunner with a slight back injury.

BF454 suffered an undercarriage collapse after swinging on take-off for a training flight late on the evening of the 13th, and although the Stirling's career was ended, Sgt Robson and his crew emerged unscathed. The busy round of non-Ruhr operations continued at the southern city of Stuttgart, for which a force of 462 aircraft was made ready on the 14th, and as for the recent Frankfurt operation, Wellingtons were again the most populous type with 146 on duty. 3 Group was represented by sixty-seven Stirlings and eight Lancasters, fourteen of the Stirlings, nine Mk IIIs and five Mk Is, made ready at Ridgewell. At briefings the crews took in the details of the plan, which involved Path Finder aircraft dropping yellow TIs as route markers at two locations, while at the target, nine Stirlings and eight Halifaxes would ground mark the aiming-point with red TIs on H2S, at the same time as releasing a short stick of flares. One Stirling and four Lancasters were then to identify the aiming-point visually and mark it with green TIs, for three Stirlings, six Halifaxes and eleven Lancasters to back up also with greens. This would leave three Stirlings, three Halifaxes and five Lancasters to bolster the efforts of the main force.

The 90 Squadron element took off between 21.30 and 21.52, each carrying an all-incendiary bomb load with deputy A Flight commander, F/L Scott DFC, the senior pilot on duty, and set course for Dungeness on the Kent coast, from where the bomber stream was to begin the Channel crossing en-route for landfall between Cayeux-sur-Mer and Dieppe. The crews of Sgts Gedak and Coombs had the French coast in sight when engine and radio issues persuaded them to turn back, leaving the others to push on in favourable weather conditions, attracting attention from the flak belts at the French coast and the Franco/German frontier. The bomber stream entered Germany under high cirrus cloud and bright moonlight to approach Stuttgart from the north-east and found it clearly visible with just a little haze to impair the vertical visibility. The Path Finder ground marker crews established their positions by H2S confirmed by visual reference, but as evidence of the shortcomings of H2S in its early form, they were actually short of the city centre when they delivered bundles of white flares, red TIs and 1,000 pounders between 00.47 and 00.56. The backers-up were carrying four green TIs, one of them of the long-burning variety, four 1,000 pounders and a single 500 pounder each, which they dropped between 00.50 and 01.14, also to the north-east of the planned aiming-point.

The main force crews were greeted by plentiful red and green TIs concentrated in a built-up area, and some would claim later to have picked out ground detail such as the River Neckar, marshalling yards, the railway station and the Bosch factory, which reinforced their belief that they were over the briefed aiming-point. The 90 Squadron crews released their incendiaries onto mostly green TIs from 9,000 to 13,000 feet between 00.55 and 01.07 and observed a concentration of fires, a large blue flash at 01.03 and smoke rising through 8,000 feet as they turned for home. On the way back, Sgt Routen and crew flew through the night-fighter belt at 400 feet in accordance with instructions for a moonlit night, and between 02.28 and 02.43 shot up three trains on a stretch of track from Noyons to Amiens, causing one locomotive to explode and another to catch fire. Debriefings gleaned little in the way of a useful assessment either of the fall of the bombs or of the raid in general, and absent from that process at Ridgewell was the crew of P/O Beldin. It emerged later that BF462 had been shot down from 11,000 feet by a BF110 and a Ju88 and had crashed some fifteen miles south-south-west of Châlons-sur-Marne. The fact that P/O Beldin alone survived to fall into enemy hands suggests that the Stirling had been outbound at the time and exploded in the air, flinging him into space attached to his parachute.

Bombing photos and post-raid reconnaissance confirmed that the Path Finders had not marked the centre of the city, and that a "creep-back" had developed, which had spread along the line of approach. Creep-back was a feature of many large raids and was caused by crews bombing the first fires they came upon, rather than pushing through to the planned aiming-point. It could work for or against the effectiveness of an attack, and on this night, worked in the Command's favour by falling across the industrial district of Bad-Canstatt, situated to the north-east of the city centre on the East Bank of the River Neckar. The bombing continued to spread further back along the line of approach onto the residential suburbs of Münster and Mühlhausen, and it was here that the majority of the 393 buildings were destroyed and more than nine hundred others severely damaged. A number of bombs did find their way into the city centre, and one killed four hundred French and Russian PoWs in an air-raid shelter. Twenty-three aircraft failed to return, among them eight 3 and 8 Group Stirlings, almost 10% of those dispatched.

Preparations were put in hand on the 16th for a major night of operations, which would see 327 Lancasters and Halifaxes head for the Skoda armaments works at Pilsen in Czechoslovakia, while a predominantly Wellington and Stirling force of 271 aircraft carried out a diversionary raid on Mannheim. 3 Group put up eighty-five Stirlings for Mannheim and eight Lancasters for Pilsen, 90 Squadron represented by fourteen Stirlings, which received bomb loads of either two 2,000-pounders and a 500-pounder or two American 1,900-pounders and a 500-pounder. The plan of attack for Pilsen called for the Path Finders to drop route markers at the final turning point seven miles from the target, which the crews were to then locate visually in the bright moonlight and bomb from as low a level as practicable. It was asking for trouble, and many crews became confused and bombed the route markers, which happened to be over an asylum at Dobrany, while the factory escaped damage. Not only was the operation an abject failure, but it also cost thirty-six aircraft, divided equally between the two types.

The 90 Squadron element departed Ridgewell for Mannheim either side of 22.00 with S/L Giles the senior pilot on duty and lost the services of Sgt Farrell and crew to the failure of both compasses shortly after crossing the Suffolk coast and F/O Mackenzie and crew because of an engine issue at the midpoint of the Channel crossing. The others pressed on in good weather conditions and those reaching the target found considerable haze blotting out ground detail. In compensation, the Path Finder marking was accurate and the subsequent bombing by the main force concentrated within the city. Heavy and light flak batteries were co-operating to good effect with searchlights as the 90 Squadron participants delivered their attacks from 9,000 to 12,000 feet between 00.52 and 01.11 and all but one returned to make their reports. F/L Scott and crew reported that their starboard-outer propeller had been shot off as they began their bombing run but continued on for the last nine miles to press home their attack and return on three engines. The absentee Stirling was BK725, which was shot down by a night-fighter and crash-landed at 02.14 in north-eastern France between Reims and Amiens, all eight occupants surviving, seven to evade capture, while the pilot, P/O White, fell into enemy hands. The rear gunner, Sgt Fitzgerald, was on the final sortie of his first tour and F/L Everiss, the navigator, had been with the squadron from the start. This was just one of seven missing Stirlings, representing a 7% loss rate for the type, in an overall loss of eighteen aircraft, which brought the combined casualty figure for the night to a new record of fifty-four. In exchange for this, post-raid reconnaissance and local reports revealed that 130 buildings had been destroyed in Mannheim, with more than three thousand others damaged to some extent, and many war industry factories had lost production.

While the Command rested on the 17th, twenty-four aircraft were made ready for mining duties off the Biscay coast, 3 Group offering four Stirlings from 214 (Federated Malay States) Squadron at Stradishall and two from 90 Squadron, the latter, bearing aloft the crews of Sgt Routen and P/O Wilson. They departed Ridgewell at 21.31 bound for the Deodar garden in the

Gironde estuary and arrived in the target area after an outward flight of almost four hours to be greeted by moonlight and a little haze. They established their pinpoints on Lake Hourtin and Pointe de la Coubre and delivered their three mines each from 2,000 and 4,000 feet at 01.25 and 01.51.

The main operation on the night of the 20/21st was directed at Stettin, the large shipbuilding port situated some thirty miles south of Swinemünde at the centre of Germany's Baltic coast. A force of 339 aircraft included eleven 115 Squadron Lancasters, while eighty-four 3 Group Stirlings and two from 7 Squadron of 8 Group were made ready for a simultaneous attack on the Heinkel aircraft works at Rostock further west along the coast. Rostock had previously been attacked with great success in a four-raid series on consecutive nights in late April 1942, when a 5 Group element had specifically targeted the Heinkel factory. 90 Squadron made ready a record seventeen Stirlings, ten Mk IIIs and seven Mk Is, and dispatched them from Ridgewell between 21.26 and 21.54 with S/Ls Giles and May the senior pilots on duty and bomb bays containing either two 2,000-pounders and incendiaries or all-incendiary loads. S/L May and crew were approaching the Suffolk coast when the port-outer engine feathered itself and sent them directly to the jettison area, while Sgt Coombs and crew had Denmark's western coast just a few miles ahead when their rear turret became unserviceable and forced them to turn back. It must have been at this point that BF346 was hit by flak and had a number of instruments shot away, despite which, P/O Crew and crew continued with a further 150 miles to travel to the target, and crossed southern Jutland with the others to reach the western Baltic. Having traversed Fyn Island, BF463 was shot down by flak and crashed at 00.19 into the waters of Storebaelt on the western edge of Zealand Island, with no survivors from the crew of P/O Cross RNZAF. Twenty-nine minutes later, BF508 came down in the sea off Zealand with fatal consequences for F/L Prioleau and crew, and curiously, the pilot's remains were interred at Odense on Fyn Island, while two of his crew were buried at Esbjerg on the western side of Jutland some seventy miles to the west. Those reaching the target area after flying out in the most favourable of weather conditions found excellent visibility but an effective smoke-screen in operation, which led to scattered bombing and an unsatisfactory outcome. Twelve 90 Squadron crews reported bombing either the factory or the town from 9,000 to 11,500 feet between 01.29 and 02.11, but P/O Elliott RNZAF and crew were absent from debriefing having disappeared into the Baltic in BF442, it is believed, close to the target. An analysis of the raid suggested that 25% of crews had attacked the factory and the remainder the town at a cost of eight Stirlings, which represented around 9% of those dispatched.

P/O Pugh and his crew were returning from a training flight in BK780 on the 25th and were approaching Ridgewell with the undercarriage deployed, when the dinghy broke loose from its stowage and interfered in some way with the landing, causing the port oleo leg to collapse and cause irreparable damage to the Stirling but not the occupants, who walked away unscathed. This was the pilot's second landing crash in the space of two weeks.

Night flying tests (NFTs) were carried out during the afternoon of the 26th in preparation for that night's operation to Duisburg as part of the Ruhr offensive, for which a force of 561 aircraft was assembled, the numbers bolstered by the inclusion of 135 Wellingtons, while 215 Lancasters represented the largest contribution by type. 8 Group was boosted by the operational debut of 97 (Straits Settlement) Squadron and 405 (Vancouver) Squadron RCAF, which had recently been transferred from 5 and 6 Groups respectively. The plan called for eight Oboe Mosquitos to drop yellow route markers and red TIs on the aiming-point and for the yellows to be backed up by others of the same colour delivered by a dozen Lancasters, while three Stirlings, five 35 (Madras Presidency) Squadron Halifaxes and seven Lancasters backed up at the aiming-point with green TIs. 3 Group detailed eighty-three aircraft, a dozen of the Stirlings provided by 90 Squadron for what was the largest raid yet on this particular target. Take-off from Ridgewell took place between 00.26 and 00.47 with S/L May the senior pilot on duty and each crew sitting on an all-incendiary bomb load. After climbing out they set course for the Dutch coast near The Hague for the northern approach to the Ruhr, joining the bomber stream as they crossed the North Sea. There were no 90 Squadron aircraft among 3 Group's six early returns, and the target area was reached after approaching from the north-east. They were greeted by largely clear skies and good visibility in which green TIs could be clearly seen backing up the reds delivered by the Oboe Mosquitos and inviting the Ridgewell participants' incendiaries from 11,000 to 14,000 feet between 02.24 and 02.44. By the end of the raid, many fires were evident, although opinions were divided as to the degree of concentration achieved. A large orange explosion was witnessed to the east of the aiming-point at 02.34, and although fires had not fully gained a hold as the last of the bombers turned away, black smoke was rising through 7,000 feet. The operation was only partially successful, daylight reconnaissance revealing that many bombs had fallen to the north-east of the city, probably as a result of some main force crews bombing too early rather than pressing-on to the aiming point at what was a recognised flak hotspot. Even so, three hundred buildings had been destroyed, and for a change, only two Stirlings were among the seventeen failures to return. Sadly for 90 Squadron, one of them was the Mk I, BF383, which was shot down by a night-fighter, it is believed while homebound, and crashed into the Ijsselmeer with no survivors from the crew of F/O Mackenzie.

Two massive mining operations were mounted on the nights of the 27/28th and 28/29th, the former employing 160 aircraft, of which thirty, mostly Stirlings, were provided by 3 Group and assigned to the Deodar and Nectarine II gardens, respectively in the Gironde estuary and the central Frisians. 90 Squadron loaded five of its Mk I Stirlings with six assorted mines each and sent them on their way from Ridgewell between 00.45 and 00.53 bound for Nectarine II with P/O Crew the only commissioned pilot on duty. All arrived safely in the target area and commented on the extreme darkness below the cloud base, but Gee assisted in establishing pinpoints and the vegetables were planted according to brief from 800 to 1,000 feet between 03.01 and 03.06.

F/L Scott was notified on the 28th that he was to receive the immediate award of a DFC for his fortitude during the Mannheim operation in mid-month, while a record mining force of 207 aircraft was made ready for that night's gardening expeditions. 3 Group contributed thirty-two Stirlings and two Lancasters, of which five Stirlings were provided by 90 Squadron and departed Ridgewell between 20.18 and 20.56 bound for the Quince garden, located in Kiel Bay off the southern tip of Denmark's Langeland Island. S/L May, a Canadian serving in the RAF, was the senior pilot on duty, and like the others, he and his crew were sitting on four assorted mines. The force encountered heavy cloud over the Danish and German coasts, which persuaded many crews to descend to low level to establish a pinpoint for the timed runs to their drop sites. This put them within range of flak ships and coastal batteries, which sprayed lethal light flak into their paths and brought down twenty-two of them, seven of them Stirlings.

Conditions had improved by the time that the 90 Squadron element reached its target area and found clear skies and good visibility aided slightly by the Northern Lights. Pinpoints were established on the southern tip of Langeland, timed runs were conducted, and the vegetables were planted from 800 to 900 feet between 23.43 and 00.12. It is not known whether or not S/L May and crew had fulfilled their brief before BF346 disappeared into the Baltic with no survivors, and just one body was recovered for burial in Kiel War Cemetery. The casualty figure on this night was the largest of the war from a mining operation, but the number of vegetables planted, 593, was also a record which would not be surpassed.

Stirlings were excluded from the month's final operation, which was by 305 aircraft against Essen on the night of the 30th, for which 3 Group contributed eleven 115 Squadron Lancasters, five of which returned early. The operation was based on Oboe skymarking over a cloud-covered target and destroyed 189 buildings, while inflicting further damage on the Krupp complex.

During the course of a very expensive month, the squadron undertook twelve operations and dispatched 108 sorties for the loss of eleven Stirlings and seven crews.

May 1943

May would bring a return to winning ways and some spectacular successes, but the first order of business for 90 Squadron was the notification on the 3rd of the award of an immediate DFC to P/O George Crew for his fortitude during the Rostock operation. 3 Group had launched its May account with a small mining effort off the Biscay coast on the 1st, which did not involve Ridgewell, but the first major operation was posted on the 4th and was the first attack during the Ruhr campaign on the city of Dortmund, an industrial powerhouse located at the eastern end of the region. At briefings across the Command, crews learned that they were to be part of a new record non-1,000 force of 596 aircraft, of which seventy-five Stirlings and a dozen Lancasters were being made ready on 3 Group stations. The plan of attack called for Oboe Mosquitos to drop yellow track markers, before eight of them ground-marked the aiming-point with green TIs, leaving two in reserve to bomb with the main force if not required for marking duties. Twenty-two Lancasters and two Halifaxes were to back up with red TIs, and all remaining Path Finder aircraft were to bomb with the main force. 90 Squadron made ready thirteen Stirlings, all but one of them Mk IIIs, although both variants continued to arrive in ones and twos from the various manufacturing sites in Belfast, Rochester, Birmingham, Cambridge and Swindon and from other squadrons. They departed Ridgewell between 22.09 and 22.34 with F/L Scott the senior pilot on duty and bomb loads of either two 2,000-pounders or five 500-pounder supplemented by assorted incendiaries. Sgt Teede and crew were east of the Dutch town of Zwolle heading for the German frontier when the port-inner engine failed followed by the mid-upper turret, forcing them to jettison the bombs and turn back. The rest of the bomber stream entered Germany over Nordhorn to the north of the Ruhr and made its way south to the target, where clear skies and good visibility prevailed with only industrial and smoke haze to spoil the vertical view.

The Oboe markers were due to go down at 01.00, but the first greens were two minutes early, after which the initial Path Finder marking was accurately placed around the city centre. Some of the backing-up fell short and inevitably attracted some bomb loads and a decoy site was also successful in luring away others, but most crews were guided by the yellow approach markers and red and green TIs on the ground. The Ridgewell crews carried out their attacks from 11,200 to 16,800 feet between 01.06 and 01.25 and all but one returned to report many sizeable explosions, including a particularly large one at 01.12, which may have been the one reported by a 50 Squadron crew that threw flame to a height of 2,000 feet and burned for ten seconds. They also described developing fires, the glow from which could be seen, according to some, from 150 miles into the return flight. Post-raid reconnaissance revealed that approximately half of the force had bombed within three miles of the aiming-point, destroying 1,218 buildings and seriously damaging more than two thousand others, while a number of important steelworks were hit, as were many facilities in the inland docks area. Local reports confirmed a death toll of 693 people, which was a record from a Bomber Command attack. It was not a one-sided affair, however, and the loss of thirty-one aircraft was a foretaste of what was in store for the bomber crews operating over "Happy Valley". The Stirlings' losses were disproportionately higher than those of the other types at almost 9% and among them was 90 Squadron's BK814, which was brought down by flak during the bombing run and crashed south of Lünen in the north-eastern suburbs with no survivors from the crew of Sgt Maxwell.

The following week was devoted to minor operations, and it was during this period on the 8th that the long-serving F/L Sayers was declared tour-expired and posted to 1665 Conversion Unit. On the 9th, 3 Group detailed twenty-one Stirlings for mining sorties off the Biscay coast, the ten 90 Squadron participants assigned to the Deodar garden in the Gironde estuary. They departed Ridgewell between 21.04 and 21.20 with P/Os Crew and Peryer the only commissioned pilots on duty and, on a night of good serviceability, all reached the target area to find up to five-tenths cloud and extreme darkness, but good enough visibility to be able to pinpoint on Pointe de Grave, Lake Hourtin and Pointe de la Coubre. They conducted timed runs to the release point at indicated air speeds of 130 to 200 m.p.h and release their three mines each into the briefed locations from 800 to 3,000 feet between 01.09 and 02.00, before returning safely after seven to eight-hour round trips.

An operation to Bochum planned for the evening of the 11th was cancelled, and the following day Duisburg was posted as the night's target, for which a force of 572 aircraft was made ready, eighty-five of them provided by 3 Group. The plan allowed for nine Mosquitos to drop yellow TIs on track as a preliminary warning and red TIs on the aiming-point, which would be backed up with green TIs by five Stirlings, five Halifaxes and twenty Lancasters. At Ridgewell thirteen Stirlings were made ready, four to carry a 2,000-pounder, two 500-pounders and selection of incendiaries, while the remainder had full loads of SBCs of incendiaries. F/L Scott was the senior pilot on duty and a late take-off slot meant that it was fourteen minutes after midnight before he and his crew started the ball rolling and 00.30 by the time that Sgt Morey and crew brought up the rear. They headed for the North Sea to rendezvous with the bomber stream and make landfall on the Dutch coast in the area of Castricum-aan-Zee, before tracking east across Holland to enter Germany some forty miles north of the target. It was at this point, at 02.05, that P/O Young and crew were attacked by a night-fighter, which knocked out the rear turret, wounded its occupant and inflicted other serious damage including bursting the main undercarriage tyres. The rear gunner was unable to return fire, but despite shattered lower legs, remained at his post to provide a running commentary on the location of the assailant and direct evasive action. The bomb load was jettisoned, the night-fighter disappeared into the darkness and the Stirling's nose was pointed in the direction of the North Sea, while the others pressed on to reach the target area guided by the yellow tracking flares.

They found ideal bombing conditions with no cloud and good visibility, which helped the Oboe and H2S crews to mark with great accuracy and focus. The main force crews were able to identify ground features and exploit the opportunity to produce a display of unusually concentrated bombing on red and green TIs, those from 90 Squadron from 10,000 to 13,000 feet between 02.25 and 02.38. P/O Young skilfully landed BF529 at Stradishall without further damage and rear gunner, Sgt Davine, was taken to hospital, where both feet would be amputated. It was more than an hour later that P/O Sheppard landed a severely damaged BF473 at Stradishall, also with a wounded rear gunner on board after being attacked by a night-fighter when fifteen miles off the enemy coast homebound. At debriefing, crews described a large explosion at 02.30, streets outlined by fire and a highly successful outcome, perhaps the first time at this target that an attack had proceeded according to plan. The crew reports were confirmed by photo-reconnaissance, which revealed extensive damage in the city centre and the Ruhrort Rhine docks, Germany's largest inland port, where thirty-four barges and other vessels had been sunk and a further sixty damaged to some extent. 1,596 buildings were totally destroyed and the Thyssen steelworks was hit, but the success was paid for by a new record loss for the campaign of thirty-four aircraft. 90 Squadron's BF523 was shot down into the Ijsselmeer while homebound at 03.28 by the night-fighter of Uffz Emil Heinzelmann of III./NJG1, killing Sgt Morey RCAF and his crew, and BK661 was lost without trace with the crew of Sgt Gedak RCAF. The loss rates by type again made interesting reading and confirmed the established food chain, the Lancasters sustaining a 4.2% loss, compared with 8.9% for Wellingtons, 7.1% for Stirlings and 6.3% for Halifaxes. Such was the level of destruction that Duisburg would now be left in peace for a year.

On the following day, 124 Lancasters of 5 Group were detailed to join forces with thirty-two other Lancasters and twelve Halifaxes of 8 Group for an attempt to rectify the recent failure at the Skoda armaments works at Pilsen. A simultaneous raid on Bochum, a city built on coal mining and situated some ten miles west of Dortmund, would involve a force of 442 aircraft, of which 3 Group contributed ninety, nine of the Stirlings made ready by 90 Squadron. They departed Ridgewell between 00.08 and 00.42 with S/L Giles and F/L Scott the senior pilots on duty and lost the services of the crews of Sgt Appelby and P/O Peryer, the former at the midpoint of the North Sea crossing because of an unserviceable rear turret and the latter due to an overheating port engine after making landfall at the Scheldt estuary. The others pressed on in favourable conditions and followed Oboe-laid yellow track markers to the target area, running the gauntlet of heavy predicted flak co-operating with searchlights to be greeted over the central Ruhr by clear skies but the usual industrial haze to obscure ground detail. The first Oboe Mosquitos dropped red TIs onto the aiming point, before a gap developed in the marking, and although the backers-up kept the aiming point marked with green TIs throughout, the bombing lacked a degree of concentration, possibly as a result of the appearance of decoy markers some fifteen minutes into the attack. The 90 Squadron crews delivered their loads of either three 1,000-pounder and incendiaries or all-incendiaries onto mostly green TIs from 11,000 to 14,000 feet between 02.19 and 02.30 and reported that the target was rocked by many explosions and appeared to be a mass of flames by the end of the raid with thick, black smoke rising and drifting to conceal the ground. Photo-reconnaissance revealed the operation to have been moderately effective and local sources admitted to the destruction of 394 buildings, with more than seven hundred others seriously damaged.

It was on the night of the 16/17th, during a nine-night lull in main force operations, that 617 Squadron wrote its page in history by attacking the Ruhr dams under Operation Chastise, and contrary to popular belief, the nineteen special Lancasters were not the only Bomber Command aircraft flying that night as eighty-six aircraft, including thirteen 3 Group Stirlings were sent mining, while a dozen SOE sorties were conducted by 138 and 161 Squadrons from Tempsford. Later, on the 17th, S/L Joseph Dugdale arrived on posting from 1657 Conversion Unit to succeed S/L Alexander as C Flight commander. At 04.25 on the 19th, as Sgt Wood and crew touched down at Ridgewell on return from a night training sortie, a tyre burst, causing BF414 to swing violently and suffer the inevitable consequence of a collapsed undercarriage. The Stirling would never fly again, but the crew walked away apparently unscathed. On the 22nd, P/O Coombs and crew carried out a sea search lasting nine hours and fifty minutes to find crews suspected to have come down during the night's mining operation, and F/O McKenzie and crew spent eight hours thirty minutes aloft for a similar cause on the 23rd.

By the time that the next major operation was posted on the 23rd, the main force squadrons had undergone an expansion with the addition to many units of a third or C Flight, which in most cases, would eventually be hived off to form the nucleus of a brand-new squadron. The giant force of 826 aircraft was the largest non-1,000 effort to date and surpassed the previous record set three weeks earlier by a clear 230 aircraft. The number of available Lancasters had leapt by eighty-eight, Halifaxes by forty-eight, Stirlings by forty and Wellingtons by forty-one, and their destination for the second time in the month was Dortmund. The Command had been restored to full health and vigour, and activity on all participating stations was hectic as preparations were put in hand to resume the Ruhr offensive. The ground crews and armourers worked tirelessly, while the aircrews attended briefings to learn of their part in the grand plan, which required eleven Oboe Mosquitos to drop yellow preliminary warning TIs on track, before marking the aiming-point with red TIs, which eight Stirlings, eleven Halifaxes and fourteen Lancasters were to back up with greens. 3 Group detailed a record 118 aircraft, and 90 Squadron achieved its best effort yet by making ready seventeen Stirlings, a dozen Mk IIIs and the rest Mk Is, which took off between 22.59 and 23.34 with W/C Claydon and S/L Giles the senior pilots on duty. They set course under cloudless skies for the Castricum region of the Dutch coast on the northern approach to the eastern Ruhr and lost Sgt Appleby and crew to engine trouble when twenty miles short of the Dutch coast.

The others all reached the target area to find clear skies but smoke already drifting across the city and combining with industrial haze to obscure ground detail, a situation, which, before the advent of Oboe, would have rendered the attack a lottery. The 109 Squadron Mosquitos marked the centre of the city accurately, after which the backers-up fulfilled their briefs to ensure that the aiming-point was maintained throughout the raid. Main force crews reported that they could observe the TIs from twenty miles away on approach, and after bombing witnessed many explosions and fires, which merged into a large area of conflagration that sent thick columns of black smoke rising up through 18,000 feet as they turned away. The 90 Squadron crews fulfilled their briefs from 11,000 to 14,000 feet between 01.07 and 01.44 and on return reported fierce night-fighter activity over the target and on the way home, and this was reflected in the high casualty rate of thirty-eight aircraft, the largest loss of the campaign to date, of which almost half were Halifaxes. Six 3 Group Stirlings failed to return, but there were no empty dispersal pans at Ridgewell. Post-raid reconnaissance and local reports confirmed massive damage in central, northern and eastern districts, where almost two thousand buildings had been destroyed and many important industrial premises had suffered a loss of production. Just like Duisburg, Dortmund would be allowed an entire year to lick its deep wounds before next hosting a visit from Bomber Command's heavy brigade.

On the 25th, the crews of P/O Pugh and Sgt MacInnes carried out sea searches over the North Sea but returned after four hours and fifteen minutes and two hours and forty-five minutes respectively having found nothing, the latter crash-landing on the airfield at Shipdham at 13.00 after losing power in yet another example of a Stirling being written off and the crew walking away. Later, in the day, preparations began to send the Bomber Command juggernaut to the southern Ruhr to attack Düsseldorf, for which a force of 759 aircraft was made ready and a plan drawn up that called for the standard procedure of Mosquito-laid yellow preliminary warning TIs on track, and red TIs delivered by Oboe onto the aiming-point. Eight Stirlings, twelve Halifaxes and twenty-three Lancasters were to back these up with green TIs, leaving five Stirlings, fourteen Halifaxes and twenty-five Lancasters to bomb with the main force. 3 Group detailed 113 aircraft, of which a new record eighteen Stirlings at Ridgewell were given a variety of loads, some all-incendiary and others with combinations of 2,000, 1000 and 500-pounders supplemented by incendiaries. They took off between 23.50 and 00.25 with S/Ls Dugdale and Giles the senior pilots on duty and set course for the Scheldt estuary for the southern approach to the Ruhr, forming into an elongated bomber stream as they made the sea crossing.

Crews expected to find the forecast favourable conditions over the target, for which a ground-marking plan had been prepared, but when the Oboe Mosquitos arrived, they were greeted by two layers of cloud with tops at 18,500 feet, and although they delivered their TIs with great accuracy, they could not be seen by the backers-up and the marking became scattered. Some main force crews arriving at the Dutch coast towards the rear of the bomber stream were able to observe feverish activity at the target, still some one hundred miles and thirty minutes flying time away. The 90 Squadron participants delivered their attacks onto red and green TIs from 11,500 to 14,500 feet between 01.41 and 02.07 and all but one returned safely to pass on their impressions to the intelligence section. Some reported a huge explosion at 01.49 as they were lining up for the bombing run and gained an impression of large fires developing beneath the clouds, despite which, many thought the raid to have been scattered. Absent from debriefing was the eight-man crew of P/O Young DFC RCAF, who had been crossing the Dutch coast homebound when EH876 was shot down by a night-fighter and disappeared into the sea. Only the remains of the rear gunner, P/O O'Connell, from the mixed RCAF, RNZAF and RAF crew were recovered for burial in Den Burg Cemetery on Texel. Post-raid reconnaissance and local reports confirmed that the raid had failed to achieve concentration, possibly as the result of the deployment by the enemy of decoy markers and dummy fire sites, and it had developed into an "old-style" scattering of bombs across a wide area. Düsseldorf suffered the destruction of fewer than a hundred buildings, in return for which, twenty-seven aircraft failed to return.

Essen was posted as the target for the night of the 27/28th, for which 3 Group detailed around a hundred Stirlings, which were suddenly cancelled after the marking plan was altered, and this left seventeen 115 Squadron Lancaster Mk IIs to represent 3 Group in the main event, while eighteen Stirlings prepared for mining duties in the Nectarine II garden off the central Frisians. The five 90 Squadron participants departed Ridgewell between 22.46 and 23.30 with S/L Dugdale the senior pilot on duty and made their way out over Cromer on course for a pinpoint on Schiermonnikoog, only to lose the services of Sgt Wood and crew within the first hour after their undercarriage instruments failed. The remaining four established their pinpoints with ease despite extreme darkness and planted six vegetables each from 750 to 1,100 feet between 00.41 and 01.08. Meanwhile, a force of 518 aircraft had departed their stations for Essen and delivered a scattered attack based on skymarking in the face of cloud cover, but still managed to destroy almost five hundred buildings.

Ten miles to the east of Düsseldorf on the southern fringe of the Ruhr, the twin towns of Elberfeld and Barmen nestle in the Wupper Valley, which gave them their joint name of Wuppertal. They had become wealthy by exploiting the rich coal deposits beneath their feet and now boasted much industry helping the German war effort. A force of 719 aircraft was assembled on Saturday the 29th to pitch against this new Ruhr target, the aiming-point for which was to be the Barmen half at the eastern end of the conurbation. On this occasion, the route markers were to be dropped by two 8 Group Stirlings and two Halifaxes, while ahead, the Oboe Mosquitos took care of ground marking with red TIs. These would be backed up by four Stirlings, eleven Halifaxes and twenty-three Lancasters with greens, at the same time as thirteen Stirlings, twenty Halifaxes and twenty-one Lancasters acted as fire raisers by dropping incendiaries. This would leave two Stirlings, five Halifaxes and seven Lancasters to bomb with the main force. 3 Group detailed ninety-nine Stirlings and sixteen Lancasters and the ground crews and armourers at Ridgewell pulled out all the stops to prepare sixteen Stirlings for what would be the squadron's final operation before moving to a new home. They took off between 23.00 and 23.19 with no senior pilot on duty and slotted into the bomber stream as it headed for the Scheldt estuary on the southern approach to the Ruhr, thereafter, to run the gauntlet of searchlights and flak in the Cologne and Düsseldorf corridor.

Those reaching the target were greeted by clear skies with the usual industrial haze extending up to 10,000 feet, and yellow tracking flares clearly identified the final turning-point as ahead the backers-up went in at 16,000 to 18,000 feet between 01.03 and 01.51 to reinforce the red TIs with greens. Meanwhile, the thirteen fire-raisers had attacked with a 2,000 pounder and 1,164 x 4lb incendiaries each, leaving the way clear for the main force to exploit the opportunity to deliver a massive blow. The operation proceeded precisely according to plan, with accurate Path Finder marking preceding concentrated main force bombing, and the 90 Squadron crews played their part, delivering their mixed high explosive/incendiary loads from 10,000 to 13,000 feet between 01.01 and 01.18. High above, the crews watched the narrow streets of the old town become engulfed in flame, which almost certainly developed into a minor firestorm and caused damage and casualties on an unimaginable scale. The defences of flak and searchlights were described by returning crews as ineffective, and a few enemy night-fighters were seen, but the impression was of a one-sided affair, when, in fact, thirty-three bombers failed to return home, in many cases having fallen victim to night-fighters. 90 Squadron's EF349 was shot down by Hptm Ludwig Meister of 1./NJG4 and crashed homebound two miles south-west of Cambrai killing P/O Letters and all but two of his crew, who were taken into captivity. EF397 had returned to the Ridgewell circuit but crashed at 04.30 two miles north of Stradishall with fatal consequences for P/O Norton and all but the rear gunner, who survived with injuries.

It was a sad way to bring to an end five months at Ridgewell, and two days later the squadron completed its move to West Wickham, a new station situated a few miles to the west of Stradishall, where it would be the first resident unit. During the course of the month the squadron took part in eight operations and dispatched 101 sorties for the loss of eight Stirlings and six crews.

June 1943

The new month began for 8 Group with the arrival of two Mosquito squadrons from 2 Group, which had left Bomber Command on the previous day to become part of a new organisation called the 2nd Tactical Air Force. 105 and 139 Squadrons had illustrious careers behind them, having been part of the AASF during the battle for France, and had served 2 Group with distinction, thereafter, flying Blenheims until the advent of the Mosquito. Unlike the Mosquitos of 109 Squadron, which operated at maximum altitude for the purpose of Oboe reception, 2 Group Mosquitos had been employed mostly in a low-level strike role against shipping and precision land targets, where speed was their greatest asset. 105 Squadron was to become the second Oboe unit, while 139 Squadron's initial role would be to drop cookies in nuisance raids on German cities as a forerunner of the Light Night Striking Force (LNSF), which would form in 8 Group with the addition of further Mosquito units in 1944. For the time being, both squadrons remained at Marham in Norfolk, which was transferred to 8 Group control, and 109 Squadron would move there from Wyton in the following month.

There were no major operations during the first week and a half of June, which provided an opportunity for training, but the Command was rarely totally operationally inactive, and 3 Group contributed Stirlings to mining operations off the Frisians on the nights of the 1st and 2nd and off the Biscay coast on the 3rd. On the last-mentioned occasion, 90 Squadron detailed ten Stirlings to participate in mining operations in the Deodar garden in the Gironde estuary, for which they departed West Wickham for the first time in anger between 22.23 and 22.38 with S/Ls Dugdale and Giles the senior pilots on duty and three mines in each bomb bay. They headed south to begin the Channel crossing at Selsey Bill with a view to making landfall on the Normandy coast near Caen and lost the services of P/O Crew and crew to compass failure at the midpoint and F/O Smith and crew to an engine issue shortly after crossing the French coast. The others arrived in the target area to find clear skies and good visibility, by which time Sgt Steel and crew had lost the use of their Gee and DR compass and, unable to positively establish their position, brought their mines home. The others pinpointed on Lake Hourtin and the Ile-de-Re and delivered their vegetables into the briefed locations from 800 to 1,000 feet between 01.15 and 01.51.

It was left to 3 Group to send a dozen gardeners back to the Nectarine I garden in the southern Frisians on the night of the 5/6th, the force consisting of eleven Stirlings and a solitary 115 Squadron Hercules-powered Mk II Lancaster. On the 7th the squadron bade a fond but sad farewell to S/L Alexander on his posting to 1665 Conversion Unit. Older than most, he had acted as a father figure to the inexperienced young men flooding into the squadron, and his wisdom and influence would be missed.

8 Group HQ moved out of Wyton on the 10th to Castle Hill House in Huntingdon, where it would remain for the rest of the war. Despite the fact that bomber crews had one of the most dangerous jobs in military service, they became bored and listless during extended periods of operational inactivity, and most preferred the dangers to the alternatives, like lectures and PT. Many cricket matches were played while the crews kicked their heels on the ground, and there was, no doubt, relief, when the operations against Düsseldorf and Münster planned for the 11th actually resulted in briefings taking place. The bomber stations from north to south became a hive of industry as ground crews and armourers got to work preparing 783 aircraft for the night's main event over the southern Ruhr and for an 8 Group show 180 miles to the north, which, in effect, was a mass H2S trial involving seventy-two aircraft. 8 Group's H2S-equipped Stirlings and Halifaxes had thus far been referred to as "special aircraft" in operational plans, but now that 83 Squadron had begun to take on H2S-equipped Lancasters, they would be referred to as "Y" aircraft. The plan for Düsseldorf would follow the standard pattern, in which Mosquito yellow preliminary warning flares would be backed up by the other 8 Group aircraft, and the Oboe-laid red TIs on the aiming-point backed up with greens. However, uncertainty concerning the weather conditions resulted in the Mosquitos also carrying target-marking red flares with green stars.

3 Group detailed 112 aircraft for Düsseldorf and seventeen 90 Squadron Stirlings had their bomb bays filled with a variety of loads that included combinations of 2,000 and 500 pounders and vast quantities of incendiaries. They departed West Wickham between 23.37 and 00.14 with S/Ls Dugdale and Scott the senior pilots on duty and flew out over Orfordness, adopting the southern approach to the region via the Scheldt estuary and Belgium. They had to contend with static and lightning conditions in towering ten-tenths cloud as they made their way across the North Sea, some reporting the tops to be at 23,500 feet. P/O Peryer and crew were soon in trouble as their port-inner engine caught fire, forcing it to be shut down and the bomb load of a 2,000-pounder and incendiaries to be dumped. It was probably at this stage, seventy-five minutes into their sortie, that F/O McKenzie and crew were persuaded to jettison their 2,000-pounder and incendiaries also in order to maintain height while experiencing icing conditions and P/O Peters and crew lost their Gee and other navigational aids to end their interest in proceedings. The cloud had largely dissipated by the time that the others reached the southern Ruhr to find just small amounts at 2,000, 5,000 and 10,000 feet, dependent upon the time of arrival on final approach. Those in the vanguard of the main force were drawn on by yellow tracking flares from 01.05 and red skymarkers with green stars at 01.16, while those a little further back in the bomber stream were guided on by red and green skymarkers. The Paramatta marking (ground-marking TIs) did not seem to appear until these crews were turning away, but they were clearly visible to the crews in the rear-guard, including those from 90 Squadron, who delivered their payloads from 11,000 and 15,500 feet between 01.45 and 01.55 and described a sea of flames covering a massive area with columns of smoke rising through 21,000 feet.

The searchlight and flak defences were at their formidable best and night-fighters were lurking to ensnare the unwary, and when all aircraft had been accounted for, thirty-eight were found to be missing, a figure that equalled the heaviest loss of the offensive to date, but included only three Stirlings. Returning crews described many large fires and huge explosions, and it was clear, that the target city had undergone an ordeal of extreme proportions. Post-raid reconnaissance revealed an area of 130 acres to have been destroyed, and local reports detailed an area of fire of eight by five kilometres covering the city centre. Almost nine thousand separate fire incidents were recorded, and massive damage was inflicted upon housing and industry, leading to the complete stoppage of production at forty-two war industry factories. The death toll in Düsseldorf amounted to almost thirteen hundred people, while 140,000 others were bombed out of their homes. This level of destruction was achieved despite the fact that an Oboe Mosquito had inadvertently dumped a bunch of TIs fourteen miles from the aiming point, which caused a proportion of the bombing to be wasted in open country.

Lancasters and Halifaxes made up the main force for a heavy raid on Bochum on the following night, when, despite complete cloud cover, Oboe skymarking allowed massive damage to be inflicted upon the city centre. The Stirling brigade spent this night at home and 90 Squadron took the next night off as well, while a number of other Stirling units contributed to a mining effort off the Biscay ports.

On the 13th, W/C Claydon and the squadron gunnery leader, F/L Ewing, each received a DFC, both highly popular awards to men whose influence had helped to shape the squadron. W/C Claydon had been notified of his posting to command the Bombing and Gunnery School at Sutton Bridge and the whole squadron paraded in a hollow square on the perimeter track with him in the centre while he delivered an emotional speech in which he thanked those present for the support that they had given him, and encouraged them to display the same commitment and loyalty to his successor, the newly promoted W/C Giles. F/L Scott was also promoted to acting squadron leader rank to fulfil the role of flight commander as a new era began. That evening, Sgt Steel and crew were sent on a sea search, and during six hours aloft over the North Sea spotted a dinghy at 19.49 from which a red Verey flare was fired. On investigating, they were able to see that it contained six men, and after alerting the rescue services they remained on scene, circling the location and maintaining watch as a Walrus seaplane landed at 20.45 and embarked the men. The Walrus then made a number of attempts to take off and a second one had to be deployed, which arrived and orbited while an Air-Sea-Rescue launch arrived at 22.15 to pick up the men from the first Walrus and return them safely to shore. The rescued airmen turned out to be members of the USAAF, who were fortunate indeed to be spotted in the vast expanse of sea, and Sgt Steel and crew received the heart-felt congratulations of the rest of the squadron. Sadly, they could not know that the cold North Sea from which they had helped to pluck six fellow fliers would be their final resting place just two weeks hence.

The main operation on the night of the 14/15th was an all-Lancaster affair at Oberhausen, the heavily industrialized Ruhr city nestling in the eastern shadows of Duisburg. Oboe Mosquitos again provided the reference, and the heavies caused major damage to the Altstadt through complete cloud cover. More than two hundred aircraft from 1, 5 and 8 Groups undertook a raid on Cologne on the night of the 16/17th, for which the marking was carried out, not by Oboe, but by sixteen Path Finder aircraft employing H2S. The experiment was not entirely successful after the late and sparse skymarking led to scattered bombing, but even so, four hundred houses were destroyed in a foretaste of what was in store for the Rhineland capital in the very near future.

In the previous October 5 Group had mounted an audacious daylight attack by more than ninety Lancasters on the Schneider armaments works at Le Creusot and its power source, the nearby Henri Paul power station at Montchanin, situated in east-central France. Labelled the French "Krupp", the company was founded by the famous family, whose name will forever be associated with the Schneider Trophy, for which Britain, France, Italy and the USA competed bi-annually in float plane speed trials between 1913 and 1931. The competition ended when Britain won the trophy outright after three straight victories, the last of which was achieved by the Supermarine S6B powered by the forerunner of the Rolls Royce Merlin engine. The attack, code-named Operation Robinson, which was believed initially to have been successful, was later shown to have caused little damage, and a new attempt to halt production of artillery pieces for use by the Germans was planned for the night of the 19/20th, when the nearby Breuil steelworks and the Mont Chanin power stations were also to be targeted.

290 aircraft were made ready on 3, 4, 6 and 8 Group stations, of which eighty-seven Stirlings were provided by 3 Group, eight of them belonging to the newly-formed 620 Squadron, which was making its operational debut. Just two Lancasters were to take part, both representing 7 Squadron, which was in the process of converting from Stirlings. The plan called for fourteen Stirlings and ten Halifaxes to drop green flares and yellow TIs as route markers by H2S, and for four Stirlings and two Lancasters to illuminate the aiming-point blindly with long sticks of flares. These and the remaining illuminators would keep the aiming-point highlighted, while the main force went about its business, before flying on to Montchanin to repeat the process. The 90 Squadron contingent of fifteen departed West Wickham between 22.01 and 22.23 with W/C Giles and S/L Scott the senior pilots on duty, and each Stirling loaded with either two 2,000 and two 1,000-pounders or six 1,000-pounders. They began the Channel crossing at the Sussex coast and Lt Farrell and crew had reached the midpoint when the rear turret was declared to be unserviceable and the six 1,000-pounders were dumped.

Time-on-target for the leading Path Finder crews was scheduled for 01.45, and there were no further early returns among the 90 Squadron element during the 450-mile outward flight. On arrival in the target area, the weather conditions were found to be excellent, enabling the crews to identify lakes and other landmarks with ease. There was no opposition, which was fortunate, as Path Finder crews would have to make up to five passes over the aiming-points, not counting dummy runs, depending upon their respective roles. The 90 Squadron crews established their positions by Gee, confirmed visually, and delivered their respective bomb loads from 4,300 to 6,000 feet between 01.55 and 02,15, ten aiming for the steelworks and four the Schneider factory. Returning crews reported explosions, fires and blue electrical flashes and the consensus was of a successful operation. However, while bombing photos revealed the attack to have fallen within three miles of the aiming-point, only about 20% of the bombs had hit the target and it was established later that drifting smoke had hampered target identification and that the Breuil steelworks had attracted most of the bombs, while the transformer station had escaped damage altogether. The problem was partly that main force crews had been trained to aim at TIs from medium to high level and were unused to identifying targets visually from medium to low level.

A hectic round of four major operations to the Ruhr in the space of five nights began at Krefeld on the 21st, for which a force of 705 aircraft was made ready, which included 113 provided by 3 Group. Situated on the western bank of the Rhine south-west of Duisburg and north-west of Düsseldorf, this was the most westerly Ruhr town to be targeted during the campaign. At briefings, the 8 Group crews were told that ten Mosquitos would ground mark the aiming-point with red TIs, and if they proved not to be visible, nine Stirlings, thirteen Halifaxes and eight Lancasters were to ground mark with yellow TIs by H2S, backed up with reds and greens by twenty-five Lancasters, six Stirlings and six Halifaxes. 90 Squadron loaded eighteen Stirlings with 30lb and 4lb incendiaries and launched them from West Wickham between 23.44 and 00.15 with F/Ls Platt and Smith the senior pilots on duty and flew out over Aldeburgh on the Suffolk coast. P/O MacInnes and crew were contending with the failure of both compasses and an inability to maintain height at 11,000 feet and turned back after reaching Moerdijk on the Scheldt. The remainder flew on to the target, which lay under cloudless, moonlit skies with just drifting smoke from fires to impair the vertical visibility. Path Finders produced a near-perfect display of target marking for the main-force crews to exploit and three-quarters of them delivered their bombs within three miles of the aiming point. The 90 Squadron element carried out their attacks on red and green TIs from 10,000 to 14,500 feet between 01.50 and 02.02 and watched a concentrated area of fire develop, which would remain visible for a hundred miles into the return journey.

At debriefings across the Command, crews described a sea of red fire giving off masses of smoke, with one particular jet-black column rising through 18,000 feet as they turned away. All were convinced of the success of the operation, and one crew likened it to the Wuppertal-Barmen raid. The searchlight and flak defences were described by most as moderate, and it was the night-fighters that were responsible for the majority of the forty-four missing bombers, a new record for the campaign. Seventeen Halifaxes were lost, six of them from 35 (Madras Presidency) Squadron of the Path Finders, and this represented an 8.1% loss rate for the type, which was marginally more than the 7.7% registered by the Stirlings, but appreciably in excess of the 3.4% for the Lancaster brigade. In return for this huge loss, Krefeld had suffered the destruction of 5,517 houses in an area of devastation in the centre representing 47% of the built-up area, leaving 72,000 people homeless and a death toll of 1,056. EE887 failed to return home and was now a smouldering wreck on the Den Helder peninsula seven miles north-west of Hoorn, after being brought down by a night-fighter with fatal consequences for the crew of P/O Peters RAAF.

Crews were back in their briefing rooms on the following afternoon to learn about that night's operation against Mülheim-an-der-Ruhr, a medium-size town situated south-east of Duisburg and south-west of Essen. A force of 557 aircraft was prepared, along with a plan that called for eight Oboe Mosquitos plus two in reserve to drop yellow preliminary warning TIs on track, before marking the aiming-point with red TIs for twenty-nine Path Finder Lancasters to back up with greens. 3 Group detailed 105 aircraft, of which eighteen Stirlings were loaded with 4lb and 30lb incendiaries by 90 Squadron and departed West Wickham between 23.15 and 23.56 with S/Ls Dugdale and Scott the senior pilots on duty. After climbing out they set course for the North Sea at Southwold to join up with the rest of the bomber stream and lost the services of Lt Farrell to oxygen supply failure at the midpoint. BK665 had just crossed the Dutch/German frontier to the north-west of the Ruhr when it was attacked by a night-fighter and terminally damaged. The wireless operator and both gunners managed to parachute into the arms of their captors, while Sgt McNair and three others perished in the wreckage at Kehrum, located between Cleves to the north-west and Wesel to the south-east. On return home after the war, the survivors testified that their pilot had been severely wounded in the legs and had remained resolutely at the controls to give his crew the best chance to save themselves. BK804 was some nine miles north-west of the target and about to start its bombing run, when it was brought down to crash in Duisburg's northern suburb of Beeck, killing F/Sgt Robson and his crew.

The others reached the target to find a thin layer of three-tenths stratus cloud at 10,000 feet, through which it could be seen that the Path Finders had produced another example of near-perfect marking. The main force crews bombed on red and green TIs, the 90 Squadron contingent from 11,000 to 16,000 feet between 01.29 and 01.39 and observed the development of many fires, while witnessing a large, red explosion at 01.34. Post-raid reconnaissance and local sources confirmed that more than eleven hundred houses had been destroyed and dozens of public buildings damaged, along with much of the town's industry, and reported that some of the bombing had spilled over into parts of neighbouring Oberhausen, to which Mülheim was linked for air raid purposes, and passage between the two by any means other than on foot was impossible. The defenders fought back again to claim thirty-five bombers, with the Halifaxes and Stirlings representing two-thirds of them and suffering a respective loss rate of 7.7% and 11.8%.

The crews of F/L Peryer and Sgt Small conducted sea searches on the 23rd but found nothing to report after patrols of three hours and three hours forty minutes respectively. Having destroyed the Barmen half of Wuppertal at the end of May in one of the most devastating attacks to date, it was time to visit the same catastrophe on the western half, Elberfeld, for which a force of 630 aircraft was made ready on the 24th. On this occasion, six Lancasters, three Stirlings and three Halifaxes of 8 Group were to deliver the yellow route markers on H2S, while seven Oboe Mosquitos marked the aiming-point with red TIs and eighteen Lancasters, seven Halifaxes and three Stirlings backed them up with greens. 3 Group supported the operation with 105 aircraft, of which sixteen of the Stirlings were provided by 90 Squadron and loaded with incendiaries. They took off between 23.10 and 23.55 with S/L Dugdale the senior pilot on duty and headed for Orfordness, only to lose the services of F/L Smith to an overheating engine within the first hour. Sgt MacInnes and crew reached enemy territory struggling to maintain height and dropped their all-incendiary load onto railway track from 12,000 feet as a last resort after turning back. The others made landfall over the Scheldt and ran the usual gauntlet of searchlights and flak from the Cologne and Düsseldorf defence zones, which were aided by the formation of condensation trails at between 18,000 and 21,000 feet to advertise the presence of the bomber stream. It seemed to some that fewer guns were firing at them over the target, where small amounts of cloud with tops at 17,000 feet were insufficient to obscure the ground.

The Path Finder marking was accurate and concentrated, and the 90 Squadron participants went in to deliver their attacks onto red and green TIs from 10,000 to 16,500 feet between 01.07 and 01.32, before a creep-back developed that hit urban areas to the west. Large explosions were observed at 01.18, 01.25 and 01.50, and those arriving at the tail end of the attack described thick columns of smoke already passing through 19,000 feet and the glow of fires visible from the Dutch coast. Post-raid reconnaissance and local sources revealed another massively concentrated and accurate attack, which had reduced to rubble an estimated 90% of Elberfeld's built-up area, including three thousand houses and 171 industrial premises. It had also severely damaged 2,500 houses and dozens of important factory buildings, and the fact that more buildings were destroyed than damaged provided a telling commentary on the conditions on the ground. The number of fatalities stood at around eighteen hundred, and some of the survivors might have been cheered to know that thirty-four bombers, containing 240 of their tormentors, would not be returning to England that night. The Stirlings suffered a 10% loss rate and missing from their ranks were two from 90 Squadron, BK628, which disappeared without trace in the North Sea with the previously mentioned Sgt Steel and his crew, and BK813, a victim of the night-fighter of Ofw Reinhard Kollak of III./NJG4. The Stirling crashed at 01.39 some four miles south-south-east of Leuven in Belgium, killing F/Sgt Teede RAAF and five of his crew, while the flight engineer, Sgt Stanton, evaded capture with the aid of the local Resistance, and was helped to reach Paris before being arrested and imprisoned and eventually sent to a Pow camp in Germany.

The German synthetic oil industry relied on two main production methods, the Bergius process, which involved the hydrogenation of highly volatile bituminous coal to manufacture high-grade petroleum products like aviation fuel, and the Fischer-Tropsch process, which produced lower-grade diesel-type fuels for vehicle, Tank, U-Boot and shipping requirements. One of the major centres for synthetic oil production was the Ruhr city of Gelsenkirchen, which was posted on the 25th as the target for the first major attack on it since 1941, when it had been a regular destination under the Oil Directive. A force of 473 aircraft was assembled and the crews briefed to focus on the Gelsenkirchener Bergwerke A G plant, which was known to the Germans as Gelsenberg A G and to the RAF as Nordstern, a Bergius-process manufacturer of aviation fuel. 8 Group was to provide seven Oboe Mosquitos plus two in reserve to drop route markers and skymark the aiming-point, and two to bomb after the main force, but none of its heavy aircraft was to be involved. The 3 Group contribution amounted to seventy-three Stirlings and a dozen Lancasters, thirteen of the former loaded with 30lb and 4lb incendiaries and sent on their way from West Wickham between 23.13 and 23.44 with S/Ls Dugdale and Scott the senior pilots on duty. S/L Scott and crew abandoned their sortie during the climb-out when the rear turret became unserviceable, and their all-incendiary load was jettisoned "safe" at Rushford to the east of Thetford in Norfolk.

The route out was the standard one for a target located on the northern side of the Ruhr, with landfall over the Den Helder peninsula, before passing to the north of Amsterdam and heading south-east across the Münsterland to the final turning point towards the south. The bomber stream arrived over the east-central Ruhr to be greeted by ten-tenths stratus with tops at 10,000 to 15,000 feet, which would not have been a problem had five of the Oboe Mosquitos not suffered equipment failures. This caused tracking flares to be late and to drop in the wrong sequence in a somewhat scattered manner at a time when the crews were contending with an intense flak barrage. Searchlights illuminated the cloud as the main force crews bombed on red flares with green stars, those representing 90 Squadron from 13,000 feet to 17,000 feet between 01.30 and 01.39, and on return they would report a large explosion at 01.43 and the glow from the target to be visible from the Dutch coast. The retreating bombers had been chased to the sea by a large deployment of enemy night-fighters, which together with flak would bring down thirty of them. 90 Squadron's EH900 was shot down at the final turning point at Legden shortly after crossing the German frontier and there were no survivors from the crew of F/O McKenzie RAAF.

The night of the 27/28th was devoted to mining operations by 1 and 3 Groups, the latter detailing fifteen Stirlings for the Nectarine I garden, six provided by 90 Squadron, which departed West Wickham between 23.50 and 23.48 with freshman crews on board. Sgt Small and crew turned back early after the failure of their Gee-box and jettisoned their six mines at the designated dumping site at Rushford, leaving the others to cross the North Sea to find ten-tenths cloud at 2,000 feet and establish pinpoints in the Waddenzee between Vlieland and Terschelling. The vegetables were planted unopposed from 1,800 to 4,000 feet between 01.27 and 01.35 and all returned safely from uneventful sorties of around three-and-a-half hour's duration.

A series of three operations against Cologne would span the turn of the month and began on the night of the 28/29th, when 608 aircraft were prepared for a late evening take-off to deliver what would be the Rhineland capital's greatest ordeal of the war to date. 3 Group contributed sixty-six Stirlings and fourteen Lancasters, fifteen of the former representing 90 Squadron, which departed West Wickham between 23.30 and 23.58 with S/L Scott the senior pilot on duty and headed for the coast at Southwold. Each had an all-incendiary load in the bomb bay, but three of these would fail to reach the target after dropping out over the North Sea, Sgt Wood and crew through oxygen failure, Sgt Callaway and crew because of an unserviceable rear turret and Sgt Brayshaw and crew after being led astray by a navigational error. These were among a dozen "boomerangs" afflicting 3 Group, while the others made landfall on the Belgian coast near Ostend, before swinging round Bruges and passing south of Antwerp with the target still 110 miles away.

The main force crews encountered ten-tenths cloud below them at 8,000 to 10,000 feet, with good visibility above, but were unaware that five of the Oboe Mosquitos had turned back and a sixth was unable to drop its skymarkers. This meant that just six were available to fulfil the initial marking role, and they were running behind schedule by seven minutes and could manage only intermittent flares. The omens for a successful attack were not good, particularly as skymarking was the least reliable method because of drift, but by the time that most of the 90 Squadron crews arrived they were greeted by red and white flares and delivered their attacks from 5,000 to 12,000 feet between 01.50 and 02.07 and deduced from the glow beneath the clouds and the presence of smoke rising through them that they had contributed to a successful operation. This was confirmed by post-raid reconnaissance and local reports, which provided details of forty-three industrial buildings and 6,374 others completely destroyed, and a further fifteen thousand sustaining damage to some extent. The death toll was put at 4,377, the greatest by far from a Bomber Command attack, and 230,000 others had lost their homes for varying periods. By recent standards, the figure of twenty-five missing aircraft could be considered moderate, but that was no consolation to the individual stations with an empty dispersal pan. 3 Group posted missing five Stirlings, two and three respectively from XV and 149 Squadrons.

At some point during the course of the month, W/C Desmond McGlinn was posted in to gain operational experience before being handed a command of his own. The squadron took part in nine operations and dispatched 128 sorties for the loss of six Stirlings and crews.

July 1943

The first two days of the new month were beset by poor weather conditions, which kept all but a few gardeners and Mosquitos on the ground and caused 3 Group gardening operations planned for the 1st and 2nd to be cancelled. The mining operation in the Nectarine I garden by fourteen Stirlings scheduled for the 3rd would go ahead under the shadow of the main event, the second attack of the current campaign against Cologne. Crews were called to briefings on all operational stations during the late afternoon as a force of 653 aircraft was assembled, the Path Finder crews listening with interest as they were told that ten Mosquitos would drop green flares four-and-a-half miles from the target as a preliminary warning, and red, green and white flares and red TIs on the aiming-point. On this night, the aiming-point was on the East Bank of the Rhine in the industrial Deutz district, where the Klöckner-Humboldt-Deutz works manufactured aero-engines and heavy and tracked vehicles for the Wehrmacht and were served by the nearby Kalk and Gremberg marshalling yards. Nine Halifaxes and twenty-four Lancasters were to back up the red TIs with greens, but in the event that cloud concealed the TIs, they were to bomb on H2S with the main force along with the remaining nine Halifaxes and seventeen Lancasters. 3 Group made ready eighty Stirlings and fourteen Lancasters, 90 Squadron loading fifteen of the former with incendiaries and two with five mines each for the crews of Sgt Brayshaw and F/L Cheek.

The two elements departed West Wickham together between 23.06 and 23.36 with S/L Dugdale the senior pilot on duty and lost the services of P/O Whitworth and crew to turret failure within the hour and Sgt Small and crew shortly afterwards because of a lack of engine power. The others continued on in the expectation of finding nine-tenths cloud from the English coast all the way to the target, as forecast by the meteorological experts, but what the leading Path Finder heavy crews actually encountered was a clear sky and red Oboe-laid TIs in the bomb sights, which they backed up with greens. There was a certain amount of haze, but this did not interfere with the accuracy of the attack, which developed in concentrated form in the face, initially, of an intense flak defence. By the time the raid reached its crescendo, it was nine-tenths smoke rather than cloud that hung over the city, through which the 90 Squadron participants delivered their loads onto red and green TIs from 12,500 to 15,500 feet between 01.30 and 01.37. Meanwhile, the mining duo had established their positions off the western Frisians by Gee-fix and planted their vegetables according to brief from 1,500 and 4,000 feet at 01.30 and 01.35.

Crews returning from Cologne described a highly successful raid, which left the city a mass of flames with smoke rising to 10,000 feet and blotting out ground detail. Some noticed a tendency to creep-back, but the overall impression was of another operation more successful than the Thousand raid against this city at the end of May 1942. Post-raid reconnaissance and local reports confirmed another stunningly accurate and concentrated attack, in which twenty industrial premises and 2,200 houses had been destroyed, 588 people had been killed and 72,000 bombed out of their homes at a cost to the Command of thirty aircraft including EH907, which was almost certainly the victim of a night-fighter while homebound and crashed near Aalst, midway between Brussels and Ghent in Belgium, killing F/Sgt Morris and five of his crew. The rear turret broke away on impact and the Germans found the occupant still inside and suffering severe injuries to which he succumbed in hospital. BK718 crashed six miles south-south-east of Bonn after being brought down by flak, and only the rear gunner from the crew of F/L Platt survived to be taken into captivity. BF504 overshot the landing at base in the hands of F/L Crew at 03.55 and was written off after the undercarriage collapsed, but the crew walked away to resume their career.

At debriefings, some crews commented on the presence over Cologne of day fighters, and this was clear evidence of the introduction of a new tactic by the Luftwaffe. The newly formed JG300 was operating for the first time, employing the Wilde Sau (Wild Boar) tactics, which was the brainchild of former bomber pilot, Major Hans-Joachim (Hajo) Herrmann. The unit had been formed in June with borrowed standard BF109 and FW190 single-engine day fighters to operate directly over a target, seeking out bombers silhouetted against the fires and TIs. On this night, the unit would claim twelve victories, but would have to share them with the flak batteries, which claimed them also. Unaccustomed to being pursued by fighters over a target, it would take time for the bomber crews to work out what was happening, and until they did, friendly fire would often be blamed for damage incurred by unseen causes.

On the following night 3 Group sent thirteen Stirlings to the Cinnamon garden off La Pallice, and followed it up on the 5th with a dozen Stirlings to mine the waters of the Nectarine II garden off the central Frisians, for which 90 Squadron contributed the crews of W/C McGlinn, P/O Wheeler, F/Sgt Candy and Sgt Worsfold. They departed West Wickham between 23.35 and 23.41, each carrying five parachute mines, and all arrived in the target area under clear skies to find excellent visibility. At the end of their timed run, W/C McGlinn and crew were unable to release the contents of the bomb bay, and although they managed to find a partial remedy and jettison one mine as a test on the way home, the remaining four resolutely refused to drop and had to be brought back. The others delivered their mines according to brief from 800 to 1,500 feet between 01.30 and 01.44 and returned safely after some four hours aloft.

The last of the three attacks on Cologne was carried out on the 8th by an all-Lancaster heavy force of 282 aircraft drawn from 1, 5 and 8 Groups, again with great accuracy, and once the dust had settled the city authorities had been able to assess that the three-raid series had caused the destruction of eleven thousand buildings, killed 5,500 people and rendered homeless a further 350,000, a massive success for the Command gained at a cost of sixty-two heavy bombers. 3 Group was also active on this night, sending a dozen Stirlings to the Deodar garden in the Gironde estuary and eight to the Cinnamon garden off La Pallice, and it was for the latter that the crews of Sgt Kinsella and P/O Mills departed West Wickham at 23.05 and 23.06, each carrying four mines. They established a visual pinpoint on Ile-de-Re and planted their vegetables from 3,000 and 3,500 feet at 01.45 and 01.46 before returning from uneventful sorties after round trips of four-and-a-half hours.

The latest raid of the Ruhr offensive was carried out against Gelsenkirchen on the 9th by an initial heavy force of 408 Lancasters and Halifaxes, which, largely as a result of Oboe failure and the errant release of skymarkers some distance from the target, resulted in a disappointing outcome. A greater weight of bombs fell on nearby Bochum and Wattenscheid than on the intended target, and despite some damage to the Scholven-Buer synthetic oil plant, damage was relatively light and spread across the southern districts. While this operation was in progress, a dozen 3 Group Stirlings made their way to the Nectarine I garden, among them the 90 Squadron crews of F/L Coombs, P/O MacInnes and Sgt Mulvey. They had departed West Wickham between 00.01 and 00.04 and established their positions by Gee-fix before planting their five vegetables each according to brief from 2,000 feet between 01.55 and 02.02.

Although two more operations to the Ruhr region would be launched late in the month, the campaign was winding down and Harris was already planning his next attempt to shorten the war by bombing alone, buoyed by the success of the spring offensive. He could look back on the past four and a half months with genuine satisfaction at the performance of his squadrons, and, as a champion of technological innovation, take particular pride in the success of Oboe, which had been the decisive factor. Although losses had been grievously high and the Ruhr's reputation as "Happy Valley" well earned, its most important towns and cities had suffered catastrophic destruction. In Britain, the aircraft factories had more than kept pace with the rate of attrition, while the training units both at home and overseas were pouring eager new crews into the fray to fill the gaps. With confidence high in the ability of his Command to destroy almost any target at will, Harris prepared for his next major campaign, the erasure from the map of a prominent German city in a short, sharp series of maximum effort raids to be launched during the final week of the month.

In the meantime, a force of 374 aircraft from all but 5 Group was assembled on the 13th for an operation that night against the Spa city of Aachen, the most westerly German city and an important railway hub and industrial centre situated right on the frontiers with Belgium and Holland. The plan called for ten Halifaxes to drop yellow TIs as route markers and six Oboe Mosquitos to ground mark the aiming-point with red TIs, backed up with greens by nineteen Halifaxes. The main force element consisted of Halifaxes, Wellingtons and Stirlings, with just eighteen Lancasters among the 8 Group contribution. 3 Group weighed in with fifty-Stirlings and eighteen Lancasters, including eight of the former belonging to 90 Squadron, which departed West Wickham between 23.46 and 23.56 with four pilots of flight lieutenant rank leading the way and each carrying an all-incendiary bomb load. Having traversed Belgium and with the frontier with southern Holland in sight, EE873 was shot down by the night-fighter of Oblt Wilhelm Telge of II./NJG1 and crashed at 01.45 at Rotem, killing F/L Coombs and six others and leaving just the mid-upper gunner, Sgt Clarke, alive in enemy hands. The others found seven to nine-tenths cloud lying predominantly over the eastern half of the city with tops at around 9,000 feet, some of the first wave having been driven by a strong tail wind to arrive at the target ahead of schedule and an unusually large number of aircraft bombed as soon as the Path Finder markers went down, giving rise to a sudden proliferation of fires. Most of the 90 Squadron crews identified the aiming point by red TIs and delivered their payloads from 12,000 to 14,000 feet between 01.51 and 02.00, and on return reported that large areas of the town seemed to burst into flames at once, commenting also on the effectiveness of the searchlights and flak and the prevalence of night-fighters. The Aachen authorities confirmed the destruction of 2,927 buildings containing more than 16,800 dwelling units, and eight large war industry factories were also hit along with many public and cultural buildings.

On the 15th F/O Ross, a member of F/O White's crew that had gone missing during the Mannheim raid in mid-April, visited West Wickham and received a tumultuous welcome from those of his former colleagues still with the squadron. He was called upon to relate his experiences and to divulge as much information as he was allowed without placing in danger those who had helped him to evade capture. On the 18th, W/C McGlinn was posted to Chedburgh to assume command of 214 (Federated Malay States) Squadron.

Hamburg had been a regular target for the Command throughout the war to date, and had been attacked, amongst other occasions, during the final week of July in 1940, 1941 and 1942. It had been spared by the weather from hosting the first "One Thousand" bomber raid at the end of May 1942, but Harris now identified it as the ideal candidate for destruction under Operation Gomorrah, the intention of which was to cause the maximum impact to the enemy's morale in a short, sharp campaign, employing ten thousand tons of bombs. Hamburg's political status was second only to Berlin's, and its value to the war effort in terms of ship and U-Boot construction and other war production was undeniable, but it suited Harris's criteria also in other respects. Its location close to a coastline aided navigation and made it accessible from the North Sea without the need to spend time over hostile territory, and its relatively short distance from the bomber stations enabled a force to approach and retreat during the few hours of darkness afforded by mid-summer. Finally, lying beyond the range of Oboe, which had proved so decisive at the Ruhr, Hamburg had the wide River Elbe and the distinctive Binnen and Aussen-Alster Lakes to provide a solid H2S signature for the navigators high above.

The first operation in the campaign was actually posted on the 22nd but cancelled during the afternoon and the same thing happened on the 23rd, by which time there had been no operations for most squadrons for nine days. By the time that 791 crews trooped into their respective briefing rooms on the 24th, they probably expected the day to end with yet another scrub. Instead, they were read a special message from the commander-in-chief to announce the beginning of the Battle of Hamburg and listened intently to the revelation that they would be aided by the first operational use of "window", aluminium-backed strips of paper of precise length, which, when released in bundles into the airstream at a predetermined point, would drift down slowly in vast clouds to swamp the enemy night-fighter, searchlight and gun-laying radar systems with false returns and render them blind. The device had actually been available for a year, but its use had been vetoed in case the enemy copied it for use against Britain. It was not realized that Germany had, in fact, already developed its own version called Düppel, which it had withheld for the same reason.

The plan of attack called for eleven Lancasters and nine Halifaxes to drop yellow TIs as route markers, before continuing on to mark the aiming-point with yellow TIs, and if conditions permitted, illuminator flares. The route markers were to be backed up by six Stirlings, thirteen Lancasters and nine Halifaxes, and six Lancasters and two Halifaxes were to use the yellow TIs as a guide, and with the aid of flares, mark the aiming-point with red TIs, which would be backed up with greens by the remaining marker crews. 3 Group detailed 115 Stirlings and seventeen Lancasters, 90 Squadron contributing seventeen of the former, the bomb bays of which were loaded with a mix of 2,000 and 500-pounders supplemented with incendiaries. They departed West Wickham between 21.45 and 22.12 with W/C Giles and S/L Dugdale the senior pilots on duty and lost the services first of F/L Peryer and crew to starboard-inner engine failure within the hour and Sgt Denton and crew much later to the inability to maintain height. The remainder continued on across the North Sea to the rendezvous point north-west of Heligoland and at the appointed moment, the designated crew member, in most cases the wireless operator, began to dispense "window" through the flare chute, beginning shortly after 00.30. The effects appeared to be immediate as few night-fighters rose to meet the approaching bombers and although a number of aircraft were shot down over the sea during the outward flight, two of them 103 Squadron Lancasters, they were off course and outside of the protection of the bomber stream and may well have been among those returning early with technical difficulties.

The efficacy of "window" was made more apparent in the target area, where the crews noticed an absence of the usually efficient co-ordination between the searchlights and flak batteries and defence appeared random and sporadic. This offered the Path Finders the opportunity to mark the target by visual reference and H2S virtually unmolested, and although the red and green TIs were a little misplaced and scattered, they landed in sufficient numbers close to the city centre to provide the main force crews with ample opportunity to deliver a massive blow. It rarely happened that aircraft arrived in strict bands according to their task, and some main force crews were already over the target from the opening of the raid at 01.00. The 90 Squadron crews carried out their attacks from 12,000 to 16,000 feet between 01.12 and 01.20 and on return reported a successful operation that had left part of the city ablaze with a column of smoke rising through 20,000 feet.

Post-raid reconnaissance revealed that a six-mile-long creep-back had developed, which cut a swathe of destruction from the city centre along the line of approach, out across the north-western districts and into open country, where a proportion of the bombing had been wasted. In fact, less than half of the force had bombed within three miles of the city centre during the fifty-minute-long raid, in which 2,284 tons of bombs had been delivered, despite which, the city had suffered a telling blow and fifteen hundred of its inhabitants lay dead. For the Command it was an encouraging start to the campaign, particularly in the light of just twelve missing aircraft, three of them Stirlings, a modest loss for which "window" was largely responsible.

On the following night, and in the expectation that Hamburg would be covered by smoke, Harris switched his force to Essen, where he could take advantage of the body blow dealt to the enemy defensive system by "window". A force of 705 aircraft was made ready and a plan prepared, which called for Halifaxes and Lancasters of 35 (Madras Presidency) and 156 Squadrons to drop preliminary yellow warning TIs on track by H2S, which would be backed up by elements of 7 and 156 Squadron. Ahead, fourteen Oboe Mosquitos would mark the aiming-point with red TIs, which nineteen Lancasters, nine Halifaxes and five Stirlings were to back up with greens. 3 Group detailed ninety-nine Stirlings and sixteen Lancasters, thirteen of the former provided by 90 Squadron, which departed West Wickham between 22.25 and 22.40 with S/L Dugdale the senior pilot on duty and for once there were no early returns. They flew out in favourable, if hazy conditions over the North Sea and visibility was good from the Dutch coast eastwards as far as the central Ruhr, where four to five-tenths cloud hung out to the west, leaving clear skies over the aiming-point and just the usual ground haze to spoil the vertical visibility. The Path Finder marking was accurate and concentrated more towards the eastern side of the city, and crews watched on as a highly concentrated attack developed, which left the ground enveloped in smoke from the many fires and explosions. The 90 Squadron crews delivered their diverse bomb loads, some with 2,000-pounders plus incendiaries and others with varying numbers of 500-pounder and incendiaries, from 13,000 to 15,000 feet between 00.42 and 00.53, observing large explosions at 00.40, 00.50 and 01.04. Other returning crews reported concentrated fires around the aiming-point in a one-and-a-half-square-mile area of the city, two large, red explosions at 00.36 and 00.39 and a column of smoke rising through 20,000 feet as they withdrew to the west, the glow remaining visible on the horizon from as far away as the Dutch coast.

Twenty-six aircraft failed to return, seven of them Stirlings, and among the latter was 90 Squadron's EE904, which disappeared into the North Sea with the mixed RAF, RAAF and RNZAF crew of S/L Dugdale DFC, the remains of three of the eight occupants eventually washing ashore on the Norfolk coast for burial. Post-raid reconnaissance and local sources confirmed the raid to be another outstanding success against this important war materials producing city, in which the complex of Krupp manufacturing sites suffered its heaviest damage of the war to date. Of 134 other industrial premises hit, fifty-one suffered complete destruction, along with more than 2,800 houses. It is believed that Dr Gustav Krupp suffered a stroke on the following day, from which he never recovered.

A night off preceded the second round of Operation Gomorrah on the night of the 27/28th, for which a force of 787 aircraft was made ready. 3 Group contributed 108 Stirlings and seventeen Lancasters and at West Wickham, seventeen Stirlings received all-incendiary bomb loads, while the crews attended briefing to learn the details of the plan. Yellow route markers would be dropped by H2S on the enemy coast and backed up, and "Y" aircraft (H2S blind markers) were to deliver red TIs and a stick of flares over the aiming-point for visual markers to confirm and back up with green TIs. The 90 Squadron element took off between 21.58 and 22.24 with F/Ls Cheek, Peryer, Sheppard and Smith the senior pilots on duty and lost the services of Sgt Luyk and crew to an undisclosed cause after around ninety minutes. The remainder pushed on towards Hansastadt (Ancient Free Trade City) Hamburg, crossing the Schleswig-Holstein coast to the north, none of them having any concept of the events that were to follow their arrival.

A previously unknown and terrible phenomenon was about to present itself to the world and introduce a new word "firestorm" into the English language. A number of factors would conspire on this night to seal the fate of this great city and its hapless inhabitants in an orgy of destruction that was quite unprecedented in air warfare. An uncharacteristically hot and dry spell of weather had left the city a tinderbox, and the spark to ignite it came with the Path Finders' H2S-laid yellow and green TIs, which fell with almost total concentration some two miles to the east of the intended city-centre aiming-point and into the densely populated working-class residential districts of Hamm, Hammerbrook and Borgfeld. To compound this, the main force, which had been drawn on to the target by yellow release-point flares, bombed with rare precision and almost no creep-back, and deposited much of its 2,300 tons of bombs into this relatively compact area. The 90 Squadron crews found three-tenths cloud in the target area and smoke already beginning to drift across the city to obscure ground detail as they delivered their attacks from 10,500 to 16,000 feet between 01.07 and 01.18. They observed many explosions and a sea of flames developing below and a ship was observed to be on fire in a dock south of the main attack. Those bombing towards the later stages of the raid observed a pall of smoke rising through 20,000 feet, and the glow of fires was reported to remain visible for up to two hundred miles into the return journey. Shortly after bombing, F/L Peryer's port-outer engine began to vibrate and continued to do so until bursting into flames as they crossed the English coast, whereupon the fire was eventually extinguished and a safe landing completed. Not so for P/O Whitworth and crew in a flak-damaged BK693, which swung off the runway on landing at Stradishall at 04.20 and collided with a parked Stirling belonging to 1657 Conversion Unit.

On the ground in Hamburg, individual fires began to join together to form one giant conflagration, which sucked in oxygen from surrounding areas at hurricane speeds to feed its voracious appetite. Trees were uprooted and flung bodily into the inferno, along with debris and people, and temperatures at the seat of the flames exceeded one thousand degrees Celcius. The defences were overwhelmed and the fire service unable to pass through the rubble-strewn streets to gain access to the worst-affected areas. Even had they done so, they could not have entered the firestorm area, and only after all of the combustible material had been consumed did the flames subside. By this time, there was no-one alive to rescue, and an estimated forty thousand people died on this one night alone. A mass exodus from the city, which would ultimately exceed one million people, began on the following morning and this undoubtedly saved many from the ravages of the next raid, which would come two nights later. Seventeen aircraft failed to return, reflecting the enemy's developing response to the advantage gained by the Command through "window". No gain was ever permanent, and the balance of power would continue to shift from one side to the other for the next year. For a change, it was the Lancaster brigade that sustained the highest numerical casualties on this night, accounting for eleven of the failures to return.

Bomber Command's heavy brigade stayed at home on the following night, while four Mosquitos carried out a nuisance raid on Hamburg to ensure that the residents' sleep was disturbed. A force of 777 aircraft was put together to continue Hamburg's torment on the 29th, while the crews attended briefings to learn of their part in the proceedings. They were told that red TIs and flares were to be employed as route markers, before seventeen Lancasters and eight Halifaxes marked the aiming-point with yellow TIs by H2S to be backed up by thirty-four Lancasters, six Stirlings and nine Halifaxes. 3 Group provided 110 Stirlings and fifteen Lancasters, seventeen of the former loaded with 30lb and 4lb incendiaries at West Wickham, and took off between 22.00 and 22.32 with F/Ls Cheek, Crew and Peryer the senior pilots on duty. Having crashed on landing at the start of the month, F/L Crew now crashed on take-off after losing control of EE916, fortunately without crew casualties. Sgt Worsfold and crew turned back within two hours after the port-outer engine caught fire, while the flight engineer in the crew of P/O Mills miscalculated fuel consumption and persuaded his captain that they would not have enough to complete the operation. The others pushed on in good weather conditions, which persisted all the way to the target, where smoke-haze was the only impediment to vertical visibility. The plan was to approach from due north to hit the northern and north-eastern districts, which thus far had escaped serious damage, but the Path Finders strayed two miles to the east of the intended track and dropped their markers just to the south of the already devastated firestorm area. Many bombs fell into the still smouldering ruins, before a four-mile creep-back rescued the situation by spreading back along the line of approach into the residential districts of Wandsbek and Barmbek, and parts of Uhlenhorst and Winterhude. The 90 Squadron crews carried out their bombing runs at 12,000 to 17,000 feet between 00.54 and 01.12 and released their loads on yellow and green TIs, before returning to report smoke rising through 17,000 feet and fires visible for two hundred miles into the homeward journey. Shortly after crossing the enemy coast homebound, F/O Day and crew were attacked by a twin-engine enemy night-fighter and took evasive action, during which the enemy closed to within four hundred feet and was hit in the nose by a two-second burst from the Stirling's rear turret. A fire erupted immediately, and the assailant was observed to break into three sections and crash in flames. The defences were very active on this night and claimed twenty-eight bombers, suggesting that they had recovered somewhat from the "window" setback.

Before the final Hamburg raid took place, the Ruhr campaign was brought to a conclusion on the 30th with an attack on the town of Remscheid, situated about six miles south of Wuppertal, where the main industries were mechanical engineering and tool-making. Up until this point, only twenty-six people had lost their lives in this town as a result of stray bombs, but it was now to face a modest force of 273 aircraft consisting of roughly equal numbers of Lancasters, Halifaxes and Stirlings with six Oboe Mosquitos to mark out the aiming-point with red TIs. Eighteen of the eighty-seven 3 Group Stirlings were provided by 90 Squadron, and each was given an all-incendiary load before departing West Wickham between 22.15 and 22.42 with F/L Peryer the senior pilot on duty. It was a bad night for the squadron's record of serviceability as the crews of P/Os Appleby and MacInnes, F/Sgt Smooth and W/O Wood all abandoned their sorties and landed between 23.43 and 02.51, two with engine issues, one because of failed bombing circuits and one after losing both compasses and Gee. The others reached the target to find clear skies and good visibility, along with pinpoint marking by Oboe Mosquitos backed up by the Path Finder heavy brigade. The main force crews bombed with great accuracy at this virtually virgin target, those from 90 Squadron from 11,000 to 16,000 feet between 01.10 and 01.19, before returning home to report many fires and explosions. Post-raid reconnaissance confirmed a devastatingly effective raid, which destroyed more than 3,100 houses and 107 industrial buildings and killed 1,120 people. It was a stunning example of what the Command could achieve with a force of moderate size and 870 tons of bombs if all went according to plan. Fifteen aircraft failed to return, eight of them Stirlings almost 10% of those dispatched, and one of those missing was 90 Squadron's BK775, which crashed somewhere in the vicinity of Mönchengladbach with no survivors from the crew of F/Sgt Small.

During the course of the month the squadron took part in eleven operations and dispatched 116 sorties for the loss of eight Stirlings and five crews.

Blenheims at Bicester

Mining (Gardening) Codenames

90 Squadron B17 Flying Fortress

Boeing B-17C, Fortress I, in RAF markings as used by 90 Squadron.

90 Squadron B17C AN530

Crash landed Fortress Mk1 90 Squadron

Fortress Mk1 AN523 of 90 Squadron taking off

The crew of a Boeing Fortress Mk I of 90 Squadron RAF putting on electrically heated flying suits at Polebrook, Northamptonshire, before taking off for a high-altitude bombing attack on the German battlecruiser Gneisenau at Brest, France. Below: Boarding for the raid.

Memorial in Bygland, Norway to the 90 Squadron Flying Fortress crew - the first B17 to fall on occupied Europe. Crew lost: F/O D A A Romans DFC, P/O FG Hart, Sgts P B Corbett, J Brown, W G Honey, H Merrill RCAF, R H Beattie.

F/O D A A Romans DFC (Photo credit: Wartime Heritage Assoc.; attribution sought.)

Admiral Scheer – target of F/O Romans' crew September 1941.

Admiral Scheer (German Heavy Cruiser, 1934-1945) Underway at sea, en route to Norway in February 1942. Photographed from the heavy cruiser Prinz Eugen. Note the air recognition marking on the latter's deck and the portable 20mm anti-aircraft gun mounting further aft.

90 Squadron B-17C

Cpl Jack King, armourer with 90 Squadron

The Denton crew (1940)

VP-Boat flotilla leaving a Dutch port during World War II

Crow's nest on a German VP Boat or Flakship.

Wing Commander P F Webster, 90 Squadron Commander, 26th July 1941 to 21st November 1941.

90 Squadron – Whitworth Crew.
L – R: Sgt Cyril Keefe (RG), P/O Peter Rushbrooke (BA), Sgt Allan Rhodes DFM (W.Op), P/O Ralph Whitworth (Pilot), Sgt Ken Forester (FE), Sgt Harry Pelham (MUG), P/O Leonard Hibbs (Nav).

On the 28th July 1943 while returning from Hamburg and on fire after being hit by flak, Ralph Whitworth's crew hit two old Stirlings and a Nissen hut when instructed by flight control to crash land on grass away from the main runway at Stradishall.

RAF Ridgewell

Nine crew from Stirling LK308 were killed when their aircraft collided mid-air with a Hurricane which was taking part in a fighter affiliation exercise on the 9th November 1943. They are commemorated on the Runnymede Memorial. - F/L R Y Rodger, F/S L Smith, Sgt E F Davany, F/O C Mitchell, Sgt R Wilson, Sgt L M Griffiths, Sgt G G Batten, Sgt M P Loyst RCAF and F/S H I Jones RAAF.

End of runway caravan at Wratting Common 1943

Sgt Colin Mitchinson with DFM which was awarded instantly for spotting an Fw190 closing in over the Baltic while the Day crew in Stirling EH908 were returning from Berlin 24th August 1943. The Stirling was heavily damaged, and the crew injured but managed to crash land at Bodney, an American Thunderbolt base in Norfolk. Mitchinson, the rear gunner, hit the Fw190 which dived and was not seen again. The pilot's report stated that the Stirling hit over 400 miles an hour in corkscrew dive to lose altitude to escape fighters.

Present day Lorient harbour. Bombed many times by Bomber Command including 90 Squadron in 1943.

The former submarine pens at Keroman, Lorient

Stirling BK784 Crew and Groundcrew of F/O Appleby

Stirling WP-H at Wratting Common 1943. Lost in May 1944 killing all crew when the Stirling swung on take-off and hit a tree. It managed to get airborne but crashed shortly after. Crew F/Sgt John Whyte, (Pilot), Sgt R L Aston (AG), Sgt H D Eggbeer (Nav), Sgt P J McCrory (AG), Sgt B Pearce (FE), Sgt L Sharpen, (W/Op), Sgt W Whalley (BA).

Sgt Guyan's photograph of a captured Junkers Ju88 at Farnborough. See page 276 for the story behind this photo.

S/L Joseph Dugdale DFC standing next to a Lancaster. He was lost with all his crew on Essen raid 25th July 1943 when their Stirling is presumed to have come down in the North Sea.

F/Sgt Samuel (Jock) Guyan, mid upper gunner in F/O Appleby's crew.

F/Sgt A J Rhodes DFM instantly awarded DFM for actions during Hamburg raid 27th July 1943.

P/O Ross Simpson, RAAF, He was killed in action on 18th November 1943 as part of a RAF bomber crew that was lost in a raid over Rhine Port and Ludwigshafen.

F/Sgt Owen Ussher   *F/Sgt Leonard Heason*

Members of P/O Simpson's crew who were all killed on the 18th November 1943 on a Mannheim raid. Remaining crew: F/O David Edward Blain, F/O Donald Arthur Brown, F/Sgt Eric Whitton Sykes, Sgt Douglas Hollamby.

Stuttgart

P/O Ernest Candy (2nd Pilot)   F/L Cyril Coombs (Pilot)   Sgt Robert Clarke (MUG)
Members of Stirling EE873 crew which was shot down by a night-fighter over Belgium on 13/14th July 1943. All crew except Sgt Clarke who evaded were killed – F/L Cyril Coombs (Pilot), P/O Ernest Candy (2nd Pilot), Sgt John Bradshaw (FE), Sgt William Dawson (BA), F/O Paul Swallow (Nav) Sgt Charles Long (WO/AG), Sgt Eric Potter (AG).   (Aircrew Remembered)

Vertical RAF photo-recce image of concentrated bomb craters at Peenemunde after the raid.

V-2 launch in Peenemünde (1943)

F/O Appleby with incendiaries

The last 90 Squadron Stirling leaving RAF Ridgewell bound for their new station RAF West Wickham.

Sgt Stan Mason and his crew doing their de-brief following a Berlin raid.

Sgt Robert Freeland KIA 4th July 1943

F/Sgt Kenneth Longmore RAAF KIA 24th August 1943.

F/L E F Mills crew and groundcrew with the high scoring Stirling EF411.

Hamburg, Germany. After the 1943 air raids, the port of Hamburg was strewn with sunken ships, like this Norwegian tramp, which was one of the 2,900 totally destroyed in the port.

Damage from 90 Squadron's raid on the Dunlop works, Montlucon, France. September 1943

The Charlottenburg Palace, Berlin was destroyed almost in its entirety by explosive and incendiary bombs. November 1943.

Soldiers were deployed in Berlin to dig splinter trenches in the public squares for the protection of the population against air raids. August 1943.

Sgt John Madge – Rear gunner in Sgt S Bradshaw's crew.

S/L Henry Kirk Ewing (known as Kirk) DFC
On S/L Ewing's second tour, he joined 90 Squadron, was awarded his DFC and became Squadron Gunnery Leader. He carried out 71 sorties throughout his three tours as rear gunner and went on to join 138 Squadron at Tempsford.

Wing Commander J H Giles
90 Squadron Commander
7th June 1943. to December 1943

Wing Commander G T Wynne-Powell
90 Squadron Commander
December 1943 to January 1944

F/O J V Newton and crew. Stirling EF497 (Lulu) West Wickham 1943

Some of 90 Squadron's wireless operators being de-briefed after a Berlin raid 1943.

August 1943

The new month began for 3 Group with mining operations off the Biscay coast, 90 Squadron briefing the crews of F/L Wilson, F/Sgts Denton and Lowe and Sgt Phillips for the Cinnamon garden off La Pallice, while Mildenhall and Downham Market provided eleven crews for the Deodar garden in the Gironde estuary. The West Wickham quartet took off between 22.08 and 22.13 and within about an hour lost the services of the Denton crew to Gee failure, which prevented them from establishing navigational pinpoints from above cloud. The others reached the target area after first pinpointing on Les Sables-d'Olonne and planted their four vegetables each in the allotted locations from 3,000 to 4,000 feet between 01.18 and 02.24.

Preparations for the last of the four rounds of Operation Gomorrah kept ground crews and armourers busy after NFTs had been completed on the afternoon of the 2nd. A force of 740 aircraft was assembled, which included 102 Stirlings and fourteen Lancasters belonging to 3 Group. At West Wickham seventeen Stirlings were loaded with SBCs of incendiaries, while their crews attended briefing to learn that the Path Finders were to mark the aiming-point with red TIs by H2S, which the visual markers would confirm with yellows, backed-up by greens for the duration of the bombing. The 90 Squadron element took off between 23.05 and 23.31 with F/L Peryer the senior pilot on duty and headed for the rendezvous point over the North Sea. The weather conditions, initially, were favourable, until the bomber stream came into contact with a towering bank of ice-bearing cumulonimbus cloud at 7° East, a not unusual feature of this regular route into north-western Germany, but on this occasion a particularly imposing one, which could not be circumnavigated and stretched upwards to 20,000 feet and beyond. Upon entering it, aircraft were thrown around by violent electrical storms characterised by enormous flashes of lightning, peels of thunder and electrical discharges that sent instruments haywire. For some it was the most terrifying experience of their lives, on the ground or in the air, and it was responsible for the early return of a massive forty-four 3 Group aircraft, seven of them belonging to 90 Squadron. The crews of P/O Mills and F/Sgt Smith were defeated by engine and rear turret failures respectively, while the remaining five abandoned their sorties because of the conditions, and this left just ten of the original starters to press on to the target. Hamburg lay under ten-tenths cloud, as a result of which the crews of F/L Peryer, F/Sgt Brayshaw and Sgt Worsfold were unable to establish a position over the primary target and sought out alternatives, which they found at Bremerhaven, Wilhelmshaven and Elmshorn respectively.

Some of those battling through the conditions to reach the target area caught a glimpse of the Elbe and isolated yellow and green Path Finder flares, which might have been jettisoned rather than placed, and the majority bombed on e.t.a., those from 90 Squadron from 9,000 to 14,000 feet between 02.08 and 02.24. Bombs were spread over a hundred miles of the Schleswig-Holstein peninsula, the town of Elmshorn, some fifteen miles to the north-west of Hamburg seeming to attract the most attention and 254 houses were destroyed. Few crews had any idea of their precise location and bombed on the glow of fires beneath the cloud and the smoke rising through it. On return, they expressed themselves to be shaken by their experiences and were unanimous in their conviction that the operation had been a total failure. The outcome was of little consequence in view of what had gone before, but the Command suffered the relatively heavy loss of thirty aircraft, some of them almost certainly having fallen victim to the weather conditions. During the course of the four raids of Operation Gomorrah, 90 Squadron despatched sixty-eight sorties, fifty-six of which reached and bombed the primary target, and none of its crews was lost. (The Battle of Hamburg. Martin Middlebrook).

On the 3rd, S/L Freeman arrived from 1651 Conversion Unit to assume command of A Flight as successor to W/C Giles. Adverse weather conditions over the ensuing days caused a number of mining operations to be cancelled until the 6th, when 3 Group detailed fifteen Stirlings for the Deodar Garden and five for Cinnamon. Six 90 Squadron crews were assigned to the former and departed West Wickham between 21.48 and 22.04 with the freshman P/O Rodger the only commissioned pilot on duty and four mines in each bomb bay. They met with five to ten-tenths cloud in the target area with a base at 1,000 feet, below which visibility was modest, while above it was fair to good. The crews of F/Sgt Gay and Sgt Luyk were unable to establish a firm pinpoint and brought their mines home, leaving four to plant theirs from 800 to 10,000 feet, according to the ORB between 00.03 and 00.47 after identifying landmarks at Ile-d'Oleron, Pointe de la Coubre and Ile-de-Re. However, the flight time to the Deodar region was normally around three-and-a-half hours, and some doubt exists, therefore, over the accuracy of the recorded timings.

Italy was now teetering on the brink of capitulation and Bomber Command was invited to help nudge it over the edge with a short offensive against its major cities. It began with the preparation of an all-Lancaster force drawn from 1, 5 and 8 Groups for an attack on Genoa, Milan and Turin on the 7th, and with preparations already in hand for, perhaps, the most important operation of the war to date to be launched in ten days' time, the Turin raid was to be used to test the merits of employing a raid controller, or Master of Ceremonies, in the manner of W/C Gibson during Operation Chastise. The man selected for the job was Group Captain John Searby, currently serving as commanding officer of 83 Squadron, and before that, Gibson's successor as commanding officer of 106 Squadron. His brief was to remain in sight of the target for the entire attack, assessing the marking and bombing and directing and encouraging the crews by VHF. It is believed that all 197 aircraft reached their respective targets after flying out in excellent weather conditions, and although the Master Bomber experiment at Turin was not entirely successful, experience was gained which would prove useful for the forthcoming Operation Hydra.

The main operation on the night of the 9/10th was directed at the city of Mannheim, for which a force of 457 Lancasters and Halifaxes was assembled. The target was found to be covered by cloud and the Path Finder marking was only marginally effective, which led to scattered bombing and a low expectation as to the outcome. Despite the doubts, this moderately-sized force set off fifteen hundred individual fires, destroyed or seriously damaged more than thirteen hundred buildings and caused a loss of production at forty-two industrial concerns.

The following night brought a return to southern Germany, this time to Nuremberg, for which a force of 653 aircraft was made ready. As far as the Halifax crews of 4 and 6 Groups were concerned, the return of Stirlings for this raid was likely to provide respite for them, as in a force of Lancasters and Halifaxes, the latter invariably came off second best. 3 Group's contribution of 116 Stirlings and fourteen Lancasters included twenty of the former belonging to 90 Squadron, which were loaded with SBCs of 4lb and 30lb incendiaries and took off from

West Wickham between 21.38 and 22.30 with five pilots of flight lieutenant rank leading the way and S/L Freeman flying as second pilot to F/L Smith. After climbing out they set course for Beachy Head to follow a route similar to that of the previous night and there were no early returns to blunt the squadron's impact. The Path Finders had been told to expect clear skies and had prepared a ground-marking plan, but conditions in the target area also reflected those of twenty-four hours earlier with eight to ten-tenths cloud at 12,000 feet, despite which, the Path Finders proceeded with the ground-marking plan. Consequently, there were no release-point flares to draw the main force crews on, but the green TIs were visible to most as the 90 Squadron participants delivered their attacks from 6,000 to 16,000 feet between 01.14 and 01.29. The main weight of bombs fell into central and southern districts, where heavy residential and industrial damage occurred in return for the loss of sixteen aircraft, three of them Stirlings, and at debriefings crews reported a good concentration of fires, the glow from which remained visible on the horizon for 150 miles into the return journey.

Briefings took place on the 12th for an attack that night on Turin by 152 aircraft of 3 and 8 Groups, while a much larger Lancaster and Halifax force attended to Milan, home to many war factories, including the Isotta Fraschini luxury car works, which had been converted to military vehicle and aero engine manufacture, the Pirelli rubber works, Alfa Romeo, the Caproni aircraft plant, the Breda locomotive, armaments and aircraft works, the Innocenti machinery and vehicle factory and out to the north-west on the shores of Lake Varese and Lake Maggiore respectively the Macchi and Savoia aircraft factories. 90 Squadron loaded twenty Stirlings with 500-pounders and mixed incendiaries and launched them skyward between 21.07 and 21.41 with S/L Freeman the senior pilot on duty for the first time. There were no early returns to West Wickham and the reward for arriving at the destination after an almost four-hour outward leg was a cloudless sky and bright moonlight. The attack took place almost unopposed from the ground, the 90 Squadron crews delivering their payloads from 13,500 to 16,000 feet between 01.13 and 01.25 and observing colossal fires and heavy explosions. It was during this operation that pilot, F/Sgt Aaron of 218 (Gold Coast) Squadron, won the posthumous award of a Victoria Cross, the second and final Stirling crewman to be so honoured. By coincidence, it had been during a previous operation to this city in November 1942 that the first and only other VC had been earned by a Stirling crew member, F/Sgt Rawdon (Ron) Middleton of 149 Squadron.

On the 13th, W/C Giles was notified of the award of a DFC in recognition of his outstanding service to date. An all-Lancaster force continued the assault on Milan on the night of the 15/16th, and the Italian campaign was brought to an end with a raid on Turin by elements of 3 and 8 Groups on the night of the 16/17th. 3 Group contributed 103 Stirlings and fourteen Lancasters, 90 Squadron loading a record twenty-one of its own with 500-pounders and incendiaries and dispatching them from West Wickham between 19.58 and 20.53 with a handful of pilots of flight lieutenant rank the most senior on duty. F/O Yates and crew turned back after an hour because of multiple engine issues, while P/O Appleby and crew were well into their passage across France when the starboard-outer engine let them down. The others reached the target area to find good weather conditions with ground haze, and those from 90 Squadron carried out their attacks from 12,000 to 15,000 feet between 00.13 and 00.30. At debriefings they would report huge explosions and very large fires spreading through the city and claim damage to the Fiat works. Conditions over 3 Group stations were unsuitable for landing, and while lobbing in at Biggin Hill in Kent short of fuel in the hands of Sgt Slade, EE900 came to grief, losing its undercarriage and damaging its wings, fuselage and all four propellers, despite which it would be repaired and returned to service. The entire force was diverted to airfields in the south of England and the time it took to recover them on the 17th meant that many would not be made ready in time to participate in one of the war's most important operations, which was to take place that night.

Since the very beginning of the war, intelligence had suggested that Germany was researching into and developing rocket technology, and although scant regard was given to the reports, photographic reconnaissance had confirmed the existence of an establishment at Peenemünde at the northern tip of the island of Usedom on the Baltic coast. The activities there were monitored through Ultra intercepts and surreptitious reconnaissance flights, and the V-1, known to the photographic interpreters at Medmenham because of its wingspan as the "Peenemünde 20", was captured on a photograph. The brilliant scientist, Dr R V Jones, had been able to gain vital information concerning the V-1's range, which would ultimately be used to feed disinformation to the enemy, largely through the double agent "Zigzag", otherwise known as Eddie Chapman. Unfortunately, Churchill's chief scientific adviser, Professor Lindemann, or Lord Cherwell as he became, steadfastly refused to give credence to the existence and feasibility of rocket weapons and held stubbornly to his viewpoint even when presented with a photograph of a V-2 on a trailer taken by a PRU Mosquito as recently as June. It required the combined urgings of Duncan Sandys and Dr Jones to persuade Churchill of the urgency to act, and Operation Hydra was planned for the first available opportunity, which occurred on the night of the 17/18th.

Earlier in the day, the USAAF 8th Air Force had carried out its first deep-penetration raids into Germany to attack ball-bearing production at Schweinfurt and the Messerschmitt aircraft plant near Regensburg, and to the shock of its leaders, had learned the harsh lesson that unescorted daylight raids in 1943 were not viable. The folks at home would not be told that sixty B17s had failed to return and further heavy and unsustainable losses during the ensuing two months would shatter American confidence in its daylight bombing policy and even persuade it to flirt with night operations on a very small scale during September.

It was vital that the Peenemünde installation be destroyed, ideally at the first attempt, and a force of 596 aircraft was assembled made up of 324 Lancasters, 218 Halifaxes and fifty-four Stirlings, sixty Stirlings short of what should have been the available number. The operation had been meticulously planned to account for the three vital components of Peenemünde, the housing estate, where the scientific and technical staff lived, the factory buildings in which the weapons were assembled and the experimental site, where testing took place. Each was assigned to a specific wave of aircraft, which would attack from medium level, with the Path Finders bearing the huge responsibility of re-directing the point of aim accordingly, for which each one of its squadrons was to provide one crew as a "shifter". That apart, once route markers had been dropped on Rügen island, the Path Finder markers and backers-up were to follow the standard routine of red, yellow and green TIs. After last minute alterations, 3 and 4 Groups were given the first-mentioned aiming point, 1 Group the second, and 5 and 6 Groups the third. The whole operation was to be overseen by a Master of Ceremonies (referred to hereafter as Master Bomber), and the officer selected for this hazardous and demanding role was G/C John Searby of 83 Squadron, who, as already mentioned, had stepped into Gibson's shoes at 106

Squadron after Gibson was posted out to form 617 Squadron. Searby's role was to direct the marking and bombing by VHF and to encourage the crews to press on to the aiming-point, a task requiring him to remain in the target area and within range of the defences throughout the attack.

In an attempt to protect the bombers from the attentions of enemy night-fighters for as long as possible, eight Mosquitos of 139 Squadron were to carry out a spoof raid on Berlin beginning at 23.00, seventy-five minutes before the opening of the main event, and would be led by the highly experienced and former 49 Squadron commander, G/C Len Slee. In the expectation of encountering drifting smoke as the last wave on target, the 5 Group crews were instructed to employ their oft-used time-and-distance approach to the aiming-point and had practiced this over a stretch of coast near the Wainfleet bombing range at the mouth of the Wash in Lincolnshire, progressively cutting the margin of error from one thousand to three hundred yards.

90 Squadron made ready fifteen Stirlings, the largest contribution by any 3 Group squadron, and the aircraft and crew captains were; EH944 S/L Freeman, BK811 F/L Cheek, EE952 F/L Crew, EE951 F/L Sheppard, EH908 F/O Day, MZ262 F/O Yates, EF443 P/O Appleby, BK781 P/O Kinsella, EE896 P/O McInnes, BF566 W/O Wood, EF446 F/Sgt Brayshaw, BK723 F/Sgt Lowe, EF426 Sgt Hilton, EH937 Sgt Luyk and BK655 Sgt Mason. Each crew was sitting on 1,000 and 500-pounders and incendiaries as they departed West Wickham between 20.28 and 20.53, the various groups making their way individually to a rendezvous point some ninety minutes flying time or three hundred miles from the English coast and sixty miles from Denmark's western coast, where they formed into a stream. The overall early-return rate was lower than normal, suggesting that crews had taken to heart the importance of the operation and there were no 90 Squadron "boomerangs". Darkness had fallen as they crossed the North Sea, and twenty miles short of landfall over the southern tip of Fanø island, south of Esbjerg, "windowing" began, in order to simulate a standard raid on a northern or north-eastern city. Southern Denmark was traversed by the Lancaster brigade at 18,000 feet, twice the altitude required for the attack, but, worryingly, in a band of cloudless sky under a bright moon, which the enemy night-fighter force failed to exploit. They adopted an east-south-easterly course and began to shed altitude gradually during the 240-mile run to the target a little over an hour away, and at the rear of the stream, the 5 Group crews focused on the island of Rügen, the ideal starting point for their timed run to Peenemünde, which lay some fifteen miles beyond to the south-east.

The skies over the target area were clear and the visibility good despite the deployment of a smoke screen, but even so, the initial marking of the housing estate went awry, and some target indicators fell onto the forced workers camp at Trassenheide, more than a mile south of the intended aiming-point. Inevitably, many of the 3 and 4 Group bombs fell here, inflicting grievous casualties on friendly foreign nationals trapped inside their wooden barracks. Once rectified, however, the attack proceeded according to plan and a number of important members of the technical staff were killed. The 90 Squadron crews had green TIs in their bomb sights as they attacked from 7,000 to 10,500 feet between 00.16 and 00.30 in accordance with the instructions from the Master Bomber, and all were satisfied that they had straddled the aiming point. The 1 Group second-wave crews encountered strong crosswinds over the narrow section of the island where the construction sheds were located, but this phase of the operation largely achieved its aims, and they were on their way home before the night-fighters arrived from Berlin, having been attracted by the glow of fires well to the north. On arrival at Rügen, the 5 Group crews began their timed run and reached the experimental site to encounter the expected smoke, before bombing on green TIs between 00.36 and 00.52. They and the 6 Group Halifaxes and Lancasters then ran into the night-fighters, which proceeded to take a heavy toll, both in the skies over the target, and on the route home towards Denmark. Twenty-nine of the forty missing aircraft came from this third wave, seventeen of them belonging to 5 Group and twelve to 6 Group, which represented a loss rate for the Canadians of 19.7%. Some had fallen victim to the new Schräge Musik (slanting or jazz music) upward-firing cannons, which were being employed by the Luftwaffe Nachtjagd for the first time. The West Wickham brigade returned safely and reported fires visible from 150 miles away and on main force stations there was praise for the work of the Path Finders and the Master Bomber. Post-raid reconnaissance revealed the raid to have been sufficiently effective to delay the V-2 development programme by a number of months and ultimately to force the manufacture of secret weapons underground at Nordhausen. The flight testing of the V-2 was eventually withdrawn eastwards into Poland, beyond the range of Harris's bombers, and thus Peenemünde had been nullified as a threat.

On the 21st West Wickham was renamed Wratting Common to avoid confusion with another RAF station with a similar name. The main operation on the night of the 22/23rd was directed at the Ruhr city of Leverkusen, situated on the Rhine just a stone's throw north of Cologne, where it was home among others to a factory belonging to the infamous I G Farben chemicals company. I G Farben, literally translated as I G Dyestuffs, or to give it its full name, Interessengemeinschaft (Common Interest Group) Farbenindustrie A G, would become infamous for its widespread use of slave labour at all of its sites, and even built production sites close to concentration camps. Among its founder members were Hoechst, Bayer, Agfa and BASF (Badische Anilin und Soda Fabrik), the last-mentioned the one which led the development and production of its chemical products. It was another subsidiary of the group that produced the Zyklon B gas employed in the extermination of Jewish people during the Holocaust. The Leverkusen site was engaged in the development and production of synthetic oil and rubber and as at all of its manufacturing sites, employed slave labour, including 30,000 from the Auschwitz concentration camp, where it had built a plant. A force of 462 aircraft carried out the raid in the absence of a 3 Group presence and failed to produce the hoped-for outcome after the Oboe signal faded.

While the above operation was in progress, thirty-seven Stirlings from 3 Group were sent mining in the Nectarine I and II gardens off the southern and central Frisians, among them five with freshman crews representing 90 Squadron. S/L Freeman was the senior pilot on duty as they departed Wratting Common between 20.25 and 20.31, four assigned to Nectarine II and F/Sgt Longmore and crew to Nectarine I and once in the target area they were to rely entirely on Gee to find their release points. As experienced by the Leverkusen force, the failure of the Gee signal prevented three crews from establishing their positions and they returned with their mines, while the Longmore crew delivered their five into the briefed location from 2,000 feet at 22.13 and Sgt Mason and crew theirs from a similar height at 22.32.

Harris had long believed that the key to ultimate victory lay in the destruction of Berlin, the seat of the Nazi government and the symbol of its power. On the 23rd, orders were received on stations across the Command to prepare for a maximum effort that night against Germany's capital city, which had not been visited by the heavy brigade since the end of March. The crews, of course, could not know that this was to be the first of an eventual nineteen raids on the "Big City", in an offensive which, with an autumn break, would drag on until the following spring. It was a campaign that would test the resolve of the crews to the absolute limit, whilst also sealing the fate of the Stirlings and the Mk II and V Halifaxes as front-line bombers. There are varying opinions concerning the true start date of what became known as the Berlin offensive or the Battle of Berlin, some commentators believing these first three operations in August and September to be the start, while others point to the sixteen raids from mid-November. However, there was little doubt in Bomber Command circles that this was it, a fact demonstrated by the comments in numerous squadron ORBs, which spoke of the "long-awaited Berlin campaign" and similar sentiments.

There would be a Master Bomber on hand for this operation, and the officer chosen was Canadian W/C "Johnny" Fauquier, the tough, grizzled and one-time bush pilot and frequent brawler, who was enjoying his second spell as the commanding officer of 405 (Vancouver) Squadron, once of 4 Group, but since April, proud to be the only Canadian Path Finder unit. The route had been planned to take the bomber stream to a rendezvous point over the North Sea, before crossing the Dutch coast near Haarlem and entering Germany between Meppen to the north and Osnabrück to the south. It would then follow a path between Bremen and Hannover to bypass the southern rim of Berlin, before turning back sharply on a north-westerly course to fly across the city centre. After bombing, they were to exit Germany via the Baltic coast and head for landfall on the Schleswig-Holstein peninsula. Seventeen Mosquitos were to precede the Path Finder and main force elements to drop route markers at key points in an attempt to keep the bomber stream on track.

A force of 727 aircraft included 124 Stirlings and thirteen Lancasters representing 3 Group, and an additional ten 139 Squadron Mosquitos were to provide a "window" screen in advance of the bomber stream. The Oboe Mosquitos were to mark the route with red and green TIs, backed up by H2S Lancasters, but as Berlin was beyond the range of Oboe, the aiming-point was to be marked with red TIs by H2S, backed up by greens. The 90 Squadron element of twenty departed Wratting Common between 20.17 and 20.55 with S/L Freeman the senior pilot on duty and carrying a mixed load each of either a 1,000-pounder or two 500-pounders and five and four SBCs respectively of 4lb and 30lb incendiaries. F/Sgt Smith and crew were on their way back to base within an hour because of an inability to maintain height, and W/O Wood and crew were the other 90 Squadron representative among twenty-seven 3 Group early returns. They arrived back in the circuit four-and-a-half hours after leaving it and like many others, cited severe icing as the reason for not continuing.

After flying out over scattered cloud, those reaching the target area found clear skies and moonlight, but the Path Finders were unable to identify the aiming-point in the centre of the city, a result of the inherent difficulties of interpreting the H2S images over such a massive urban sprawl and marked the southern outskirts instead. It would be established later, that many main force crews had cut the corner to approach the city from the south-west rather than south-east, and this had resulted in the wastage of many bombs in open country and on outlying communities. The 90 Squadron crews aimed their bombs at the centre of green TIs from 12,000 to 16,000 feet between 23.59 and 00.10, and on return described large explosions, many fires and a pall of smoke rising to meet them as they turned towards the north-west. The glow from the burning city remained visible for at least 140 miles into the homeward flight, and, curiously, only a few crews commented on hearing the Master Bomber and finding his instructions helpful. S/L Freeman and crew reported combats with three enemy night-fighters as they departed the target area and claimed one as probably badly damaged, while P/O Mills and crew went one better by claiming to have played a part in the destruction of their assailant. A Do217 had attacked during the bombing run and after return fire from the Stirling was seen with its port wing on fire, held in a searchlight cone and under fire from flak, an experience which it failed to survive. The Mills crew landed at Coltishall short of fuel and displaying evidence of flak damage.

It had been a bad night for the Command, which registered a new record loss of fifty-six aircraft, made up of twenty-three Halifaxes, seventeen Lancasters and sixteen Stirlings, representing a percentage loss rate respectively of 9.1, 5.1 and 12.9, which perfectly reflected the food chain when all three types operated together. The Stirling losses were disproportionately high, and this continued to sound alarm bells at Bomber Command HQ, where the type, as previously mentioned, was already unpopular with Harris because of its low operating ceiling and inability to carry anything larger than a 2,000 pounder in its split bomb bay. The 3 Group statistics of a 20% rate of early returns and 12.4% failure to return made uncomfortable reading at 3 Group HQ at Exning. Two empty dispersal pans at Wratting Common should have been occupied by BK779 and EH937, the former having crashed into the North Sea north-west of Cuxhaven, condemning Sgt Mulvey RCAF and two of his crew to eight days in their dinghy as the only survivors, before being rescued by the enemy and taken into captivity. EH937 had been brought down over the Ijsselmeer with no survivors from the crew of F/Sgt Longmore RAAF.

Despite the difficulty in marking, this was the most successful raid to date on Berlin and resulted in the destruction of or serious damage to 2,611 buildings in mostly residential districts. A few bombs did fall in the centre, into the government quarter, and the industrial districts of Marienfelde and Mariendorf were also hit. The death toll on the ground stood at 854, and an unusually high number of these were civilians, who had declined the opportunity to enter their allocated air-raid shelters.

On the following night, 3 Group sent nine Stirling and two Lancaster freshman crews mining in the Nectarine I garden, that of F/Sgt Langford representing 90 Squadron and departing Wratting Common at 20.50. They planted six vegetables according to brief from 1,800 feet at 22.13 aided by ideal weather conditions and good visibility and returned safely from an uneventful trip.

Orders were received on the 27th to prepare for an operation that night against Nuremberg and a force of 674 aircraft was duly assembled, which included a contribution from 3 Group of 112 Stirlings and ten Lancasters, nineteen of the former made ready at Wratting Common, where each bomb bay was filled with eight SBCs each of 4lb and 30lb incendiaries. They took off between 21.07 and 21.59 with F/L Smith the senior pilot on duty, he now acting as B Flight commander. F/Sgt Denton became unwell early on and returned to base ninety minutes after leaving it, while the others joined the bomber stream as it flew out in cloud, which dispersed to leave clear skies and good horizontal visibility in the target area but extreme darkness that obscured ground detail. The Path Finders had been briefed to check their H2S equipment by dropping a 1,000 pounder on Heilbronn, and some crews complied, while others, it seems, experienced technical difficulties. Despite accurate initial marking, a creep-back developed, which the backers-up and the Master Bomber could not correct. The 90 Squadron crews observed red, yellow and green TIs and most had the greens in their bomb sights as they let their loads go from 12,000 to 15,000 feet between 00.45 and 01.03. Many concentrated fires were reported and the consensus of returning crews was of an effective raid, which would not be entirely supported by an analysis and local sources that revealed that many bomb loads had fallen into open country, while others had hit south-eastern and eastern districts. Thirty-three aircraft failed to return, eleven of each type, which again confirmed the vulnerability of the Stirlings and Halifaxes when operating alongside Lancasters. The loss rate on this night was 3.1% for the Lancaster, 5% for the Halifax and a disproportionately high 10.6% for the Stirlings. 90 Squadron was represented by EF439, which crashed outbound at Hesselberg, clearly the victim of a night-fighter over a heavily wooded and sparsely populated region to the east of Heilbronn, and only the mid-upper gunner in the crew of F/Sgt Phillips survived to fall into enemy hands.

The main event on the night of the 30/31st was a two-phase attack on the twin towns of Mönchengladbach and Rheydt, the first time that either would experience a major Bomber Command assault. Situated some ten miles west of the centre of Düsseldorf in the south-western Ruhr, they would face an initial force of 660 aircraft of four types, in what for the crews, was a short-penetration trip across the Dutch frontier and a welcome change from the recent long slogs to eastern and southern Germany. The plan called for the first wave to hit Mönchengladbach, before a two-minute pause in the bombing allowed the Path Finders to head south to mark Rheydt. 3 Group put up 107 Stirlings and eleven Lancasters, nineteen of the former provided by 90 Squadron, their crews having been briefed to bomb in the first wave. They departed Wratting Common between 00.04 and 00.44 with W/C Giles and the newly promoted and appointed C Flight commander, S/L Wilson, the senior pilots on duty and each crew sitting on twenty-four SBCs divided equally between 4lb and 30lb incendiaries. P/O Mills and crew returned early because of an unserviceable rear turret, leaving the others to continue on over seven to nine-tenths cloud, which persisted all the way across Holland to lie at 8,000 feet over the target, but without impairing the good visibility. The operation proceeded according to plan with scarcely any creep-back, the 90 Squadron crews delivering their attacks from 11,000 to 15,000 feet between 02.15 and 02.27 and contributing to the destruction of approximately half of the built-up area of each town. This amounted to more than a thousand buildings in Mönchengladbach and almost thirteen hundred in Rheydt, at a cost to the Command of twenty-five aircraft.

The month ended with preparations for the second of the Berlin operations on the night of the 31st, for which 622 aircraft were made ready, more than half of them Lancasters. 3 Group detailed 101 Stirlings and five Lancasters, nineteen of the former belonging to 90 Squadron, which were loaded with a mixture of high explosives and incendiaries before departing Wratting Common between 19.50 and 20.17 with S/L Wilson and F/L Smith the senior pilots on duty. The route on this night took the bomber stream on an east-south-easterly heading across Texel to a position between Hannover and Leipzig, before turning to pass to the south-east of

Berlin and approach the city-centre aiming-point on a north-westerly track. The return leg would involve a south-westerly course to a position south of Cologne for an exit over the French coast, but despite the attempts to outwit the enemy night-fighter controller, he would be able to predict to some extent where to concentrate his night-fighters. This would be the first occasion on which the Command registered the German use of "fighter flares" to mark out the path of the bombers to and from the target.

The 3 Group effort was depleted by the early return of a massive twenty-five aircraft for a variety of reasons and among them were five of the 90 Squadron contingent, which landed between 22.11 and 23.05, three citing technical failures and two a lack of power. The Path Finders encountered five to six-tenths cloud in the target area, which combined with H2S equipment failure and a spirited night-fighter response to cause the markers to be dropped well to the south of the planned aiming-point. The main force crews reported between four and nine-tenths thin cloud and bombed on green TIs, those from 90 Squadron from 11,500 to 15,000 feet between 23.43 and 23.55 and observing many fires over a wide area. It was noted by some that two groups of green TIs were ten miles apart, and both attracted bomb loads, which possibly contributed to an extensive creep-back stretching some thirty miles into open country and outlying communities. The outcome was a major disappointment, brought about by woefully short marking, and resulted in the destruction of just eighty-five houses, a figure in no way commensurate with the effort expended and the loss of forty-seven heavy bombers. The lower-flying Stirlings were particularly vulnerable to both night-fighters and flak, and this was demonstrated by the loss of seventeen of them or 16%, among which was 90 Squadron's EE871. This came down somewhere in the Berlin defence zone with fatal consequences for W/O Callaway and all but the mid-upper gunner, who alone survived to fall into enemy hands.

On the 31st, S/L Scott was posted to 1665 Conversion Unit at the conclusion of his tour, but he would return for a second tour. During the course of the month the squadron took part in thirteen operations and dispatched 186 sorties for the loss of four Stirlings and crews.

September 1943

September began for the Command with extensive mining operations on the night of the 2/3rd, for which 3 Group detailed twenty-five Stirlings and a single Lancaster, some of the former provided by the group's most recent additions, 620, 622 and 623 Squadrons. 620 and 623 Squadrons were destined for short careers in Bomber Command, the former transferring to 38 Group for transport duties in November and the latter undergoing disbandment in December.

The Stirling malaise of collapsing undercarriages accounted for 90 Squadron's EE951 on return from an air test on the 3rd of September, which had been carried out in preparation for a mining sortie that night. There were no casualties among the crew of W/O Mason, but they were not among the five and three crews respectively assigned to the Nectarine I and Deodar gardens, which departed Wratting Common that evening between 19.58 and 20.05 with S/L Freeman the senior pilot on duty. In the event, only two of the Nectarine-bound crews managed to plant their vegetables, from 4,000 and 4,500 feet at 21.44 and 21.46, before the Gee signal faded to prevent the others from establishing a pinpoint. The crews of F/L Freeman, P/O Mills and W/O Wood fared better in the Gironde estuary, pinpointing on a small lake some twelve miles south of Grave Pointe and delivering their stores from 4,000 to 6,000 feet between 22.52 and 23.04.

The main operation on this night was the third and last in the current series against Berlin, which probably as a result of the heavy losses incurred by the Halifaxes and Stirlings in the two previous raids, involved an all-Lancaster heavy force of 316 aircraft, just four provided by 3 Group. Much of the effort fell short, but local sources confirmed severe damage, principally in the largely residential districts of Tiergarten, Wedding, Moabit and Charlottenburg, but also in the industrial Siemensstadt, which resulted in a significant loss of war production. Twenty-two Lancasters failed to return, 7% of those dispatched, demonstrating that in the absence of Halifaxes and Stirlings, the type was equally vulnerable to night-fighters.

Whether by design or as a result of the losses sustained, Berlin was now shelved for the next ten weeks, while Harris sought other suitable targets, of which there were many. He would shortly begin a four-raid series against Hannover stretching over a four-week period, but first he focused on southern Germany, beginning on the 5th with the twin cities of Mannheim and Ludwigshafen, which face each other from the eastern and western banks respectively of the Rhine. The plan was to exploit the creep-back phenomenon that attended most large operations, by approaching the target from the west and marking the eastern half of Mannheim, with the expectation that the bombing would spread back along the line of approach across western Mannheim and into Ludwigshafen. A force of 605 aircraft was assembled, which included 111 Stirlings, the crews of which learned at briefing that the blind marker crews were to identify the target area with red TIs and flares, by means of which the visual marker crews would confirm and back up the aiming-point with yellow and green TIs.

The twenty-one-strong 90 Squadron element departed Wratting Common between 19.20 and 19.51 with S/Ls Freeman and Wilson the senior pilots on duty and each Stirling carrying ten SBCs, six of 4lb and four of 30lb incendiaries. F/Sgt Kirk and crew turned back within the first hour because of engine issues, and an hour after they landed, W/O Wood and crew joined them on the ground citing a burst oil pipe in the rear turret as the reason behind their "boomerang". The bomber stream tracked across France to a point five miles south of Luxembourg, where route markers established the final turning point for a direct run on the target. The Path Finders were routed in over Kaiserslautern some thirty miles due west of Mannheim, from where they were to carry out a timed run to the aiming-point, benefitting from almost clear skies and excellent visibility, which enabled them to carry out their tasks according to brief and prepare the way for the approaching main force. The invitation to exploit the opportunity was accepted and the 90 Squadron crews delivered their attacks from 11,000 to 14,500 feet between 23.10 and 23.35, those arriving towards the later stages of the raid drawn on by the burgeoning fires fifty miles ahead. A number of large, red explosions were observed at 23.12, 23.23 and 23.27, the last of which was followed by a purplish-red mushroom of fire. Searchlights were numerous but the flak negligible, and it was the abundance of night-fighters that posed the greatest risk to life and limb. Black smoke was rising through 15,000 feet as the bombers withdrew to the west, and the glow from the burning cities was visible on the horizon for 150 miles into the return journey, which thirty-four aircraft would fail to complete.

Thirteen Lancasters, an equal number of Halifaxes and eight Stirlings were missing, and the percentage loss rates continued to tell the same story, a 7.2% loss rate for the Stirling, compared with 6.6% for the Halifaxes and 4.3% for the Lancasters. 90 Squadron's EF129 came down at Limbergerhof, some four miles south-south-west of Ludwigshafen, killing W/O Smith and his crew, and it is not possible to determine whether or not they had bombed. Local reports confirmed that both Mannheim and Ludwigshafen had suffered catastrophic destruction, with almost two thousand fires in the latter alone, 986 of them classed as large. Mannheim's reporting system broke down completely, and little detail emerged of this raid, although it would recover in time for the next assault in fewer than three weeks' time. What is known, is that the main railway station in Mannheim and three suburban stations were destroyed, and the tank and military tractor factories belonging to Heinrich Lanz and Josef Vogele respectively sustained serious damage, as did the Rashig & Sulzer chemicals plant.

Four hundred Lancasters and Halifaxes targeted Munich on the night of the 6/7th and scattered bombs over the southern districts in the face of extensive cloud cover. In the absence of Stirlings, thirteen Halifaxes were lost, a percentage loss rate of 8.8, compared with 1.2 for the Lancasters. The 90 Squadron stalwarts, F/Ls Cheek, Crew, Peryer and Sheppard were posted out on the 7th at the end of their tours and over the ensuing six months at least would pass on their skills to new crews at training units.

Operation Starkey was an attempt to mislead the enemy into believing that an invasion was imminent and had begun in mid-August with highly visible troop movements and the assembly of landing craft and gliders. It involved British, Canadian and American forces, and intimated that the area around Boulogne was to be the landing ground. Harris was not amused at being ordered to participate in what he considered to be play-acting, and most of the other service chiefs were of like mind, but bad weather provided Harris with a temporary "get-out" of the planned Bomber Command involvement during the final week of August. It was not until the night of the 8/9th of September that the opportunity arose for him to carry out his orders to bomb heavy gun emplacements at either end of the small resort town of Le Portel near Boulogne. Perhaps in a gesture of his attitude towards the whole Starkey affair, he committed only his two Oboe Mosquito squadrons and two heavy Path Finder units, along with the Stirlings of 3 Group and Wellingtons from the Polish 300 Squadron and the training units in an overall force of 257 aircraft. Phase I was aimed at the northern site, code-named Religion, and phase II at the southern site, code-named Andante and 90 Squadron assigned ten of its Stirlings to each. A bomb load of six 1,000 and eight 500-pounders was winched into each bomb bay, before the phase I element departed Wratting Common between 20.40 and 21.00 with S/L Freeman the senior pilot on duty, and they were followed into the air between 21.26 and 21.38 by the second element led by S/L Wilson.

They arrived in the target area to find clear skies and a little ground haze and pinpointed on the red and green TIs delivered by the Oboe Mosquitos, which were experimenting with a new technique. The marking proved to be inaccurate, which led to wayward bombing, delivered by the 90 Squadron participants in the first wave from 6,000 (S/L Freeman) to 15,000 feet between 22.04 and 22.20 and the second wave from 12,050 to 15,000 feet between 22.46 and 22.52. Returning crews reported numerous large explosions but few fires, and it seemed to them to have been a successful operation. In fact, neither battery had been hit, but the town of Le Portel had suffered extensive damage and many casualties. (For a detailed analysis of this operation, see the excellent book, The Starkey Sacrifice, by Michael Cumming, published by Sutton).

Generally adverse weather and fog ensured that the crews remained on the ground over the ensuing few days, and they were kept busy at most stations with lectures, PT and escape and evasion exercises. It was during this period on the 9th, that navigator S/L Levien was posted in from Bomber Command HQ to assume command of B Flight, which had been overseen by F/L Smith DFM, who was soon to depart for 623 Squadron and elevation to the rank of acting squadron leader. There was, no doubt, relief when the weather improved, and crews were called to briefing on the 15th to learn of that night's operation to attack a Dunlop factory at Montluçon in the Vichy region of central France. It was to be carried out by 369 aircraft of 3, 4, 6 and 8 Groups, with Halifaxes and Stirlings making up the main force element, 3 Group contributing 120 of the latter. At Wratting Common fourteen of them had 1,000 pounders and incendiaries loaded into their bomb bays, before taking off between 20.20 and 21.13 with no senior pilots on duty and only P/Os Mills and MacInnes of commissioned rank. They all reached the target area, where eight to nine-tenths cloud at 4,000 feet failed to prevent a view of the factory and the red, green and yellow TIs marking it out. A Master Bomber in the person of W/C "Dixie" Deane of 35 (Madras Presidency) Squadron was on hand to direct the attack and the 90 Squadron crews complied with his instructions to bomb in bright moonlight from 4,500 to 10,000 feet between 23.38 and 23.46. It wasn't long before black smoke was rising through 12,000 feet from the developing fires, and it was clear to all that the factory complex had been severely damaged. Opposition was negligible, and just two Halifaxes and a single Stirling failed to return. Post-raid reconnaissance confirmed that every building in the factory area had been hit, for which some of the credit must go to the Master Bomber.

As previously mentioned, the confidence of the US Eighth Air Force to deliver daylight attacks on military and war production targets in Germany had been shaken by the high loss rates, which were not sustainable. They had been toying with the idea of operating at night and this operation brought the maiden participation by five B17s launched under the control of 3 Group.

On the following day, the same groups were alerted to an operation that night against the important and extensive railway yards at Modane, situated on the main line between France and Italy in the foothills of the Alps in south-eastern France. A force of 340 aircraft was assembled, which included 127 Stirlings and five B17s, seventeen of the former made ready at Wratting Common and loaded either with four 1,000-pounders or six SBCs of 4lb incendiaries and seven of 30lbs. The marking was to be dependent upon a visual reference, but in case the conditions in the target area proved to be unfavourable, red spotfires were to be dropped on Grenoble. A careful timed run from there would culminate in the delivery of red TIs on e.t.a., followed by backing-up throughout the raid with green TIs. The 90 Squadron element took off between 19.50 and 20.16 with S/Ls Freeman and Wilson the senior pilots on duty, and all reached the target area to find between zero and two-tenths cloud at 10,000 feet with good visibility and moonlight. Zero hour was set for 00.01, but a patch of cloud right over the aiming-point delayed the start for a brief period. The target was situated in a steep valley, which presented the Path Finders with difficulties that they were unable to overcome, but most of the main force crews arriving early believed that they had identified it visually, assisted by the red TIs backed up by greens in a good concentration. Bombing was carried out by the 90 Squadron participants from

12,200 to 16,000 feet and they turned for home to report an apparently highly successful attack attended by heavy explosions and large fires, which appeared to be spreading. However, the confidence in the success of the operation was not borne out by post-raid reconnaissance, which revealed that the marking had been inaccurate and that the yards had escaped damage.

On the 21st, 3 Group detailed thirteen Stirlings for mining duties in the Nectarine I and II gardens, three of them representing 90 Squadron and departing Wratting Common between 18.58 and 19.04 with five mines of various types in each bomb bay. The ORB did not record to which garden the freshman crews of P/O Birdsall, F/Sgt Hinde and Sgt Young had been assigned and no map references were provided to offer a clue, but they fulfilled their briefs from 1,300 to 2,500 feet between 20.54 and 20.55 and returned safely from uneventful sorties of around four hours duration.

When the tannoys called the faithful to prayer on the 22nd after a five-night break, crews learned that they were to be part of a force of 711 aircraft, including 137 Stirlings and seven Lancasters of 3 Group plus five B17s, to attack the ancient city of Hannover, situated in northern Germany midway between the Dutch frontier and Berlin. They were told that it was home to much war industry, as detailed earlier in this narrative, and that the plan of attack called for the Path Finder blind marker crews to use their H2S to mark the general target area with red TIs and illuminator flares, and that the visual markers would confirm the exact aiming-point with yellow TIs, which the backers-up were to maintain throughout the attack with green TIs. What was not known at the time among the Allies was that the region was also the location of seven Nazi concentration camps.

According to Martin Middlebrook and Chris Everitt in Bomber Command War Diaries, the first two operations produced concentrated bombing, but mostly outside of the target, while only the third one succeeded in causing extensive damage, which, if the figures are to be believed, seem to be massively out of proportion. The author contends that the reports of the crews after the first two operations suggest strongly that the damage to Hannover was accumulative over the first three raids and did not result from just one, as will be explained in the following narrative. The telling feature is, perhaps, that no reports came out of Hannover to corroborate the testimony of the crews on the first two raids, although post-raid reconnaissance by the RAF after the second one did show that some of the bombing had fallen into open country and the Path Finders did admit to at least one poor performance.

The nineteen-strong 90 Squadron element departed Wratting Common between 18.32 and 19.09 with W/C Giles and S/Ls Freeman and Wilson the senior pilots on duty and each Stirling loaded with two 1,000-pounders and six and five SBCs respectively of 4lb and 30lb incendiaries. As they climbed out the starboard-inner engine of MZ262 burst into flames, which spread to a fuel tank and at 19.16 the Stirling exploded at 500 feet, scattering wreckage over Breckley Green to the south of Newmarket. Sgt Hayman and five of his crew died instantly and the mid-upper gunner succumbed soon afterwards to his injuries. The others headed for the coast and the North Sea, where they would rendezvous with the rest of the bomber stream, but not all would complete the 430-mile outward leg, the crews of W/O Mason and P/O Mills among fourteen from 3 Group to return early, both because of engine issues. Clear skies and good visibility prevailed as the attack began on schedule at 21.30 and the first red TIs were observed three minutes later, before another was seen to cascade over the city after overshooting it by an estimated four miles. This was followed by other red TIs overshooting by one to four miles with many greens falling among them and yellows seeming to undershoot the reds by two miles and fall closer to the city centre aiming point. Stronger-than-forecast winds were also playing their part in pushing the marking and bombing towards the south-east, but the main force crews could only bomb on the TIs that presented themselves and those from 90 Squadron carried out their bombing runs from 11,000 to 15,500 feet between 21.33 and 21.49 in the face of intense searchlight activity and heavy flak bursting at their level.

90 Squadron's BF566 failed to arrive home after falling victim to the night-fighter of Hptm August Geiger of III./NJG1 and crashing at 22.35 at Gestorf, some ten miles south of Hannover, killing P/O Birdsall and his crew. Meanwhile, a life and death drama was taking place in EH944 after it had been badly shot up in an engagement with a night-fighter, during which one crew member was killed. Two others baled out while the Stirling was in freefall, but W/O Denton regained control, and with the help of the three remaining members of the crew set about nursing the damaged aircraft home, eventually crash-landing at Lakenheath at 01.40. For their gallant efforts W/O Denton was awarded the DFC, flight engineer Sgt Jones the CGM and navigator Sgt Suddens the DFM. Twenty-six aircraft failed to return, five of them Stirlings, but the Halifaxes again sustained the highest numerical losses, this time, at 5.3%, even exceeding the Stirlings' loss rate.

At debriefings, some main force crews reported a line of fires developing from west to east with smoke rising through 14,000 feet, while others claimed that fires ran from the aiming-point in a north-north-westerly direction across the city. One 101 Squadron crew made the comment, "Excellent attack – should be the end of Hannover". All, it seems, were unanimous that the raid had been highly successful, and confirmed that the glow of fires remained visible from the Dutch coast two hundred miles away. So, let us now consider the claim that the main weight of bombs fell two to five miles south-south-east from the city centre, and that the operation largely failed as a result. Firstly, two to five miles in any large city means that the bombing fell within the boundaries, and therefore, within the built-up area. Secondly, the majority of crews, if not all, reported a highly successful raid with fires right across the city, smoke rising to 14,000 feet as they left the scene and the glow visible on the horizon from the Dutch coast. It is true that crews were very frequently mistaken in their belief that an attack had been successful, but the evidence on this occasion would seem to confirm their testimony. Decoy fire-sites did not produce a glow visible from a distance of two hundred miles, or sufficient volumes of smoke to reach bombing height during the short duration of a raid in a density visible at night. In fact, fifty-six factories had sustained damaged, railway installations had been severely disrupted, the line to Hildesheim cut and a four-track railway bridge brought down as the result of a direct hit.

On the 23rd, and for the second time in the month, Mannheim was posted as the target and a force of 628 aircraft assembled, 3 Group providing 116 Stirlings, six Lancasters and five USAAF B17s. At the Wratting Common briefing, while eighteen aircraft were being loaded with SBCs of 4lb and 30lb incendiaries, the crews learned that Mosquitos were to drop red and green route markers, before the Path Finder blind marker crews delivered flares and red TIs over the target by H2S to guide the visual marker crews to the precise aiming-point. That was located in the less-severely afflicted northern districts, which they would mark with yellow TIs, followed by the backers-up with greens. The 90 Squadron element took off between 19.00 and 19.40 with S/L Freeman the senior pilot on duty, and there were no early returns to blunt the squadron's impact. The bomber stream adopted the familiar route across France and entered Germany south of Luxembourg, where it encountered largely clear skies and good visibility. Zero hour had been set for 21.45, and following a competent performance by the Path Finders, the 90 Squadron crews bombed on green TIs from 10,000 and 15,000 feet between 21.50 and 22.03. At debriefing, crews reported a successful operation with heavy explosions and large, concentrated fires spreading towards the west, from which smoke had reached around 6,000 feet as they turned away. They also claimed that the glow of fires remained visible for 150 miles into the return journey and commented on the abundance of night-fighters, which were involved in a number of skirmishes with 3 Group aircraft. Thirty-two aircraft failed to return and this time, eighteen of them were Lancasters, compared with seven Halifaxes and seven Stirlings. This provided a somewhat topsy-turvy and unusual loss-rate of 5.7%, 3.6% and 6% respectively. 90 Squadron's EF458 was homebound when crashing at Kaifenheim, some forty miles south of Cologne, and there were no survivors from the crew of Sgt Haynes. Post-raid reconnaissance and local reports revealed that the marking had been accurate and concentrated, although later bombing had spilled over into the northern fringe of Ludwigshafen and out into the nearby towns of Oppau and Frankenthal, where much damage resulted. A total of 927 houses and twenty industrial premises had been destroyed in Mannheim, and the I G Farben factory in Ludwigshafen had been brought to a standstill.

Minor operations on the 25th included a mining effort by ten Stirlings in the Nectarine I garden off the western Frisians, for which the 90 Squadron crews of Sgts Dalton and Blyfield departed Wratting Common at 18.58, each carrying five B200 mines. They established their positions by Gee, before planting their vegetables according to brief from 1,500 and 3,500 feet at 20.26 and 20.30.

There were three briefings at Wratting Common on the 27th, the first involving four freshman crews, who were to join eight others from 3 Group to mine the waters in one of the Silverthorn gardens in the Kattegat off Jutland's Baltic coast. The second briefing was of the lone crew of Sgt Wright, who, along with six others, were assigned to the Nectarine I garden off the western Frisians, while a dozen others were to take part in the main event, the second of the series against Hannover. The crews of F/Sgt Hinde and Sgts Blyfield, Dalton and Young took off between 16.36 and 16.58 bound for the Baltic, and we know only that the Kullen Light on the Swedish coast was one of the pinpoints and Knudshoved another, but the two are separated by around a hundred miles with the Danish Zealand Island between them, on the eastern seaboard of which lies the city of Copenhagen. All four sorties were successful in delivering three mines each into the briefed locations from 5,000 to 6,000 feet between 20.17 and 20.40. Sgt Wright took off at 19.00 bound for Nectarine I and despite encountering ten-tenths cloud and rain, planted five B200 mines from 4,000 feet at 20.25.

The bombing contingent departed Wratting Common between 19.40 and 20.16 with S/Ls Freeman and Wilson the senior pilots on duty as part of a force of 678 aircraft, for which 3 Group had contributed 111 Stirlings and five USAAF B17s. At briefing, they had learned of their part in the overall plan, while out on the dispersals the armourers spent the late afternoon loading nine and ten SBCs respectively of 4lb and 30lb incendiaries into the Stirlings' bomb bays. The Steinhuder Lake to the north-west of the city was to be employed again by the Path Finder blind marker crews as the starting point for a timed run to the aiming point, which would be marked with yellow TIs on H2S and identified visually by the backers-up and marked with reds and greens. They climbed out through ice-bearing cloud before setting course towards poor weather conditions over the North Sea, the bomber stream pressing on behind the Path Finder spearhead, who were unaware that the weather forecasts on which their performance would be based were incorrect. The result of that would be to push the marking some five miles from the city centre towards the north of the city, but at least the weather improved markedly over northern Germany to present the crews with clear skies at the target. The main force crews carried out their attacks on green TIs, those from 90 Squadron from 12,500 to 15,000 feet between 22.13 and 22.19 and observed widespread fires and black smoke rising through 12,000 feet. F/L Freeman and crew failed to make debriefing after EF952 collided with trees during final approach to land and crashed at 00.17 at Horseheath, within three miles of the runway. S/L Freeman and four of his crew died at the scene, while the flight engineer and mid-upper gunner survived with injuries.

Returning crews reported a city on fire with the glow visible from the Dutch coast and confidence in the success of the operation was unanimous across the Command, giving lie to the claim that little damage resulted. Post-raid photos did reveal many bomb craters in open country, but also that the main force crews had performed with distinction to hit fifteen square miles within the built-up area and achieve 130 tons of bombs per square mile. Again, the fire and smoke evidence did not support decoy fire-sites, but no local report was forthcoming to shed further light. The ground defences were described as ineffective, but night-fighters were very much in evidence and P/O Mills and crew reported being engaged twice by a BF110 during the bombing run and inflicting damage upon it sufficient to discourage a further attack. The loss of thirty-eight aircraft was probably something of a shock, but common sense had returned to the statistics to re-establish the status-quo after the topsy-turvy outcome of the Mannheim raid. Seventeen Halifaxes, ten Lancasters, ten Stirlings and one Wellington failed to return, giving loss-rates for the four-engine types of 9% for the Stirling, 7.3% for the Halifax and 3.2% for the Lancaster.

During the course of the month the squadron took part in eleven operations and dispatched 139 sorties for the loss of seven Stirlings, four complete crews and members of others.

October 1943

The first week of the new month would place a heavy burden on the Lancaster squadrons, which would be called upon to operate five times in the first seven nights. It began at Hagen in the Ruhr on the night of the 1/2nd and moved on to Munich twenty-four hours later. While the latter was in progress, extensive mining operations involved 117 aircraft plying their trade between the Biscay coast and the Baltic. 3 Group assigned thirty-nine Stirlings to two Baltic regions, the Kraut garden in Lim Fjord between Hals and Aalborg off Jutland's north-eastern coast and one of the Silverthorn gardens in the Kattegat, and a further eighteen Stirlings and a Lancaster to the Nectarine region off the Frisians. 90 Squadron made ready six of its Stirlings to divide equally between Nectarine I and, based on the map reference for a pinpoint, Silverthorn VII, the latter, the crews of P/Os Wood and Brayshaw and W/O Hilton, departing Wratting Common first between 17.40 and 17.45, each sitting on three H802 mines. The crews of P/O Whitworth and F/Sgts Simpson and Tyler remained on the ground for more than an hour before taking off between 18.53 and 18.56 for the short trip to the western Frisians each with five B200 mines beneath their feet. They relied on Gee to establish their positions and carried out their briefs from 1,500 to 4,000 feet between 20.13 and 20.20, shortly before the Baltic brigade arrived in their target area to pinpoint on the brightly illuminated city of Gothenburg, before running west to the release point and delivering their stores from 5,500 to 6,000 feet between 20.36 and 20.46. The return route from the Baltic passed through an electrical storm, which provided the only excitement during otherwise uneventful sorties.

The Halifaxes and Stirlings were included on the order of battle for the next operation, which was against the highly industrialised city of Kassel on the 3rd, for which a force of 547 aircraft was assembled that consisted of 223 Halifaxes, 204 Lancasters, 113 Stirlings and seven Mosquitos. 90 Squadron provided eighteen of the Stirlings, which were loaded with fifteen SBCs split more or less equally between 4lb and 30lb incendiaries and departed Wratting Common between 18.25 and 19.00 with a whole host of pilots of flight lieutenant rank leading the way. The plan of attack called for the Mosquitos to provide route markers and for the Path Finder H2S crews to mark the target blind by H2S with yellow TIs and flares. The visual markers were then to identify the aiming-point and mark it with red TIs for the backers-up to maintain with greens. For Kassel, the industrial city located some eighty miles to the east of the Ruhr, this night's visit would be the first of two during the month, which forever after would leave their mark upon it. As home among other war industry concerns to the Henschel and Fieseler aircraft factories and the Henschel tank works where the much-feared Tiger Tank was in production, it was a priority target that needed to be dealt with. The Fieseler company would also be responsible for the design and construction of the V-1 flying bomb that would be unleashed on London in the summer of 1944 and become known as the "Doodlebug" or "Buzzbomb".

F/Sgt Luyk and crew turned back when the rear gunner found his turret to be unserviceable during testing over the North Sea, leaving the others to traverse Holland and the Münsterland in favourable weather conditions to reach the target area. They were met by largely clear skies but thick ground haze, which should not have, but did cause the Path Finder blind markers to overshoot the planned aiming-point. The light from the flares reflected off the haze to prevent the visual markers from determining the location of the aiming-point, and as a consequence, they withheld their red TIs. The Germans were operating decoy markers, which together with the absence of the red TIs, conspired to lead a quarter of the main force crews astray and waste their bombs outside of the built-up area. The 90 Squadron crews carried out their part in the operation from 12,000 to 15,000 feet between 21.24 and 21.32, F/Sgt Kirk and crew coming under attack by a FW190, which, during a three-minute engagement, rendered both turrets inoperable, but not before return fire had persuaded the enemy pilot to break off the chase. As the bombers turned away from what appeared to be a good concentration of fires, crews observed a pall of smoke rising through 10,000 feet, suggesting that the operation had been a success. In fact, the main weight of the attack had fallen onto the western suburbs, where the Henschel aircraft and tank factories and the Fieseler aircraft plant were hit, but also onto woodland beyond. However, a stray bomb load had fallen onto one of the largest ammunition dumps in Germany, situated three miles north-east of the aiming point at Ihringshausen, close to the suburb of Wolfsanger, and the resulting explosion at 22.06 devastated the area and attracted more bomb loads. A second explosion ten minutes after the first added to the destruction and left eighty-four buildings on the site flattened and the ground pockmarked by craters, one of which was three hundred feet in diameter. Twenty-four aircraft failed to return, fourteen Halifaxes, six Stirlings and four Lancasters, which gave a loss-rate of 6.3%, 3.2% and 2.9% respectively. 90 Squadron had two empty dispersal pans to contemplate with the arrival of dawn, one of which should have been occupied by BK723, which crashed in the North Sea when outbound and took with it to their deaths the crew of Sgt De Meillac. The other absentee was EE901, which crashed at Krefeld on the western edge of the Ruhr, and there were no survivors from the mixed RAF/RCAF crew of Sgt Dalton RCAF.

The busy schedule of operations continued with the posting of Frankfurt as the target for 406 aircraft on the 4th, for which 3 Group detailed sixty-nine Stirlings and three USAAF B17s in what was to be their final night operation. The Americans could not be convinced to become nocturnal, and October would turn into their blackest month of the war, during which, between the 8th and 14th alone, they would lose 152 bombers on daylight operations, 11.3%, and in the month as a whole, a total of 214 B17s and B24s, almost 10% of those dispatched, with many more sustaining severe damage. It was a hammer blow to American morale and would result in restricted operations until they were able to provide adequate protection with the arrival of the Merlin-powered P51D Mustang in 1944. Crews learned at briefing that they would be following a somewhat circuitous route, which departed England over the Sussex coast and tracked across France as if heading for southern Germany, before swinging to the north-east and passing to the west of Frankfurt for the final run-in of around eighty miles. This added significantly to the mileage but avoided the flak hotspots from the Dutch coast and the Ruhr's southern defence zone. Eight 90 Squadron Stirlings departed Wratting Common between 18.40 and 18.53 with pilots of flight lieutenant rank still leading the way, and set course for the Channel, each carrying an all-incendiary bomb load. They reached the target after a four-hour outward flight, up to an hour of which was accounted for in climbing-out and gaining height before setting course. Frankfurt was found to be clear of cloud, and the Path Finder crews excelled to deliver the H2S-laid markers and illuminator flares all within three miles of the aiming-point and the visual markers within a mile-and-a-half, leaving the city at the mercy of the main force crews.

Bombing was carried out by the 90 Squadron participants on red and green TIs from 12,000 to 15,000 feet between 21.38 and 21.46 in the face of searchlights co-operating with night-fighters, which were very much in evidence. A large red explosion was observed at 21.37, which threw flames up to 3,000 feet, and smoke was rising through 8,000 feet as the bombers turned away, some crews reporting the glow from the burning city to be visible for up to 150 miles into the homeward leg. A modest ten aircraft failed to return, just two of them Stirlings, and post-raid reconnaissance revealed massive damage in the eastern half of the city and in the inland docks area, both of which were described locally as a "sea of flames". This was the first major success for Bomber Command at this target.

There were many accounts of "friendly fire" incidents involving convoys, which invariably fired at anything that flew within range, and one such example on the night of the 7/8th centred around a 90 Squadron Stirling and crew. 3 Group had detailed forty-two Stirlings for mining operations in Lim Fjord, the Kattegat and the Frisians, and it was for the last-mentioned that the crews of Sgts Phillips and Jones, F/Sgt Timlin and P/O Newton took off between 18.20 and 18.23, each carrying six mines for delivery to the Nectarine I garden. Sgt Phillips and crew lost the use of their Gee shortly after crossing the Suffolk coast and turned back, leaving the others to fulfil their briefs from 1,500 to 4,000 feet between 20.05 and 20.07. On the way home EF179 came under fire from a convoy and sustained sufficient damage to force F/Sgt Timlin to ditch off Cromer, and all but the wireless operator, Sgt Miller, made it safely into the dinghy and were picked up by a destroyer at around 03.15.

The main operation on this night, at the end of a busy first week of the month, was directed at Stuttgart, for which a force of 343 Lancasters was drawn from 1, 3, 5, 6 and 8 Groups. A new weapon in the Command's armoury was introduced for the first time in numbers on this night with the participation of a night-fighter-communications-jamming device called "Jostle" fitted in 101 Squadron Lancasters. It required a specialist operator in addition to the standard crew of seven, who, though not necessarily a German speaker, could recognise the language and on hearing it, jam the signals on up to three frequencies by broadcasting engine noise over them. At 101 Squadron the device was referred to as ABC or Airborne Cigar, and once proved to be effective, ABC Lancasters would be spread throughout the bomber stream for all major operations, whether or not 1 Group was otherwise involved. The Lancaster would also carry a full bomb load reduced by 1,000lbs to compensate for the weight of the equipment and its operator. The operation was inconclusive in the face of ten-tenths cloud but cost a remarkably modest four aircraft, and whether or not the presence of the radio-countermeasures Lancasters was responsible could not be proved, but it was a promising start and would lead ultimately to the formation of the dedicated 100 RCM Group in November.

The following night brought the third raid in the series against Hannover, for which a force of 504 aircraft was made ready, thirteen of the Lancasters representing 3 Group in the absence of the Stirling brigade. Twenty-six Wellingtons from the Polish 300 Squadron and the Canadian 432 (Leaside) Squadron were included, for what would be the type's bombing swansong. 3 Group had been asked to provide ninety-five Stirlings and twelve Mk II Lancasters as the main force for a diversionary raid on Bremen, some seventy miles north-west of the main target, and the sixteen 90 Squadron participants departed Wratting Common for the last time in anger between 22.28 and 22.56, again with pilots of flight lieutenant rank the most senior on duty. They were carrying a mix of bomb loads, some with one or two 1,000-pounders and others with up to ten 500-pounders supplemented with incendiaries, and only Sgt Young and crew returned early after losing their starboard-outer engine. The others reached north-western Germany to find eight to nine-tenths thin cloud at 6,000 feet, through which the Path Finder markers were clearly visible. The 90 Squadron contingent fulfilled their briefs by bombing on red and green TIs from 12,000 to 16,000 feet between 01.10 and 01.19 and observed some fires, while remaining unable to form a clear impression of the outcome. The accuracy of the bombing was not of overriding importance on a spoof raid, the primary purpose of which was to confuse the night-fighter controller and split the defences. Three Stirlings failed to return, and among them was BK655, which crashed at 01.25 at Rhade, some twenty miles to the north-north-east of Bremen, and there were no survivors from the crew of F/L Yates.

Meanwhile, Hannover had been found to be clear of cloud and a highly successful operation ensued, in which all parts of the city, except for the western districts, sustained massive damage.

Local reports claimed that 3,932 buildings had been destroyed and thirty thousand others damaged to some extent, figures which seem excessive for a single operation in which fewer than five hundred aircraft had bombed. There was also an absence of the kind of enthusiastic remarks at debriefings that had followed the two previous attacks and no mention of the glow from the burning city remaining visible from the Dutch coast. This lends weight to the author's contention that the earlier raids, which had been dismissed largely as failures, had in fact caused much destruction and the above figures were accumulative over the three raids. Despite the Bremen diversion, night-fighters appeared on the scene while the raid was in progress and twenty-seven aircraft failed to return.

A spate of training accidents now afflicted the squadron, beginning on the 12th, when EF426 crashed at Wratting Common during a three-engine landing and W/O Hilton and five of his crew died at the scene, while the rear gunner survived with injuries. On the 13th, the squadron changed address for the final time when taking up residence at Tuddenham, a new station located three miles south of Mildenhall, and on the 16th, S/L King arrived from 1651 Conversion Unit to assume command of A Flight.

The Path Finder and main force squadrons would effectively stand down now for a period of ten days, while Mosquitos of 8 Group took the war to Germany. For a time at least, Stirlings would be precluded from deep penetration forays into the Reich and 90 Squadron would spend the rest of the month engaged in mining operations. Poor weather conditions hampered training and operations, and it was the evening of the 17th before four crews managed to get away, those of F/L Smith and Sgt Wright at 17.53 bound for the Deodar garden in the Gironde estuary, while the crews of Sgts Jones and Nixon set off at 18.01 and 18.11 respectively for Cinnamon, off La Pallice, and Nectarine I, off the western Frisians. EF497 was hit by lightning, which wiped out the trailing aerial and rendered the compass unserviceable, forcing the Jones crew to turn back. The Deodar crews pinpointed on the western end of the Ile-de-Re and planted four vegetables each from 2,000 and 4,000 feet at 21.07 and 21.09, while the Nixon crew fulfilled their brief off Vlieland from 4,000 feet at 19.36 and all returned safely to make their reports.

On the 18th, F/L Appleby was posted to 17 O.T.U after being declared tour-expired, and that night, the final events in the mini-campaign against Hannover were played out, when a force of 360 Lancasters produced scattered bombing, much of which fell into open country at a cost of eighteen aircraft. The series against Hannover had involved 2,253 sorties from which 110 aircraft had been lost, in return for which, much of the city had been reduced to ruins. On the 20th, Sgt Jones and his crew were killed when EF492 clipped trees and crashed at 16.30 near Benson aerodrome in Oxfordshire during an air test. The operation for which they had been preparing was a mining foray in the Nectarine I garden involving a dozen Stirlings, while fourteen Lancasters from 115 Squadron supported the night's main event, the first major attack on the eastern city of Leipzig. 90 Squadron briefed the crews of S/L King, P/O Adams and F/Sgt Chapple for gardening duties and sent them on their way from Tuddenham between 18.04 and 18.12, each carrying two A102 and three B200 mines, which they delivered according to brief from 1,500 to 3,000 feet between 19.35 and 19.41. Unfortunately, the Leipzig raid was hampered by appalling weather conditions, and the bombing was scattered and probably ineffective.

The main event on the 22nd was the second raid of the month on Kassel, for which a force of 560 Lancasters and Halifaxes was assembled. No one could have predicted the scale of destruction that took place within the city on this night, but a tragedy of extreme proportions was played out on the ground, out of sight of the bomber crewmen, for whom this was just another operation against an industrial city and one more towards the end of their tour. 4,349 blocks of flats containing 26,782 apartments were destroyed and a further 6,743 blocks with 26,463 apartments were damaged, rendering 63% of the city's living accommodation unusable. Vast numbers of industrial, public, administrative and military buildings were also destroyed or damaged, the transport systems were put out of action, and 5,600 people lost their lives. The city's three Henschel factories, engaged at the time in the construction of the Tiger tank, locomotives and aircraft under licence, and the Fieseler works, where the V-1 flying bomb was in development, were also severely damaged, and this would impact the introduction of the new weapon and the numbers initially available to unleash on London. It was, perhaps, fortuitous for the Stirlings that they were not included in the operation, which claimed twenty-five Halifaxes and eighteen Lancasters. One can only imagine the carnage amongst Stirlings, had they been available for the night-fighters to target.

While the above was in progress, 3 Group sent nine Stirlings and a Lancaster to the Nectarine I garden, the 90 Squadron pair of P/O Blake and Sgt Smith and their crews departing Tuddenham at 18.10 and 18.12, each carrying two A102 and three B200 mines. They found favourable conditions in the target area to the west of Vlieland and released their vegetables on a Gee-fix from 1,500 and 3,000 feet at 19.35 and 20.07, before returning safely from uneventful sorties.

The squadron operated for the final time during the month on the night of the 24/25th, when contributing the crews of Sgt Wright, F/Sgts Nixon and Simpson and P/O Newton to a 3 Group mining effort off the Frisians involving eighteen Stirlings. The Tuddenham quartet took off between 17.47 and 17.57 bound for Nectarine III, the most easterly Frisians off the German coast and established their positions by Gee-fix, before depositing their payloads in the briefed locations from 5,200 to 6,000 feet between 19.39 and 19.46.

During the course of the month the squadron undertook nine operations and dispatched sixty-five sorties for the loss of five Stirlings, three complete crews, six members of another and one airman from the ditching.

November 1943

The next four months would bring the bloodiest, hardest-fought air battles between Bomber Command and the Luftwaffe's Nachtjagd and test the hard-pressed crews to the limit of their endurance. In a minute to Churchill on the 3rd, Harris stated, that with the participation of the American Eighth Air Force, he could "wreck Berlin from end to end". He estimated that the campaign would cost the two forces between four and five hundred aircraft, but that it would cost Germany the war. This would remove the need for the kind of bloody, expensive and protracted land campaign, which he had personally witnessed during the Great War and had prompted him to "get into the air" at the earliest opportunity. It should be remembered that this was the first time in the history of air warfare, that the means had existed to prove the theory, that an enemy could be defeated by bombing alone. It is only in the light of more recent experiences that we have learned of the need, in a conventional conflict at least, to occupy the enemy's territory to secure submission. The Americans, however, were committed to victory on land, where film cameras could capture the glory, and would not accompany Harris to Berlin.

The unfavourable weather conditions that had kept the squadron at home during the final days of October continued into November, relenting sufficiently on the 3rd to allow eighteen Stirlings to go mining off the Frisians, although none from Tuddenham. The main event on this night involved a force of 577 Lancasters and Halifaxes at Düsseldorf, and while the raid was in progress, thirty-eight Mk II Lancasters of 3 and 6 Groups conducted the first large-scale test of the G-H bombing system against the city's Mannesmann Rohrenwerke (tubular steel works) on the northern outskirts. In the event, five returned early, sixteen suffered G-H equipment failure, two were lost and only fifteen bombed the factory, destroying in the process a number of assembly halls. Development of G-H would take a considerable time and it would be a further twelve months before it was unleashed to great effect on the enemy in the hands of 3 Group. Central and southern districts of the Ruhr giant bore the brunt of the main attack, and all the indications were that it had been a successful operation at a cost of eighteen aircraft. A destructive diversionary raid was also mounted by 8 Group against Cologne.

On the following night 3 Group detailed twenty Stirlings for mining duties in the Kattegat and Lim Fjord and it was for the latter that the 90 Squadron crews of F/Sgt Kirk and W/O Gay departed Tuddenham at 16.01 and 16.08 each carrying three mines for delivery, it is believed into the Silverthorn II garden between the Island of Anholt and the northern coast of Jutland. Dense low cloud prevented them from establishing a pinpoint, and both jettisoned one mine between Viborg and Holstebro as they recrossed northern Jutland and returned the others to the station store.

There would be no further operations for 90 Squadron for two weeks, while other Stirling squadrons were required occasionally for mining duties, and 3 Group's main focus was on special, top-secret operations conducted by 138 and 161 Squadrons at Tempsford on behalf of the Special Operations Executive (SOE) and the Secret Intelligence Service (SIS). On the 9th, LK380 collided with a Hurricane near Mildenhall during a fighter affiliation exercise and crashed at Sedge Farm to the north-west of the aerodrome killing F/L Rodger and the other eight occupants. The Hurricane pilot managed to abandon his aircraft but sustained broken legs during the landing. Three days later EH908 crashed five miles north-east of Haverhill in Suffolk while training, and the newly promoted W/O Timlin, who had survived a ditching a month earlier, was killed with one of his crew. The accident was attributed to a jammed control column.

Undaunted by the American response to his invitation to join the Berlin party, Harris would return alone, and the rocky road to Germany's capital city was re-joined by an all-Lancaster heavy force on the night of the 18/19th, while a predominantly Halifax and Stirling contingent of 395 aircraft acted as a diversion by raiding Mannheim and Ludwigshafen three hundred miles to the south-west. An innovation for the Berlin operation was a shortening of the bomber stream to reduce the time over the target to sixteen minutes. When the first Thousand Bomber raid had taken place in May 1942, with an unprecedented twelve aircraft per minute crossing the aiming-point, there was consternation at the high risk of collisions. The number had since been increased to sixteen per minute, with large raids lasting up to forty-five minutes, but on this night, twenty-seven aircraft per minute were to pass over the aiming-point.

The diversionary force consisted of 248 Halifaxes, 114 Stirlings and thirty-three Lancasters drawn from 3, 4, 6 and 8 Groups, 90 Squadron making ready seventeen Stirlings loaded with a 2,000-pounder and eight and four SBCs respectively of 4lb and 30lb incendiaries. They departed Tuddenham between 16.56 and 17.18 with S/L Wilson the senior pilot on duty and B Flight commander, S/L Levien, flying as bomb-aimer in the crew of Sgt Wright. They lost the services of the crews of F/Sgts Kirk and Sgt Wright to engine issues within the first ninety minutes, leaving the rest of the bomber stream to be driven by stronger-than-forecast winds to arrive at the target a little ahead of time, which upset the planned schedule to a degree and may have led to what became a scattered attack. Crews were greeted by clear skies, ground haze, and a fairly active ground defence backed up by numerous night-fighters, and some were able to make a visual identification of the aiming-point after following yellow route markers. The Path Finders confirmed their positions by H2S, while the main force crews relied on the red and green TIs, those from 90 Squadron bombing from 13,000 and 18,000 feet between 20.30 and 21.00 and observing fires and black smoke. The main weight of the attack fell into the northern districts, where 330 buildings were destroyed and a similar number seriously damaged and the Daimler-Benz car factory suffered a 90% loss of production for an unknown period.

Returning crews described large, concentrated fires and huge explosions, and a number reported inconclusive encounters with night-fighters. Nine Stirlings, 7.9% of those dispatched, were among twenty-three aircraft that failed to return, and EH996 and LK379 belonged to 90 Squadron. The former, captained by F/L Smith RAAF, crashed at Fussgönheim, some six miles west-south-west of Mannheim and of the eight men on board, only the flight engineer survived to fall into enemy hands. The latter came down some six miles north of Mannheim at Lampertheim and there were no survivors from the crew of F/Sgt Simpson RAAF. Four members of the RNZAF also lost their lives in the two aircraft. It is believed that the Smith crew was on its bombing run when shot down and that the Simpson crew was leaving the target, but this is speculation, and the reverse could be the case.

Crews returning from Berlin had nothing useful to pass on to the intelligence section at debriefing, and most considered the bombing to have been scattered and probably ineffective. Local sources confirmed that there had been no concentration and catalogued the destruction of 169 houses and a number of industrial units, with many more damaged to some extent. The loss of a relatively modest nine Lancasters was credited partly to the diversion at Mannheim, but the night's overall losses were still high.

On the 19th, 3, 4, 6 and 8 Groups combined to put together a force of 266 aircraft, 170 Halifaxes, eighty-six Stirlings and ten Mosquitos to attack the city of Leverkusen, situated on the eastern bank of the Rhine on the south-western fringe of the Ruhr a few miles north of Cologne. The Tuddenham element of fifteen Stirlings took off between 16.59 and 17.18 with S/Ls King and Wilson the senior pilots on duty, and a bomb load each of a 2,000-pounder, a long-delay-fused 1,000-pounder, ten SBCs of 4lb incendiaries and four of the 30lb denomination. After F/L Mills and crew had returned early with an engine issue, the others joined the bomber stream and adopted the southern route to the Ruhr, passing north of Antwerp. They found ten-tenths cloud in the target area with tops at 10,000 to 12,000 feet but no TIs to guide them to the aiming point, a situation caused by mass Oboe equipment failure among the Mosquito element and the decision by the backers-up not to confuse the issue by releasing their markers. Sparce and scattered marking caused bombs to be sprayed over a wide area to the north, the 90 Squadron participants attacking from 12,000 to a lofty 18,000 feet between 19.15 and 19.23, before returning safely. Sgt Blyfield and crew were set upon by two FW190s as they left the target, but effective corkscrewing and a long burst of fire from the rear turret persuaded both assailants to break off their attacks, one with damage to its fuselage. According to local sources, twenty-seven towns reported bombs falling and fortunately for the Command, the failure was not compounded by high losses, which amounted to four Halifaxes and a single Stirling. On return, fog in the 3 Group region forced most crews to land away, and ten of the 90 Squadron crews spent the night at Thorney Island near Portsmouth.

Harris called for a maximum effort on Berlin on the 22nd, and 764 aircraft were made available, of which fifty Stirlings and eighteen Lancasters were provided by 3 Group, six of the former belonging to 90 Squadron. They each received a bomb load of a single 1,000 pounder and nine SBCs of 4lb and 30lb incendiaries before departing Tuddenham between 16.59 and 17.05 with F/L Mills the senior pilot on duty. After climbing out they adopted an outward route similar to that employed by the all-Lancaster force four nights earlier, which took the bomber stream from Texel to a point north-west of Hannover, where a slight dogleg to port put them on a due-easterly heading directly to the target. Unlike the previous raid, however, rather than the circuitous return south of Cologne and out over the French coast, they would come home via a reciprocal route. This was based on a forecast of low cloud and fog over Germany, which would inhibit the night-fighter effort, while broken, medium-level cloud over Berlin would facilitate ground marking. An additional bonus was the availability to the Path Finders of five new H2S Mk III sets, while a new record of thirty-four aircraft per minute passing over the aiming-point would be achieved by abandoning the long-standing practice of allocating aircraft types to specific waves. On this night, aircraft of all types would be spread through the bomber stream, and this was bad news for the Stirlings, which, by the very nature of their design, would be below the Lancaster and Halifax elements and in danger of being hit by friendly bombs.

F/Sgt Phillips and crew turned back within the first hour because of the failure of the intercom, while the others pressed on over ten-tenths cloud which persisted all the way to the target and topped out at around 12,000 feet, in defiance of the meteorological forecast that had been offered at briefing. The blind marker crews employed H2S to establish their positions before releasing both red TIs and skymarkers, but the TIs disappeared as soon as they hit the cloud and were largely ineffective. This meant that the least reliable Wanganui (skymarking) method was all that was available to the main force crews as they began their bombing runs in the face of intense predicted flak and a mass of searchlights. The Path Finder backers-up maintained the aiming point with red flares with green stars and also released green TIs, which the 90 Squadron crews bombed from 13,000 to 18,000 feet between 20.12 and 20.22, observing the glow of fires beneath the clouds and a very large explosion that lit up the sky at 20.10. They flew home with a notion that they had taken part in a successful operation, but a meaningful assessment had been impossible, and they would have to wait for post-raid reconnaissance to reveal the truth. This and local reports would confirm that Berlin had suffered its most destructive raid of the war to date, which had left a swathe of destruction from the city centre through the western residential districts of Tiergarten and Charlottenburg as far as the suburb town of Spandau. A number of firestorm areas were reported, and the catalogue of destruction included three thousand houses and twenty-three industrial premises. Many thousands more sustained varying degrees of damage, costing 175,000 people their homes and an estimated two thousand their lives, and by daylight on the 23rd, the smoke had risen to almost 19,000 feet.

Twenty-six aircraft failed to return, eleven Lancasters, ten Halifaxes, and five Stirlings, which amounted to a loss-rate among the types respectively of 2.3%, 4.2% and 10.0%, and as far as Harris was concerned, the Stirling losses proved to be the final straw for a type, which, unlike the Lancaster and Halifax, lacked development potential. It was immediately withdrawn from future operations over Germany in a major blow to 3 Group, which had always been at the forefront of Bomber Command operations. Now, with just 115 and 514 Squadrons operating the Hercules-powered Mk II Lancaster, it would have to wait until sufficient of its other squadrons had converted before resuming its rightful place in the front line. The Stirling would still have an important role to play on secondary duties, which included bombing over occupied territory and mining, and eventually in 1944, it would replace the Halifax to become the aircraft of choice for the two SOE squadrons at Tempsford. In the meantime, they would be able to lend support to Tempsford, and as conversion to the Lancaster released Stirlings for other duties, many would find their way to 38 Group, where they would give valuable service as transports and glider-tugs for airborne landings.

Having heard preliminary reports of the previous night's success, Harris ordered another immediate attack on Berlin, a decision that would stretch the nerves of the aircrew, who were still in recovery mode. A heavy force of 365 Lancasters and ten Halifaxes was made ready with some difficulty on the 23rd, because such back-to-back long-range operations also put a strain on those charged with the responsibility of getting the aircraft off the ground. At Ludford Magna, for example, the armourers would be unable to load all nineteen 101 Squadron Lancasters with the intended weight of bombs, and would have to send them off 2,000lb short. In further manifestations of the effects of back-to-back long-range operations, forty-six aircraft returned early, and others intending to continue on to the target dumped part of their loads over the North Sea to gain more height. It involved largely those from 1 Group, who were shedding their cookies in protest at their A-O-C's policy of loading each Lancaster to its absolute maximum all-up weight at the expense of altitude. The slogan "H-E-I-G-H-T spells safety" could be found on the walls of most bomber station briefing rooms at the time.

Berlin was found to be covered by ten-tenths cloud with tops at between 10,000 and 15,000 feet, and guided by the glow of fires still burning beneath the clouds from the night before, the Path Finders located the town of Rathenow on H2S and carried out a thirty-five-mile timed run to the city centre. Skymarkers were released and red and green TIs formed a triangle into which the bulk of the bombing fell and returning crews described a column of smoke reaching 20,000 feet and the glow of fires visible again from the Hannover area some 150 miles from the target. Fake broadcasts from England, which had begun a few nights earlier, caused annoyance to the night-fighter force by ordering them to land because of fog over their bases. There were arguments between the fake and real controllers as each claimed to be the legitimate voice, but despite the confusion, night-fighters still played a major hand in the bringing-down of twenty

Lancasters. Post-raid reconnaissance and local reports confirmed that this operation had destroyed a further two thousand buildings and killed around fifteen hundred people.

The removal of Stirlings from operations over Germany was not immediately communicated to 3 Group squadrons and 75(NZ) Squadron was ordered to make ready four for Frankfurt, which was posted as the target for the night of the 25/26th. These were cancelled and the operation, which was only moderately effective, went ahead with a main force of 236 Halifaxes from 4 and 6 Groups. 3 Group did operate on this night, when sending thirty-two Stirlings to mine the sea lanes off the French coast from the Gironde estuary in the south to the ports of Le Havre and Cherbourg in the north. 90 Squadron briefed the crews of P/Os Adams, Blake and Johnston and Sgt Gardiner for the Deodar garden and the crew of F/Sgt Greenwood for Greengage, off Le Havre, and sent them on their way from Tuddenham between 17.12 and 17.20, the Deodar quartet because of the longer distance with four mines in each bomb bay, while the short hop across the Channel to the Normandy coast allowed the carriage of six. Ten-tenths cloud off the Biscay coastline thwarted the efforts of P/O Adams and crew to establish a pinpoint and they returned their mines to the station store, while the others pinpointed on Lake Hourtin and planted their vegetables according to brief from 4,000 to 5,000 feet between 20.32 and 20.53. Meanwhile, three hundred miles to the north, the Greenwood crew had encountered more favourable conditions and had delivered their mines into the allotted locations from 6,000 feet at 19.14.

The Nectarine gardens around the Frisian Island chain provided the destination for nineteen Stirlings on the following night, 90 Squadron contributing five for the Nectarine I garden, for which they departed Tuddenham between 16.53 and 17.02 with F/O Clark the senior pilot on duty. Again, the short dash across the North Sea allowed six mines to be carried in each bomb bay, three B200s and three A114s, which were dispensed from heights of 1,800 to 3,000 feet between 18.41 and 18.43 after establishing positions by Gee-fix. P/O Lange and crew flew back across the North Sea at low level, before climbing to cross the East Anglian coast on a heading for Tuddenham. On a windless night, the crew encountered a thick blanket of fog, and began a gentle descent, the bomb aimer, F/Sgt Porth RCAF, taking up station next to the pilot, while the navigator stood up to lend his eyes to the search for the ground. As the Stirling broke through the murk at what turned out to be Flempton, four miles north-west of Bury St Edmunds, the crew members were immediately aware of trees on either side and a field ahead, but before the throttles could be applied, the aircraft struck the ground in a landing profile at 20.55. This catapulted the pilot, bomb aimer and navigator through the Perspex, causing each of them to sustain quite severe injuries, and the rear gunner was also hurt, while the three crew members in the mid-section were able to walk away, shaken, but uninjured. The Australian pilot and the navigator, Sgt Hartley, remained unconscious for a number of days before recovering, and all of the injured were eventually transferred to Ely hospital. (I am indebted to former F/Sgt Wilf Porth RCAF for providing details of this incident. Following convalescence for his spinal injuries, he returned to Canada).

The main event on this night had been the next assault on Berlin, where the marking was misplaced and fell around six miles north-west of the city centre. Even so, most of the bombing fell within the city boundaries and caused much further damage to residential property, while destroying thirty-eight factories in the Siemensstadt district.

The month's operations concluded for 90 Squadron on the evening of the 30th, when four crews were sent to lay mines in the Deodar garden in the Gironde estuary and two in the Elderberry garden off Biarritz as part of a 3 Group effort involving twenty-nine Stirlings. They departed Tuddenham between 17.10 and 17.21 with P/Os Adams and Johnston the commissioned pilots on duty and arrived at their destinations more than four hours later to find largely favourable conditions. The Deodar contingent planted their three vegetables each from 4,500 to 6,000 feet between 21.42 and 21.49 after pinpointing on Lake Hourtin, while the crews of P/O Johnston and F/Sgt Hinde were guided by the brightly-lit Spanish resort of San Sebastian, from where they headed north to the drop zone to deliver their mines from 4,000 feet at 22.21.

During the course of the month the squadron operated on just seven occasions and dispatched fifty-six sorties for the loss of five Stirlings, three complete crews and two members of another.

December 1943

The new month began for the squadron with participation in a 3 Group mining operation on the 1st, which involved nineteen Stirlings plying their trade in the Kattegat region of the Baltic off northern Jutland. The five participating Stirlings from Tuddenham were assigned, it is believed, to the Silverthorn II garden between the coast and Anholt Island, a belief based on landfall on the western coast over Bredning Lake, followed by a due easterly course across Jutland and passage over Mariager Fjord to reach the Bay of Aalborg with Anholt ahead some thirty miles out into the Baltic. They departed Tuddenham between 15.02 and 15.22 with F/L Mills the senior pilot on duty, but his compasses failed as he crossed Jutland's western coast and the vegetables were planted instead in the Hawthorn II garden at the northern extremity of the Wadden Sea from 6,000 feet at 17.58. The others reached the target area to find ten-tenths cloud, which prevented F/Sgt Phillips and crew from establishing a pinpoint, and they brought their mines back to a landing, along with many others, at Acklington in Northumberland. The crews of W/O Luyk and P/O Blake were able to establish pinpoints visually and delivered their mines from 6,000 and 5,000 feet at 18.31 and 18.39 respectively. Shortly after leaving the western coast of Jutland behind, the Luyk crew was attacked by a Do217 at 19.20 at 7,000 feet and EH906 sustained damage to the starboard elevator and wing. Return fire from the rear gunner hit home between the starboard engine and wing root, and as the enemy broke away in a climb, both turrets scored hits on its belly from 150 yards, after which it was observed to dive steeply to starboard before falling vertically into cloud to be claimed as a "probable". EF191 failed to return with the crew of W/O Nixon, having crashed without survivors in the Ringkøbing Fjord area on Jutland's western coast.

The Berlin campaign continued on the night of the 2/3rd, when a predominantly Lancaster main force delivered a scattered attack across mainly southern districts and open country, although a number of war industry factories in the east and west also sustained damage. It was an expensive operation for the Command, which lost forty aircraft, or 8.7%. Amends were made on the following night, when Leipzig was targeted by a force of more than five hundred aircraft and much destruction occurred in both residential and industrial districts at a more modest cost of twenty-four aircraft. 3 Group supported both operations with twenty-one and eleven Mk II Lancasters respectively from 115 and 514 Squadrons.

3 Group contributed twenty Stirlings to a force of forty-eight aircraft sent mining in the Nectarine II garden on the 4th, 90 Squadron briefing five crews and sending them on their way from Tuddenham between 22.35 and 22.44 with F/O French the senior pilot on duty. Each was carrying six mines, many of which would not end up where intended after Gee was successfully jammed almost from the start of the North Sea crossing. The crews of F/O French, F/Sgt Greenwood and Sgt Symmons brought their loads or at least part of them back, leaving the crews of F/Sgt Wood and Sgt MacDonald to fulfil their briefs from 3,000 feet at 00.41 and 5,000 feet at 00.46 respectively.

On the 6th, W/C Giles was posted to Nº 11 Course at the RAF Staff College at the end of a successful tour as commanding officer, and he was succeeded by the twenty-eight-year-old Toronto-born W/C Wynne-Powell DFC, who a week earlier had relinquished command of 623 Squadron, leaving his successor just seven days in post before its disbandment. Wynne-Powell was becoming something of a Stirling unit journeyman overseer, having begun his operational career as commanding officer of 199 Squadron in early 1943, before the recent short spell with 623 Squadron and his time at Tuddenham would also last only one month. I am indebted to my good friend and leading 3 Group authority, Steve Smith, for providing the information that Wynne-Powell was the middle of five Powell brothers, all serving in the RAF, the Wynne part of his name having been acquired at boarding school through a clerical error, which he had never got round to changing. His eldest brother was Group Captain John "Speedy" Powell, the gung-ho, high-spirited, uncompromising RAF officer who had commanded 149 Squadron in 1941. During his spell as Feltwell station commander, his sometimes-abrasive personality created a division between him and some of the New Zealanders, which would contribute to a dip in 75(NZ) Squadron morale. He had been very prominent in the film documentary "Target for Tonight, which cast genuine serving RAF personalities in the appropriate roles and starred the legendary W/C Percy "Pick" Pickard as the pilot of F for Freddy, Powell as the squadron commander and G/C "Bull" Staton, the former 10 Squadron commanding officer, as the station commander.

On the 9th, six Stirlings and their crews were assigned temporarily to "special duties" and flew over to the "hush-hush" 3 Group station at Tempsford, which lay nine miles to the east of Bedford, having been built by John Laing and Sons between late 1940 and the last days of the summer of 1941 on what might be termed a reclaimed bog. As time was to prove, this was a fact that would be difficult to ignore for pilots who put a wheel off the concrete taxiways. The airfield was spread across what had once been Gibraltar Farm, a name that would persist throughout its occupation by the RAF. A few of its buildings were retained and used as offices and stores, and they acted as a natural camouflage to casual onlookers from the air. To these were added the necessary hangers, a control tower and nissen hut accommodation, and a standard triangulation of runways, two of which terminated just short of the main LNER London to Edinburgh railway line running along its western boundary. Since 1942 it had been home to Bomber Command's two "Moon" Squadrons, 138 and 161, which operated in 3 Group, but on behalf of the Special Intelligence Service and the Special Operations Executive, the latter a shadowy, anonymous organisation run out of offices in Baker Street. The two squadrons were responsible for the delivery of agents and supplies into the occupied countries, mostly by parachute, although both Squadrons employed Lysanders and occasionally other small aircraft to enable them to land in fields to disgorge agents and pick up others to bring home. The main role, particularly for 138 Squadron, was to deliver agents, arms and equipment by parachute to the resistance organisations fighting the Nazis, and they operated in all weather conditions over France, Belgium, Holland, Scandinavia, Poland and even Germany and Austria, sometimes remaining airborne for up to fourteen hours. They operated predominantly for two weeks each month during the moon period, and such was the demand upon their services by this stage of the war, that other squadrons were called upon to contribute aircraft and crews to supplement their efforts. *(A full account of 138 Squadron's wartime history can be found in RAF Bomber Command Profiles, Vol 6. 138 Squadron, by Chris Ward and Piotr Hodyra, published by Aviation Books Ltd, formerly Mention the War Publications, in 2017.)*

Tempsford had not been the first choice of those seeking a permanent home for the "Moon" Squadrons, Graveley, the home at the time of 161 Squadron, had been preferred until someone suggested that it was not ideally suited to the launching of heavily laden Halifaxes. It should be mentioned, however, that 35 (Madras Presidency) Squadron experienced no difficulty in launching its heavily laden Halifaxes and later Lancasters from Graveley from August 1942 right through to the end of the war. One senses, perhaps, the hand of Harris manipulating matters, for he was, after all, the C-in-C Bomber Command and in the overall scheme of the strategic bombing offensive, the "Moon" Squadrons were, in his eyes at least, entirely alien entities with no useful part to play. The temptation in such a situation was probably to find a backwater for them to play in, and this was Tempsford. Ironically, as the war progressed and the Allies began preparing to invade Fortress Europe, Harris, as now, actually found himself doing the unthinkable and lending aircraft and crews to an increasingly busy Tempsford, particularly from the Stirling squadrons of 3 Group, although this was only after they had been withdrawn from operations over Germany.

When the 90 Squadron crews climbed out of their Stirlings on arrival at Tempsford, they would have noticed three weirdly configured Lancasters bearing the AJ code of 617 Squadron, which had taken part in Operation Chastise against the Ruhr dams in May and had flown over from Coningsby that day. Unimaginably, Harris had sanctioned a very short-term loan to Tempsford for these aircraft, which were temporarily, at least, without a purpose, lacking as they were a mid-upper turret and bomb doors and retaining the calliper arms used to secure the Upkeep "bouncing" bomb. One of them, ED825, the last-minute "spare" in which Joe McCarthy and his now famous bomb-aimer, the late "Johnny" Johnson, had attacked the Sorpe Dam, even retained its ventral gun position, unique to this particular aircraft. ED906 was credited with the destruction of the Möhne Dam in the hands of F/L David Maltby and crew and ED886 had attacked the Ennepe Dam with Townsend at the controls and had survived a return journey across Holland in broad daylight to be the last home from Operation Chastise. As Lancasters were an unknown quantity at Tempsford, sixteen ground crew personnel accompanied the detachment.

Tempsford had been dormant as always during the dark period of each month and was scheduled to resume operations on the night of 90 Squadron's arrival, only for adverse weather conditions to intervene and shut down all activity. A further attempt was made on the following night, the 10/11th, when ten aircraft took off, including the three from 617 Squadron bound for destinations in France. Such was the level of secrecy surrounding operations from Tempsford that the 90 Squadron ORB is devoid of information relating to the activities of its crews. This is sad, as no restrictions were placed on the 75(NZ) Squadron ORB scribe and that squadron's SOE sorties are well documented. We know from the 3 Group ORB that nine Stirlings were among the thirty-four sorties launched from Tempsford and that some of them belonged to 214 (Federated Malay States) Squadron, one of which crashed on take-off. Four aircraft failed to return, including two of the 617 Squadron Lancasters, but we can only assume that some or all of the 90 Squadron crews took part on a night of continuing poor weather conditions, which denied many sorties a successful conclusion. According to the 3 Group ORB, there were no further Stirling sorties from Tempsford before the 90 Squadron element returned to Tuddenham on the 20th.

In the meantime, poor weather conditions had settled over the bomber counties since early in the month and it was left to the Mosquitos of 8 Group to roam around Germany, harassing in particular the residents of the Ruhr cities. Major operations resumed on the night of the 16/17th, when an all-Lancaster heavy force containing twenty-six Mk IIs from 3 Group returned to Berlin, while the Stirling force was divided between a "special" operation against a flying bomb site and gardening duties around the Frisians and off the Biscay coast. The former involved a force of twenty-six Stirlings targeting a site near Abbeville, and the latter twenty-seven Stirlings, 90 Squadron supporting both with five and four aircraft respectively. The first departures from Tuddenham between 16.53 and 17.00 were those of the crews of F/Sgts Greenwood and Chapple and F/O Clark, who were bound for the Deodar garden in the Gironde estuary, each with three mines beneath their feet. Ten minutes later, P/O Johnston and crew took off for the Nectarine I garden carrying six mines, leaving the bombing quintet on the ground until they took to the air between 18.01 and 18.10, each with twenty-one 500 pounders in the bomb bay, two of them with long-delay fuses. F/Sgt McCarthy and crew turned back early because of engine issues, leaving just four to continue on across the Channel.

F/Sgt Greenwood and crew were unable to establish a pinpoint in the Deodar garden after encountering ten-tenths cloud at 600 feet on arrival in the target area, and they returned their mines to store after an unproductive round trip of more than seven hours. The others planted their vegetables according to brief from 6,000 feet at 20.36 and 20.43, by which time P/O Johnston and crew had done likewise from a similar height at 18.35.

Operation Crossbow was a joint RAF/USAAF response to the proliferation of flying-bomb launching and storage sites in the Pas-de-Calais region of north-eastern France, and because of the nature of the targets would require extreme bombing accuracy to eliminate them. While the Stirling element attended to its target at Tilley-le-Haut, near Abbeville, nine 617 Squadron Lancasters under the command of W/C Leonard Cheshire targeted a similar objective at Flixecourt situated to the south-east of the town. Both aiming points were to be marked by Oboe Mosquitos with red spotfires backed up by red and green TIs, and at Tilley the 90 Squadron participants delivered their payloads from 10,500 to 15,000 feet between 19.34 and 19.35, observing little of the outcome. At Flixecourt, 617 Squadron obliterated the markers but failed to destroy the target, which was separated from the markers by 450 yards. The frustration born out of this failure and others before the turn of the year would lead to a radical new approach to bombing within 5 Group, which would change the face of bombing for the remainder of the war and render 5 Group effectively independent from the rest of the bomber force.

This night will forever be remembered for the very low cloud that blanketed the airfields as the bombers returned from Berlin and the other operations, and it was the 1, 3, 6 and 8 Group airfields that were most severely affected. The tired crews stumbled around in the murk seeking somewhere to land, most without the reserves of fuel to reach other regions of the country, and twenty-nine Lancasters and a Stirling either crashed or were abandoned by their crews, and around 150 airmen lost their lives in these tragic circumstances when so close to home and safety.

On the 20th, 3 Group detailed twenty-two Stirlings for mining duties in the Nectarine I garden, for which 90 Squadron provided the three freshman crews of F/Sgts Arrowsmith and Poynton and Sgt Azouz, who departed Tuddenham between 17.16 and 17.22. Some seventy minutes later they arrived in the target area to find excellent weather conditions and planted six vegetables each from 2,000 to 6,000 feet between 18.34 and 18.40. The main event on this night was a major raid on Frankfurt involving a force of 650 aircraft, which was compromised by unexpected eight-tenths cloud. Anticipating clear skies, the Path Finders had prepared a ground-marking plan, and the challenges resulting from this were exacerbated by a decoy fire site lit five miles south-east of the city, which attracted some bomb loads. A creep-back rescued the situation, spreading back across part of the city to destroy 466 houses and seriously damage almost two thousand others.

On the 22nd, a second attempt was made to hit the flying bomb site at Tilley-le-Haut with twenty-nine Stirlings, five of which returned early, leaving the others to locate and bomb the target. Eleven 617 Squadron Lancasters had been assigned to another site, possibly Flixecourt, but it remained elusive in the prevailing weather conditions and no attack was carried out. 90 Squadron was not involved and instead dispatched the crews of F/Sgts Arrowsmith, McCarthy and Phillips between 17.14 and 17.16 to join five others from the group for mining duties in the Cinnamon II garden located off the Ile-de-Re on the approaches to the ports of La Pallice and La Rochelle. The Phillips crew turned back early after losing the intercom connection to the rear turret and jettisoned two of their four vegetables, while the others found favourable conditions in which to fulfil their briefs from 5,000 to 6,000 feet between 20.01 and 20.08.

The fifth wartime Christmas was observed in traditional style across the Command and 90 Squadron's festivities were uninterrupted until the 29th, when the freshman crews of F/Sgts Davey, Harper and Thomas were briefed for mining duties in the Nectarine 1 garden and the crews of F/Sgt McDonald and Sgt Symmons for the Deodar garden in the Gironde estuary as part of an overall 3 Group effort involving twenty-eight Stirlings. The main event on this night was an operation by 712 aircraft, including thirty-six Lancasters from 3 Group, against Berlin, for what would be the first of three raids on the capital over a five-night period spanning the turn of the year. It was another moderately effective attack, which produced disappointing results in view of the size of the force deployed, and it cost twenty aircraft. The 90 Squadron elements departed Tuddenham between 17.00 and 17.07 and the McDonald crew was an hour out and passing to the south-east of the Isle of Wight when engine issues ended their interest in proceedings. They returned their four mines to the station store, where they would be joined eventually by those carried by the Symmons crew, who reached the target area only to be thwarted by ten-tenths cloud that prevented them from establishing a pinpoint. The Frisian-bound crews fared better, and each was able to plant six vegetables in the briefed locations from 6,000 feet between 18.45 and 18.47.

Minor operations on the 30th included another attempt by 617 Squadron to hit the flying-bomb site, which again escaped damage when the markers fell two hundred yards wide. 3 Group detailed twenty Stirlings for mining duties and six representing 90 Squadron were assigned to three gardens, Deodar the most distant for the crews of F/Sgts McDonald and Thomas and Sgt Azouz, while the crews of F/Sgts Arrowsmith and Wright were handed Juniper in the western Scheldt and F/O French Anemone off Le Havre. B Flight commander, S/L Levien, again occupying his usual place as bomb-aimer with the Wright crew. Those bound for the more local destinations departed Tuddenham between 17.15 and 17.33 and arrived in their respective gardens at around the same time, at Juniper to plant six vegetables each from 1,000 to 1,200 feet at 18.38 and at Anemone five from 1,200 feet at 18.46, each having employed Gee to establish their positions. They all returned safely and had retired to bed by the time that the Deodar element took off between 02.06 and 02.13 to deliver four mines each into the briefed locations also by means of a Gee-fix. They arrived home between 08.24 and 09.25, and after debriefing and a meal would do their best to catch up on sleep while the work of the day went on around them.

During the course of the month DFCs were awarded to pilots F/Ls Appleby, Blake, MacInnes and Whitworth and W/O Luyk and the DFM to F/Sgt Kirk. Elements of the squadron operated from Tuddenham on seven nights and from Tempsford on one and lost one Stirling and crew. It had not been a year on which 3 Group could look back with pride, the Mk III Stirling having succeeded the Mk I, but remaining subject to the same malaises and restrictions and suffering disproportionately high casualties, while the loss of its designated and somewhat protected slot in the bomber stream sounded the death knell for the type over Germany. 3 Group's conversion to Lancasters was under way and XV Squadron would begin operations in mid-January, but it would be a protracted process and September 1944 before the final bombing operation by a 3 Group Stirling took place.

January 1944

One can assume with some degree of certainty, that the beleaguered residents of Berlin and the hard-pressed crews of Bomber Command shared a common hope for the coming year, that Germany's capital city would cease to be the focus of Harris's attention. Proud to be Berliners first and Germans second, the residents were a hardy breed, and just like their counterparts in London during the blitz of 1940, they bore their trials with fortitude and humour. During this, their "winter of discontent," they paraded banners in the streets, which proclaimed, "You may break our walls, but not our hearts", and the melodic song, Nach jedem Dezember kommt immer ein Mai, After every December there's always a May, was played endlessly over the air waves, hinting at a change of fortunes with the onset of spring. Both camps would have to endure for some time yet, however, and before New Year's Day was over, a force of 421 Lancasters would be winging its way towards the "Big City", most of them to arrive overhead in the very early hours of the 2nd. Cloud and poor quality skymarking led to a scattering of bombs over southern districts and the operation was a dismal failure that destroyed twenty-one houses at a cost to the Command of twenty-eight Lancasters.

This first season of the New Year must have seemed strange to the Stirling crews of 3 Group, when, all around them the Command was fighting its way to Berlin and to other distant targets as the winter campaign ground on. News was, no doubt, filtering through from other stations of the grievous losses incurred in the process, and the strain of back-to-back long-range operations was beginning to drain morale, a situation reflected in the increasing number of early returns. For the time being, the Stirling units would continue to be restricted to mining duties, with occasional "special" bombing operations in northern France. There is no question that mining was a vital part of Bomber Command's work, but 3 Group had been at the forefront of operations from the very start, and it was a matter of pride that they resume their rightful place as soon as possible. As mentioned, 3 Group was being represented over Germany by the two MK II-equipped Lancaster squadrons, 115 and 514, but it must almost have felt as though they were gate-crashing a 1, 5 and 8 Group party. However, XV and 622 Squadrons were in the final stages of their conversion to Mk I/III Lancasters and would soon be available for operations.

As 383 aircraft, mostly Lancasters, were being prepared for the return to Berlin on the 2nd, 90 Squadron's F/Sgt Poynton and crew departed Tuddenham at 18.43 bound for the Deodar garden in the Gironde estuary, where they would meet ten-tenths cloud but make a visual coastal pinpoint before planting three vegetables from 6,000 feet at 23.35. They were still outbound when the freshman crews of Sgts Duncliffe, Field and Hodges and F/Sgt Edinborough took off between 22.06 and 22.11 and headed towards the east on course for the Nectarine I garden off the western (southern) Frisians. Each was carrying six mines, which through the genius of H2S would find their way into the allotted locations from 5,000 to 6,000 feet between 23.31 and 23.35 despite the presence of eight to ten-tenths cloud. There was a very late departure for the Berlin brigade, among which were five 90 Squadron pilots flying as "second dickeys" on board 115 Squadron Lancasters, and while only three would reach the target to bomb, the experience was useful to all and provided a taste of what was in store for 90 Squadron come the summer. The operation was another failure that destroyed a meagre eighty-two houses at a cost to the Command of twenty-seven Lancasters.

The night of the 4/5th was busy for the Stirling squadrons as fifty-seven aircraft were made ready for "Crossbow" operations to be conducted against flying bomb sites in northern France, while sixteen others were assigned to gardening duties in the Deodar and Elderberry gardens in the Gironde estuary and off Biarritz in France's south-western coastal region. The 90 Squadron ORB referred to the flying bomb sites as "constructional works", a term which would endure right through to the liberation of France in August 1944, and which aptly described some of the larger concrete structures used for both storage and launching of V-Weapons. There were two targets for this night, "Robin" and "Blackcap", the former, according to the Bomber Command War Diaries, located at Bristillerie near Cherbourg, a name that does not appear on any modern maps, while the latter was near Abbeville in the Pas-de-Calais and was probably the previously attacked site at Flixecourt. The weather conditions were marginal as the crews of F/Sgt Edinborough and Sgts Duncliffe and Hodges departed Tuddenham between 23.48 and 23.51 bound for the Deodar garden, each with three mines beneath their feet, and they were two-thirds of the way to their destination before the fourteen-strong bombing element took to the air between 02.26 and 02.49.

The ORB entries for the bombing element are subtly different in their designation of the targets, five aircraft assigned to "French Coast area" and nine to "Coast of France area", and whether this was significant in identifying the allotment of aircraft between the two targets or was simply a quirk of the scribe's recording style cannot be determined. The latter would seem to be the most likely and it is reasonable to assume that aircraft would be assigned according to the Base system established in 1943, in which a main station had satellites and the resident squadrons would tend to operate together. In the case of 3 Group by the start of 1944, after a repurposing and or a general rearrangement of statuses, the main station for 31 Base was Stradishall with its satellites mostly but not entirely engaged in training, while the 32 Base main station was Mildenhall with Newmarket, Methwold and Tuddenham as satellites and Waterbeach acted as 33 Base main station with Mepal and Witchford as satellites.

F/Ls Blake and Mason were the senior pilots on duty as the 90 Squadron contingent headed for the south coast to begin the Channel crossing in improving weather conditions, each with twenty-three 500-pounders in the bomb bay. The bombing and mining elements reached their respective target areas at around the same time, the latter pinpointing on a wood at Pointe-de-la Negade on the Atlantic coast of the Medoc peninsula that separates the ocean from the estuary. They planted their vegetables in relatively poor visibility from 6,000 feet between 04.15 and 04.38, before returning safely to offer their impressions to the intelligence sections after around eight hours aloft. We do not know which target, "Robin" or "Blackcap", was the destination for the 90 Squadron participants, we know only that they arrived at the French coast to find clear skies and low-lying mist, through which the red TIs delivered by Oboe Mosquitos and backed up by Path Finder Lancasters were clearly visible and bombed from 8,000 to 11,000 feet between 04.10 and 04.18. Both targets were dealt with effectively in the face of slight opposition, and no aircraft were lost.

This was the first occasion on which Bomber Command recorded activity launched from Tempsford by 138 and 161 Squadrons and other elements lent to it for SOE and SIS operations, and in this night, it was the turn of 214 (Federated Malay States) Squadron to supplement the resident squadrons' efforts with six Stirlings. W/C Wynne-Powell was posted to 31 Base on the 6th, to perform administrative duties until late in the year, when he would be granted command of 620 Squadron, the former 3 Group Stirling unit which had been posted out of Bomber Command in November 1943 for transport duties with 38 Group. On the 9th, W/C Milligan arrived from 31 Base, where he had been since his week-long stewardship of 623 Squadron, the disbandment of which he had overseen on the 6th of December.

Adverse weather conditions would keep most of the Command on the ground for the next ten days, but not before a force of 348 Lancasters and ten Halifaxes had set off for the first major assault on the distant port-city of Stettin since the previous April. They departed their stations either side of midnight on the 5/6th, and those reaching the target succeeded in destroying 504 houses and twenty industrial buildings in central and western districts, and seriously damaging a further 1,148 houses and twenty-nine industrial buildings, while also sinking eight ships in the harbour.

It was the 14th before the Lancaster crews were next called to arms for a raid by 496 of them on Braunschweig (Brunswick), the historic and culturally rich city to the east of Hannover in northern Germany. It would be the first major operation to this target, and it would also be the maiden Lancaster operation for 3 Group's XV and 622 Squadrons. While preparations were in hand for this, fifty-nine Stirlings were detailed, and their crews invited to briefings to learn of their participation in another series of attacks in the Crossbow series against targets in the Cherbourg and Abbeville regions. The Stirlings were to be accompanied by ten Oboe Mosquitos and twelve Path Finder Halifaxes belonging to 35 (Madras Presidency) Squadron, the former to mark the aiming points at Ailly, Bonneton and Bristillerie, and the latter to support the main force. It is believed that 33 Base was assigned to the last-mentioned, while elements of 32 Base attended to the others, the fourteen-strong 90 Squadron contingent departing Tuddenham between 17.25 and 17.43 with S/L King the senior pilot on duty, B Flight commander, S/L Levien, occupying his usual place as bomb-aimer to F/Sgt Wright and W/C Milligan flying as second pilot. They followed closely on the heels of the crews of F/Sgt Greenwood and Sgt Azouz, who had taken off a few minutes earlier bound for the Nectarine I garden in company with four other Stirlings. The bombers were each carrying twenty-three 500-pounders, all of which arrived in the target area under clear skies and in excellent visibility to be dropped onto Oboe TIs from 8,000 to 9,700 feet between 19.27 and 19.40. Returning crews were uncertain as to the effectiveness of their efforts, and while scattered marking at Cherbourg had led to a disappointing outcome, the attacks in the Abbeville region appeared to be effective. The gardeners, meanwhile, had fulfilled their briefs in favourable conditions by planting six vegetables each from 6,000 feet at 18.58 and 19.00.

Braunschweig had been a sobering occasion for the Lancaster squadrons, after thirty-eight failed to return home from what was a highly disappointing raid, which all but missed the city on its southern extremity. The Path Finders, in particular, had suffered a torrid time since the turn of the year, and 156 Squadron alone had lost fourteen Lancasters and crews from the two Berlin and the Braunschweig operations, creating a manpower crisis for 8 Group. One solution, in addition to sideways postings to maintain a leavening of experience, was to draft in the cream of the new crews emerging from the training units rather than wait for them to gain operational experience at a squadron.

Another Stirling unit was removed from 3 Group on the 16th, when 214 (Federated Malay States) Squadron was transferred to 100 Group to perform a radio-countermeasures (RCM) role. A force of 769 aircraft assembled on the 20th for the next round of the Berlin offensive included sixty-two 3 Group Lancasters, while twenty-one Stirlings were made ready for mining duties. 90 Squadron loaded five Stirlings with six mines each and sent them off to three different gardens off the Dutch coast, F/L French and crew to Juniper in the Westerschelde at 17.02, F/L Ralph and crew to Limpet, off the Island of Texel at 17.05, and the crews of Sgt Duncliffe and F/Sgts Davey and Edinborough to Nectarine I between 17.04 and 17.09. In contrast to the seventeen 3 Group early returns from the Berlin force, there was none among the gardeners and all of the vegetables departing Tuddenham found their way into their allotted locations after being delivered in largely favourable conditions from 4,000 to 6,000 feet between 18.28 and 18.33. Meanwhile, the Lancasters and Halifaxes were fighting their way through night-fighters both to and from Berlin and lost thirty-five of their number in the process. It was established later that the main weight of the attack had fallen in an eight-mile swathe across the eastern districts from Weissesee in the north to Neukölln in the south, where substantial but not excessive damage had resulted.

On the following day, a record twenty-three Stirlings were made ready at Tuddenham and each loaded with twenty-one 500-pounders for an attack on one of three flying bomb sites assigned to 3 Group. The 3 Group ORB specifies eighty-nine Stirlings divided equally between targets at Abbeville, Hazebrouck and Cherbourg, for which the 90 Squadron contingent took off between 18.48 and 19.31 with S/L King the senior pilot on duty. EH958 survived a collision with an unidentified aircraft on the way out and F/Sgt Symmons attempted to continue, reaching approximately the midpoint of the Channel crossing before accepting that the damage was too severe and dumping the bomb load. Not far behind, W/O Gardiner and crew turned back when the starboard-outer engine and Gee failed, while W/O Blyfield and crew were unable to locate the target because of the failure of their navigational aids, and their perfectly serviceable bomb load joined the others on the seabed. Based on the plotting of the few map references provided, it is believed that the 90 Squadron target was at Cherbourg, the most westerly, where six-tenths cloud prevailed, through which the bombs were delivered with accuracy from 11,000 to 13,000 feet between 21.17 and 21.26. There was five-tenths cloud at Abbeville, which affected the accuracy of the bombing, and mostly clear skies over Hazebrouck, which was bombed effectively, and no aircraft were lost.

The main operation on this night was the first major attack of the war on the eastern city of Magdeburg, for which a force of 648 aircraft included forty-three 3 Group Lancasters and took off in mid-evening. The operation was a failure in return for a new record loss of fifty-seven aircraft, the Halifaxes suffering a 15.6% casualty rate.

On the 23rd, 3 Group detailed three Stirlings for mining duties in the Greengage garden off Cherbourg, for which the 90 Squadron crews of F/Sgt Davey RAAF and P/O Langford RAAF departed Tuddenham at 21.53 and 21.55 respectively, the former carrying six D412 vegetables and the latter six of the B230 variety. They encountered between two and eight-tenths cloud below them as they established their positions on a Gee-fix and released their payloads from 3,500 and 5,500 feet at 23.38.

The same three Crossbow sites were targeted again on the night of the 25/26th, when 3 Group detailed fifty-six Stirlings, ten of them representing 90 Squadron, which departed Tuddenham between 00.29 and 00.46 with W/C Milligan the senior pilot on duty for the first time. Reading between the lines of the 3 Group ORB, it seems that the squadron effort was directed at the Cherbourg site, which was covered by five to eight-tenths cloud with tops at 5,000 feet, through which each delivered twenty-one 500-pounders from 11,000 to 13,000 feet between 02.22 and 02.34. Meanwhile, the attacks at Abbeville and Hazebrouck were not proceeding according to plan after the late arrival of the Path Finder elements and the failure of their equipment led to sparse and scattered marking. A high wind added to the difficulties at Abbeville, making it a challenge for aircraft to remain on station as they waited for the markers, and the expectation of success was low.

On occasions during the Battle of Berlin, a large force of mine-layers would be sent up ahead of the main force to mislead the enemy night-fighter controller. If he could be persuaded that they represented the main threat, the night-fighters might be on the ground refuelling and re-arming as the bomber stream passed through. This ruse was partially successful on the night of the 27/28th, when a total of 140 aircraft took part in extensive diversionary and support operations ahead of a five hundred-strong all-Lancaster heavy force making its way to the capital. 3 Group detailed seventy-four Stirlings to mine the waters of the Rosemary, Silverthorn and Yewtree gardens, situated respectively in the Heligoland Bight and in the Kattegat off Denmark's Baltic coast. Fifty-two were assigned to the first-mentioned, seven to the second and eight to the third, 90 Squadron supporting Rosemary with fifteen and Yewtree, located in the strait between Jutland's Baltic coast and Læsø Island with four. With further to travel to the Baltic, the latter took off first between 16.46 and 16.55, each with three mines in the bomb bay, and they were followed into the air between 17.02 and 17.18 by the second element, among which W/C Milligan was the senior pilot. The Rosemary element was reduced by one when F/L French and crew turned back because of excessive fuel consumption caused by a vain attempt to maintain height. The others found the weather conditions to be excellent, apart from a little sea haze, and the operations proceeded according to plan with almost no opposition off Heligoland, although several of the squadron's crews strayed a little too close to the island and almost drew the attention of a few patrolling enemy aircraft. The 90 Squadron crews planted their five vegetables each in the Rosemary garden from 13,000 to 15,500 feet between 19.18 and 19.33 and in the Yewtree garden from 1,000 to 2,000 feet between 20.02 and 20.11, and while they were attracting the attention of the night-fighter controller, the Berlin-bound Lancasters slipped across the northern coast of Holland and headed south-east as if threatening an attack on Hannover, Brunswick, Magdeburg or Liepzig. At a point south of Hannover, they turned abruptly to the north-east to make for Berlin, while Mosquitos maintained the fake course dropping flares. The diversionary measures were successful in delaying the arrival of the night-fighters, but they still scored heavily over Berlin and on the way home, claiming the bulk of the thirty-three Lancasters that failed to return.

A force of 673 Lancasters and Halifaxes, including thirty-nine of the former belonging to 3 Group, was assembled on the 28th for a return to Berlin for the second of three attacks on the city in the space of an unprecedented four nights. As part of the diversionary measures, 3 Group contributed sixty-three Stirlings to mining operations in the Forget-me-not and Quince gardens in Kiel Bay, 90 Squadron loading fifteen Stirlings with three mines each for delivery to the latter. They departed Tuddenham between 18.29 and 18.49 with S/L King the senior pilot on duty and when some ninety miles north of the eastern Frisians encountered ten-tenths ice-bearing cloud, which persuaded some of the mining force to jettison their loads and turn for home. The 90 Squadron crew of S/L King sought out an alternative drop zone and planted their vegetables in the Rosemary III garden off the Island of Sylt from 9,000 feet at 21.34, while F/Ls Blake and Whitworth also planted, but in reality, effectively dumped their mines outside of the shipping lanes. F/Sgt Wright and crew reached the target only to suffer the frustration of the bomb doors failing to open, leaving S/L Levien with his thumb on the tit but unable to press it and the mines were returned to the station store. Ten others from the squadron carried out their briefs in the face of variable weather conditions of five to ten-tenths cloud and ineffective anti-aircraft fire from 8,500 to 17,000 feet between 21.32 and 21.41, having pinpointed on Ærø Island. There was also some night-fighter activity, and shortly after releasing their load, W/O Gardiner and crew effectively evaded the attentions of a twin-engine night-fighter and a BF109. The return of EF443 was awaited in vain and the crew of F/Sgt Greenwood RAAF duly posted missing, their fate never to be determined. It had been another expensive night for the Command, which lost forty-six aircraft on the Berlin raid.

After a night's rest, 534 aircraft, including forty-four 3 Group Lancasters, set out once more for Berlin, while a dozen 3 Group Stirlings made their way south-west to the familiar waters of the Deodar garden in the Gironde estuary. The six 90 Squadron participants had departed Tuddenham between 16.44 and 16.55 with F/L French the senior pilot on duty and had encountered adverse weather conditions of ten-tenths cloud and poor visibility in the target area, which persuaded all to bring their mines home. Just one crew from the entire force completed its sortie as briefed but was unable to confirm the deployment of the parachutes through the cloud. A further thirty-three aircraft failed to return from Berlin after this final concerted effort to bring the capital to its knees, and just two further operations would be mounted against it before the winter campaign drew to a close at the end of March.

During the course of the month the squadron took part in twelve operations and dispatched 118 sorties for the loss of a single Stirling and crew.

February 1944

Although major operations were planned early in February, none took place for the first two weeks, and the only event of significance was an attack by 617 Squadron on the Gnome & Rhone aero-engine factory at Limoges on the night of the 8/9th, which tested and proved the efficacy of the low-level marking technique employing Mosquitos. Further successful live trials would see 617 Squadron marking for 5 Group operations and ultimately 5 Group's virtual independence from the main force by late spring. For the entire month, 90 Squadron operations from Tuddenham would be exclusively of a horticultural nature, but first, six Stirlings and crews were sent to Tempsford on the 2nd, where they would be joined by a seventh four days later.

The details of the activities of the Tempsford detachment are not available, and we know only that the first extensive deployment of 3 Group Stirlings involved twenty-seven aircraft on the 4th and twenty-nine on the 5th, on both occasions in company with Tempsford's own Halifaxes and other types. SOE/SIS operations were entirely different from any other type of activity undertaken by Bomber Command crews and required particular skills and even personal characteristics not necessary for the success of main force operations. At a time when large bomber forces were failing to locate huge urban areas like Berlin, SOE crews were flying hundreds of miles alone and at low level in moonlight and hopefully but not always in favourable weather conditions to identify a specific field, where, if all went to plan, a reception committee from the local resistance network would be waiting to receive by parachute much-needed supplies or, perhaps, an agent. Before any drop could take place, the reception committee had to arrive in secret and in time at the designated location to mark out the drop zone and then flash the correct signal to the approaching aircraft, failure to do so, or any slight deviation from the plan to cause suspicion, resulting in the abandonment of the drop. With the invasion of France planned for later in the year, the urgency to supply the resistance organisations increased, hence the need to draft in assistance from outside sources. More sorties ended in failure than success, but this was the lot of the SOE crew, to spend sometimes ten hours aloft with nothing to show for it and in the knowledge that it might have to be repeated on the following night. The operations handed to the 3 Group detachments were the least demanding and likely involved destinations exclusively in France.

Operations from Tuddenham began on the 4th, when six crews were called to briefing to learn that they and six others from 75(NZ) Squadron would be undertaking the long round-trip to the Deodar garden in the Gironde estuary. The distance meant a payload of just three mines in each bomb bay, although F/L Ralph and crew would be carrying four G710s and one G714, which suggests that they were a lighter calibre of weapon. They departed Tuddenham between 18.42 and 18.56 and all arrived in the target area to encounter a layer of ice-bearing ten-tenths cloud at between 4,000 and 7,000 feet with excellent visibility below and pinpointed on Lake Hourtin and the headland south of Grave Point, before planting their vegetables according to brief from 2,500 to 5,200 feet between 23.25 and 23.46. A little light flak was thrown up from the northern tip of the lake, but nothing troublesome and all returned home safely to report a successful night's work. We do not know the extent of 90 Squadron's activities from Tempsford on this night, only that twenty-eight Stirlings, seventeen Halifaxes and six other aircraft were detailed for SOE operations, and this effort resulted in twenty-five successful sorties and thirteen failures.

Tuddenham would remain operationally inactive now until the 11th and in the meantime, operations from Tempsford on the 5th involving thirty-one Stirlings and seventeen Halifaxes resulted in twenty-seven successful sorties, twenty-one failures and the loss of a 149 Squadron Stirling. On the 8th, nineteen Stirlings and sixteen Halifaxes successfully completed twenty-eight assignments and failed in twelve, and on the 10th, twenty Stirlings, four Halifaxes and four other aircraft managed to complete eight drops but failed in twenty others. While eighteen Stirlings, seven Halifaxes and two other aircraft were conducting ten successful sorties, eleven unsuccessful and five with unknown outcomes from Tempsford on the 11th, 3 Group Stirlings were engaged in mining duties off the French coast, two in the Scallop garden in Le Havre harbour, two in Upas Tree off Morlaix, two in Hyacinth off St-Malo, eleven in Deodar in the Gironde estuary, nine in Elderberry off Bayonne and three in Young Elderberry, at the mouth of the River Adour, astride which the town of Bayonne sits.

Fourteen 90 Squadron crews answered the call, twelve with the Deodar garden as their destination and two the Scallop garden. They departed Tuddenham together between 18.02 and 18.46 with the Scallop-bound S/L Hogg DFC the senior pilot on duty, having arrived on posting from 31 Base on the 1st. He and his crew were accompanied by the freshman crew of F/Sgt Waltrich, while five pilots of flight lieutenant rank led those heading for south-western France. Ten-tenths cloud over Le Havre with a base at 1,000 feet required a Gee-fix to establish positions, and each planted six vegetables from 6,000 feet between 20.00 and 20.01. They were homebound and already over England by the time that their colleagues reached their designated region of the Biscay coast having traversed France over ten-tenths cloud. This had diminished to five-tenths with a base at 3,500 feet as they began searching for a suitable pinpoint from which to carry out a timed run, easily establishing their positions on the usual ground features of Lake Hourtin and Grave Point before planting their vegetables in the briefed locations from 4,000 to 6,000 feet between 21.27 and 21.41.

On the 12th, 3 Group detailed thirteen Stirlings for mining duties, two in the Greengage garden off Cherbourg and the remainder in Nectarine III off the eastern (northern) Frisians, for which 90 Squadron loaded each of its five aircraft with six assorted mines. The crews of F/Ls Clark,

Johnston and Ralph and F/Sgts Azouz and Waltrich departed Tuddenham between 18.05 and 18.18, and all arrived in the target area to find eight-tenths low cloud with tops at 6,000 feet. Positions were established by Gee-fix followed by timed runs of between three and sixteen miles and the planting of vegetables from 4,000 to 6,000 feet between 19.50 and 19.51.

The penultimate major raid on Berlin, and the first large-scale activity of the month, turned all of the bomber stations into hives of activity on the 15th. A force of 891 aircraft was made ready for the main event, and this represented not only the largest force ever sent against Berlin, but also the largest non-1,000 force to date. 90 Squadron was to play its part by contributing fifteen Stirlings to the forty-nine from 3 Group assigned to mining duties in the Forget-me-not garden in Kiel Bay and Young Elderberry garden at the mouth of the River Adour as part of the support and diversionary measures put in place to confuse the enemy. The Tuddenham contingent took off between 17.11 and 17.30 with S/L Hogg the senior pilot on duty, and on a night of poor serviceability, the crews of F/Sgt Wright, with S/L Levien as bomb-aimer, F/Sgt Azouz and F/L Adams returned early within thirty minutes of each other with compass, engine and fuel feed issues respectively. Path Finder aircraft were not normally involved in gardening operations unless they were diversions, as on this night, when they guided the mining crews to the target area with red route markers released 20.14 to create some visible presence and attract the German controller's attention. The 90 Squadron participants delivered between them thirty-six mines in a ten-minute slot from 20.19 to 20.29, in what was a highly successful operation. The diversions and the wide sweep over Denmark of the Berlin-bound bomber stream succeeded in keeping the night-fighters at bay until the capital was reached, from which point on they scored steadily, and forty-three aircraft were lost in return for a very destructive attack on central and south-western districts, which set off more than eleven hundred medium to large fires, destroyed a thousand houses and 526 temporary wooden barracks and caused damage to war-industry factories in the Siemensstadt district.

While the above operations were in progress, twenty-nine Stirlings and twenty-one Halifaxes ventured out from Tempsford in doubtful weather conditions, which ultimately prevented all but eight drops from being successfully completed, and a 199 Squadron Stirling failed to return.

The eastern city of Leipzig was posted as the target for a force of 823 aircraft on the 19th, including seventy 3 Group Lancasters, and among the diversions was another mining effort in the Forget-me-not garden in Kiel Bay. Now back to full strength after the return of its Tempsford detachment, 90 Squadron loaded eighteen Stirlings with four mines each as part of a 3 Group mining effort of forty-five Stirlings and sent them on their way from Tuddenham between 22.43 and 23.27 with S/L Hogg the senior pilot on duty. F/L Blake and crew were contending with an engine issue as they approached the western coast of Jutland and decided at 01.40 to turn back, dropping their mines from 15,000 feet at 01.52 into the Rosemary II garden as an alternative. The others reached the target area to find eight to nine-tenths cloud with tops at 6,000 feet, and once more Path Finder markers pinpointed the drop site, allowing each to plant their vegetables from 12,000 to 17,000 feet between 02.30 and 02.46. In contrast to the success of the mining operation, the Leipzig raid was a disaster, which cost the Command a staggering seventy-eight aircraft, the largest loss to date by a clear twenty-one aircraft. A 13.3% loss rate amongst the Halifaxes proved to be the final straw and the less efficient Merlin-powered Mk II and V variants were immediately withdrawn from further operations over

Germany, thus substantially reducing 4 Group's contribution to the main offensive until the Hercules-powered Mk III could be made available to all of its squadrons.

Despite the losses, a force of 598 aircraft was put together on the following night for a raid on the southern city of Stuttgart, while twelve 90 Squadron crews attended briefing for another night of horticultural activities, this time off the Frisians and Le Havre. 3 Group detailed twenty-eight Stirlings, twenty for nectarine II and eight for four locations off the northern coast of France. The ten 90 Squadron crews assigned to the former departed Tuddenham between 17.56 and 18.25 bound for Nectarine II, the central Frisians, with W/C Milligan the senior pilot on duty and six mines in each bomb bay. The map references recorded in the ORB are in the North Sea and some distance to the north-west of the island chain, suggesting a lengthy timed run to the point of release, all the time scraping the base of the ten-tenths cloud at 2,000 to 3,000 feet and establishing their positions by Gee. The vegetables were planted from that height between 20.26 and 20.39, but in the extreme darkness no parachutes were observed to deploy. The crews of F/Sgts Prowd and Tickner were assigned to the latter, the Scallop garden, the Seine estuary at Le Havre, and took off at 18.53 and 19.02 also with six mines each beneath their feet. They encountered eight to ten-tenths cloud in the target area with a base at around 2,000 feet, which required a Gee-fix to establish a pinpoint, before they released their payloads from 6,000 feet at 20.35 and 20.37. Meanwhile, some 375 miles to the east, the Stuttgart raid was achieving some very useful industrial damage, and in contrast to the previous night, resulted in the loss of a more modest nine aircraft.

On the 22nd, 3 Group detailed an unknown number of Stirlings for mining duties in the Baltic, for which fifteen 90 Squadron crews were briefed and assigned to the Daffodil garden, located in "The Sound", or Oresund, south of the strait between the Danish Saltholm Island, situated just off Copenhagen, and the Swedish city of Malmö. They departed Tuddenham in the late afternoon and had been airborne for up to two-and-three-quarter hours when recalled because of doubts over the weather in the 3 Group region at landing time.

A major operation against the city of Schweinfurt was posted on the 24th and a force of 734 aircraft made ready. Located seventy miles to the east of Frankfurt in south-central Germany, it was the centre of the ball-bearing industry, which was vital to the war effort, and contained four manufacturing plants. The largest was Kugelfischer-Georg-Schäfer and the others Fichtel & Sachs, Vereinigte Kugellagerfabriken A G and Deutsche Star GmbH, and together were responsible for 50% of Germany's total ball-bearing output. The Americans had attacked it famously in daylight in mid-August 1943 and suffered catastrophic casualties on the same day that Bomber Command went to Peenemünde, and when they went back in October they lost equally heavily. They caused significant damage on both occasions, but the loss of production was temporary and further attacks were required. At briefings across the Command crews were told of a new tactic to be employed in an attempt to reduce the recent heavy losses to night-fighters. The force was to be divided into two waves with a two-hour interval between them, in the hope of catching the night-fighters on the ground re-arming and refuelling as the second wave passed through. They would be following on the heels of another raid by the USAAF the day before, this time with more adequate protection from escort fighters. As part of the diversionary measures, 3 Group detailed fifty Stirlings for mining duties in the Forget-me-not garden in Kiel Bay, for which 90 Squadron contributed fifteen of its own.

They departed Tuddenham between 16.48 and 17.07 with F/Ls Adams, Mills and Ralph the senior pilots on duty and three mines in each bomb bay and lost the services of W/O Thomas and crew early on to an engine issue and later F/L Mills and crew, who had progressed to within a hundred miles of Jutland's western coast when the starboard-inner engine failed and curtailed their sortie. F/Sgt Davey and crew had fallen thirty-five minutes behind schedule after being caught out by a change in the wind and knowing that they could not reach the target area in time to benefit from the Path Finder markers, returned their mines to the station store. The others arrived in the target area to find ten-tenths cloud topping out at 6,000 feet with good visibility above and delivered their payloads on red skymarkers from 12,500 to 14,500 feet between 21.36 and 21.48. F/Sgt Prowd's EF196 was hit by flak and the rear gunner wounded, but he remained in his turret to provide his captain with a running commentary on a night-fighter that appeared immediately afterwards. Meanwhile, three hundred miles to the south, the main event did not proceed as intended after some of the Path Finder backers up dropped their markers short and attracted much of the main force effort. Local sources reported nominal damage and a combined figure of 362 fatalities resulting from the American and RAF raids. On a more positive note, Bomber Command's second phase force lost 50% fewer aircraft than the first in an overall casualty figure of thirty-three, and this suggested some merit in the tactic of dividing the force.

The following night was devoted to an attack on Augsburg, the beautiful, culturally significant and historic city in southern Germany, which had been the scene in April 1942 of the audacious daylight raid by 44 and 97 Squadron Lancasters on the M.A.N diesel engine factory. A force of 594 aircraft was assembled and the crews briefed for another two-phase operation, while thirty-three Stirlings were detailed for mining duties in the Daffodil garden at the southern end of Oresund (The Sound) off the eastern seaboard of Zealand, the large Danish island upon which Copenhagen is situated. 90 Squadron loaded eight of its Stirlings with three mines each and dispatched them from Tuddenham between 19.45 and 19.55 with S/L Hogg the senior pilot on duty. They flew out in favourable conditions and F/Sgt Waltrich and crew were some one hundred miles short of Jutland's western coast when the compasses failed, leaving them with no choice but to return their mines to the station store. The others pressed on in continuing excellent weather conditions to find the target area under clear skies and plant their vegetables from 13,000 to 15,000 feet between 23.04 and 23.22, some after pinpointing visually on coastal features having failed to spot the green skymarkers. On return and while cautiously descending through cloud west-south-west of Bury St Edmunds, EF198 struck trees on top of a 250-foot-high hill and crashed at 02.55 at Denham Castle, killing F/Sgt Davey RAAF and four of his crew, including two members of the RCAF. The two RAF gunners survived with injuries, the rear gunner sustaining two broken legs. The Augsburg raid was one of those rare occasions when all facets of the plan came together in perfect harmony and the devastatingly concentrated and accurate bombing destroyed forever centuries of cultural history and priceless treasures, while also hitting some of the city's important war-industry factories in northern districts.

During the course of the month the squadron took part in operations on nine nights from Tuddenham, dispatching 108 sorties for the loss of a single Stirling at home and five of its crew. We do not know how many sorties were launched from Tempsford.

March 1944

By the beginning of March only four Stirling units remained in 3 Group, 75(NZ), 90, 149 (East India) and 218 (Gold Coast) Squadrons and a new task was about to be handed to them to supplement their mining and SOE responsibilities. The new month began for the Command with the second of three large-scale attacks on Stuttgart on the night of the 1/2nd by an initial force of 557 aircraft, and those reaching the target produced destructive bombing through cloud, which hit central, western and northern districts and claimed some important industrial scalps, including the Bosch electronics factory and the Daimler-Benz motor works.

With D-Day, the planned invasion of France, now just three months away, SOE operations were stepped up substantially to the extent that Tempsford was unable to accommodate all of the aircraft required, which meant that some Stirlings would operate from their home stations. On the 2nd, 3 Group detailed twenty-six Stirlings to supplement the fifteen Halifaxes and a Hudson for SOE operations and eight for mining duties off the northern coast of France and off the Den Helder peninsula. The 90 Squadron crews of F/Sgt Towers and W/O Field were briefed for the Upas Tree garden off Morlaix, and departed Tuddenham at 18.16 and 18.24 respectively with six B230 mines each beneath their feet. They encountered ten-tenths cloud with a base at 3,000 feet and established their positions by Gee, confirmed by a visual sighting of the Ile-de-Batz and the coastline, after which the Field crew planted their vegetables from 3,000 feet at 20.29 and the Towers crew from 4,000 feet five minutes later, neither observing the splash of impact. They had just turned for home when seven of their fellow crews departed Tuddenham between 20.40 and 20.58 bound for France to fulfil their SOE briefs. The fact that they were operating from Tuddenham means that we have a little more detail than previously, although the specific operations and destinations were not recorded in the ORB. The senior pilots were of flight lieutenant rank, but the senior officer on duty was B Flight commander and bomb-aimer, S/L Levien, whose pilot, formerly F/Sgt Wright, had recently been elevated to warrant officer rank. They all returned safely after six to seven hours aloft, and we are told only that "special operations were carried out as ordered". According to the 3 Group ORB, twenty of forty-eight details were completed successfully.

On the following night, 3 Group detailed eight Stirlings to continue mining off the Normandy and Brittany coasts and twenty-six, including nine from 90 Squadron, to assist with Tempsford's workload, which on this night involved sixty-five details over France and Belgium. They departed Tuddenham over an extended period between 18.49 and 20.31 with pilots of flight lieutenant rank leading the way and returned some seven to eight hours later claiming to have fulfilled their briefs, the long duration of their sorties suggesting that either southern France had been their destinations or that they had spent a long time searching for the drop zone and raising a reception committee.

A busy night of SOE operations on the 4th required the services of fifty-six Stirlings to supplement Tempsford's programme, and eighteen were provided by 90 Squadron, which departed Tuddenham between 19.56 and 21.40. The crews of F/L Ralph and F/Sgts Chapple and Symmons returned after fifty minutes, ninety minutes and a hundred minutes respectively for undisclosed reasons and were among eleven Stirling and four Halifax "boomerangs", while all but one of the others arrived home safely after sorties lasting around eight hours. The absent crew was that of F/L French in EH906, which was hit by flak at 500 feet and crash-landed at St-Hilaire-de-Gondilly, some twenty miles east-south-east of Bourges in central France, killing the pilot and delivering three crew members into enemy hands, while three others evaded a similar fate. Eighty details were attempted during the night, of which thirty-one were concluded successfully.

Forty-nine Stirlings were required for SOE duties on the 5th, 90 Squadron contributing six, which departed Tuddenham between 18.54 and 21.19 with S/L King the senior pilot on duty and returning after around six to seven hours to report successful outcomes. This time it was the crew of W/O Edinborough who failed to appear at debriefing, after EF147 was engaged and hit by light flak batteries located on high ground while homebound, and despite dropping to treetop height, continued to take hits, resulting in a fire in the bomb bay. W/O Edinborough put the Stirling down on a ploughed field some four miles east-south-east of Abbeville with the coast almost in sight, and he and all but the Canadian rear gunner evaded capture. Of sixty-nine SOE details attempted on this night, thirty-six were successful.

For the fifth night in succession, SOE operations demanded the support of Stirlings on the 6th, when a reduced number of six were called into action, three of them at Tuddenham. The crews of F/Ls Blake, Johnston and Kirk took off at 19.56, 20.01 and 20.09 respectively and lost the services of the Blake crew for an undisclosed reason after being outbound for around two hours. The others returned after eight hours to report successful outcomes and were among sixteen out of thirty that had been able to fulfil their brief.

It was on this night that the opening salvoes were fired in the Transportation Plan, the pre-invasion campaign to dismantle by bombing thirty-seven railway centres in France, Belgium and western Germany to prevent their use by the enemy to bring forces to bear to counter the Allied landings. While the Lancaster and Mk III Halifaxes were fully engaged in the continuing winter offensive, it was left initially to the demoted types, the Stirling and MK II and V Halifaxes, to carry the torch and it was a force of 261 Halifaxes of 4 and 6 Groups that undertook the maiden operation against the marshalling yards at Trappes, situated some ten miles west-south-west of Paris. The attack was highly successful and caused extensive damage to track, rolling stock and installations. The excellent work there was repeated on the following night further west at Le Mans, when 242 Halifaxes of 4 and 6 Groups and fifty-six Lancasters of 3 and 8 Groups inflicted heavy damage upon the cloud-covered target.

Another busy night of SOE operations was laid on for the night of the 10th, for which seventy-three Stirlings were made ready, seventeen of them by 90 Squadron at Tuddenham. They took off between 19.46 and 21.59 with S/L King the senior pilot on duty, and the crew of F/L Langford had not even left the circuit when an issue of some sort curtailed their sortie, and their return was followed within two hours by those of F/Ls Adams and Mills and their crews for undisclosed reasons. Thirteen crews landed after sorties lasting eight hours or more and at debriefing reported successful outcomes, and this left just S/L King and crew unaccounted for. They were carrying fifteen containers of supplies when LJ509 crashed some fifteen miles south-west of Dijon in east-central France, killing all but the navigator, F/Sgt Squance, who was assisted by locals to evade capture.

The 11th brought another night of minor operations with a reduced demand for SOE flights, 3 Group providing ten Stirlings for supply drops and nineteen for mining duties in the Deodar and Elderberry gardens off the south-western Biscay coast. 90 Squadron briefed the crews of F/Ls Adams, Langford and Mills and sent them on their way from Tuddenham between 19.55 and 20.34, and welcomed them back between 03.49 and 05.05, the Langford crew having been airborne for ten hours and ten minutes. All reported successful outcomes, but the 3 Group ORB recorded just one successful sortie after low cloud was encountered in the target areas. It had been known for some time that Lancasters were coming to 75(NZ) Squadron at Mepal, and the first example arrived on the 13th.

3 Group detailed six Stirlings for SOE work that night, when only a quarter of twenty operations were concluded successfully. A further twenty-five Stirlings were made ready for gardening duties off France's northern and Biscay coasts, 90 Squadron assigning two aircraft each for four regions, the Greengage garden off Cherbourg, Scallop off Le Havre, Hyacinth off St-Malo and Cinnamon II off the Ile-re-Re on the approaches to La Rochelle and La Pallice. The first six, each with a freshman crew on board and six mines in the bomb bay departed Tuddenham between 18.40 and 19.11 for the short dash across the Channel to northern France and back, which four would complete in under four hours and two in under five. In fact, three crews had landed before the more experienced crews of F/L Mills and W/O Blyfield took off shortly after 22.30 bound for the Biscay coast for what would be a five-and-a-half hour round trip. The skies over northern and western France were clear and those with target areas on the Normandy and Brittany coasts established their positions by Gee-fix before planting their vegetables according to brief from 5,000 to 6,000 feet between 20.39 and 21.09. To the south-west, pinpoints were obtained visually on the resort of Sables d'Ollone, from where a timed DR run took them to the point of release for four mines each from 5,000 and 6,000 feet at 00.57 and 01.07.

The 15th was the final day of the current moon period, after which the entire Stirling brigade could be released for other duties until the next moon period came around on the 30th. It was to be a busy night with the main event the third and final raid of the series on Stuttgart, for which a massive force of 863 aircraft included seventy-six 3 Group Lancasters. A second force of ninety-four Halifaxes and thirty-eight Stirlings would be active 280 miles to the north-west over Amiens in north-eastern France, where the railway yards were the target, while nineteen Stirlings took part in SOE operations. Together with minor and mining operations, the number of sorties involved in the night's activities amounted to a record 1,116. At Tuddenham 90 Squadron briefed twenty crews for Amien and loaded their Stirlings with twenty-two 500-pounders each, before sending them on their way between 18.50 and 19.16 with W/C Milligan the senior pilot on duty. P/O Lange and crew were back in the circuit within ninety minutes with a dead engine, and they were joined on the ground an hour later by F/L Adams and crew for a similar reason. The others were greeted at the target by six to seven-tenths thin cloud, through which the red TIs delivered by the Oboe Mosquito element onto the aiming point were clearly visible. The 90 Squadron participants carried out their attacks from 10,000 to 12,000 feet between 20.59 and 21.06 and observed a number of large explosions between 21.01 and 21.04, before returning home to file their reports. Absent from debriefing was the crew of F/Sgt Spring in EH989, who had been preparing to land when colliding with a Wellington of 11 O.T.U at 22.47 and crashing at Astwell Park in Northamptonshire with no survivors. F/Sgt Spring was just eighteen years-old and must have been amongst the youngest pilots to lose his life in

Bomber Command service. The Wellington came down north-west of Aylesbury, it is believed also with fatal consequences for the occupants.

The Stuttgart operation was not successful and cost the Command thirty-seven aircraft after night-fighters fell upon the bomber stream just short of the target. Some bombs hit the city centre, but much of the effort fell short and was wasted in open country to the south-west of the city. Although the attack on Amiens had been claimed by Bomber Command as successful, another assault was planned for the following night, for which a force of eighty-one Halifaxes and forty-one Stirlings was assembled. The twelve-strong 90 Squadron element departed Tuddenham between 19.48 and 20.05 with S/L Pickford the senior pilot on duty after arriving on posting the day before from 31 Base. On a night of poor serviceability for the squadron, a third of them, the crews of P/O Stewart, F/Sgt Hodges, F/O Wheate and F/Sgt Hadlow, returned early between 21.53 and 23.48 for a variety of reasons including engine and intercom issues and an inability to maintain height. The others reached the target to find largely clear skies and good visibility and delivered their twenty-two 500-pounders each onto red TIs from 10,000 to 11,000 feet between 22.01 and 22.29, before returning safely to report their impressions to the intelligence section.

The main event on the 18th was the first of two heavy raids on the city of Frankfurt, for which a force of 846 aircraft was assembled, 3 Group providing seventy Lancasters, while thirty-nine Stirlings were made ready to join a large-scale mining diversion involving ninety-eight aircraft in the Rosemary garden in the Heligoland Bight. 90 Squadron's fifteen Stirlings each received a payload of five mines, before departing Tuddenham between 18.55 and 19.09 with S/L Pickford the senior pilot on duty but lost the services of W/O Poynton and crew to starboard-inner engine failure within the first hour. The others reached the target area, where they found eight to ten-tenths cloud in two layers, one topping out at 6,000 feet and the other a thin layer of stratocumulus at 10,500 feet. As this activity was part of the diversionary measures and needed to attract the attention of the night-fighter controller, Path Finder aircraft were on hand to dispense green TIs in pairs to guide the gardeners in. The 90 Squadron participants conducted timed runs from whichever pair of TIs they selected and planted their vegetables from just below the upper cloud base at 10,500 feet between 21.00 and 21.15 and had little to report at debriefing. The attack on Frankfurt was devastating and left around six thousand buildings of all types destroyed or seriously damaged in eastern, central and western districts, and this was just a precursor for what lay in store four days hence.

On the following night 3 Group detailed nineteen Stirlings for mining duties off the south-western Biscay coast from the Gironde estuary to the Franco-Spanish frontier and off the Den Helder peninsula, and it was for the Deodar garden that twelve 90 Squadron Stirlings were made ready and loaded with three mines each, before departing Tuddenham between 18.49 and 19.02 with F/Ls Adams, Blake, Ralph and Whitworth the senior pilots on duty. The freshman crew of F/Sgt Bowling RNZAF had six mines in the bomb bay when they took off at 19.26 bound for Schulpengat, located on the eastern shore of the Ijsselmeer just north of the Ketelmeer, for which there was no named garden, the nearest being Trefoil some thirty miles to the west and a little south of Den Helder. They established a pinpoint on Gee at 20.38 and planted their vegetables according to brief from 2,500 feet after a timed run of four minutes, before returning home from an uneventful sortie. Meanwhile, F/O Stewart and crew had abandoned their sortie within the first hour after losing their starboard-inner engine, leaving the others to establish a pinpoint on Pointe-de-la-Negade in conditions more favourable than forecast and plant their vegetables from 5,000 to 6,500 feet between 23.09 and 23.40.

The second major assault on Frankfurt was posted on the 22nd and a force of 816 aircraft assembled, among which were seventy-one 3 Group Lancasters. The diversionary measures included a mining effort by a force of 128 Halifaxes and eighteen Stirlings operating in the Radish garden in the Baltic's Fehmarn Strait located between the Bay of Kiel to the west and Bay of Mecklenburg to the east. 90 Squadron's fourteen Stirlings departed Tuddenham between 17.39 and 17.55 with S/L Pickford the senior pilot on duty and four mines in each bomb bay. W/O Blyfield and crew turned back within the first hour because of a leak in N° 5 fuel tank, leaving the others to press on across the North Sea and southern Jutland and arrive in the target area to find varying amounts of thin cloud at heights up to 10,000 feet. F/Sgt Bowling and crew reached the target area at 21.10 but failed to spot any TIs and orbited to await developments. When TIs appeared well behind, they realised that they had overshot the drop zone and headed back, by which time the TIs had burned out and rather than plant in the wrong location, brought their mines home. The others planted their vegetables according to brief from 12,000 to 13,000 feet between 21.25 and 21.30. The diversion was not successful in distracting enemy night-fighters from the Frankfurt force, which suffered the loss of thirty-three bombers, but inflicted upon the city a second massive blow, which this time deprived half of the city of gas, electricity and water for an extended period. Thirty-six hours later, 162 B17s of the American 8th Air Force would bomb Frankfurt as a secondary target and add to the destruction, after which, according to local commentators, the city that had grown up since the Middle Ages ceased to exist.

On the 23rd, 143 aircraft drawn from 3, 4, 6 and 8 Groups were made ready to continue the interdiction campaign with a two-wave raid on the marshalling yards at Laon in north-eastern France. Forty-eight Stirlings were detailed, of which the seventeen belonging to 90 Squadron each received a bomb load of eighteen 500-pounders before departing Tuddenham between 19.24 and 19.42 with S/L Pickford the senior pilot on duty. They had been preceded into the air at 18.35 and 18.40 by the freshman crews of F/O Joseph and F/Sgt Brown, who were carrying five mines each to the Sultana garden located in the strait between Ushant Island and the headland west of Brest. They pinpointed on Ushant to the north and the Ile-de-Beniguet to the south and planted their vegetables according to brief from 3,500 and 5,000 feet at 21.24.

The bombers, meanwhile, had lost the services of F/L Whitworth and crew to the failure of their port-inner engine after ninety minutes, while the rest carried on to find clear skies and good visibility in the target area but an absence of TIs to mark out the aiming points. This was caused by an Oboe ground station going offline just before the marking was due to begin, which resulted in an absence of red TIs and provided just two greens for bomb-aimers to latch onto. The five 90 Squadron crews in the first wave carried out an attack from 11,000 to 12,000 feet between 22.02 and 22.12, but the eleven in the second wave were forced to orbit for ten minutes before abandoning their sorties and returning their payloads to the station dump. According to local sources, half of the bombing hit the marshalling yards and cut some track, which was repaired later that day, probably by pressganged civilians, while the rest was scattered in an area up to two miles away.

On the 24th, orders were received across the Command to prepare for what would be the final operation of the war by RAF heavy bombers against Berlin. 811 Lancasters, Halifaxes and Mosquitos took off in the early evening and encountered for the first time what would become known as "Jetstream" winds. These were previously unknown currents of air at higher altitudes moving at speeds in excess of one hundred mph, which, if not detected, would drive the bomber stream wildly off course, break its cohesion and ruin the operation. Each squadron had designated "wind-finder" crews, whose job was to ascertain wind speed and direction during the course of the operation and transmit their findings back to HQ, where the readings would be collated and broadcast back to the bombers. Such was the strength of the wind on this night, however, that wind-finder crews felt unable to trust their readings and modified them down before sending them to group. At group the amended figures were disbelieved and were further modified, so that navigators were working with false information, and many were unaware of the degree to which they were being driven south of their intended track. The result was that only in Berlin's south-western districts was there significant damage, largely to housing, while much of the effort was wasted on 126 outlying communities. The wind continued to push the homeward-bound bombers towards the south and many strayed inadvertently over the heavily-defended Ruhr region, where the flak batteries claimed two-thirds of the massive total of seventy-two failures to return. 3 Group posted missing seven of its sixty-three Lancasters on a night when the Stirling brigade remained on the ground.

On the following day, while the main force licked its wounds, preparations were put in hand for an attack on the marshalling yards at Aulnoye in north-eastern France. A mixed force of 192 aircraft was made ready, which included thirty-seven Stirlings, eighteen of them provided by 90 Squadron, which also detailed three others for mining duties, two in the Scallop garden at the mouth of the Seine at Le Havre and one in the Whelk garden off the Dutch port of Ijmuiden. The bombing element and the Scallop-bound crews of F/Sgts Brown and Sankey departed Tuddenham between 19.01 and 19.23 with S/L Pickford the senior pilot on duty and eighteen 500-pounders in each bomb bay. As they neared the French coast, the gardeners peeled off towards the west, while the bombers pressed on past Lille to the target located close to the Belgian frontier. The skies were clear and the visibility good, despite which the Path Finders failed to accurately mark the marshalling yards, a detail not appreciated by the main force bomb-aimers, who released their payloads on red and green TIs laid out in a row, assuming them to be across the aiming point. The 90 Squadron crews delivered their attacks from 8,500 to 9,000 feet between 21.57 and 22.03, observed explosions and smoke rising through 8,000 feet, and returned after round-trips of five to six hours to report what appeared to be a well-concentrated attack. What they did not realise was that the bombing had been concentrated largely outside of the target, for which the Path Finders were held responsible. Meanwhile, at Le Havre, the gardening duo had pinpointed on the Normandy coast precisely where the British and Canadian landings would take place on D-Day and conducted a timed run on a north-easterly heading to the drop zone, where they delivered between them ten mines from 5,000 and 6,000 feet at 20.58 and 21.01. F/L Kinch and crew had been last to depart Tuddenham, at 21.55, bound for the busy port of Ijmuiden, which acted as Amsterdam's gateway to the North Sea and was home to large concrete bunkers providing shelter for U-Boots and E-Boots. They established their position by Gee-fix and planted six B230 vegetables from 6,000 feet at 23.10, before returning safely from an uneventful sortie.

A force of 702 aircraft was made ready for Essen on the 26th, while 3, 4, 6 and 8 Groups put together seventy Halifaxes, thirty-two Stirlings and seven Mosquitos for an attack on the railway yards at Courtrai (Kortrijk) in north-western Belgium. The assault on Essen took place through complete cloud cover, the effects of which were negated by Oboe, and more than seventeen hundred houses were destroyed and forty-eight industrial buildings seriously damaged, thus continuing the remarkable run of successes against this once elusive target since the introduction of Oboe a year earlier. Meanwhile, twenty-one 90 Squadron Stirlings departed Tuddenham between 19.27 and 19.50, seventeen bound for Courtrai with S/L Pickford the senior pilot on duty and twenty-two 500-pounders in each bomb bay, and the others with four mines on board. All reached their respective target areas under clear skies, the bombers to aim at two clusters of red TIs from 9,500 to 10,000 feet between 20.59 and 21.03 and observing what appeared to be a successful attack. In fact, the bombing spread across the town, where 313 buildings were destroyed and 252 civilians killed, and whilst the marshalling yards sustained damage, the Germans drafted in 1,650 local workers to carry out repairs, and they were operating again three days later. While this was in progress, almost four hundred miles to the south-west the gardeners were pinpointing on the Ile-de-Re and Ile-d'Oleron and running for up to eleven minutes to release their mines from 5,000 to 6,000 feet between 22.21 and 22.35. Shortly after setting a course for home, EH947's starboard-inner engine failed and later the port-inner lost power, persuading F/Sgt Hadlow to land at Tangmere in Sussex.

The final operation of the long, bitterly-fought and costly winter campaign was directed at Nuremberg on the night of the 30/31st, the first night of the new moon period. This was to be a standard deep-penetration operation for which 795 aircraft were made ready. Under normal circumstances the operation would be planned by 8 Group and would incorporate feints, diversions and a circuitous route to the target to keep the enemy controllers guessing. This plan, however, offered a 5 Group-inspired direct route, which would involve a 250-mile straight leg across Germany to a point fifty miles north of Nuremberg, from where the final run-in would commence, and was based on the belief that a layer of high cloud would protect the bomber stream from the moonlight, but that the target area would be clear. The A-O-Cs of the Lancaster-equipped groups were happy with the plan, but AVM Roddy Carr of 4 Group was less enamoured about the prospects for his Halifaxes, even though they were the new Hercules-powered Mk III version, and AVM Bennett, the 8 Group A-O-C, was apparently incandescent with rage and, it is said, predicted a disaster.

A report from a Meteorological Flight Mosquito cast doubt on the weather forecast, particularly the amount and altitude of the cloud, and many expected the operation to be scrubbed. It was not, and what had been planned as a sixty-eight-mile-long bomber stream, which would pass across the aiming point in seventeen minutes, made its way in late-evening towards the fulfilment of Bennett's prediction. It was not long before the crews began to notice some unusual, unsettling and, perhaps, even freak features about the conditions, which included uncharacteristically bright moonlight. This created crystal clear visibility, which enabled the crews to see other aircraft around them, something to which they were not accustomed. Often, they would feel totally alone all the way to the target and only as they funnelled towards the aiming point would they become aware of the presence of other aircraft. They also noted the fact that the forecast high cloud was absent, and instead, a layer of white cloud below them acted as a backdrop to silhouette them like flies on a tablecloth. The two final insults were the formation of condensation trails to further advertise their presence in the hostile skies, and the close proximity of the route to two night-fighter beacons. All of these circumstances served to hand the bomber stream on a plate to the waiting night-fighters, and the route to the target could be traced by the burning wreckage on the ground of Lancasters and Halifaxes.

The carnage began at Charleroi in Belgium and continued all the way to the target, and at least eighty aircraft were lost during the outward leg. The same "Jetstream" winds that had so adversely affected the Berlin raid in the previous week, were also present, only this time from the south, and those crews who either failed to notice or refused to believe the evidence, were driven up to fifty miles north of the planned route. Again, the windfinders and groups did not believe the findings, as the result of which, many crews turned towards Nuremberg from a false position and when they came across Schweinfurt and observed some Path Finder markers, they believed it to be the target. These and the losses reduced dramatically the numbers bombing at Nuremberg, and the city escaped serious damage. When all returning aircraft had been accounted for, ninety-five were missing, and many others had been written off in crashes at home or with battle damage too severe to repair.

While this tragedy was on-going, thirty-one aircraft took off to carry out supply drops over France on behalf of SOE, 90 Squadron providing all five of the Stirlings, which departed Tuddenham between 20.01 and 20.40. The crews of F/Ls Langford and Whitworth returned within ninety minutes because of engine failure, and it was more than two hours later before F/L Gay and crew joined them on the ground after failing to maintain height as they traversed France. This left just the crews of F/Ls Kirk and Ralph to complete their sorties after round-trips of eight and six hours respectively.

During the course of the month the squadron carried out twenty operations and dispatched 213 sorties for the loss of four Stirlings and crews.

April 1944

The winter campaign had brought the Command to its low point of the war and was the only time when the morale of the crews was in question. What now lay before the hard-pressed men of Bomber Command was in marked contrast to that which had been endured over the seemingly interminable winter months. In place of the long slog to Germany on dark, often dirty nights, shorter range hops to France and Belgium in improving weather conditions became the order of the day. However, these operations would be equally demanding in their way, and would require of the crews a greater commitment to accuracy, to avoid casualties among friendly civilians. Despite this, a decree from on high insisted that such operations were worthy of counting as just one third of a sortie towards the completion of a tour, and for a time afterwards, the hint of a mutinous air would pervade the crew rooms. In fact, the number of sorties to complete a tour would fluctuate between thirty and thirty-eight from this point until the end of hostilities. Despite the horrendous losses of the winter campaign, the Command was in remarkably fine fettle to face its new challenge, with 3 Group well on its way towards phasing out Stirlings in favour of Lancasters and the much-improved Hercules-powered Halifaxes equipping 4 Group and half of 6 Group. Harris was now in the enviable position of being able to achieve what had eluded his predecessor, namely, to attack multiple targets simultaneously with enough strength to be effective. Such was the hitting-power now at his disposal, he could assign targets to individual groups, to groups in tandem, or to the Command as a whole, as dictated by operational requirements. Although invasion considerations would now take priority over all others, Harris would never entirely shelve his favoured policy of city-busting and would sneak one in whenever an opportunity arose.

The first 75(NZ) Lancaster operation would take place a few days hence, leaving just three operators of the Stirling, and it would be some time yet before they could rejoin the main offensive. Operations began for 3 Group on the 5th with SOE activity involving thirty-eight aircraft, including Stirlings on loan, while twenty-four Stirlings were sent mining off the southern Biscay coast. 90 Squadron detailed six Stirlings for SOE duties and eight for mining, five in the Elderberry garden off Bayonne, two further south in the Furze garden off the Franco-Spanish frontier and one to the north in Cinnamon II off the Ile-de-Re. The gardeners departed Tuddenham between 20.39 and 20.55 with F/L Kinch the senior pilot on duty and they were followed into the air two minutes later by the first of the SOE crews, whose take-offs were spread over forty minutes. The supply containers carried by W/O Poynton and crew would not reach their destination in France and were back on the ground within the first hour after the failure of the starboard-inner engine. The Elderberry-bound W/O Wheate and crew were defeated by a rear turret issue and landed at Lyneham after three hours having jettisoned their four mines. The five SOE crews returned after an average of seven hours aloft to report a successful conclusion to their efforts. The miners were airborne for a similar length of time and all but one landed at Thorney Island near Portsmouth, the other at Lyneham. F/L Kinch and crew reported three tenths cloud and good visibility at Cinnamon II, where they planted their four vegetables between the Ile-de-Re and the mainland from 3,000 feet at 23.50. The crews of F/Sgts Sankey and Towers also enjoyed unlimited visibility under clear skies in the Furze garden and delivered their three vegetables each from 3,000 feet at 01.00, while the Elderberry quintet pinpointed on Cap Higuer and let their mines go from 900 to 4,000 feet between 00.59 and 01.05.

As already documented, the Transportation Plan had been prosecuted since early March, largely by elements of 3 and 4 Groups employing aircraft withdrawn from the main battle, but now the campaign could get into full swing with the availability of the entire bomber force. The weather at the start of the month had not been conducive to main force operations, and most stations operating heavy bombers were effectively stood down until the 9th, when, to the relief of the bored crews, two operations were posted. One was to target the Lille-Delivrance goods station in north-eastern France with a force of 239 aircraft from 3, 4, 6 and 8 Groups, while the other was to be directed at the marshalling yards at Villeneuve-St-Georges on the southern outskirts of Paris and would involve 225 aircraft drawn from all groups. In addition to these operations, a large mining effort would be mounted in the Baltic by forty-seven and fifty-six Lancasters respectively from 1 and 5 Groups. 3 Group's contribution to the night's activities amounted to twenty-three Lancasters for Paris, twenty-two Stirlings for Lille and thirty Stirlings for SOE duties. 90 Squadron made ready twenty-one of its Stirlings, seventeen for SOE and four for Lille, the latter carrying twenty 500-pounders each as they departed Tuddenham between 22.09 and 2225 with F/L Kinch the senior pilot on duty. The special duties element took off over a two-hour period between 21.41 and 23.43 with S/L Pickford the senior pilot on duty and returned up to eight hours later to report successful outcomes on a night when thirty-five of forty-nine sorties were completed according to brief.

This was a momentous occasion for 75(NZ) Squadron, which would be operating Lancasters for the first time, although only at Paris, while its Stirlings took part in the attack on Lille. The weather conditions were good as the two forces flew out to cross the French coast at 14,000 feet and returning crews would confirm clear skies over both targets and concentrated marking. At Lille, crews were greeted by up to seven-tenths patchy cloud at 8,000 feet, but good visibility and favourable bombing conditions, and were guided to the aiming point by red and green TIs dropped by six Oboe Mosquitos and backed up by the Path Finder heavy brigade. The 90 Squadron quartet delivered their attacks from 12,000 to 12,500 feet between 00.51 and 00.56 and would learn later that forty-nine bombs had fallen into the target area, destroying 2,124 items of rolling stock, more than two-thirds of what was present in the yards, and also damaging buildings and tracks. Many crews witnessed two particularly noteworthy explosions at 00.52 and 00.53, the former accompanied by an uprush of orange flame that reached several thousand feet and lasted for a few seconds before fading to leave a pall of black smoke. Crews arriving towards the end of the attack reported another violent explosion at 01.04, by which time the smoke was passing through 10,000 feet. Unfortunately, much of the effort strayed into the nearby built-up area, particularly the residential district of Lomme, where five thousand houses were damaged and 456 people killed. The problem of collateral damage would never be solved, but the French people stoically accepted such casualties as a price that had to be paid to gain liberation from a hated enemy.

On the following day, Monday the 10th, a further five railway yards were posted as the targets for that night, four in France and one in Belgium, and assigned to individual groups. Eighty-four 3 Group Lancasters joined other aircraft from 6 Group to act as the main force at Laon, while fifty Stirlings were detailed for SOE operations, 90 Squadron dispatching nineteen of its own between 20.29 and 22.59. A whole host of flight lieutenant captains led the way but B Flight commander, S/L Levien, was the senior officer on duty, occupying his usual position as bomb-aimer to W/O Wright. Four crews were recalled after their drops were cancelled, fourteen crews returned to report successfully carrying out their briefs and LJ460 failed to return after being brought down by light flak. F/L Gay RNZAF and crew had been briefed to supply a resistance cell at Bourges some 120 miles south of Paris, and while flying at 500 feet over Gien ran into light flak and crash-landed at 03.00 fifty miles short of the drop zone on the southern bank of the Loire, falling into enemy hands. On return to base, EH947 was flying the crosswind leg in the circuit at 600 feet when both outer-engines failed and caused it to crash at 05.15 at Icklingham, seven miles north-west of Bury St Edmunds. The rear gunner, Sgt Powell, was killed, while the rest of the crew walked away.

Aachen, Germany's most westerly city, was a major railway centre with marshalling yards at both the western and eastern ends, but the attack planned for the night of the 11/12th was clearly designed also as a city-busting exercise for which a force of 341 heavy aircraft was drawn from 1, 3, 5 and 8 Groups. While 3 Group committed thirty-nine Lancasters to this main event, nine Stirlings were assigned to SOE duties and eight to mining, 90 squadron supporting both with seven and five aircraft respectively. The latter departed Tuddenham between 19.56 and 20.14 with six mines in each bomb bay, the crews of F/Ls Joseph and Wheate and W/O Wright bound for the Jellyfish garden in the mouth of the estuary leading to the port of Brest and the crews of F/L Kinch and F/Sgt Sankey for the Sultana garden located between the Island of Ushant and the Finistere (Brest) headland. The SOE element took off between 22.06 and 23.49 with F/Ls Blake and Whitworth the senior pilots on duty and returned safely to report successful outcomes from sorties lasting between four and eight hours. F/L Kinch and crew were thwarted by thick fog or cloud in the Ushant strait, and after searching for fifteen minutes for a pinpoint, despite Gee confirming that they were in the correct general location, they abandoned the attempt and headed home, leaving the Sankey crew to plant their vegetables according to brief from 3,500 feet at 22.58. Twenty miles to the east, the Jellyfish trio fulfilled their orders from 1,500 to 6,500 feet between 22.44 and 22.54 and returned safely after around five hours aloft.

Meanwhile, the Aachen force climbed to between 18,000 and 20,000 feet by the time it reached the Belgian coast at 3° East and maintained that altitude all the way to the target, where six to ten-tenths thin cloud was encountered at 7,000 to 8,000 feet. Red and green TIs identified the aiming point and the main force crews attacked it from 17,000 to 20,000 feet either side of 22.45, setting off many bomb bursts and fires, which suggested that the attack was accurate. The crews maintained height on the way home until fifty miles from the coast, at which position they began a gentle descent to exit enemy territory at 15,000 feet or above. Post-raid reconnaissance and local sources revealed that Aachen had experienced its most punishing attack of the war, in which central and southern districts bore the brunt as fires took hold, and severe damage was inflicted also upon communications and utilities, while more than fifteen hundred people lost their lives. However, post-raid reconnaissance revealed that the railway yards had not been destroyed and would require further attention.

The Command entered a period of minor operations thereafter, 3 Group detailing eleven Stirlings for SOE support and ten for mining duties on the 12th, 90 Squadron providing respectively eleven and four, the latter for the Nectarine I garden off the western Frisians. The mining quartet departed Tuddenham first between 20.55 and 21.07 with F/L Stewart the senior pilot on duty, and they all reached the target area under clear skies to establish their positions on Gee, before planting their six vegetables each in the briefed locations from 6,000 feet between 22.45 and 22.53. They were well on their way home by the time that the SOE element took off between 23.00 and 23.25 with F/Ls Adams and Ralph the senior pilots, and they were bound for northern France with containers of supplies for the resistance in their preparations for D-Day. Nine Stirlings returned to Tuddenham after sorties of five to six-and-a-half hours duration to claim the only successful outcomes on a night of unfavourable weather conditions. It was established later that EF162 had crashed nine miles north-west of Laon with fatal consequences for F/Sgt Bowling RNZAF and four of his crew, leaving both gunners in enemy hands. LJ483 came down near Roye in the Hauts-de-France region, some twenty miles south-east of Amiens and there were no survivors from the crew of W/O Gardiner.

On the 14th, the Command became officially subject to the orders coming from the Supreme Headquarters of the Allied Expeditionary Force (SHAEF), under the command of General Dwight D Eisenhower, and would remain thus shackled until the Allied armies were sweeping towards the German frontier at the end of the summer.

On the 17th, the squadron was ordered to prepare seventeen Stirlings for SOE duties, but this activity was cancelled and two were assigned instead to nickelling (leaflet) sorties over Belgium and three to mining in an unspecified sector of one of the Nectarine gardens. The crews of F/Sgts Sankey, Hadlow and Brown departed Tuddenham between 20.25 and 20.34 carrying four mines each and established their positions by Gee-fix before planting their vegetables in favourable conditions from 5,500 to 6,000 feet between 22.11 and 22.15. The nickelling crews of P/O MacDonald and W/O Poynton took off at 21.46 and 21.51 respectively, each carrying a load of ninety-two packages of B5 propaganda leaflets in French and Flemish for delivery to eleven locations across Belgium. They encountered up to eight-tenths cloud, through which large quantities of what Harris described as "toilet paper" fluttered down from 12,000 to 14,000 feet between 23.07 and 00.05. The skill was to assess the wind speed and direction and position the aircraft upwind accordingly, and while the activity had limited strategic value and was despised by Harris, it was a useful way to introduce rookie crews to operations.

The 18th was to be extremely busy on stations across the Command as 1,125 aircraft were made ready for the night's operations, which involved 811 Lancasters and Halifaxes and thirty-nine Mosquitos assigned to four marshalling yards in France, 3 Group detailing eighty-nine Lancasters for Rouen. A further 168 aircraft, including forty-eight Stirlings, were to be sent mining in the Baltic, and it was for this that 90 Squadron made ready sixteen Stirlings, while six pilots were sent to Mildenhall to gain valuable experience flying as second pilots on board XV and 622 Squadron Lancasters, a type shortly to arrive at Tuddenham. The mining effort was a diversion and the presence of target marking pyrotechnics delivered by Path Finder aircraft would have the desired effect in attracting some night-fighters away from France. The target area was Kiel Bay and probably focused on the Forget-me-not and Quince gardens, although there is no specific reference to either in the ORBs. The 90 Squadron contingent took to the air between 20.28 and 20.47 with S/L Hogg the senior pilot on duty and lost F/Sgt Arrowsmith and crew immediately to port-outer engine failure. The engine gremlins had attached themselves to 90 Squadron on this night as the crews of W/O Blyfield, F/Sgt Sankey and F/L Whitworth dropped out successively having respectively reached seventy miles out from the Humber, sixty miles north of the central Frisians and the islands on the western coast of Jutland. F/L Kinch and crew arrived in the target area early ahead of the Path Finders and rather than orbiting as the lone target for the heavy predicted flak batteries, abandoned their sortie and jettisoned one of their three mines. The others fulfilled their briefs from 11,000 to 13,500 feet between 23.42 and 23.50 aided by favourable weather conditions and effective marking and on return reported on the presence of night-fighters. Some intruders had infiltrated the bomber stream and followed it back to England, where two 3 Group aircraft were shot down in the circuit and the crews killed. F/O Wheate and crew also had an encounter as they prepared to land, but no damage resulted, and the six pilots returned safely from Rouen.

Another busy night of operations on the 20th would require 1,155 sorties, 357 Lancasters and twenty-two Mosquitos from 1, 3, 6 and 8 Groups targeting Cologne in the main event, while 5 Group was to carry out a full-scale major test of its low-level marking method against marshalling yards at La Chapelle to the north of Paris. Three other railway yards in France would provide targets for elements of 3, 4, 6 and 8 Groups, but it was mining off the Dutch and Biscay coasts that would occupy thirty Stirlings, including fourteen belonging to 90 Squadron. Two aircraft received a load of six mines each to deliver to the Whelk garden off Ijmuiden, four would take a similar load to Sultana between Ushant Island and the Finistere coast (Brest) and eight were loaded with five vegetables each for planting in the Gorse garden in Quiberon Bay located between Lorient and St-Nazaire. With the furthest to travel, the Gorse contingent departed Tuddenham first between 20.36 and 20.46 with F/L Lange the senior pilot on duty, and they were followed into the air between 20.47 and 20.51 by the Sultana-bound quartet, consisting of the crews of F/Ls Blake, Ralph and Young and F/Sgt Arrowsmith. Finally, the crews of Sgt Rawlings and F/Sgt McCollah lifted off at 21.26 and 21.31, only for the latter to lose Gee to jamming when over the North Sea with the island of Texel in sight. They returned their mines to the station store, while the Rawlings crew continued on and established a Gee-fix before fulfilling their brief from 6,000 feet at 22.42. Largely clear skies off the Finistere coast enabled crews to establish a pinpoint on Ushant Island and conduct timed runs of two-and-a-half to seven minutes to deliver their payloads from 4,000 to 6,000 feet between 23.20 and 23.25. Further south, clear skies and good visibility provided ideal conditions for establishing pinpoints on the Ile-de-Groix and planting vegetables from 6,000 feet between 00.01 and 00.09. In all on this night, 3 Group Stirlings successfully delivered 130 out of 146 mines into the briefed locations.

Post-raid reconnaissance and local sources in Cologne confirmed an outstandingly destructive operation, during which a record 4,500 tons of bombs had been dropped mostly in northern and western districts and had destroyed 1,861 houses or apartments and damaged 20,000 others, and there was damage to some extent also to 192 industrial premises and 725 dwelling houses with commercial units attached. Many public buildings, including schools and churches, were caught in the bombing and more than 1,200 fires had to be dealt with.

The 21st provided a brief respite for the heavy brigade, while minor and mining operations occupied small numbers of aircraft. 3 Group detailed eighteen Stirlings for mining duties in the Nectarine I and Limpet gardens, respectively the western Frisians and off Texel, of which four and two aircraft respectively were provided by 90 Squadron, while four others were loaded with propaganda leaflets for delivery to Dijon (P/O Wheate), Clermont-Ferrand (F/Sgt Brown), Lyon (F/L Stewart) and St-Etienne (F/O Joseph), all located in central France. They departed Tuddenham at intervals between 21.05 and 22.40 and those heading eastwards ran into low cloud and poor visibility in which they established their positions by Gee. In Nectarine I they planted five vegetables each from 1,500 to 6,000 feet between 22.26 and 22.31 and off Texel six each from 6,000 feet at 22.29 and 22.54. The nickellers headed towards Selsey Bill to begin the Channel crossing and lost F/L Stewart and crew to intercom failure before reaching it. The others arrived in their respective target areas under clear skies and dispensed thirty-five packets of OSF 46 leaflets each from 14,000 feet between 01.41 and 02.13, before returning home from uneventful sorties of an average duration of six hours.

On the 22nd a force of 596 aircraft, including eighty-seven 3 Group Lancasters, was assembled to attack Düsseldorf as Harris continued to pursue his own city-busting agenda on what was to be another very busy night for the Command. At the same time, a 5 Group force of 238 Lancasters and seventeen Mosquitos crews was to test the low-level Mosquito-based marking system for the first time at a heavily-defended German city, for which Braunschweig had been selected. Finally, 181 crews from 3, 4, 6 and 8 Groups were briefed to attack the marshalling yards at Laon in north-eastern France in a two-phase operation involving forty-eight Stirlings, twenty of them provided by 90 Squadron at Tuddenham, where each was loaded with nineteen 500-pounders. They were part of the second wave and took off between 21.52 and 22.21 with S/L Pickford the senior pilot on duty and lost LJ579 to a take-off crash, from which the crew of W/O Symmons walked away, and the Stirling eventually returned to service. The others reached the target area to find clear skies and the luxury of a Master Bomber in the person of W/C Cousens, the commanding officer of 635 Squadron, on hand to oversee the raid and provide guidance on where to bomb. The Path Finders illuminated the aiming point with flares and marked it with yellow and green TIs, after which the 90 Squadron crews carried out their attacks from 6,500 to 8,000 feet between 00.06 and 00.15 in accordance with the Master Bomber's instructions. They contributed to a highly effective raid, which caused considerable damage to the yards at a cost of nine aircraft, most, if not all, falling victim to night-fighters. It is believed that Sgt Dobson and crew were homebound in EF159 when shot down by the night-fighter of Oblt Dietrich Schmidt of III./NJG1 to crash some twelve miles west-south-west of Soissons without survivors. Another casualty was the Lancaster in which Master Bomber, W/C Cousens, lost his life.

Meanwhile at Düsseldorf, 2,150 tons of bombs rained down predominantly onto the northern districts of the city, where two thousand houses were either destroyed or severely damaged, fifty-six large factories were hit, of which seven were reduced to rubble, and more than a thousand people lost their lives. Night-fighters penetrated the bomber stream, and the failure to return of twenty-nine aircraft was a reminder that the Ruhr was still a dangerous place to visit.

On the following night, 114 aircraft were detailed for mining duties in five Baltic regions, 3 Group contributing thirty Stirlings for the Radish garden located in the Fehmarn Belt in the south between the Bays of Kiel to the west and Pomerania to the east. 90 Squadron dispatched fifteen Stirlings from Tuddenham between 20.33 and 20.51 with pilots of flight lieutenant rank the most senior and B Flight commander, S/L Levien, flying as bomb-aimer as usual with W/O Wright, while the five Stirlings representing 75(NZ) Squadron were operating for the final time. As they climbed out, P/O McDonald and crew noticed oil leaks from two engines and proceeded directly to the jettison area off the coast to relieve themselves of the unwanted weight of their four mines. Shortly after crossing the English coast, F/Sgt Hadlow's navigator complained of feeling unwell and sometime later, at 22.15, he passed out, by which time they would have been somewhere in the Heligoland Bight area, one of the Rosemary gardens, where the vegetables were planted from 6,000 feet at 22.47. The others found patchy cloud in the target area but good visibility and were guided by green flares as they established positions and fulfilled their briefs from 11,500 to 14,000 feet between 23.35 and 23.39.

90 Squadron rested on the 24th, when Karlsruhe was posted as the target and the 1, 3, 4, 6 and 8 Group stations responded by preparing 637 Lancasters, Halifaxes and Mosquitos, eighty-six of the Lancasters provided by 3 Group. Meanwhile at 5 Group, 234 Lancasters and sixteen Mosquitos were made ready for another test of its low-level marking technique at a heavily defended Munich 150 miles to the south-east, to which destination they would be accompanied by ten 101 Squadron Lancasters from 1 Group to perform a Radio Countermeasures (RCM) role. The Karlsruhe raid was partially successful and that on Munich very successful after W/C Leonard Cheshire had delivered the initial markers by Mosquito and escaped at rooftop height through a hail of flak.

The 25th was a quiet day on most stations and just twenty-three Stirlings were detailed by 3 Group for mining duties off the Biscay coast, 90 Squadron making ready four for the Artichoke garden off Lorient and six for the Cinnamon garden off La Pallice/La Rochelle and loading each with four mines. They departed Tuddenham between 21.29 and 21.55 with S/L Pickford the senior pilot on duty and lost the services of Sgt Rawlings and crew after a deviant compass had taken them too far to the west of track and left them with insufficient time to catch up. The others arrived in their respective target areas under clear skies and planted their vegetables according to brief from 6,000 to 7,000 feet between 00.19 and 00.45.

After a night off on the 26th, while more than a thousand sorties were launched on major operations against Essen, Schweinfurt, the marshalling yards at Villeneuve-St-Georges and minor and support operations, 90 Squadron would see out the month supporting SOE on four consecutive nights. 3 Group detailed twenty-four Stirlings for SOE duties on the 27th, the fourteen belonging to 90 Squadron departing Tuddenham between 21.22 and 21.48 with S/L Hogg the senior pilot on duty. They all returned after six to eight hours, which suggested that their destinations had been deep in central France and claimed to have fulfilled their briefs on a night in which 3 Group recorded sixteen successful sorties out of forty-four. Thirteen crews attended briefing at Tuddenham on the 28th to learn that they and ten others in Stirlings would be operating over France, for which they took off between 21.26 and 21.56 with S/L Pickford the senior pilot on duty. F/O Joseph and crew were back in the circuit within three hours for an undisclosed reason and the others landed between 03.23 and 06.01, having completed their sorties, leaving EE974 and the crew of F/Sgt Towers unaccounted for. News soon confirmed that the Stirling had crashed at 05.35 some two miles north-east of Stradishall and that five of the crew were safe after taking to their parachutes, but that F/Sgt Towers and the rear gunner, Sgt Milligan, had died in the wreckage. They had been airborne for more than eight hours and it is possible that they had run out of fuel, but they had opportunities to land sooner if that had been the case and we can only speculate that some kind of technical emergency had overtaken them. It was only three weeks since this same crew had survived a crash in which their rear gunner had lost his life, and Sgt Milligan had been in the mid-upper turret. According to the 3 Group ORB, forty drops were attempted and sixteen were successful.

Twelve Stirlings were detailed by 3 Group for SOE support on the 29th and nine of them were provided by 90 Squadron, which sent them on their way from Tuddenham between 21.17 and 21.52 with S/Ls Hogg and Pickford the senior pilots on duty. The former returned early after a little more than two hours and was soon joined on the ground by F/L Kinch and crew and no details of the cause of their abandoned sorties were recorded. The remaining seven returned safely, some after more than eight hours in the air, and a few of them at least would have been among the eight out of eighteen sorties to report successful outcomes. The month ended with the detailing of twenty-four Stirlings for SOE support, 90 Squadron dispatching thirteen of its own from Tuddenham between 21.38 and 22.04 only to lose F/Sgt Hodges and crew to a crash-landing almost immediately, from which all eight occupants walked away. The others returned safely, some after more than eight hours aloft on what was a relatively successful night, which resulted in a positive outcome from thirty-three of forty-six attempted drops.

During the course of the month the squadron operated on sixteen nights and dispatched 109 SOE sorties, eighty-one mining sorties, twenty-four bombing sorties and six nickelling sorties for the loss of six Stirlings, four complete crews, a pilot and two gunners.

May 1944

With the invasion now just five weeks away, the new month would be devoted to attacks on railway targets and coastal defences, and in the case of the latter, the focus would be on the Pas-de-Calais region of north-eastern France, to try to reinforce the enemy's mistaken belief that the landings would take place there. The month began with six small-scale operations over France on the night of the 1/2nd, three directed at railway targets and three at specific factories, 3 Group providing a main force of eighty Lancasters and sixteen Stirlings to attack the main railway stores and repair depot at Chambly. 3 Group also detailed fourteen Stirlings for SOE duties, all from Tuddenham, to supplement the Tempsford effort, and it began with the departure of the crews of Sgt Kelly and F/Sgt Mellors at 21.25 and 21.27 respectively to carry out mining duties in the Nectarine I garden off the western Frisians. Two minutes later the first of the SOE sorties began to roll and they continued until 22.21, leaving F/Sgt Rawlings and crew on the ground until 01.50, by which time the gardeners had returned to report establishing their positions by Gee-fix and planting their five vegetables each from 2,000 feet at 23.04 and 23.16 in favourable conditions. The SOE contingent, in which S/L Pickford was the senior pilot on duty, was depleted by the early return of the crews of W/O Blyfield at 22.38, P/O Chapple at 22.44 and F/L Ralph at 22.47, all for undisclosed reasons, and all of the others were back home by 05.53 having contributed to the successful conclusion of twenty-seven of forty attempted drops.

On the 2nd, 3 Group detailed thirteen Stirlings for mining duties off the Dutch coast from Ijmuiden in the south to Nectarine I further north, 90 Squadron dispatching the crew of F/O Fritz at 22.03 and those of F/O Donnan and Sgt Whyte at 22.09 and 22.14, the former bound for Nectarine I with five mines on board and the latter for the Whelk garden off Ijmuiden with six each. Eight-tenths cloud lay over the Dutch seaboard with a base at between 2,200 and 6,000 feet, beneath which conditions were favourable and positions established by Gee-fix before planting took place from 1,000 to 3,500 feet between 23.23 and 23.27.

On the 5th, 3 Group detailed thirty SOE sorties, 90 Squadron responsible for all six by Stirlings, which departed Tuddenham between 21.44 and 22.28 with F/L Young the senior pilot on duty. F/O Joseph and crew returned early at 23.24, and the others arrived back between 04.29 and 05.56 having contributed to twenty-five successful drops out of thirty-six attempted. Similar fare on the following night involved seven 90 Squadron SOE sorties among fourteen by Stirlings and nineteen by others from Tempsford. They departed Tuddenham between 21.45 and 22.01 with S/L Hogg the senior pilot on duty for the last time and S/L Levien occupying his usual spot in the crew of W/O Wright. The latter and that of F/Sgt Hodges returned early, leaving the others to fulfil their briefs among a total of twenty-seven successful drops out of thirty-eight attempted, and return safely between 03.07 and 05.28. Also on this night, 3 Group sent six Stirlings mining off the Biscay coast, five of them belonging to 90 Squadron, one departing Tuddenham at 21.54 bound for the Cinnamon garden off La Pallice and four between 21.57 and 22.04 for the Beech garden off St-Nazaire. The latter arrived first at their destination to find clear skies and pinpointed on Le Croisic, before running to the drop zone to deliver their four mines each from 6,000 feet between 00.38 and 00.44. Frustratingly, F/Sgt Fawcett was unable to open the bomb doors and had to bring his payload home. Some ninety miles further south along the coast, F/Sgt Rawlings and crew pinpointed on the Ile-de-Re and Isle-d'Oleron before planting four vegetables off La Pallice from 6,000 feet at 00.50.

Over the ensuing four nights 90 Squadron found itself occupied exclusively on SOE business, contributing fifteen of twenty-three Stirlings to add to the sixteen aircraft operating out of Tempsford on the 7th. They departed Tuddenham between 21.32 and 22.13 with F/Ls Stewart and Young the senior pilots on duty and S/L Levien the senior officer, and there were no early returns to deplete their effectiveness. They all made it back safely to land between 04.14 and 06.00 having played their part in the success of twenty-seven drops out of forty-two attempted. Earlier in the day, S/L Pickford had been rewarded for his outstanding service as a flight commander at 90 Squadron with a posting to a command of his own at 149 (East India) Squadron at Lakenheath, but soon to move to a new home at Methwold. On the 8th 90 Squadron was responsible for twelve Stirlings out of twenty-one of the type operating in support of twenty aircraft out of Tempsford. They departed Tuddenham between 21.41 and 22.04 with F/Ls Adams and Young the senior pilots on duty, and when they returned between 04.10 and 06.07, the crew of F/Sgt Rawlings was not among them. News was eventually received that BF524 had crashed west of the Loire at St-Aignant-le-Jaillard, some thirty miles south-east of Orléons and sixty miles south of Paris and that four members of the crew had lost their lives, while the pilot and both gunners had survived to fall into enemy hands. On a night of favourable weather conditions this was the only SOE casualty and two-thirds of forty-five attempted drops were successful.

On the 9th, 3 Group detailed twenty-one Stirlings and twenty-two other aircraft from Tempsford, mostly Halifaxes, to attempt forty-four assignments. The twelve-strong 90 Squadron element departed Tuddenham between 21.42 and 22.02 with F/L Adams the senior pilot on duty and S/L Levien the senior officer and lost the services of F/Sgt Parry and crew to the failure of an engine when about ninety minutes out. Nine others returned between 04.04 and 06.03 after successfully fulfilling their briefs, and this left the crews of P/O Chapple RAAF and F/O Joseph unaccounted for. The former had crossed the Normandy coast at low level and at some point, was hit by light flak, which proved to be terminal and EF509 was crash-landed at Tinchebray on the main road between Vire to the north-west and Flers to the south-east. All seven occupants survived, the pilot and four others to evade capture, while their two colleagues were not so fortunate. Many miles to the south-east, EF254 crashed to the east of Bourges, killing the pilot and four others and delivering the bomb-aimer and rear-gunner into enemy hands. A Halifax also failed to return on a night when once more, two-thirds of the assignments were concluded successfully.

On the 10th the squadron welcomed S/L Lee-Warner, who had been posted in from XV Squadron at Mildenhall to succeed S/L Pickford as a flight commander. While he settled into his new surroundings, six crews attended briefing for the last official night of the moon period and learned that they would be part of an SOE effort involving a dozen Stirlings to supplement fourteen Halifaxes, a Hudson and a Lysander operating out of Tempsford with a total of thirty assignments between them. The 90 Squadron element departed Tuddenham between 22.09 and

23.32 with F/L Lange the senior pilot and S/L Levien the senior officer on duty, and this time all returned safely between 04.36 and 05.35 to report fulfilling their briefs and contributing to twenty-one successful outcomes.

Having operated on six successive nights, most of the Squadron enjoyed a night off on the 11th, while nine pilots went to Mildenhall to operate with XV and 622 Squadrons against Louvain marshalling yards in Belgium, from which they returned safely. There would be a diet thereafter of mining operations as excitement mounted at the prospect of soon going to war in Lancasters, while all around the pre-invasion campaigns against railways and coastal batteries continued with gathering pace. While the rest of 3 Group stayed at home on the 12th, 90 Squadron briefed the freshman crews of Sgts Kelsey and Page for mining duties in the Greengage garden off Cherbourg and the more experienced crews of F/Os Elliot and French for the Scallop garden at the mouth of the River Seine at Le Havre. They departed Tuddenham between 21.49 and 22.00, each carrying five mines, and arrived at the French coast to find clear but hazy conditions and extreme darkness in the absence of a moon. Positions were established by Gee-fix and the vegetables planted in the briefed drop locations from 5,500 to 6,000 feet between 23.41 and 23.47. On the 13th, S/L Hogg was posted out at the conclusion of his tour and would "rest" at 30 O.T.U. During a quiet night on the 14th, 90 Squadron was once more the only 3 Group unit in action when dispatching the crews of F/Os Donnan and Elliot at 22.11 and 22.22 respectively, each sitting on four mines to deliver to the Cinnamon garden off La Pallice. They encountered seven-tenths cloud at 5,000 feet and established a Gee-fix on the Ile-de-Re, before fulfilling their briefs from 2,000 and 4,500 feet at 01.00 and 01.04.

The squadron ORB announced "conversion" on the 15th, from which point Lancasters would begin to arrive at Tuddenham to make 90 Squadron the forty-second operational unit in the Command to receive the type. However, operations for the remainder of the month would be conducted in Stirlings and continued that night with a return to the Cinnamon garden by the crews of Sgt Kelly and F/O French, while the crews of F/O Fritz and Sgts Page and Kelsey were to fly an extra thirty miles to the Deodar garden in the Gironde estuary. They departed Tuddenham between 22.16 and 22.43 to deliver four mines each and lost the services of the Kelly crew to air-speed-indicator (a.s.i) failure during the Channel crossing. The French crew reached the target area to find clear skies and haze and pinpointed on the Ile-d'Oleron, from which they headed to the drop zone, only to find on arrival that the bomb-release system was faulty, and they were forced to bring their payload home. Sgt Kelsey and crew had just crossed the Normandy coast at 10,000 feet over what in three weeks' time would be the D-Day landing grounds, when the rear gunner reported that his guns had jammed, an inconvenience that persuaded them to turn back. The remaining two crews arrived at their destination under clear skies and established a Gee-fix before running for between six and seven minutes at 6,000 feet to release their mines into the briefed locations at 01.32 and 01.48.

On the 18th, S/L Hodgson arrived on posting from 1657 Conversion Unit to fill the vacancy created by the departure of S/L Hogg, and on the following day, five pilots headed over to Mildenhall to fly as second pilots with XV and 622 Squadron crews against the marshalling yards at Le Mans. The operation was successful but cost the Command two highly decorated crews from 7 Squadron, captained by W/C Barron DSO & Bar DFC DFM RNZAF and S/L Dennis DSO DFC, who were the Master Bomber and Deputy. Fraser Barron was an outstanding bomber pilot and inspirational leader and was on his eightieth sortie, while one of his crew was on his eighty-sixth. On the 21st, two pilots gained Lancaster experience when flying as second pilots from Mildenhall on the first major attack on Duisburg for a year, which involved a heavy force of 510 Lancasters, 109 of them provided by 3 Group. Just like Duisburg, Dortmund had not been visited by the heavy brigade for a year when it was posted on the 22nd to face an all-Lancaster heavy force of 361 aircraft drawn from 1, 3, 6 and 8 Groups, while 5 Group targeted Braunschweig.

3 Group's contribution to the main event amounted to eighty-four Lancasters, while twenty-one Stirlings and seven Lancasters were sent mining off the French coast, the Frisians and in the Baltic. 90 Squadron briefed five crews for the Frisians, it is believed in the Nectarine II garden, and four for Deodar in the Gironde estuary and sent them on their way from Tuddenham between 22.17 and 22.32 with F/Ls Burton and Kinch respectively the senior pilots on duty. F/O Robinson and crew were in sight of Schiermonnikoog when their Gee failed and the mines were jettisoned, leaving the others to continue on to encounter seven to ten-tenths cumulus cloud with a base at around 2,000 feet. They established positions by Gee-fix and conducted runs of between four and twenty miles to plant their five vegetables each from 5,000 to 15,000 feet between 00.10 and 00.17. Meanwhile, almost four hundred miles to the south-south-west three-tenths cloud and good visibility prevailed, which enabled crews to confirm the accuracy of their Gee-fixes by visual coastal references. A total of sixteen mines fell by parachute from 4,000 to 6,000 feet between 01.34 and 01.44 and all aircraft were back on the ground at Tuddenham by 04.43.

Minor operations on the 23rd included nine Stirlings mining in the Nectarine I garden off the western Frisians, seven of them belonging to 90 Squadron, which departed Tuddenham between 22.40 and 23.04 with F/O Robinson the only commissioned pilot on duty and six mines in each bomb bay. BK784 swung on take-off in the hands of F/Sgt Whyte, but somehow left the ground and clipped a tree, before crashing at Chippenham, some four miles west of the airfield, killing all on board. Unlike its relatively inexperienced crew, the Stirling was a veteran of fifty-four sorties, one of only twenty-seven of the type to survive past fifty. Those reaching the target area found around seven-tenths cloud above 3,000 feet and good visibility below and established their positions by Gee-fix before planting their vegetables from 2,000 to 5,500 feet between 00.26 and 00.32.

A major assault was mounted on the 24th against the two large marshalling yards in Aachen to prevent their use in transporting troops and equipment to the invasion area. 3 Group contributed forty-three Lancasters and a further forty-eight to an attack on a coastal battery at Boulogne as part of the deception plan. The Stirling brigade remained on the ground on this and the following night and was next called into action for mining duties on the 26th, when 90 Squadron provided all eight of the type for action in three regions. The crews F/Ls Harper and MacDonald and W/O Wright, including S/L Levien, were assigned to Whelk, off the port of Ijmuiden, the crews of F/Ls Lange and Johnston to Nectarine II in the central Frisians and those of F/Sgts Cooper, Hadlow and Sankey to Cypress Tree II off Gravelines, a small port located at the mouth of the River Aa between Calais and Dunkerque. They departed Tuddenham together between 22.54 and 23.29 and from under clear skies at their respective gardens planted a total of forty vegetables from 600 to 800 feet between 00.25 and 00.30.

The Whelk and Cypress Tree II gardens were the destinations also on the following night for three and four 90 Squadron crews respectively, while six Stirlings and six Lancasters from 3 Group operated elsewhere. The Tuddenham elements took off between 23.27 and 23.46 and arrived at their respective gardens to find favourable condition and good visibility despite a little haze. A total of ten vegetables found their way into the briefed locations from 600 to 800 feet between 00.28 and 00.35 and all crews were back on the ground by 01.37. It was similar fare for the Stirling brigade on the 28th, when the crews of P/O Cooper and F/Sgt Hendry departed Tuddenham at 22.33 and 22.41 bound for the Upas Tree garden off Morlaix and were followed into the air at 22.52 by Sgt Page and crew, whose destination was the Cinnamon garden off La Pallice. The latter pinpointed on the southernmost point of the Ile-de-Re and planted four vegetables from 5,000 feet at 01.54, while two hundred miles to the north the pinpoint was Pointe-de-Primel, from where timed runs culminated with the delivery of twelve mines from 800 to 1,000 feet at 00.47 and 00.52.

A new moon period began on the 30th and six 90 Squadron Stirlings were assigned to SOE support duties, while, according to the squadron ORB, seven others were to mine the waters off the Belgian port of Knokke. Most guides to mining areas identify Knokke as the Flounder Garden, but the 3 Group ORB for this date refers to the Iris II garden. Iris was a later addition to mining areas and was probably a subdivision of Flounder and was certainly close by. Curiously, the 3 Group ORB makes no mention of SOE sorties during this night, but the 90 Squadron participants departed Tuddenham between 22.26 and 22.42 with F/Ls Harper and MacDonald the senior pilots on duty and S/L Levien the senior officer and flying with W/O Wright. They were followed into the air between 23.20 and 23.35 by the gardening fraternity, who arrived off the Belgian coast under clear skies and established their positions by Gee-fix before completing timed runs and planting their vegetables from 600 to 800 feet between 00.29 and 00.31, most observing the splash as they entered the water. They had been debriefed by the time that the SOE crews returned safely between 02.45 and 04.21 to report successful outcomes to their sorties.

On the 31st, the crews of S/L Lee-Warner, F/L Lange and F/Sgt Arrowsmith were sent on a sea-search in Lancasters R5692, NE178 and NE149 respectively and were airborne for up to four hours and forty-five minutes. That night, the crews of S/L Hodgson, F/Sgt McClone and F/L Robinson departed Tuddenham in that order between 22.44 and 22.40 in Stirlings bound for one of the Nectarine gardens off the Frisians, each with six mines in the bomb bay. Based on the flight times of between three hours and eight minutes and three hours and fifty minutes, the likelihood is that it was Nectarine I. They were followed into the air at 23.16 by F/L Burton and crew, whose destination with five mines beneath their feet was the Oyster garden off the Hook of Holland. They arrived at their respective target areas at the same time to find clear conditions and good visibility beneath the 3,000-foot cloud base and planted their vegetables according to brief from 600 to 800 feet between 00.27 and 00.33.

During the course of the month the squadron took part in twenty-one operations and dispatched 144 sorties for the loss of three Stirlings and crews, a few individuals from which were on the run and on their way home.

90 Squadron - F/L Day Crew.
Back L – R: Sgt J Morris (Nav), Sgt R A James (MUG), Sgt J Fenn (W/Op), F/Sgt C A Mitchinson DFM, (RG. Front L – R: Sgt T Fitzsimmons (FE), F/L W Day DFC (Pilot), F/O D Beaton (BA)

90 Squadron Crew with X-X Ray. L – R: Sgt Ken Gandy (RG), F/Sgt Phillip Green (Nav), F/Sgt Wilf Hodgson (BA), Sgt Roy Pask (W.Op) F/Sgt David Chapple RAAF (Pilot), Sgt Charles Potten (FE), Sgt Jack Cochrane (MUG). Tuddenham March 1944.

90 Squadron F/Sgt Towers' Crew.
F/Sgt J Towers, F/O L A Waller (Nav), F/Sgt E Webster (BA), P/O I Entwistle (W.Op/AG), Sgt R S Park (MUG), Sgt A Milligan (RG), Sgt W Burns (FE). On the 29th April 1944, their Stirling crashed on return killing the pilot F/Sgt Jack Towers and rear gunner Sgt Andrew Milligan. The remaining five of the crew had already baled out and were uninjured,

Sgt Jack Towers' original crew at Tottenham. Bill Burns on left. F/Sgt Towers third from left. Rear gunner Jimmy Powell next to Towers was killed on the 11th April 1944 when his aircraft crashed landed at Icklingham as the turret separated from the aircraft on impact after a SOE drop.

Kleve, Germany after its one major bombing attack.

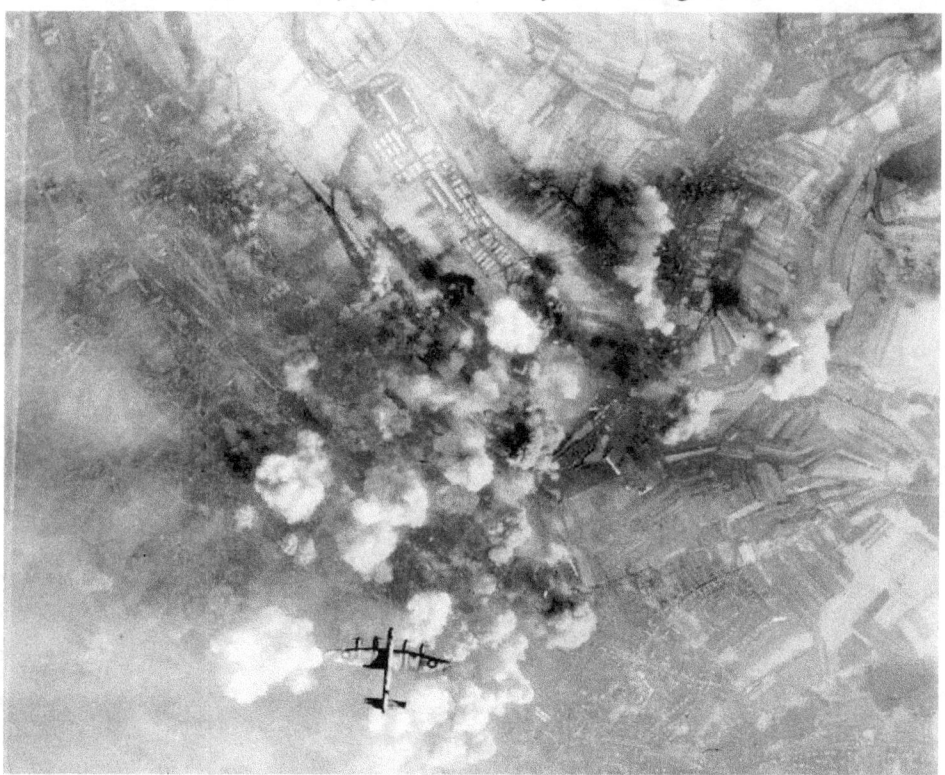

Clouds of smoke from exploding bombs rise into the air as an Avro Lancaster flies over the target area during a daylight raid by 153 aircraft of No. 3 Group, including 90 Squadron on Trier, Germany, 23rd December 1944. Trier central railway station is in the centre, the snow-covered Petrisberg is visible in the upper part of the picture.

Saarbrücken above and Münster below

F/L Jack Ralf DFC

F/O Frank McGlone. Killed on a Homberg raid 21st July 1944.

The McGlone Crew
Back L-R: F/Sgt G D Williams (BA), Sgt D A Bassett (FE), Sgt J W Simpson, F/Sgt J A McKim (Nav). Front: Sgt C C Cannon (RG), F/O F McGlone (Pilot), Sgt J E W Dickinson (MUG). All killed when their Lancaster LM189 was shot down by a night-fighter.

The F/O Bogle Crew of Lancaster ME852
Back L-R: Sgt M Kelly, Sgt C S Gilbert, F/Sgt R B McCormack, F/O C S Bogle. Front: Sgt P W Jones, Sgt J C Hines, F/Sgt R S Camier. (Sgt F Myers had replaced Sgt Kelly as flight engineer when the crew were all killed on the 13th August 1944 while on a Braunschweig raid).

F/O K C Forester and F/L N G Jones April 1944

The Edmunds Crew and three of their groundcrew (right middle).
F/O W B Edmunds RCAF (Pilot), F/O J B Barker RCAF (Nav), F/O J N Ferguson (BA), Sgt A N Bishop (WO/AG), F/Sgt A T Kendall RCAF (MUG), Sgt D E Brown (RG)

Wratting Common armourers stop for a tea break (Church Army Mobile Canteen) in the bomb dump, Cadgers Wood.

The crew of a Short Stirling B Mark III of 90 Squadron RAF relax by their aircraft on a hard standing north of the main runway at West Wickham/Wratting Common, Cambridgeshire, while other Stirlings of the Squadron are prepared for the night's operation.

F/Sgt Peter Latchford, Wireless Operator in F/L S Gay's crew. All crew taken prisoner on 10th April 1944 when their Stirling was hit by flak and crashed as they were dropping supplies to the Maquis in northern France.

F/L Reg Prior, navigator in Sid Gay's crew after return from Stalag Luft III at RAF Cosford, the prisoner receiving base.

Members of 90 Squadron – Centre F/L Vernon Barry (pilot), right F/L Thomas Jones DFC (BA) and possibly F/O Don Aylard (Nav) to the left.

Rawlings Crew - Brandrick, Daniels, Higgins, Rawlings, 'Wilbert' and, in front, Lithgow.
Left: F/Sgt H S Rawlings

The Rawlings' Crew
L-R: Sgt Derek Brandrick (KIA), W/O Ken Lithgow (POW), Sgt Bernard Daniels (POW), 'Wilbert', F/Sgt Henry Rawlings (POW), Sgt Edward Bray (KIA). Also killed were P/O Leslie Higgins and F/Sgt Harold Isles. ('Wilbert' is probably P/O Higgins or F/Sgt Isles). Their Stirling BK524 was shot down by a night-fighter while on an SOE operation on the 9th May 1944.

90 Squadron E for Easy

The Lane crew of Lancaster LM185.
Back: possibly Sgt Peter Richardson, F/Sgt Hugh Brown, possibly Sgt Arthur Marshall, Sgt Edward Flaherty. Front – probably Sgt William Morgan, F/Sgt William Lane, probably Sgt Reginald Naylor.

Flak stand at the Seeburg on Düsternbrooker Weg, Kiel. The anti-aircraft stand was spared after repeated bombing at the start of 1944.

Tuddenham's Flying Control Staff 1944/45

Crew and ground crew of 90 Squadron Lancaster F- Freddie.

90 Squadron Poynton Air and Ground Crew.
Standing L-R: Sgt Jimmy Kerevan, Wilf, Tommy, Tich and Jock. Front: Sgt Ronnie Stewart, Sgt George Bailey, Sgt A F Thomas, Sgt J Hazard, W/O Reg Poynton, P/O Jack Smith.
Below: Poynton Crew on 'faithful and well tried' H for Harry.

P/O L H Arrowsmith DFC RAAF

Sgt E Jeffery

Doc Lyon

90 Squadron Stirlings RAF Tuddenham

Sgt A P Thomas, (flight engineer) at RAF Tuddenham. The small photos are 'escape' photos for use in forged documents if shot down and evading.

Lancaster NE177 WP-H with Sgt Harry Holt at the crash site. P/O T A Burnett RAAF, Sgt C A Page, and Sgt D A F Mundy were killed when they came down in France. Sgts J F Clinton, Holt and W/O G A Hartwig evaded and Sgt Gallivan was taken into captivity, 11th June 1944.

90 Squadron Lancaster LM588 WF-F

Direct hit. Adolfplatz Kiel 1944

Tuddenham's answer to FC Barcelona 1943/1944

Railway marshalling yard at Tours following a Bomber Command raid on 10/11th April 1944

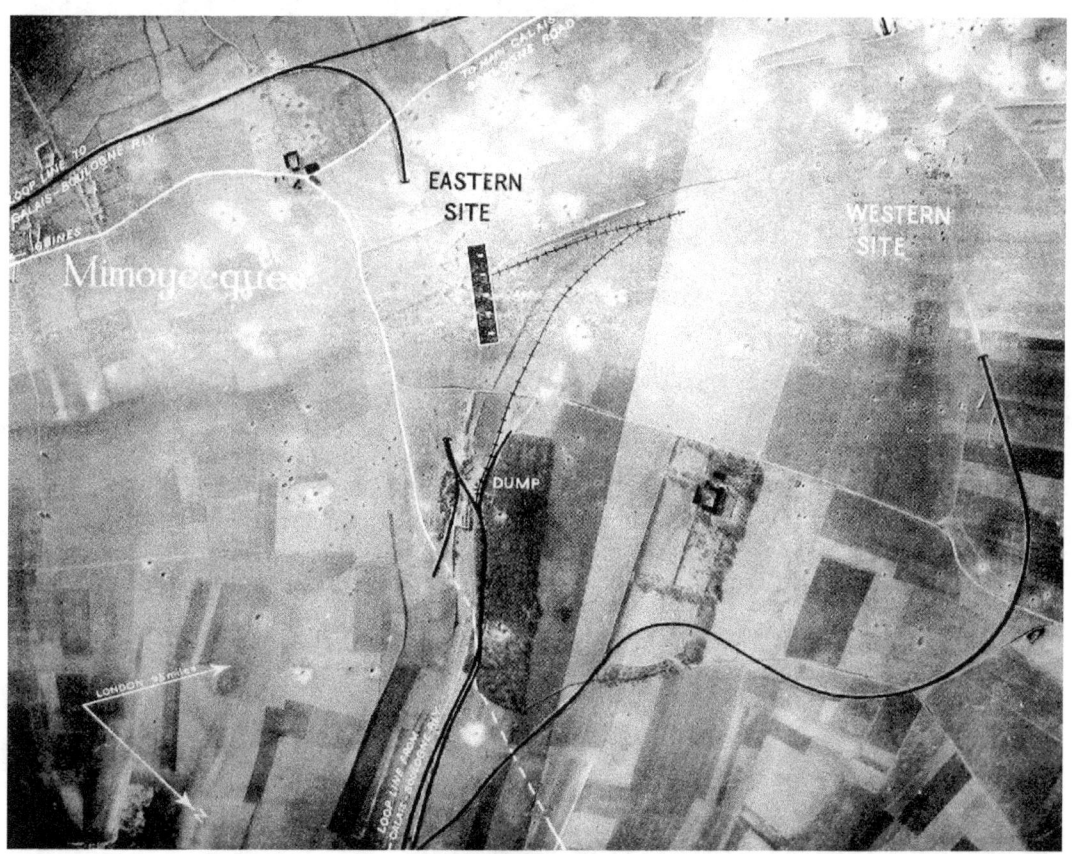

Photo map of the area around the two Mimoyecques sites and the crater evidence of the bombing carried out by Bomber Command including 90 Squadron.

Blockhaus d'Éperlecques - World War II V2 Rocket Assembly and Firing Facility

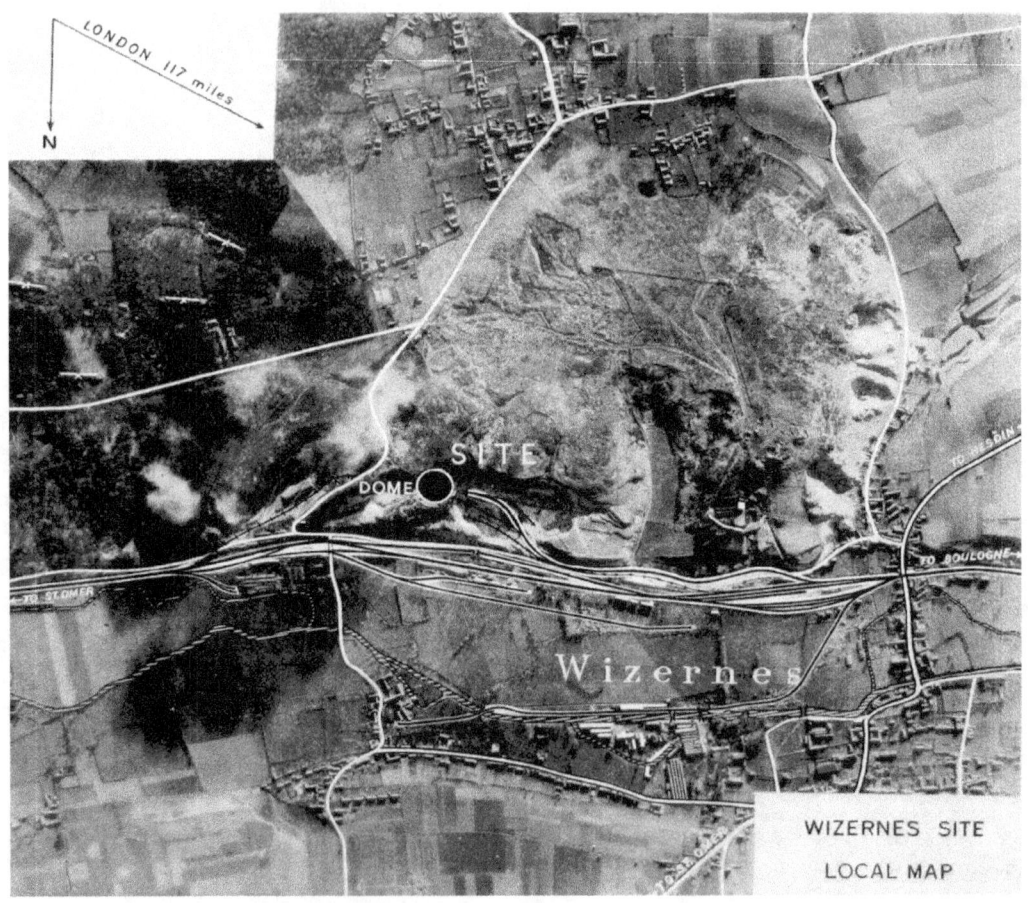
Site of V weapon site of La Coupole dome at Wizernes, northern France.

Inside WAAF Hut Tuddenham Christmas 1944.

Christmas Dinner, Sergeants' Mess 1944.

RAF Tuddenham 1945

The airfield has almost disappeared from the geography of the area - the World War II runways and the Thor emplacements are shown.

Believed to be the crew of Lancaster NN762. F/O NP Babey (Pilot). F/O W F Clayson (Nav), F/Sgt W A Lett (AB), Sgt J F Benson (WO/AG), Sgt A R Coombs (MUG), Sgt W McAllister (RG), Sgt P W R Fox, (FE).

The German cruiser Admiral Scheer capsized in the docks at Kiel after being hit in an RAF raid on the night of 9/10th April 1945 in which 90 squadron was involved.

Tuddenham FIDO system 1945

Tuddenham Watch Office 1945

Flying Control Staff with duty pilot that day W/O Reg Poynton (left

The Garbutt Crew
F/Sgt Beer (RG), F/Sgt Nowak (MUG), F/O MacDougal (BA), F/L Garbutt (Pilot), F/Sgt Blacklaw (Nav), Sgt Reeve (FE).

A bleak February Tuddenham 1945

Dortmund 1945. Bombed by 90 Squadron January 1945.

F/Sgt Roydon Derwent Woods, 90 Squadron. Before entering service with the RAAF at age 26, on 12th August 1942, Flt Sgt Woods was a clerk living in Hornsby, New South Wales. He left Australia on 17th October 1942 and took part in a number of bombing raids with the Bomber Command 3 Group. F/Sgt Woods was promoted to Flight Lieutenant and in 1945, he was awarded the Distinguished Flying Cross for his courage, fortitude and devotion to duty. F/L Woods survived the Second World War and was discharged on 14th December 1945.

F/Sgt Roydon Woods

River Pregnitz choked by debris and unable to supply war factories in nearby Nuremberg. Below: Nuremberg 1945.

Tuddenham Fancy Dress Ball V E Day 1945.

June 1944

June was to be a hectic month and make great demands on the crews, and the first week was dominated by unsettled weather, which caused concerns for the impending launch of Operation Overlord. The bombing of coastal batteries and signals stations was to be the priority during the first few days leading up to D-Day, and crews were briefed on the 1st for two sites, a battery at Brutelles and a radar-jamming station at Berneval-le-Grand, both of which were cancelled. 3 Group added fourteen Stirlings to the twenty-four Halifax and two Hudson SOE sorties for that night, and the seven representing 90 Squadron departed Tuddenham between 22.24 and 22.53 with F/L Kinch the senior pilot on duty. They all arrived back safely between 04.33 and 05.29 and were able to report successful outcomes.

On the following night 3 Group called upon the entire front line Stirling strength, detailing fifty-nine to maintain the deception by attacking a coastal battery at Wissant, a few miles down the coast from Calais, fifteen for mining duties off the Belgian coast between Seebrugge and Knokke in what was probably one of the recently constituted Iris gardens, and fifteen to supplement the twenty-one Halifaxes on SOE operations from Tempsford. 90 Squadron supported the SOE effort with eight Stirlings, half of them captained by pilots of flight lieutenant rank, and contributed eight also to the horticultural activities, dispatching the former from Tuddenham between 22.39 and 22.54 and the latter between 23.26 and 23.49 with S/L Hodgson the senior pilot on duty. F/Sgt Hadlow and crew abandoned their SOE sortie early on, while S/L Hodgson and crew had reached a point some twenty miles short of the Belgian coast when the Gee signal faded and persuaded them to turn back. They were joined at base shortly afterwards by F/L Rossington and crew who had been similarly compromised, but the others managed to maintain a Gee signal and arrive at the Belgian coast under clear skies to plant their five vegetables each from 4,000 to 4,500 feet between 00.43 and 01.04. After six of the SOE element had landed between 04.02 and 05.00, the crew of F/L MacDonald remained unaccounted for, and news eventually filtered through to confirm that EF294 had crashed between Amiens and St-Quentin at 01.35 and that the entire crew had survived, five falling into enemy hands, while the pilot and bomb-aimer evaded a similar fate. This was the last of fifty-eight Stirlings to be lost in 90 Squadron service, which now had just two weeks to run.

On the 3rd, 3 Group detailed thirty Lancasters to attack a coastal battery near Calais, probably at Wissant or Sangatte, while ten Stirlings and four Lancasters attended to mining duties in the Iris II garden off the Belgian coast at Knokke. 90 Squadron supported the latter with five aircraft, which departed Tuddenham between 23.36 and 23.54 with S/L Hodgson the senior pilot on duty and five or six mines in each bomb bay. The weather conditions in the target area were favourable as each crew established its position by Gee-fix and the vegetables were planted unopposed from 2,000 to 4,000 feet between 00.41 and 00.57.

Operation Overlord and already been put back by twenty-four hours when the decision was taken to launch it during the early hours of the 6th. It was with trepidation in view of the anticipated choppy sea conditions that the executive order was issued, and 1,211 crews across Bomber Command were called to briefings late on the 5th to learn of their part in attacks on coastal defences and in support and diversionary operations. No mention was made of the impending invasion, but strict guidelines were put in place which probably alerted them to the fact that a momentous night lay ahead. They were told that more than a thousand aircraft would be operating throughout the night, and that they must adhere to assigned flight levels and not jettison bombs over the Channel. The 3 Group Stirling squadrons had important roles to play in deception and diversionary operations in Phase A, while Phase B involved 107 of its Lancasters in an attack at dawn on the coastal battery at Ouistreham, situated on the Normandy coast at the eastern end of the invasion area, where Sword and Juno Beaches would be the scene of the Anglo-Canadian landings. Phase A, Operation Titanic I, involved four Stirlings of 149 Squadron and eleven Halifaxes from Tempsford's 138 and 161 Squadrons, whose brief was to create the impression of an airborne landing behind enemy lines in the Yvetot region to the east of the landing grounds by dropping dummy parachutists, rifle-fire simulators, "window" and other devices to draw attention away from the beaches. Operation Titanic III required three 149 Squadron Stirlings to carry out similar sorties to the west of the landing grounds in the Maltot and Baron regions, while Operation Titanic IV was to be conducted by fifteen Stirlings of 90 Squadron and a single Halifax of 138 Squadron with a similar purpose in the Marigny region, also located to the west of the landing grounds at the base of the Cherbourg peninsula. Operations Glimmer and Taxable would be carried out respectively by Stirlings of 218 (Gold Coast) Squadron and Lancasters of 5 Group's 617 Squadron, flying meticulously-timed circuits over the Channel dispensing "window", to create on German radar screens the appearance of large invasion fleets advancing towards the French coast on a ten-mile front either side of Boulogne.

The 90 Squadron contingent departed Tuddenham over an extended period between 22.22 and 23.43 with S/L Hodgson the senior pilot on duty and there were no early returns to blunt their contribution to this momentous night's activities and achievements. The squadron ORB Form 541 provides no detail of their individual sorties, only that they carried out their briefs and returned safely between 03.00 and 04.28. It was those operating as dawn approached that perhaps caught a glimpse through gaps in the cloud of the giant invasion fleet sedately ploughing its way at a steady eight knots across the Channel below and most, like the rest of the Allied world, would learn of the purpose behind their efforts through the BBC's radio news broadcasts later in the morning.

Another thousand aircraft were aloft on D-Day night to attack road and railway communications leading to the beachhead, for which 3 Group detailed a hundred Lancasters to target a railway junction in the town of Lisieux, some twenty miles to the east of Caen. They bombed through a thin layer of cloud at 5,000 feet, which obscured the aiming point, but the Oboe TIs could be seen clearly, and the bombing was accurate and concentrated. Post-raid reconnaissance confirmed the success of the attack in cutting the railway lines, but also revealed heavy damage within the town itself. Elsewhere, 3 Group detailed fourteen Stirlings for mining duties in the Brest and La Pallice areas and along the Belgian coast and around the western Frisians and a further fourteen Stirlings to supplement Tempsford's Halifax brigade. 90 Squadron briefed six crews for SOE sorties and eight for mining, four of the latter for the Nectarine I garden and two each for the Iris garden off Knokke and the Oyster garden off the Hook of Holland. The SOE and Nectarine I elements departed Tuddenham between 23.01 and 23.26, and the other two mining duos between 00.01 and 00.11, BK781 swinging on take-off and failing to leave the ground in the hands of F/O Fritz. The others reached their respective target areas, where F/L Rossington and crew found their Gee signal fading and preventing them from establishing a reliable fix. Their decision to bring their six mines home left F/O Donnan and crew to carry out their brief in the Iris garden from 1,000 feet at 01.03, three minutes after Sgt Kelly and crew had planted their six vegetables in the Oyster garden from a similar height. At the same time in Nectarine I all four crews had established a firm Gee-fix and released their stores from 900 to 1,800 feet between 00.59 and 01.06. The SOE crews returned between 01.45 and 04.45 having completed their tasks and as usual, no details were provided.

3 Group operations on the night of the 7/8th involved a force of sixty-six Lancasters in an attack on a railway junction at Massy-Palaiseau, south-south-west of Paris, three Stirlings mining between Ushant and the Brest peninsula and six Stirlings supplementing seventeen Halifax sorties from Tempsford. The 90 Squadron crews of W/O Wright, with S/L Levien as bomb-aimer, F/Sgts Hodges and Kelsey and Sgt Page departed Tuddenham between 22.53 and 23.10 bound for SOE drops and returned between 03.15 and 04.41, the crews of Sgt Page and F/Sgt Kelsey landing at Newmarket. Sgt Page and crew were unsuccessful, and mention of a combat report suggests that their sortie was terminated after an encounter with an enemy night-fighter. F/Sgt Hodges and crew were also unable to fulfil their brief on a night when fourteen of twenty-seven attempted drops were completed.

The much anticipated 90 Squadron Lancaster operational debut arrived on the 10th, when seven were made ready and loaded with eighteen 500-pounders for use against the marshalling yards at Dreux, some twenty-five miles west of Paris, one of four similar targets earmarked for destruction. They departed Tuddenham between 23.10 and 23.30 with S/L Lee-Warner the senior pilot on duty, probably with a misplaced confidence in their new equipment that was common to most after converting from the less efficient Halifaxes and Stirlings. However, like those before them, they would soon learn the harsh reality that Lancasters were equally vulnerable to enemy defences, and for 90 Squadron that lesson would come soon. They climbed out over the station eventually to join up with eighty-three other 3 Group Lancasters heading for the Channel coast, on the French side of which the weather conditions were favourable and crews were able to identify the aiming point visually and by white, green and yellow TIs. A Master Bomber was on hand to direct the attack and he instructed the crews to bomb the yellows, the 90 Squadron crews complying from 6,000 to 7,000 feet between 00.59 and 01.03. The bombing was initially scattered but became more concentrated as the raid progressed and smoke began to drift across to obscure the ground from view. Night-fighters began to arrive during the attack, continuing to harry the returning bombers until they reached the Channel Islands, and five Lancasters failed to return. There must have been shock at Tuddenham at the failure to return of the crews of F/L Thatcher and P/O Burnett RAAF, and it would be some time before news of their fate filtered through. There were no survivors from the former in NE149, which crashed a dozen or so miles west of the target, but four escaped with their lives from NE177, which came down at Grandvilliers some ten miles further north. The pilot, navigator and mid-upper gunner lost their lives, while the flight engineer, bomb-aimer and wireless operator were helped by the local resistance to evade capture and the rear gunner fell into enemy hands.

The squadron was not called to arms on the 11th for a raid by fifty 3 Group Lancasters on a railway junction at Nantes, but with just one flight fully converted, managed to offer six Lancasters on the 12th, the night on which Bomber Command's workload increased substantially with the addition of new responsibilities to its already busy schedule. Still immersed in the campaign against the enemy's transportation system, and on hand to support the breakout of the invasion forces, two new offensives against Germany's oil industry and V-Weapons storage and launching sites were introduced, beginning on this night with the first salvoes against the former. It was to be a hectic night generally for the stations, those of 4, 5 and 6 Groups concentrating on preparing more than six hundred Halifaxes and Lancasters for attacks on communications targets, while 1, 3 and 8 Groups put together a force of 286 Lancasters and seventeen Mosquitos to attack the Bergius-process Gelsenkirchener Bergwerke A G oil plant, known to the bomber crews as Nordstern and to the Germans as the Gelsenberg A G. *(A.G stands for Aktien Gesellschaft or production company. See the chapter on June 1943 for an insight into Germany's synthetic oil manufacturing processes)*. Path Finder Mosquitos and Lancasters would be on hand to provide the marking at all of the night's targets, and together with the minor operations taking place, 1,083 aircraft would take to the air on this night.

The 90 Squadron participants departed Tuddenham between 23.21 and 23.31 with S/L Lee-Warner the senior pilot on duty and a cookie (*4,000lb high-capacity blockbuster*) and sixteen 500-pounders in each bomb bay. They set course for the east coast to rendezvous with the rest of the heavy brigade at the midpoint of the North Sea at 18,000 feet, before climbing to 20,000 to 22,000 feet for the run to the target. and then shedding height during the final approach to bomb from 18,000 feet. F/Sgt Fawcett and crew turned back after an hour when the rear turret became unserviceable, leaving the others to press on to find the skies over the Ruhr to be clear. The first TIs were estimated to be eight miles south of the target and attracted thirty-five bomb loads, before the main Path Finder effort marked out the intended aiming point with reds and greens. The 90 Squadron crews delivered their payloads from what for them represented the unprecedented height of 18,000 to 20,000 feet between 01.05 and 01.10, and they could see the bombing become concentrated around the TIs and the resultant large fires emit copious amounts of black smoke. The ground defences were not as troublesome as had been anticipated, but night-fighters chased the bombers home, scoring steadily over Holland's Ijsselmeer and Gelderland regions in particular, and seventeen Lancasters were lost. Tuddenham had another empty dispersal pan to contemplate in the light of dawn, the one that had earlier been occupied by LM158, which crashed at Eerbeek, midway between the German frontier and Utrecht in the Gelderland region of central Holland, and only the bomb-aimer from the predominantly RCAF crew of F/O Elliott RCAF survived to fall into enemy hands. Post-raid reconnaissance and local sources confirmed that a highly destructive operation had taken place, which halted all production at the plant for several weeks at a cost to the German war effort of one thousand tons of aviation fuel per day.

The heavy squadrons enjoyed a rare night off on the 13th, which the 90 Squadron crews, no doubt, took advantage of to visit the local watering holes perhaps in Cambridge or the less distant towns of Thetford, Bury St Edmunds and Newmarket. The first major daylight operation since the departure from Bomber Command of 2 Group a year earlier was mounted against Le Havre on the evening of the 14th in a two-phase attack involving 221 Lancasters and thirteen Mosquitos of 1, 3, 5 and 8 Groups. The targets were destroyers, U-Boots, minesweepers and the fast, light surface vessels (E-Boots) that posed a threat to the Allied shipping supplying the Normandy beachhead. A predominantly 1 Group force was to take the first of the evening shifts, with 3 Group following up later after nightfall, and elements of 617 Squadron were also on hand with their Barnes Wallis-designed 12,000lb Tallboy earthquake bombs, but only for use if absolutely required. Eight Lancasters were made ready at Tuddenham and took off between 23.45 and 23.53 with F/L Lange the senior pilot on duty and each carrying a bomb load of eleven 1,000 and four 500-pounders. They arrived at the target under clear skies, finding it to be on fire from the earlier assault and bombed with the rest of the group from 14,000 to 15,000 feet between 01.15 and 01.19, achieving in the process great concentration and contributing to a highly successful raid from which few enemy vessels escaped intact.

A similar operation was mounted on the following evening against enemy craft at Boulogne, also with highly satisfying results, but 3 Group did not take part, having been assigned instead to attack the marshalling yards at Valenciennes in north-eastern France, and Lens, twenty-five miles away to the west. The latter was a Stirling affair involving thirty aircraft as the main force, eight belonging to 90 Squadron, with Path Finder Lancasters to provide the marking. At Tuddenham, each received a bomb load of eighteen 500-pounders, as did six of the squadron's Lancasters as part of the force of ninety-nine 3 Group Lancasters for Valenciennes. The two elements departed Tuddenham together between 23.13 and 23.39 with F/Ls Harper, Rossington and Thomas the senior pilots on duty in the Lens-bound contingent and S/L Levien the senior officer, while F/L Lange was the senior Lancaster pilot. On arrival at their target the Lancaster crews were greeted by a cloud base at 7,000 feet and an invitation from the Master Bomber to descend to that level, where they noticed the initial markers to be scattered, and he delayed the start of the bombing until the aiming point had been remarked. However, the second set of TIs undershot slightly, causing the Master Bomber to call for the bomb-aimers to allow a two second overshoot, which caused a degree of confusion, partly as a result of aircraft running in on a variety of headings. The 90 Squadron crews did their best to comply from 7,000 to 10,000 feet between 00.35 and 00.41, but the operation was only moderately effective and cost five Lancasters. Meanwhile, at Lens, up to ten-tenths cloud lay in a wedge over the target area with a base at around 9,000 feet and tops at 15,000, and the aiming point was marked out by red and green TIs and yellow and white spotfires, at which the 90 Squadron bomb-aimers focused their attention and released the contents of their bomb bays from 8,000 to 10,000 feet between 00.49 and 00.59. Both operations appeared to be effective but cost between them eleven Lancasters, six belonging to 8 Group at Lens and four 3 Group and one 8 Group Lancaster from the Valenciennes force.

Plans were put in hand on the 16th to launch 829 sorties that night against a number of targets, including four flying-bomb launching and storage sites in the Pas-de-Calais/Hauts-de-France regions of north-eastern France. Just three days earlier, the first V-1 flying bombs had landed on London, and this prompted a response in the form of a second new campaign to open during the month against this revolutionary new menace. As previously described, the V-1 targets were of two types, launching sites in the form of small buildings shaped like the letter J or a ski, which were attached to a launch ramp and referred to as "ski-sites", and large concrete storage facilities known in Bomber Command parlance as "constructional works", and many were, indeed, still under construction with additional work in progress to provide road and rail links. 3 Group's Lancasters remained on the ground on this night, while eight Stirlings were sent mining off the Frisians and Biscay coast. Elsewhere on this night, a force of 321 aircraft from

1, 4, 6 and 8 Groups continued the campaign against oil with an attack on the Ruhr-Chemie synthetic oil refinery at Sterkrade-Holten in Oberhausen.

Three railway targets were selected for the attention of elements from 1, 3, 4 and 8 Groups on the night of the 17/18th, 3 Group providing seventy-seven Lancasters and twenty Stirlings for one at Montdidier in north-eastern France. 90 Squadron briefed seven Lancaster and seven Stirling crews on the occasion of its final Stirling operation, and they departed Tuddenham between 00.50 and 01.20 with eighteen 500-pounders in each bomb bay and pilots of flight lieutenant rank leading the way. P/O Field and crew turned back early because of an issue with LK516's rear turret, leaving the others to reach the target in the minutes either side of 03.00 and encounter ten-tenths cloud at between 1,500 and 8,000 feet, conditions which were not conducive to accurate bombing. This situation would not have impeded an attack on a German target, but with collateral damage in mind and possible French civilian casualties, the Master Bomber ordered the force to orbit while he considered his options and ultimately called a halt to proceedings after just twelve aircraft had bombed. The 90 Squadron element returned with bomb loads intact and brought to an end the Stirling era, which left just 149 (East India) and 218 (Gold Coast) Squadrons as the only Stirling flag bearers in the group, and these too would shortly begin conversion to Lancasters. The withdrawal of the Stirling allowed 3 Group to regain its rightful place in the Command's order of battle, and to throw off the restrictions of the past seven months.

Three flying bomb sites were assigned to elements of 3, 6 and 8 Groups on the evening of the 21st, and as some squadron ORBs pointed out, this was to be the first full daylight operation since 1941. The target for a hundred 3 Group Lancasters was a V-Weapon storage site at Domleger, situated east of Abbeville in the Pas-de-Calais region of north-eastern France, where, as previously mentioned, large concrete storage and supply sites were springing up and were in various stages of completion. The plan called for aircraft to form into loose pairs in squadron order as they headed south to rendezvous with the leader at 9,000 feet over Braintree in Essex. The sixteen-strong 90 Squadron element departed Tuddenham between 17.57 and 18.11 with S/Ls Hodgson and Lee-Warner the senior pilots on duty and once in contact with the rest of the force, gained height to 14,000 feet over the Channel with the intention of bombing from between 12,000 and 14,000 feet. Unfortunately, ten-tenths cloud in the target area prevented even a faint glow from the TIs and the Master Bomber was forced to send the force home with its bombs. Despite this setback, valuable experience had been gained in formation flying in daylight, which would prove to be useful from the autumn onwards. Later on, during this night, 5 Group entered the oil campaign with attacks on the refineries at Wesseling, near Cologne, and Scholven-Buer in the Ruhr. Cloud at both targets rendered the low-level marking system unworkable, and night-fighters got amongst the Wesseling force to contribute to the massive loss of thirty-seven Lancasters, or 27.8%.

3 Group detailed a hundred Lancasters on the 23rd for an attack that night on another constructional works at L'Hey, situated some fifteen miles south of Dunkerque, for which 90 Squadron loaded a dozen Lancasters with eleven 1,000 and four 500-pounders each before sending them on their way from Tuddenham between 22.58 and 23.08 with S/Ls Hodgson and Lee-Warner the senior pilots on duty. They reached the target a little ahead of schedule, which led to some congestion, and were faced with ten-tenths cloud with tops at 5,000 feet, through

which the glow from the well-placed markers allowed the main force crews to bomb accurately in accordance with the Master Bomber's instructions, those from 90 Squadron from 8,000 to 9,000 feet between 00.15 and 00.17. The operation was concluded for the loss of a single Lancaster, which probably fell victim to coastal flak.

On the 24th, 3 Group assembled a force of one hundred Lancasters to attack a "constructional works" at Rimeux, situated in the Hauts-de-France region some twenty miles inland from the little port of Etaples. This was just one of seven such sites to be attacked on this night, for which 739 Lancasters, Halifaxes and Mosquitos were made ready. The sixteen 90 Squadron Lancasters each received a bomb load of eighteen 500-pounders before departing Tuddenham between 23.07 and 23.23 with S/L Hodgson the senior pilot on duty and arrived at the target under clear skies and bright moonlight to deliver their attacks on well-placed red TIs. A considerable night-fighter presence in the various target areas and on the routes home led to the loss of twenty-two Lancasters, two of which belonged to 3 Group. One of them was 90 Squadron's LM179, which crashed south-east of the target after bombing with no survivors from the crew of F/Sgt Mellors, whose flight engineer, Sgt Tollit, was an ancient thirty-eight years old and would have been known in the squadron as "Grandad".

On both the 25th and 26th 3 Group squadrons were put on standby to provide aircraft for an attack on constructional works at Zudausques in the northern area of the Pas-de-Calais, but the weather prevented any operation from taking place. On the 27th, W/C Milligan was posted to 3 Group HQ at the conclusion of his tour as commanding officer and W/C Ogilvie came in the opposite direction as his successor. Briefings took place that day for an attack on a "constructional works" supply site at Biennais, situated twenty miles south of Dieppe, for which 90 Squadron loaded a dozen of its Lancasters with eighteen 500-pounders each as part of a 3 Group force of one hundred. They departed Tuddenham between 23.29 and 23.43 with S/L Lee-Warner the senior pilot on duty and eighteen 500-pounders in each bomb bay, and after climbing out, joined up with the rest of the force as they headed for the Channel coast. They found the target to be hidden by ten-tenths cloud, through which the glow of the red TIs was just visible and the Tuddenham crews bombed from 13,000 to 14,000 feet between 01.09 and 01.16. A large explosion suggested that the bombing had found the mark, and then the crews had to fight their way through considerable night-fighter activity on the return journey, only to be warned of intruder activity at home. P/O Todd and crew had entered the Tuddenham circuit in NE145, when they were shot down crashed without survivors at Canada Farm near Icklingham, seven miles north-west of Bury St Edmunds. LM164 also came under attack and sustained damage, and after it had landed safely in the hands of F/L Burton, his rear gunner, Sgt Smith, was found to have been fatally wounded.

Preparations were put in hand on the 30th for a daylight attack on a road junction at Villers-Bocage, a village perched across a main road on the western approaches to Caen, through which two German Panzer divisions were planning to pass that night on their way to the beachhead. 3 Group assembled a record 127 Lancasters as part of an overall 3, 4 and 8 Group force of 266 Lancasters, Halifaxes and Mosquitos, the nineteen 90 Squadron Lancasters each receiving a bomb load of eleven 1,000 and four 500-pounders before departing Tuddenham between 17.59 and 18.16 with S/Ls Hodgson and Lee-Warner the senior pilots on duty. The bombers formed into loose pairs as they flew south to rendezvous with the 4 and 8 Group elements and reached the target under the protection of a Spitfire escort provided by 11 Group. They intended to carry out the attack from between 12,000 and 14,000 feet, until the presence of some broken cloud persuaded many crews to descend to 4,000 feet under the guidance of the Master Bomber, but poor communications meant that not all were able to pick up his broadcasts and the 90 Squadron participants were spread between 4,000 and 12,000 feet as they carried out their attacks on green TIs between 20.00 and 20.05. They observed the flash of bursting bombs and black smoke rising to meet them and it was clear that a highly successful attack had taken place, which entirely achieved its purpose and elicited messages of congratulations from the American and British army commanders. There was moderate flak to contend with, and S/L Lee-Warner and crew lost an engine as they left the target and P/O Kelly's LM188 was also hit, but both returned safely to base.

On the 30th S/L Levien was posted to 32 Base at Mildenhall at the conclusion of his tour and his pilot, acting W/O Wright, would follow him out of the squadron on posting to 85 O.T.U on the 7th of July. During the course of the month the squadron participated in nineteen operations and dispatched seventy-four Stirling sorties and 111 by Lancasters for the loss of five Lancasters and a single Stirling, six complete crews and a rear gunner.

July 1944

The first week of the new month would be dominated by the campaign against flying-bomb sites, and a main force of 307 Halifaxes from 4 and 6 Groups opened proceedings in daylight on the 1st. On the following afternoon 374 Lancasters of 1, 3 and 8 Groups were assigned to three sites, 3 Group contributing 119 Lancasters to Beauvais, situated twenty-five miles south-west of Amiens. *(The 90 Squadron ORB incorrectly recorded the target as Beauvoir, a location much further west in Normandy.)* The nineteen aircraft provided by 90 Squadron each received a bomb load of eleven 1,000 and four 500-pounders and departed Tuddenham between 12.50 and 13.14 with W/C Ogilvie displaying excellent leadership qualities by leading the squadron into battle very early in his stewardship, with S/L Hodgson the other senior pilot on duty. They met up with a fighter escort from 11 Group as they approached the Channel and reached the target area to find good conditions with three to eight-tenths cloud, through which the yellow TIs were clearly visible, if a little late in going down. The bombing by the Tuddenham crews was carried out in accordance with the instructions of the Master Bomber from 8,000 to 14,000 feet between 14.36 and 14.39 and was entirely unopposed from the ground or in the air. At debriefings some crews commented on confusing messages from the Master Bomber, but the bombing appeared to be concentrated and effective, particularly in the north-western corner of the site, where launching ramps had been destroyed.

Some 3 Group squadrons were on standby from the early hours of the 5th and right throughout the day for an attack on the "constructional works" at Biennais, but poor weather conditions prevented the operation from taking place. Eventually the target was changed to other "constructional works", the rocket launching site at Watten, situated a dozen miles south-east of Calais and the huge domed storage facility at Wizernes six miles further south, for which 3 Group contributed eighty and thirty-nine Lancasters respectively, 90 Squadron supporting both with ten Lancasters each. Elements of 4, 6 and 8 Groups were also in action on this night against the four designated targets, bringing the total number of sorties to 542. At Tuddenham all twenty Lancasters received a bomb load of eleven 1,000 and four 500-pounders, those bound for Watten taking off between 22.37 and 22.48 with F/L Burton the senior pilot on duty, to be followed into the air by the second element between 22.56 and 23.06 led again by W/C Ogilvie. By the time that they reached their respective target areas the skies over north-eastern France had cleared to leave bright moonlight but also some ground haze, and three groups of red TIs presented themselves at Watten, the 90 Squadron crews selecting those in the centre for attention in accordance with the Master Bomber's instructions. They bombed from 8,000 to 12,000 feet between 00.08 and 00.13 and were on their way home by the time that the Wizernes contingent delivered their attacks from 8,000 to 11,000 feet between 00.25 and 00.32. All four operations were concluded successfully at a cost of four Lancasters, each of which was observed to be shot down, but each site would require further attention over the ensuing two months.

A major assault on enemy positions in fortified villages north of Caen was carried out by 460 aircraft of 1, 4, 6 and 8 Groups on the evening of the 7th in support of British and Canadian ground forces. The two locations were well-plastered under the control of Master Bombers, but the choice of aiming points was flawed and rendered the operation ineffective, causing extensive damage to the outskirts of Caen which would prove to be a hindrance rather than a help in the effort to break out.

A proposed attack on the marshalling yards at Vaires, east of Paris, on the previous night had been cancelled because of adverse weather conditions, and this was now reinstated and handed to a hundred Lancasters of 3 Group and twenty-three Lancasters and five Mosquitos of 8 Group to provide the marking. 90 Squadron briefed nineteen crews while their chariots out on the dispersals were being loaded with eleven 1,000 and three 500-pounders each, and they departed Tuddenham between 22.24 and 22.47 with S/L Lee-Warner the senior pilot on duty. Among seven 3 Group early returns were the crews of P/O Cooper and F/O Cooper, the former because of an indisposed mid-upper gunner and the latter with W/T failure. The others found the target under clear skies and carried out their attacks on red, green and yellow TIs from 12,000 to 13,000 feet between 01.30 and 01.39 in compliance with the master Bomber's instructions and with excellent results and no losses. This was in stark contrast to a simultaneous 5 Group attack on flying-bomb storage caves at St-Leu-d'Esserent, north of Paris, where night-fighters got amongst the bombers and shot down twenty-nine Lancasters and two Mosquitos, a massive 14% of the force.

Six flying-bomb launching sites were earmarked for attention by daylight on the 9th, for which 347 aircraft from 3, 4, 6 and 8 Groups were made ready, 3 Group detailing fifty Lancasters from 33 Base for the site at Lisieux. The target was obscured by ten-tenths cloud and the TIs difficult to see and most crews bombed on either a Gee-fix or DR, which led to a scattered and unsuccessful raid. It was a similar story on the following day, when 3 Group detailed 130 Lancasters to target "constructional works" at Nucourt, located some twenty-five miles north-west of Paris. 90 Squadron contributed a record twenty-four Lancasters, each of which received a bomb load of eleven 1,000 and four 500-pounders before departing Tuddenham between 03.27 and 03.57 with W/C Ogilvie and S/L Lee-Warner the senior pilots on duty. F/L Burton and crew were back home within two hours after losing their communications systems, leaving the rest to reach the target area, where the Master Bomber issued instructions in the face of complete cloud-covered to bomb on Gee-fix or DR. The 90 Squadron participants complied from 13,000 to 16,000 feet between 06.00 and 06.13 and reporting on their return that they spotted the TIs only as they turned away. Inevitably, the attack was scattered and ineffective and would have to be repeated.

Flying bomb sites occupied more than two hundred aircraft of 4, 6 and 8 Group on the 12th, while 110 Lancasters of 3 Group and forty-three from 1 and 8 Groups joined forces for another swipe at the marshalling yards at Vaires. The 90 Squadron armourers loaded eighteen 500-pounders into each of eighteen Lancasters before they departed Tuddenham between 17.26 and 17.57 with W/C Ogilvie and the newly promoted S/L Burton the senior pilots on duty. There were no early returns, and all reached the target area to be confronted by nine-tenths cloud, which, according to the Master Bomber's assessment, put adjacent residential districts in jeopardy and he decided to abandon the attack. By this time the crews of W/C Ogilvie and F/Sgt Arrowsmith had spotted red and yellow TIs and a stretch of railway line and had released their payloads from 16,000 feet at 20.00, followed a minute later by F/Sgt Hendry and crew, who caught a glimpse of the TIs and bombed from 14,000 feet. The others responded to the Master Bomber's instructions to abandon the operation and take their bombs home, and at debriefings it emerged that a further nine crews from other squadrons had carried out an attack. W/C Ogilvie was scathing about the planning of routes and times and the fact that two streams of bombers had met head-on at the same height.

The weather caused planned daylight attacks on the marshalling yards at Villeneuve-St-Georges to be cancelled on the 13th, and at Vaires on the 14th and 15th, and it was the evening of the 15th before a planned operation could go ahead against marshalling yards at Chalons-sur-Marne in the Champagne region of France to the east of Paris. 90 Squadron was called upon to contribute twenty Lancasters, each of which received a bomb load of eighteen 500-pounders before departing Tuddenham between 21.17 and 21.43 with W/C Ogilivie and S/L Hodgson the senior pilots on duty. F/Sgt Hendry and crew soon returned with intercom failure and they were followed home within two hours by P/O Parry because of an engine issue and finally F/Sgt Kluczny and crew because of an unserviceable mid-upper turret. The others arrived in the target area to find ten-tenths cloud above 8,000 feet but conditions below favourable enough for most to be able to identify the aiming point visually. The Master Bomber gave clear instructions to bomb on the red TIs and the 90 Squadron crews complied from 8,000 to 12,000 feet between 01.30 and 01.37, observing bomb bursts and a large column of smoke rising to meet them. At debriefing F/L Shepherd and crew reported that they had orbited until hearing the Master Bomber's broadcast and had then descended to 7,500 feet only to fail to spot any TIs and had brought their bombs home. Post-raid reconnaissance confirmed that severe damage had been inflicted upon the yards.

The squadron detailed twenty-two Lancasters on the 16th for another crack at the Vaires marshalling yards, but the raid was cancelled, only to be rescheduled for the morning of the 17th. They departed Tuddenham at around midday but were recalled shortly afterwards and on return were refuelled and told to stand-by for a tactical target, which in the event did not materialise until the following dawn.

The tactical target turned out to be five enemy strongholds in the villages of Colombelles, Mondeville, Sannerville, Cagny and Manneville, all situated to the east of Caen and standing in the path of the advancing British 2nd Army, which was about to attack under Operation Goodwood. This was Montgomery's plan for a decisive breakout into wider France as a prelude to the march towards the German frontier, and a force of 942 Bomber Command aircraft was made ready on the 18th to operate alongside its American counterparts. 3 Group detailed 129 Lancasters for three aiming points without identifying to which base each target had been assigned, and the 90 Squadron ORB simply states Caen as the target for the twenty Lancasters standing ready at Tuddenham as the first streaks of light appeared in the eastern skies. They took off between 04.00 and 04.25 with S/Ls Hodgson and Lee-Warner the senior pilots on duty and each bomb bay containing eleven 1,000 and four 500-pounders. All aiming points were marked initially by Oboe and backed up with yellow TIs and the bombing carefully controlled by Master Bombers, whose instructions were complied with by the 90 Squadron crews as they carried out their attacks from 6,500 to 8,500 feet between 06.09 and 06.16. Two German divisions, the 16th Luftwaffe Field Division and the 21st Panzer (armoured) Division were hit particularly hard, and Bomber Command was responsible for 5,000 of the 6,800 tons of bombs dropped at the five locations. The ground defences were soon overwhelmed and only five Lancasters and a Halifax failed to return.

The day's work was not yet done, as more than nine hundred aircraft were involved that night in attacks against synthetic oil refineries at Wesseling and Scholven-Buer, while others targeted railway centres at Revigny and Aulnoye. The Revigny raid had already been attempted twice by 1 Group but on each occasion it had been abandoned because of unfavourable weather conditions in the target area, a disappointment compounded by a combined loss to Luftwaffe night-fighters of seventeen Lancasters. On this night it was left to 5 Group to complete the job, which it accomplished, but at the high price of twenty-four Lancasters, 22% of the force. Meanwhile, 3 Group detailed 127 Lancasters for an attack on the Aulnoye marshalling yards, situated close to the Belgian frontier, for which 90 Squadron loaded its twenty-three participating Lancasters with a bomb load each of eighteen 500-pounders. They departed Tuddenham between 22.12 and 22.39 with S/Ls Burton and Hodgson the senior pilots on duty, and after climbing out, set course for the Suffolk coast and the North Sea crossing, intending to enter French airspace at 17,000 feet before descending to between 8,500 and 9,500 feet for the bombing run. F/Sgt Rouse and crew lost their W/T while still over base and proceeded as far as the coast in the vain hope, as it turned out, that the problem could be rectified. Clear skies prevailed over the target area and green TIs burned on the ground as eighteen of the 90 Squadron crews attacked from 8,000 to 9,000 feet between 00.54 and 01.00 under the guidance of a Master Bomber. W/O Rowell and crew picked up the Master Bomber's instruction to bomb green TIs and spent ten minutes searching for them before giving up and heading home, while F/Sgt Modeland and crew saw only reds and also turned away. F/O Kirsch and crew suffered the frustration of a complete hang-up and brought their bombs back with a view to jettisoning two off the coast at Southwold to lighten the load, but when the bomb-aimer pressed the tit, the whole lot went! F/L Shepherd and crew fell behind schedule somewhere and all activity had ceased by the time they reached the target, and they too returned their bombs to the station dump. Post-raid reconnaissance revealed that the railway track to the front had been cut at a cost of two Lancasters.

The pressure on Bomber Command was demonstrated on the night of the 20/21st, when more than nine hundred aircraft were involved in attacks associated with three of the four on-going campaigns. Three hundred aircraft were made ready to attack a triangular railway junction at Courtrai in Belgium, a further three hundred for oil refineries at Bottrop and Homberg in the Ruhr and yet more for V-Weapon sites at Ardouval and Wizernes, while support and minor operations accounted for over two hundred other sorties. 3 Group made ready 128 Lancasters to target the Rheinpreussen (Meerbeck) Bergius process oil refinery located on the western bank of the Rhine at Moers/Homberg, opposite Duisburg, and they would be joined by fourteen ABC Lancasters from 1 Group's 101 Squadron and five Lancasters and eleven Mosquitos from 8 Group to take care of the marking. 90 Squadron loaded a record twenty-six Lancasters with a cookie and sixteen 500-pounders each and dispatched them from Tuddenham between 22.58 and 23.31 with S/L Lee-Warner the senior pilot on duty. There were four early returns, but none from among the 90 Squadron contingent, and the force was, therefore, largely intact as it approached the target area in conditions of good visibility. It was at this point that the first night-fighters arrived on the scene, after which they would remain in contact all the way to the Dutch coast on the way home. The red and green TIs were clearly visible to the bomb-aimers as the 90 Squadron participants released their loads from 15,000 to 20,000 feet between 01.21 and 01.27 and watched them fall in concentrated fashion in and around the refinery, causing a mushroom of thick, black smoke to spread and rise through 15,000 feet as the raid developed. Returning crews expressed confidence that they had taken part in a successful operation but were shocked when they learned that eighteen of their number had failed to return. 75(NZ) Squadron had been the hardest-hit and had seven empty dispersal pans to contemplate at Mepal on the following morning, while there were four at Waterbeach, home of 514 Squadron, and three at Tuddenham. LM189 crashed at around 01.25 some four miles north-north-east of the target and there were no survivors from the crew of F/O McGlone. F/L Rossington and crew were well on their way home in LM183, heading westwards towards Tilburg and the Scheldt estuary when their lives ended at around 01.40 near Boxtel, and five minutes later LM185 crashed nearby, killing F/Sgt Lane and his crew. Post-raid reconnaissance and local reports confirmed the effects of the raid, which had caused massive damage to a plant, which, only weeks earlier, had been producing six thousand tons of aviation fuel per day, but was now fluctuating at between 120 and 970 tons.

There were no operations for most of the Command on the 22nd, but the 23rd would be busy and generate 1,188 sorties, the bulk of which would be involved in night-time activity, while there was an early start for twenty-four 3 Group Lancaster crews, a third of them belonging to 90 Squadron. The target was a flying-bomb site at Mont Candon, located some seven miles to the south-west of Dieppe, for which the 90 Squadron element departed Tuddenham between 06.44 and 06.50 with W/C Ogilvie the senior pilot on duty and eighteen 500-pounders in each bomb bay. This attack and another of similar size by 8 Group Lancasters at Forêt-de-Croc involved a new "Mosquito leader" technique, in which the Lancasters formed a gaggle behind an Oboe Mosquito and released their bombs when the leader fired off a green verey flare and his bombs were seen to fall away. They encountered ten-tenths cloud over the target, which was not critical in terms of accuracy because of Oboe, but would prevent an immediate assessment of results, and all released their bombs from 16,000 to 17,000 feet between 09.00 and 09.01 and appeared to achieve concentration. This was a mini version of the G-H system, which was still in development but would be ready to roll out to 3 Group in the autumn.

After a two-month break from city busting, Harris had sanctioned a major raid on the naval and ship-building port of Kiel for that night, for which a force of 629 aircraft was made ready, a hundred of the Lancasters provided by 3 Group. 90 Squadron loaded some of its eighteen Lancasters with ten 1,000 and three 500-pounders each and others with a cookie, eight 500-pounders and six J-Type cluster bombs before sending them on their way from Tuddenham between 21.29 and 21.51 with F/L Shepherd the senior pilot on duty. Imaginative routing and changes of height helped to keep the night-fighters at bay, and a large RCM effort by 100 Group enabled the force to appear suddenly and with total surprise from behind a "Mandrel" screen. There was complete cloud cover over the target, forcing crews to bomb on red skymarkers with green stars and their own navigational aids, the 90 Squadron participants from 18,000 to 21,000 between 01.19 and 01.31, but the attack found the mark anyway, causing damage in all parts of the town, with particular focus in the port area, where the Krupp-Germania, Deutsche Werke and Howaldtswerke U-Boot construction yards and naval facilities were hit. Returning crews reported seeing the glow of fires from the west coast of Jutland as they flew home.

A second pair of "Mosquito leader" operations was briefed out on the 24th, one against a flying-bomb site at Acquet, situated a dozen or so miles to the north-east of Abbeville, for which eight 90 Squadron crews departed Tuddenham between 09.30 and 09.41 to act as the main force with S/L Hodgson the senior pilot on duty and a total of 144 x 500-pounders to do the damage. As they ran across the target the Mosquito's bomb doors were seen to open, but no bomb fell away, and when a second Mosquito took over, no verey flare was fired and the operation was abandoned.

The first of a three-raid series on Stuttgart was scheduled for the night of the 24/25th, for which a force of 614 aircraft was assembled, 3 Group contributing ninety-nine Lancasters, fifteen of them representing 90 Squadron. Each received a bomb load of seven 1,000 and four 500-pounders before departing Tuddenham between 21.48 and 22.02 with no senior pilot on duty and lost the services first of F/Sgt Page and crew during the climb-out because of a fuel leak and F/O Hadlow shortly after crossing the Normandy coast when the rear turret became unserviceable. The others pushed on across France and into south-western Germany and arrived in the target area over ten-tenths cloud with tops at 5,000 feet, into which the ground marker TIs disappeared to leave only a dim glow. This compelled the main force crews to bomb on e.t.a., H2S and drifting green skymarkers with yellow stars, the 90 Squadron crews bombing in accordance with the Master Bomber's instructions from 18,000 to 22,000 feet between 01.48 and 01.55. No local report came out of Stuttgart for this night, but the glow of fires beneath the cloud indicated that it was clearly a successful and destructive raid, although gained at a cost of seventeen Lancasters and four Halifaxes, many of them falling victim to night-fighters waiting for them south-east of Paris. There was no post-raid reconnaissance, and when local sources eventually provided a report, it combined the results from all three attacks.

A force of 550 aircraft was made ready for a return to Stuttgart on the following night, when 3 Group contributed eighty-nine Lancasters, a dozen of them belonging to 90 Squadron, which departed Tuddenham between 21.34 and 21.51 with S/Ls Hodgson and Lee-Warner the senior pilots on duty and seven 1,000 and three 500-pounders in each bomb bay. They set course for the Channel, where ice-bearing cloud between 7,000 and 15,000 feet contributed to an alarming twenty-three 3 Group early returns, four of them involving Tuddenham aircraft. Between 00.22 and 01.27 the crews of F/Sgts Kelsey, Hendry and Modeland and W/O Rowell landed at base in that order, two because of icing, one with an indisposed rear gunner and one with a jammed throttle lever, leaving the others to press on to the target through the layer cloud, which provided excellent protection from night-fighters. However, this dispersed to leave clear skies over Stuttgart, which allowed most crews to identify the target visually, with the red and green TIs clearly evident through the ground haze. The 90 Squadron participants delivered their attacks from 17,000 to 21,000 feet between 01.54 and 02.09 and observed explosions, five large fires and others in a line across the city. Again, there was no post-raid reconnaissance, but local reports emerged eventually to confirm that this had been a highly destructive raid, which had devastated the city centre and destroyed most of its remaining cultural and public buildings.

The last of the Stuttgart series was scheduled for the night of the 28/29th and involved an all-Lancaster heavy force of 494 aircraft drawn from 1, 3, 5 and 8 Groups, while 307 Halifaxes, Lancasters and Mosquitos from 1, 6 and 8 Groups targeted Hamburg 330 miles to the north. 3 Group provided 120 Lancasters, twenty-five of them belonging to 90 Squadron, which departed Tuddenham between 21.30 and 21.54 with W/C Ogilvie and S/Ls Burton and Hodgson the senior pilots on duty and six 1,000 and four 500-pounders in each bomb bay. Among ten 3 Group early returns were the crews of F/L Shepherd and F/O Cooper because of engine failures and F/Sgt Kluczny after a fire in the electrical system knocked out their W/T. In contrast to the previous trip to this location, there was bright moonlight to assist the enemy night-fighters to infiltrate the bomber stream and many bomber crews took advantage of a layer of cloud between 5,000 and 7,000 feet over France to hide themselves. This exposed them to light flak from the ground, which proved to be troublesome, particularly in the area around Orleans as the outward route passed well to the west of Paris. The stream turned sharply to port at this point to adopt a course slightly north of east to the frontier, and night-fighters began to score heavily all the way from there to the target. The 90 Squadron crews of F/Ls Fritz and Kinch, F/Os Kirsch and Sankey and F/Sgt Smith were engaged and all survived, while three of their assailants were claimed as destroyed.

A thin layer of ten-tenths cloud lay over the target at 8,000 feet, through which the red and green TIs were clearly visible and two distinct areas appeared to be marked about three miles apart, one having undershot the aiming point, while the other one was assessed by the Master Bomber as accurate, and both inevitably attracted bombs. The 90 Squadron crews attacked both red and green TIs from 18,000 to 21,000 feet between 01.49 and 01.58 in accordance with the Master Bomber's instructions and observed explosions and scattered fires. Thirty-nine Lancasters failed to return, and among them was 90 Squadron's PB198, which crashed near Bulgnéville in the Grand Est region of France some seventy miles from the German frontier near Strasbourg. The crew of F/Sgt Morton RCAF was predominantly Canadian with a RAF flight engineer and wireless operator, and there were no survivors. The crews of W/O Rowell and F/O Jennings arrived back with damage from heavy flak, the latter's fuselage having been peppered by splinters as it crossed the French coast homebound. The Hamburg force had run into heavy night-fighter activity on the way home, and twenty-two aircraft were lost, making this a very expensive night for the Command.

692 crews were roused from their beds early on the 30th for daylight operations against six enemy positions facing mainly American forces in the Villers-Bocage-Caumont area southwest of Caen. Twenty-two 90 Squadron crews were briefed for a target, it is believed at Amaye-sur-Seulles, and departed Tuddenham between 05.20 and 05.39 with S/Ls Burton and Hodgson the senior pilots on duty and eighteen 500-pounders in each bomb bay. Cloud interfered with four of the attacks, which were based on Oboe ground marking, but it seems that all went according to plan at the 3 Group aiming point, where the bombing was carried out from low level under the precise instructions of a Master Bomber. The 90 Squadron crews released their loads from 1,400 to 3,330 feet between 07.48 and 07.52 and along with the others appeared to achieve concentration, the bombing, as intended, creeping southwards as it developed. Crews saw nothing of the results other than clouds of smoke and had little of value to pass on at debriefing. Fewer than four hundred aircraft released their bombs because of the conditions, the remainder returning theirs to store, and just four Lancasters failed to return.

During the course of the month the squadron took part in eighteen operations and dispatched a record 319 sorties, including those recalled, for the loss of four Lancasters and crews.

August 1944

The first week of the new month was dominated by operations against flying-bomb sites and oil production and storage facilities, and it began on the 1st when 777 aircraft took off for daylight raids on numerous examples of the former, only for adverse weather conditions to intervene and prevent all but seventy-nine aircraft from carrying out an attack. 3 Group had been assigned to two sites, one at Coulonvillers, located some ten miles east-north-east of Abbeville, for which a force of fifty Lancasters included a dozen belonging to 90 Squadron, and the other a "constructional works" at Le Nieppe five miles to the east of St-Omer for which eleven 90 Squadron Lancasters departed Tuddenham as part of a force of forty-nine Lancasters. The two elements flew out across the Channel only to encounter ten-tenths cloud in their respective target areas, and although a few of those arriving at the head of the stream did attack at Le Nieppe, the Master Bomber sent all 90 Squadron crews home with their loads intact.

A similar target at Noyelle-en-Chausee was scheduled for attention by elements of 3 Group on the 2nd, but the raid was called off. The weather in the Paris area had improved sufficiently on the 3rd to provide clear skies for an attack on the flying bomb supply dump at L'Isle Adam (Bois-de-Cassan) to the north of the French capital. 3 Group detailed 113 Lancasters, twenty-four of them departing Tuddenham between 11.10 and 11.33 with W/C Ogilvie and S/L Burton the senior pilots on duty and eleven 1,000 and two 500-pounders in each bomb bay. On the way out the bombers picked up a Spitfire escort provided by 11 Group and reached the target to find ideal conditions and clearly visible TIs, at which the 90 Squadron element aimed their ordnance from 17,000 feet between 14.03 and 14.04, contributing to a concentrated and accurate raid.

An intended operation against another flying bomb site in the Foret-de-Nieppe on the 4th was cancelled in favour of an attack on an oil storage facility at Bec d'Ambes, situated on the west bank of the Dordogne River near its separation from the Gironde estuary ten miles north of Bordeaux. A second force of 1 Group Lancasters was assigned to a similar target at Pauillac, on the west bank of the Gironde estuary, ten miles further north, and both targets were to be marked by 8 Group Lancasters. The plan routed the two forces out over Land's End to fly at 1,000 feet to a point at 06° West, continuing south before turning towards the French coast and climbing from 02° West to a bombing height of 7,000 to 9,000 feet. The seventeen 90 Squadron Lancasters each received a bomb load of seven 1,000 and three 500-pounders before departing Tuddenham between 13.17 and 13.37 with S/L Hodgson the senior pilot on duty, and flew out in clear conditions, which persisted all the way to the target. P/O Beaune and crew found themselves in the 1 Group stream and bombed at Pauillac from 8,000 feet at 18.03 before realising their error, while the others carried out their attacks from just above the five-tenths cloud at 8,000 to 9,000 feet between 18.00 and 18.04. The presence of a fighter escort, provided for the first time by "Serrate" night-fighter Mosquitos of Bomber Command's 100 Group, ensured that the bombers went about their tasks unmolested, while 11 Group Spitfires provided cover for the return trip across the Brest peninsula. All crews arrived safely home between 21.05 and 21.36, highly satisfied with their day's work and reported many fires and explosions with smoke rising to 10,000 feet.

On the following day 3 Group detailed 106 Lancasters for a return to the Gironde estuary to attack an oil storage facility located within five miles of the centre of Bordeaux at Bassens to the north-east of the city. 1 and 8 Groups were also to be active in the area at Blaye and Pauillac, and this meant a total of 306 Lancasters heading out and adopting a similar route and tactics as for twenty-four hours earlier. 100 Group again provided the escorting Mosquitos, while two squadrons of Mustangs patrolled the target area and Spitfires would cover the return route over the Brest peninsula. The twenty-four 90 Squadron Lancasters each received a bomb load of seven 1,000 and four 500-pounders before departing Tuddenham between 14.08 and 14.38 with W/C Ogilvie and S/Ls Burton and Hodgson the senior pilots on duty. The only departure from the previous day's tactics was a climb to between 15,000 and 17,000 feet for bombing because of the expected heavy flak so close to the port of Bordeaux. Weather conditions were good with five-tenths cloud at between 5,000 and 15,000 feet over the target, and this allowed the crews to identify the aiming point visually, those from 90 Squadron carrying out their attacks from 3,000 to 11,000 feet between 18.59 and 19.06. On return they reported a concentrated raid which caused several large explosions and much smoke and commented that they had faced less flak than had been anticipated.

More than a thousand aircraft were detailed on the 7th for operations in support of ground forces still trying to break out of the Caen area. Twenty-one Lancasters were made ready at Tuddenham as part of a 100-strong 3 Group element, and they took off between 21.34 and 21.57 with S/Ls Burton and Hodgson the senior pilots on duty and each crew sitting on eleven 1,000 and three 500-pounders. Their aiming point was a troop concentration and road at Mare-de-Magne (untraced), which was just one of five enemy strongpoints to be attacked. The marking was assisted by a pre-arranged use of searchlight coning, star shells and Bofors tracer to provide a reference for the Path Finder element, and the attack went ahead in clear conditions onto a well-defined target. All of the attacks were closely controlled by a Master Bomber and while the 90 Squadron participants delivered their attacks from 7,000 to 8,000 feet between 23.39 and 23.49, 360 other aircraft brought their bombs home because of uncertainty as to the accuracy of the marking. Ten Lancasters failed to return, four of them from 3 Group, and among these were two belonging to 90 Squadron. LM111 was hit by flak and crashed eight miles north-north-west of Lisieux in an area to the east of Caen, and all but the pilot, F/L French, escaped with their lives, four to evade capture and two to fall into enemy hands. LM164 disappeared without trace with the crew of F/O Brooks, and it must be assumed that they found a final resting place in the Channel.

The target for a 3 Group force of 104 Lancasters on the evening of the 8th was an oil storage facility behind enemy lines in the Forêt de Lucheux in north-eastern France, which was one of two similar targets, the other, at Aire-sur-Lys, assigned to 1 Group and both would receive 8 Group support. 90 Squadron loaded each of its fourteen Lancasters with eighteen 500-pounders before sending them on their way from Tuddenham between 21.50 and 22.15 with S/L Lee-Warner the senior pilot on duty. F/L Dobinson and crew failed to complete the climb-out because of an engine issue and proceeded directly to the jettison area, while the others flew out in favourable conditions under clear skies to cross the French coast at 17,000 feet, before shedding height quickly and passing through a forest of searchlights to bomb on red, green and yellow TIs from 11,000 to 12,000 feet between 23.50 and 23.53. The concentrated and accurate bombing set off three large explosions at 23.52 and left many fires burning and columns of smoke rising through 9,000 feet as the bombers turned away. There was little flak, and despite clear evidence of night-fighters only one Lancaster from 115 Squadron failed to return.

A force of 311 Lancasters, Halifaxes and Mosquitos of 1, 3, 6 and 8 Groups was detailed on the 9th for operations against four flying-bomb launching sites and one storage site, the latter at Fort-d'Englos, situated four miles west-south-west of Lille, described in the group and squadron ORBs respectively as a petrol storage site and army fuel depot. The details mattered little to the one hundred 3 Group crews attending briefings, twenty of them at Tuddenham, where their Lancasters each received a bomb load of fourteen 1,000-pounders before taking off between 21.45 and 22.10 with S/L Hodgson the senior pilot on duty. They all reached the target to find clear conditions, but the marking was scattered and the instructions from the Master Bomber confusing, which led to poor early bombing. Matters improved somewhat later, and the 90 Squadron crews delivered their attacks from 13,000 feet between 23.13 and 23.16. Returning crews were able to report a large conflagration, which suggested that the target had been hit and there were no missing aircraft.

Railway targets dominated on the 11th, for which 459 Lancasters, Halifaxes and Mosquitos of 1, 3, 4 and 8 Groups were assigned to three marshalling yards and a bridge. Twenty-two Lancasters were made ready at Tuddenham and loaded with eleven 1,000 and four 500-pounders each before taking off between 13.55 and 14.14 as part of a 120-strong 3 Group force bound for the yards at Lens in north-eastern France. S/Ls Burton and Hodgson were the senior pilots on duty as they flew out in good weather conditions under a fighter escort and arrived in the target area to find six-tenths cloud with tops at 8,000 feet, through which the aiming point could be identified visually and by red and yellow TIs. All but one of the 90 Squadron crews delivered their attacks from 15,000 to 17,000 feet between 16.32 and 16.35, while F/Sgt Myers and crew jettisoned their load over the target "safe", after the fusing switch failed. Returning crews reported accurate and concentrated bombing, which caused explosions and fires and left smoke rising through 8,000 feet and the negligible opposition from the ground and in the air was reflected by the absence of losses.

A major night of operations on the 12th would involve more than 1,150 sorties at widely dispersed locations in Germany and France, the largest of which was an experiment to gauge the ability of main force crews to locate and attack an urban target on the strength of their own H2S equipment in the absence of a Path Finder element. The huge volume of operations generated by the four concurrent campaigns, each of which called upon the finite resources of 8 Group, compelled it, in the short term at least, to spread itself more and more thinly. The conclusion of the flying-bomb campaign at the end of the month, together with the end of tactical support for the ground forces, would remove the pressure and the planned independence of 3 Group through the G-H bombing system from the autumn would solve the problem altogether. In the meantime, however, no one knew what demands might be made of the Command, and it would be useful to see what main force crews could do when left to their own devices and H2S. The target was to be the northern historic city of Braunschweig (Brunswick), for which a force of 379 aircraft was assembled from all but 8 Group, while a second large operation over Germany involved 297 aircraft to target the Opel factory at Rüsselsheim, situated two hundred miles to the south. The factory had been building heavy trucks for the Wehrmacht until production switched to tanks and aircraft parts in 1942 and was one of Nazi Germany's most important production facilities, despite being a subsidiary of America's General Motors. 90 Squadron briefed twenty-one crews for Braunschweig and loaded each of its Lancasters with a cookie and sixteen 500-pounders, before sending them on their way from Tuddenham between 21.32 and 22.07 with S/L Hodgson the senior pilot on duty.

The Braunschweig force made landfall on Germany's north-western coast over the Ems estuary and arrived at the target to find ten-tenths cloud with tops at 7,000 to 10,000 feet but good visibility. They established their positions by H2S, and the 90 squadron participants delivered their bombs from 15,000 to 23,000 feet between 00.07 and 00.19 and observed what appeared to be a concentrated attack that caused explosions and fires. In fact, the bombing had been scattered with no point of concentration, and even though extensive damage occurred in central and southern districts, much fell onto outlying communities up to twenty miles to the south. The local flak defence were moderate in intensity, but night-fighters were much in evidence and their efforts would complete an expensive night for the Command and take a toll of seventeen Lancasters and ten Halifaxes, 7% of the force. ME852 failed to return to Tuddenham with the mixed RAF/RAAF crew of F/O Bogle RAAF, after crashing somewhere in northern Germany without survivors. The performance, generally, confirmed that main force crews were not yet able to perform to the highest standard without a Path Finder presence, although previous raids on this city during 1944, either with a Path Finder presence or employing the 5 Group low-level marking system, had also failed to deliver a telling blow.

The Rüsselsheim force crossed France to arrive at the target at the same time as the above raid and found a small amount of thin cloud with haze below. The attack opened punctually with illuminating flares and green TIs, the former rendered more or less ineffective by the haze, while a visual identification of the aiming-point was hindered by the diffused glow from early incendiaries. Green TIs were scattered initially to the north and south until a degree of concentration was eventually achieved and a number of fires developed covering a circular area approximately one-and-a-half miles in diameter. The main force bombing was carried out from around 16,000 to 19,000 feet either side of 00.20, but a detailed assessment was not possible, and the force headed home uncertain as to the outcome and harried by enemy night-fighters. It was left to post-raid reconnaissance to ascertain that a number of buildings had been damaged within the Opel factory complex, but nothing vital to production, and fires had spread through a wood three miles away and adjacent housing estates to the south-east. There were also many bomb craters in open country, confirming that the target would need further attention, and this was a disappointment compounded by the loss of twenty aircraft.

While the above operations were in progress, a "rush job" after midnight called upon the services of 144 crews to attack German troop concentrations and a road junction north of Falaise and south of Caen. F/O Cooper and crew took off at 00.20 as the lone 90 Squadron representative and delivered eleven 1,000 and four 500-pounders onto red and green TIs from 8,000 feet at 02.19, observing what appeared to be concentrated bombing around the markers. Post-raid reconnaissance confirmed that the area around the junction was heavily cratered and the roads leading from it mostly blocked.

The 14th was devoted to the support of British, Canadian and Polish Divisions as they closed in on German forces in the Falaise area in an attempt to encircle them and close the avenue of their escape through the towns of Trun and Chambois. Bomber Command assembled forces that together totalled 805 aircraft, which were to target seven aiming points, with the 3 Group element of one hundred Lancasters assigned to Hamel. There are a number of locations in France called Hamel, but all are too far east to be the one cited in the group and squadron ORBs, and it is believed that it was situated on the eastern outskirts of Falaise itself. Nineteen Lancasters of 90 Squadron each received a bomb load of eleven 1,000 and four 500-pounders before departing Tuddenham between 13.31 and 13.46 with S/L Hodgson the senior pilot on duty. All arrived in the target area to find clear weather conditions, which aided the Master Bomber at each aiming point to carefully control proceedings. The Master Bomber at Hamel was described as particularly good, directing the bombing skilfully and with concise instructions as bombing by most of the 90 Squadron contingent took place on red, green and yellow TIs from 7,000 to 9,000 feet between 15.53 and 15.55. F/Ls Kinch and Fritz withheld their bombs, the former having been confused by the frequently changing instructions of the Master Bomber, which had them zig-zagging until they overshot the aiming point and were sent home before completing a second orbit. The latter failed to pick up any instructions and eventually ran out of time. The bombing was seen to be accurate, but smoke and dust from other aiming points began to drift across the target in the later stages, denying some crews a clear view and they brought their bombs home. Some confusion arose at another aiming point resulted in bombs falling into a large quarry occupied by Canadian troops. This "friendly fire" incident cost thirteen lives, while a further fifty-three soldiers were wounded, and many guns and vehicles were hit.

Now that his primary responsibility to SHAEF had been fulfilled, Harris could start directing more of his resources towards industrial Germany, whilst remaining on hand to support the ground forces as required, particularly in their quest to recapture the German-held ports of France and Belgium. In preparation for his new night offensive against Germany, Harris called for operations against enemy night-fighter airfields in Holland and Belgium, in response to which a list of eight such targets was drawn up. Those at Eindhoven, Soesterberg, Volkel, Melsbroek, St-Trond, Tirlemont-Gossancourt and Le Culot were to be targeted in daylight during the course of the morning and early afternoon of the 15th, and Venlo that night, involving in all 1,004 aircraft. 3 Group contributed one hundred Lancasters to the attack on St-Trond in Belgium and nineteen of them departed Tuddenham between 09.49 and 10.07 with W/C Ogilvie and S/L Hodgson the senior pilots on duty, S/L Hodgson undertaking his eighth sortie of the month since the 4th. The weather conditions were ideal as the bombing took place in a perfectly executed, unopposed attack, during which the 90 Squadron crews each delivered eleven 1,000 and four 500-pounders from 14,000 to 16,000 feet between 12.05 and 12.10. There was no opposition and all 3 Group aircraft returned safely to their home stations, where their crews reported observing the bombs to impact the runways. The other aerodromes were also bombed accurately, and it remained to be seen what effect this effort would have on night-fighter operations over the ensuing weeks.

S/L Burton was rewarded for his outstanding service with the award of a DSO on the 16th. the day selected by Harris as the start of the new assault on Germany, for which Stettin and Kiel were posted as the targets for forces of 461 and 348 aircraft respectively. 3 Group detailed ninety-seven Lancasters for the former, of which a dozen were made ready at Tuddenham and each loaded with a 2,000-pounder and twelve J-Type 500lb cluster bombs before taking off between 21.00 and 21.22 with no senior pilot on duty. Departing Tuddenham at the same time were six other Lancasters, which were 3 Group's contribution to the extensive diversionary and support operations involving more than three hundred aircraft, including eighty-nine bound for mining duties in the Baltic. F/Ls Dobinson and Fritz were the senior pilots on duty as the 90 Squadron sextet set course for northern Jutland with a view to entering the Baltic in the Kattegat region before heading south to their assigned target area, the Sweet Pea garden in the Bay of Mecklenburg. F/L Dobinson and crew had reached Jutland's eastern seaboard when their H2S failed and forced them to turn back, retaining four of their five mines. The others continued on to plant their vegetables by H2S from 14,000 to 16,000 feet between 00.30 and 00.48 and return safely after round-trips of up to seven hours.

The port-city of Stettin, now Szczecin in Poland, lies at the southern end of an inland sea that feeds into the Odra River and finally into what is now called the Dammscher See some thirty miles south of the Baltic coast at Swinemünde. The bombers approached it at around 1,000 feet to remain under the enemy radar, before climbing to the intended bombing height, where they encountered seven-tenths cloud at between 15,000 and 20,000 feet. This impaired the marking to some extent, causing the TIs to become scattered, and the Master Bomber's performance was criticised for failing to communicate clearly his order to the crews to bomb from 14,000 feet. W/O Smith and crew were the only 90 Squadron crew to comply at 01.16, while the others attacked from 15,000 to 20,000 feet between 01.03 and 01.23. Three areas of fire were reported by returning crews, who were unaware initially of the actual extent of the damage inflicted on an urban target which never seemed to escape heavy punishment at the hands of Bomber Command. Fifteen hundred houses and twenty-nine factories were destroyed, a thousand houses and twenty-six factories seriously damaged, and 1,150 people lost their lives. In the port area five ships were sunk and a further eight damaged, and it is unlikely that the Oderwerke AG U-Boot construction yard emerged unscathed. The raid on Kiel was moderately successful, and inflicted severe damage in the port area, but much of the bombing also fell outside of the town.

Bremen was posted as the target on the 18th, for which a relatively small heavy force of 281 Lancasters and Halifaxes was made ready, with seven Mosquitos to deliver the initial markers.

3 Group provided 120 of the Lancasters, twenty of which departed Tuddenham between 21.39 and 22.11 with no fewer than seven pilots of flight lieutenant rank leading the way and a cookie and 30lb and 4lb incendiaries in each bomb bay. Thus far during the month the squadron's record of serviceability had been good, but on this night three crews turned back and landed between 00.33 and 01.10, W/O Smith and crew with engine issues in a brand-new Lancaster, F/L Cooper with a dead port-outer engine and W/O Rowell after the oxygen supply to the rear turret failed. The others pressed on to a city, which for the first three years of war had been one of the Command's most frequently-visited destinations, but since September 1942 had been left in peace by the heavy brigade. The attack took place in clear conditions, the 90 Squadron element delivering their payloads on red and green TIs from 17,000 to 20,000 feet between 00.12 and 00.20 and observing large explosions and extensive fires in central and north-eastern districts which sent a column of smoke rising through 13,000 feet. A reconnaissance Mosquito over Bremen at 01.05 reported an area of intense and unbroken fire covering 4 x 1½ miles with black smoke rising by then through 23,000 feet. It was confirmed later that the 1,100 tons of bombs had devastated central and north-western districts, including the docks, destroying 8,635 "dwelling houses", mostly in the form of apartment blocks and too many industrial units to count, while sinking eighteen ships in the harbour. The death toll probably exceeded eleven hundred people, and this was the start of a torrid time for Germany's cities, which would last until war's end, as Bomber Command grew in strength and Germany's ability to defend itself waned.

It was on this day, that G/C John "Speedy" Powell DSO DFC OBE, the brother of 90 Squadron's former commanding officer, W/C Wynne-Powell, lost his life while flying in a Beaufighter of 19 Squadron SAAF in the Balkan theatre.

The heavy squadrons spent the greater part of the ensuing week away from the operational scene, as a number of further attacks on Stettin were posted then cancelled because of the weather. Major operations resumed on the 25th, when preparations were put in hand to make ready more than nine hundred aircraft to launch against three major targets, while four hundred others would be engaged in a variety of smaller endeavours. The largest operation was to be the all-Lancaster affair involving 412 aircraft from 1, 3, 6 and 8 Groups in a return to the Opel tank works at Rüsselsheim, while 334 others attended to eight coastal batteries between Brest and the islands to the south of Lorient, leaving 5 Group to focus on Darmstadt, a university city renowned as a centre of scientific research and development, and one of a few almost virgin targets considered to be worthy of attention. 90 Squadron was responsible for twenty-five of 3 Group's 130 Lancasters and they departed Tuddenham between 20.18 and 20.43 with S/Ls Burton and Lee-Warner the senior pilots on duty and a cookie and eleven 500lb cluster bombs in each bomb bay. F/Sgt Modeland and crew were heading south across the London area when the intercom failed, and they proceeded directly to the jettison area, leaving the others to adopt the familiar route across France to enter Germany south of Luxembourg.

Clear conditions awaited them as they ran in on the red and green TIs at 17,000 to 20,000 feet to release their loads between 00.59 and 01.12 and observe explosions, fires and a pall of smoke rising through 14,000 feet. F/Sgt Perrett and crew were at the final turning point when they became ensnared in a searchlight master beam and then by the whole cone, and during evasive action the Lancaster fell into a spin which sent the instruments haywire. They overshot the target, glimpsing TIs to port, and realising that they would not be able to bomb accurately, jettisoned the contents of their bomb bay as they headed north-west between Mainz and Frankfurt. Shortly after bombing, ME862 was attacked from below by an unidentified enemy night-fighter, which destroyed the rear turret and H2S cupola and left the rear gunner severely wounded. F/O Jennings threw the Lancaster into a violent corkscrew, which threw off the assailant and enabled them to return home to land at Hartford Bridge in Hampshire, where Sgt Jameson was removed to hospital, sadly to succumb to his wounds later on the 26th. Absent from the debriefing process were fifteen crews, two of them from 90 Squadron, one highly experienced and the other in the early stages of their first tour. ME802 and LM588 both crashed in the general target area with the crews respectively of S/L Lee-Warner and F/Sgt Simmons and there were no survivors. It was established later that the forge and gearbox assembly shop had been put out of action for several weeks, but the assembly line was operating again within days with production barely affected because of a stockpile of ready-made components.

Kiel was the target for 372 Lancasters and ten Mosquitos of 1, 3 and 8 Groups on the following night, for which 90 Squadron made ready twenty-five aircraft as part of a 3 Group contribution of 124. Each received a bomb load of a cookie supplemented by thirteen-and-a-half SBCs of 30lb incendiaries and ten of the 4lb denomination, before departing Tuddenham between 20.04 and 20.28 led by pilots of flight lieutenant rank. They flew out over the North Sea at below 2,000 feet, and it was at this stage that F/Sgt Perrett and crew turned back with a generator issue and unserviceable DR compass, while the others pressed on to reach 05° East, when they began to climb in the clear skies to between 17,000 and 19,000 feet for the passage across the Schleswig-Holstein peninsula. The ground in the target area was concealed by a smoke screen, but the Path Finders were able to mark the aiming point clearly and a concentrated attack ensued in the face of a moderate heavy flak barrage, the 90 Squadron contingent delivering their loads from 16,000 to 20,000 feet between 23.12 and 23.19, guided by flares and red and green TIs. HK604 failed to return with the crew of W/O Halstead, and the washing ashore of three crew members on the Island of Sylt confirmed that the Lancaster had gone down in the Waddensee. Returning crews reported accurate bombing, which hit the town centre and surrounding districts and a strong wind helped to fan and spread the fires.

The final operations against V-1 launching and storage sites were mounted on the 28th, when 150 aircraft carried out twelve small-scale attacks in the absence of a 3 Group participation. The Pas-de-Calais region would return to Allied hands within a matter of days, and only then could a proper examination of these structures take place.

In recognition of his fine service both with 90 Squadron and before, the now departed S/L Levien was awarded a DSO on the 29th. This was the day on which Stettin was earmarked for its second visit of the month, for which a force of 402 Lancasters and a single Mosquito of 1, 3, 6 and 8 Groups was assembled. 3 Group put up eighty-eight Lancasters, including eighteen representing 90 Squadron, while a further six Lancasters at Tuddenham and six at Mepal were loaded with five mines each to deliver into the Privet and Spinach gardens, respectively off the ports of Gdynia and Danzig (now Gdansk in Poland) in the Gulf of Danzig under cover of the main operation. The gardeners departed Tuddenham between 20.16 and 20.31 with F/Ls Fritz and Kelly the senior pilots on duty and were followed into the air by the bombing brigade between 20.58 and 21.17 led by W/C Ogilvie, each with a cookie in the bomb bay along with seven-and-a-half SBCs of 30lb incendiaries and five-and-two-thirds of 4-pounders. They flew out over cloud for most of the way to the target, and F/O Stevens and crew had reached a point off Sweden's south-eastern coast more than four hours after take-off when he became unwell and complained of giddiness. He took the sensible option to turn back, jettisoning the vegetables on the way, and they landed safely after more than eight hours aloft. The remaining gardeners established their positions by H2S and planted their vegetables through ten-tenths cloud from 12,000 to 14,000 feet between 01.12 and 01.21, and while the ORB does not specifically identify which of the two gardens had been assigned to 90 Squadron, a map reference provided by the Fritz crew strongly suggests that it was Privet, off Danzig.

Meanwhile, 170 miles to the west, the skies over Stettin had cleared and the aiming point, which had been marked with red and green TIs, could be identified visually as the 90 Squadron payloads went down from 12,000 to 20,000 feet between 02.00 and 02.11. On return, LM128 emerged from low cloud and crashed at 07.14 near Freckenham, some five miles south-west of Mildenhall, injuring the entire crew of P/O Sullivan, the flight engineer, bomb-aimer and rear gunner sadly succumbing to their injuries in hospital. Twenty-three Lancasters failed to return, and among them was LM184, which had crashed at Aalestrup in northern Jutland with fatal consequences for F/O Sumsion and his crew. It had been another highly successful operation which destroyed 1,569 houses and thirty-two industrial premises, sank a 2,000-ton vessel in the harbour and damaged seven others. The death toll was again high and amounted to 1,033 people.

Although the V-1 threat had been largely nullified, the V-2 menace was very much in the minds of the British authorities and a force of 601 aircraft was assembled on the 31st to attack nine sites in Northern France, where the Germans were believed to be storing the weapon. 3 Group made available a hundred Lancasters, seventeen of them at Tuddenham, to attack a site at Pont-Remy situated four miles south-east of Abbeville. The 90 Squadron participants took off between 15.50 and 16.05 with S/L Hodgson back on the order of battle for his ninth sortie of the month, and eleven 1,000 and four 500-pounders in each bomb bay. F/Sgt Perrett and crew lost an engine early on and abandoned their sortie, leaving the others to continue and reach the target area to find cloud partially obscuring the markers, which forced most crews to orbit the aiming point two or three times before drawing a bead on it. All but one of the 90 Squadron contingent released their loads from 13,000 to 16,000 feet between 18.05 and 18.12, while F/L Kelly and crew arrived too late and returned most of their ordnance to the bomb dump. The bombing appeared to be scattered and the expectation of success was not high among returning crews, but there were reports of a large explosion followed by a column of black smoke.

During the course of the month the squadron carried out twenty-one operations and dispatched 353 sorties for the loss of six Lancasters, five complete crews and four other crew members.

September 1944

The destructive power of the Command was now almost beyond belief with each of its heavy bomber groups capable of laying waste to a German city at one go, and from now until the end of the war, this would be demonstrated in awesome and horrific fashion. Much of the Command's effort during the new month, however, would be directed towards the liberation of the three French ports remaining in enemy hands, Le Havre, Boulogne and Calais. Germany's oil industry and its railway communications would continue to occupy elements of the Command, and when the opportunities presented themselves, urban targets in Germany also. Operations against six airfields in southern Holland, which had been cancelled because of the weather on the 2nd, were mounted on the 3rd by 675 aircraft, of which fifty Lancasters were provided by 3 Group from 33 Base stations.

A force of 348 aircraft was assembled on the 5th to carry out the first operations against enemy strong points around the port of Le Havre, 313 Lancasters from 1, 3 and 8 Groups representing the bulk of the heavy brigade, accompanied by five Stirlings of 149 Squadron, the last of the type in service with a bomber unit three days ahead of its retirement in favour of Lancasters. 8 Group provided thirty Oboe Mosquitos for marking duties and 3 Group 136 of the Lancasters, twenty-three of them at Tuddenham, each of which received a bomb load of eleven 1,000 and four 500-pounders, before taking off between 16.46 and 17.12 with S/Ls Burton and Hodgson the senior pilots on duty. The attack was to be delivered in six waves, with groups assigned specifically, and each was controlled by a Master Bomber and Deputy and two marker backers-up were on hand if required. Nine-tenths cloud lay over England, but as the formations made their way towards the Sussex coast at Worthing, it began to break up and over the target it was at no more than three-tenths with tops at around 6,000 feet. The vertical visibility was excellent and the main force crews of the first wave experienced no difficulty in identifying the aiming point visually, although the expected green TIs were absent, and the Master Bomber ordered the force to orbit until the first red TIs were seen at 18.07. The 90 Squadron element had been assigned to the final waves and carried out their attacks on red TIs from 12,000 to 13,700 feet between 19.02 and 19.06 having established their positions visually on ground features. The bombing appeared to be concentrated where intended, despite smoke enveloping the target from time to time and hiding it from view, and a westerly breeze kept blowing it away to reveal the TIs again. A post-raid analysis suggested that around 90% of the bombs had fallen within the six defined target areas.

On the following day, a force of 344 aircraft was assembled for a return to Le Havre and among them were 130 Lancasters from 3 Group, which according to the 75(NZ) Squadron ORB, had been handed the German Army HQ as its aiming point. As before, there were six aiming points, each served by four Path Finder Lancaster and five Oboe Mosquitos to provide the marking. 90 Squadron loaded each of its participating Lancasters with the standard bomb load for this type of operation, eleven 1,000 and four 500-pounders, before sending them on their way from Tuddenham between 15.59 and 16.39 with S/L Hodgson the senior pilot on duty. They climbed into poor weather conditions and encountered ten-tenths cloud over the Channel with a base at 11,000 feet, before crossing the French coast at 7,000 feet, still with thick cloud above. At the target they encountered a layer of rain cloud at between 7,000 and 8,000 feet and fires still burning in the town from the previous day and from the earlier waves. The Master Bomber invited the main force element to descend to beneath the cloud base and the 90 Squadron crews complied to bomb unopposed from 6,000 to 8,000 feet between 18.22 and 18.24.

There was an early start for crews participating in the next round of attacks on five German positions around Le Havre on the 8th, for which 3 Group put up 120 Lancasters and four Stirlings in an overall 1, 3 and 8 Group force of 333 aircraft. The Stirlings belonged to 149 Squadron at Methwold, which was in the final stages of converting to Lancasters, and they would be the very last in Bomber Command service to conduct bombing sorties. Curiously, the 3 Group ORB makes no mention of their involvement in this operation, which for the 3 Group element was a two-wave attack on enemy defensive positions at Doudeville, situated some thirty miles to the north-east of Le Havre. Twenty 90 Squadron Lancasters each received a bomb load of eleven 1,000 and four 500-pounders before departing Tuddenham between 05.33 and 06.00 as part of the first wave, with S/L Hodgson the senior pilot on duty. They arrived at the target to find ten-tenths cloud with a base at 3,000 feet, which created considerable difficulty in identifying the aiming point, but most of the 90 Squadron crews managed to find red TIs to aim at and delivered their attacks from 2,500 to 5,500 feet between 07.32 and 07.38. However, with the close proximity of Allied troops in mind, the Master Bomber decided to call an early end to proceedings and the crews of F/Os Britton and Law and F/Sgt Kluczny were instructed to withhold their bombs. The second wave found more favourable conditions in the early stages, but as the bombing began to overshoot late on, the Master Bomber called a halt and sent a proportion of the force home with their loads intact. At debriefings it was reported that considerable light flak and machine gun fire had been encountered in the target area, and this was an expected consequence of attacking at low-level.

3 Group was not involved in the operations against Le Havre on the 9th, which were abandoned by the Master Bomber because of poor visibility. On the 10th, the squadron was briefed for an attack on a position at Montivilliers, situated five miles to the north-east of the port, and this was just one of eight German strong-points occupying the attention of 992 aircraft during the afternoon and evening. The aiming-points were given the names of car manufacturers, Buick 1 and 2, Alvis 1, 2, 3 and 4 and Bentley 1 and 2. Twenty-five Lancasters were dispatched from Tuddenham between 15.16 and 15.39 with six pilots of flight lieutenant rank the most senior on duty and each crew sitting on the standard bomb load. Conditions in the target area were ideal for bombing and a negligible amount of opposition allowed a highly concentrated attack to take place, the 90 Squadron participants delivering their payloads from 10,000 to 12,000 feet between 17.40 and 17.44. Not a single aircraft failed to return from any of the sites attacked on this penultimate day of operations against occupying forces around Le Havre. The final operations in this campaign were carried out on the following day in the absence of a 3 Group contribution, and shortly afterwards the German garrison surrendered to the two advancing British divisions.

On the 11th 3 Group detailed one hundred Lancasters to carry out an attack on the Chemwerke-Steinkohle synthetic oil refinery at Bergkamen on the north-eastern rim of the Ruhr. They were part of an overall force of 379 Lancasters, Halifaxes and Mosquitos assigned to some of the Ruhr's oil production sites, the rest of the force divided between the Klöckner Werke AG plant at Castrop-Rauxel and the Nordstern refinery in Gelsenkirchen. The three sites lay in a twenty-five-mile south-west to north-east straight line and the bombers would be shepherded all the way to their respective targets by a fighter escort of twenty Spitfire, three Mustang and three Tempest squadrons. The sixteen 90 Squadron Lancasters departed Tuddenham between 16.00 and 16.15 with F/Ls Cooper and Shepherd the senior pilots on duty and a cookie and sixteen 500-pounders in each bomb bay and flew out in formation to join up with the others, They found the target in excellent weather conditions and many crews were able to pick out ground detail as they approached in pairs, line astern. The red TIs were well-placed and clearly visible and the 90 Squadron crews carried out their attacks in accordance with the instructions of the Master Bomber from 17,000 to 20,000 feet between 18.39 and 18.43. The highly successful attack left clouds of black smoke rising to 15,000 feet as the bombers withdrew and they were approaching the Dutch coast homebound when ten 90 Squadron Lancasters took off between 19.31 and 19.40 bound for the long round-trip to the Geranium garden off the Baltic port of Swinemünde in the Bay of Pomerania. They were among thirty Lancasters of 3 Group assigned to four Baltic locations, and F/Ls Dobinson, Jennings and Stevens were the senior pilots on duty as they made their way across the North Sea, nine with five mines on board and one with six. They all reached the target area, where conditions were favourable to gardeners and night-fighters alike, and positions were established by H2S before the vegetables were planted from 11,000 to 12,000 feet between 23.21 and 23.29. ME838 failed to return with the crew of P/O Perrett, and the washing ashore in Sweden of one member of the crew confirmed that the Lancaster had found a final resting place in the Baltic.

Also on this night, 5 Group laid waste to the southern university city of Darmstadt, which was engulfed in a firestorm that killed in excess of twelve thousand people and rendered seventy thousand others homeless out of a population of 120,000.

The oil offensive continued on the 12th with the briefing of 412 crews on 4, 6 and 8 Group stations for daylight raids in the Ruhr on the Hydrierwerke refinery at Scholven-Buer to the north of Gelsenkirchen, the Krupp Treibstoffwerke at Wanne-Eickel to the east and the Hoesch-Benzin plant a dozen miles further east in the Wambel district of Dortmund. While these operations were in progress, preparations were in hand for major raids on the southern cities of Frankfurt and Stuttgart for forces respectively of 378 and 204 aircraft, the former of 1, 3 and 8 Groups and the latter predominantly of 5 Group. 3 Group put up 119 Lancasters, of which twenty-two represented 90 Squadron and took off between 18.20 and 18.45 with F/Ls Cooper, Dobinson, Jennings and Stevens the senior pilots on duty and a cookie and twelve 500lb cluster bombs in each bomb bay. F/O Hooper and crew lost their port-outer engine on take-off and proceeded directly to the jettison area, while the others joined the bomber stream heading south and exited the English coast at Beachy Head on course for landfall near Dieppe, enjoying clear skies all the way to the target. They had to run the gauntlet of night-fighters from 6° East, and it is likely that it was at this stage of the outward flight that PB193 was brought down to crash at Vitry-les-Nogent in the Haute Marne region of north-eastern France with no survivors from the crew of F/O Law. Favourable conditions prevailed at the target, where the many searchlights were supported by heavy flak, but this was not overly troublesome, and the crews were able to pick out ground detail such as the River Main and the railway yards. The first markers had fallen towards the south-west, but this was soon corrected by the Master Bomber and the main weight of bombs then fell into the more-industrialized western districts, those from the 90 Squadron contingent from 14,000 to 20,500 feet between 22.58 and 23.06. Fires began to spread rapidly, and it was clear to the crews that a successful raid had taken place. This would be the last major raid of the war on Frankfurt, and it cost seventeen Lancasters, including a second one from Tuddenham, HK605, which crashed in southern Germany with no survivors from the mixed RCAF/RAF crew of F/L Kirsch RCAF.

Meanwhile, some one hundred miles to the south, Stuttgart was also undergoing an ordeal, during which, according to a local historian, a firestorm occurred that erased the northern and western areas of the city centre and killed more than eleven hundred people.

With the Montgomery-inspired but ultimately ill-fated Operation Market Garden about to be launched to capture the Rhine bridges, in what history records as "The bridge too far" endeavour at Arnhem, Bomber Command prepared to support it with attacks against communications targets during the night of the 16/17th. 3 Group detailed forty-eight Lancasters to attack a railway bridge across the Hollandsch Diep at Moerdijk in the Scheldt estuary region of south-western Holland, and twenty-four of them were made ready at Tuddenham and loaded with eleven 1,000 and four 500-pounders each before taking off between 21.13 and 21.53 with F/Ls Cooper, Jennings, Shepherd and Stevens the senior pilots on duty. They found the precision target in favourable weather conditions and identified the aiming point visually and by red TIs, before releasing their bombs from 8,000 to 9,000 feet between 22.55 and 23.01. LM169 failed to return to Tuddenham with the crew of F/O Tooley, and it was established later that it had collided with 115 Squadron Lancaster, LM693, and both had crashed near Dordrecht, to the north-east of the target, without survivors. Photographic reconnaissance confirmed a successful operation and revealed that the bridge had been severed.

With Le Havre safely back in Allied hands and the work to make it useable progressing, attention turned upon Boulogne, for which a force of 762 aircraft was made ready for a morning attack on the 17th, a day celebrated as "Battle of Britain Sunday". 3 Group detailed a hundred Lancasters divided between two aiming points, the first of which was attacked from below the cloud base at 3,500 feet and was called off by the Master Bomber as the initial bombing became scattered. It is assumed that the second aiming point was also attacked from low level, as the light flak was described as troublesome. Returning crews reported that they had been able to identify landmarks and described the bombing as accurate. The attacks on German positions around Boulogne, during which three thousand tons of bombs were dropped, had the desired effect and the garrison surrendered shortly afterwards.

90 Squadron had not taken part in the above but was alerted later in the day to prepared twenty Lancasters to take part in a special operation, "Martet", a diversionary action in support of Operation Market Garden for which 3 Group provided forty Lancasters. The Tuddenham contingent each received a load of seven SBCs of incendiaries and took off between 19.13 and 19.27 with W/C Ogilvie the senior pilot on duty and the German frontier town of Emmerich, situated on the northern bank of the Rhine, as their destination. All reached the target, establishing their positions by Gee-fix, and all but one carried out an attack from 2,500 feet between 20.54 and 21.04. F/Sgt Shepherd and crew had to bring their SBCs home after a master switch on the navigator's table had been disabled during "windowing" and prevented their release. All returned safely with little to report, F/O Smith and crew returning LM618 to its ground crew with a few holes in a wing courtesy of light flak from Dordrecht aerodrome.

The long-serving F/L Kinch and crew had completed their first tour and Kinch was posted to 12 O.T.U on the 19th to pass on his skills to the incoming eager new crews. The first of six operations against enemy strong points around Calais was scheduled for the 20th, and a force of 646 aircraft made ready, of which 158 Lancasters were provided by 3 Group. The force was split among five aiming points, two to receive two visits, but there is no record of which were assigned to 3 Group and 90 Squadron's twenty-six Lancasters, each of which received a bomb load of eleven 1,000 and four 500-pounders before departing Tuddenham between 14.29 and 14.50 with F/Ls Cooper, Jennings and Shepherd the senior pilots on duty. They climbed away into cloudy conditions, which improved as they crossed the Channel, and had broken up considerably by the time that the target hove into view through a blanket of haze. The Tuddenham crews were in the first wave and identified the target visually and by red TIs as they carried out their attacks from 3,000 to 4,500 feet between 16.20 and 16.32. The squadron scribe had taken to providing extremely limited entries against each crew on the Form 541, and this was a common problem at various times within 3 Group, but it seems that the bombing was accurate and concentrated and represented a promising start to the campaign.

The weather remained unfavourable over the ensuing days, keeping most squadrons on the ground or restricted to training flights until the afternoon of the 23rd, when twenty-five crews were called to briefing at Tuddenham to be informed of an operation that night to Neuss, a city on the western bank of the Rhine opposite Düsseldorf on the south-western edge of the Ruhr. They were to be part of a force of 549 aircraft drawn from 1, 3, 4 and 8 Groups, of which 3 Group's contribution was 159 Lancasters, and each received a bomb load of eleven 1,000 and four 500-pounders before departing Tuddenham between 18.50 and 19.27 with F/Ls Cooper, Jennings and Stevens the senior pilots on duty, along with F/L Scott, who had been posted in from 31 Base two days earlier as a flight commander elect. F/O Hendry and crew lost their starboard-outer engine during the climb-out and proceeded to the jettison area, before landing at 20.15, and over the ensuing fifty-four minutes the crews of P/O Modeland, F/O Rowell and F/O Walton joined them on the ground, either because of a sick crew member or a technical failure. The others had set course for the Essex coast at Clacton-on-Sea, from which point the high cloud dispersed to leave ten-tenths cumulus all the way to the target area, where a standard ground-marking plan had been prepared. However, the sensitivity of the Oboe equipment led to the early return of ten Mosquitos, leaving the others to drop their red TIs into the tops of the ten-tenths cloud lying over the target at up to 10,000 feet. In the absence of skymarkers, crews could either aim at the glow of red TIs through the cloud or rely on H2S and Gee to establish their position, and some decided to bomb nearby Düsseldorf, which was more easily identified on H2S. All but two of the 90 Squadron participants carried out their attacks from 18,000 to 22,000 feet between 21.21 and 21.27, while those of F/Os Myers and Phillips were unable to positively identify either the target or an alternative and returned their bombs to the dump. At debriefings, crews reported explosions, flashes and the impression of fires beneath the cloud but an assessment was impossible. Bomber Command claimed that the main weight of the attack had fallen into the Rhine docks and factory areas, while a local report gave a figure of 617 houses and fourteen public buildings destroyed or seriously damaged.

The attacks on Calais resumed on the 24th as the poor weather continued, and 188 aircraft were assembled of which just thirty were provided by 3 Group. 90 Squadron loaded ten of its Lancasters with the usual load of 1,000 and 500-pounders and sent them on their way from

Tuddenham between 17.00 and 17.11 with F/L Cooper the senior pilot on duty. The low cloud and rainy conditions that accompanied the bombers on their way south improved somewhat in the target area, where the bombing was carried out by the 90 Squadron crews in good visibility from 1,800 to 2,000 feet between 17.49 and 17.53. Light flak was troublesome at such low level and a number of aircraft were hit, F/O Walton's PA167 sustaining damage to the port tailplane leading edge, the port wing, the port side of the nose and the starboard undercarriage. The pilot was wounded but was able to remain in his seat to bring the Lancaster home to a landing at Martlesham Heath, while fifteen miles to the north-east HK607 crash-landed at Friston in the hands of F/O Smith and the mid-upper gunner was treated for flak splinter wounds. Both Lancasters would be returned to duty.

The campaign intensified on the 25th, when 872 aircraft were made ready for a morning assault on enemy positions, for which 3 Group contributed 138 Lancasters including nineteen belonging to 90 Squadron. Each received the standard bomb load before departing Tuddenham between 08.01 and 08.17 with the newly promoted acting S/L Scott the senior pilot on duty. By the time that the French coast hove into view, 287 aircraft had already bombed through gaps in the low cloud, which the 90 Squadron crews found to be at 1,000 to 2,000 feet, which made it impossible to bomb from above because of an inability to see the ground, or from below because of the danger from the lethal light flak batteries. The Master Bomber had no option but to abandon the attack and send the remaining crews home with their bomb loads intact, and as no further operations were planned for the day, some no doubt took advantage of a night off to visit local watering holes.

It is to be hoped that they didn't overindulge, as 722 crews were hauled out of their beds very early on the following morning to get ready for a return to Calais. 90 Squadron crews were allowed to slumber on as they were not invited to be part of the one-hundred-strong 3 Group contingent. Of the seven aiming points, four were coastal batteries at Cap Gris Nez and three were closer to the town and all were accurately bombed unopposed from low level.

1, 3, 4 and 8 Groups joined forces to put together a force of 341 Lancasters and Halifaxes on the 27th, 120 of the former provided by 3 Group divided 40/80 between the two aiming points. The eighteen 90 Squadron Lancasters departed Tuddenham between 07.39 and 07.54 with F/L Jennings the senior pilot on duty and the usual bomb load on board, and all reached the target, where the Master Bomber instructed them to descend to 5,000 feet. The 90 Squadron crews largely complied and from that altitude were able to make a visual identification of the aiming point as they delivered their attacks from 5,000 to 6,000 feet between 08.56 and 08.59, contributing to effective attacks at both aiming points. The final operations against enemy positions around Calais took place on the 28th, when four were earmarked for attention, while six coastal batteries at Cap Gris Nez occupied the remainder of the 494 participating aircraft. 3 Group detailed eighty Lancasters split equally between two aiming points, for which the Tuddenham element of twelve Lancasters took off between 07.31 and 07.46 with W/C Ogilvie and S/L Scott the senior pilots on duty. They arrived in the target area to find a continuation of the unhelpful weather conditions, but chanced upon a gap in the cloud, through which they dropped their eleven 1,000 and four 500-pounders each from 4,000 to 7,000 feet between 09.01 and 09.09 before the gap closed. They were among sixty-eight crews to bomb at Calais, while the rest of the force was instructed to orbit for an extended period to allow the Master Bomber to consider his options. Ultimately, he sent them home with their bombs, as did the Master Bomber at Cap Gris Nez after two-thirds of the three-hundred-strong force had bombed. Canadian ground forces moved in shortly afterwards to accept the surrender of the German garrison, and thus all of the Channel ports were now back in Allied hands.

Acting S/L Burton was posted from the squadron at the end of an outstanding tour on the 28th, his destination SDL, the meaning of which has not been ascertained. During the course of the month the squadron took part in fifteen operations and dispatched 283 sorties for the loss of four Lancasters and crews.

October 1944

The new month began for 3 Group with stations on stand-by on the 1st and 2nd to support ground forces, but nothing came of it. During the previous month, preparations had been put in hand to capture the heavily-defended island of Walcheren in the Scheldt estuary, which was barring the approaches to the much-needed port of Antwerp. The coastal battery at Domburg had been the main target, but it had been decided now to attack the sea wall at Westkapelle, and allow the sea to inundate the land to make it difficult to defend when the ground forces went in. A force of 252 Lancasters and seven Mosquitos was made ready on the 3rd, and these included 120 of the former belonging to 3 Group and an element from 617 Squadron carrying Tallboys for use if necessary. The plan called for eight waves of thirty bombers each to attack the walls, and the seventeen representing 90 Squadron were divided seven/ten between the first two waves, departing Tuddenham between 11.45 and 11.55 and 12.15 and 12.21, with S/L Shepherd the senior pilot on duty and a cookie, six 1,000-pounders and a single 500-pounder in each bomb bay. They found cloud in the target area with a base at 3,000 to 4,000 feet and some crews had to make several attempts before releasing their bombs, mostly from 5,000 feet under the instructions of a Master Bomber, the 90 Squadron crews carrying out their attacks from 5,000 to 10,000 feet between 13.03 and 13.35. The first breach occurred during the fifth wave and subsequent attacks widened it to more than a hundred yards to leave flood water encroaching into the town of Westkapelle as the last crews retreated westwards.

The long-serving S/L Hodgson had now completed his outstanding tour as a flight commander, during which he had inspired his crews by leading from the front on many occasions, and was posted now for a much deserved rest to 22 O.T.U on the 4th. The mining of northern waters continued that night, when 90 Squadron contributed five of fifteen 3 Group Lancasters to gardening duties in one of the many Silverthorn gardens in the Kattegat off north-eastern Jutland. S/L Shepherd was the senior pilot on duty as they departed Tuddenham between 16.53 and 17.06 with five or six mines in each bomb bay and made their way across the North Sea to make landfall on Jutland's western coast. No clues were provided in the group and squadron ORBs to identify the garden in play, we know only that the 90 Squadron crews established their positions by H2S before fulfilling their briefs from 6,000 to 8,000 feet between 21.38 and 21.54.

While a 5 Group force carried out a scattered attack on Wilhelmshaven on the morning of the 5th, 531 other aircraft of 1, 3 and 8 Groups were being prepared for a two-phase operation that night against Saarbrücken in south-west-central Germany, the first attack on this city since September 1942. It was in response to a request from the American Third Army, which was advancing towards the German frontier in that region. The purpose of the first phase, to be delivered by 121 Lancasters of 3 Group with thirteen 101 Squadron ABC Lancasters providing RCM support, was to hit the marshalling yards to cut enemy rail communications, while the second phase by 239 Lancasters of 1 Group and sixty-three of 3 Group two hours later was to be directed at the city. 8 Group's ninety-six Lancasters and twenty Mosquitos were to be divided equally between the two phases to establish and maintain the aiming-points. They encountered ten-tenths low cloud over France until shortly before crossing the German frontier, when it became thin and broken and ground haze added to the visibility problems. The marking of the marshalling yards appeared to be compact, and the bombing took place on red and green TIs from an average of 15,000 feet shortly after 20.30, until at 20.36, the Master Bomber issued the code-word "Marmalade", the signal to cease bombing. It has been suggested that this was because of the close proximity of US ground forces, but other sources point to the fact that the Master Bomber and Deputy were unable to agree on which markers to aim for, and the squabble led to the abandonment of the attack after only half of the force had bombed.

The twenty-five participating 90 Squadron aircraft were assigned to the second phase, and each received a bomb load of nine 1,000 and four 500-pounders, before departing Tuddenham between 18.59 and 19.19 with S/L Scott the senior pilot on duty. They lost the services of F/O Smith and crew over the Reading area when the rear turret became unserviceable, leaving the others to traverse France and enter Germany to the south of Luxembourg and encounter three-tenths cloud at the target, through which the red and green TIs were clearly visible. The 90 Squadron crews carried out their attacks from 12,000 to 16,000 feet between 22.30 and 22.42 and most observed a large explosion at 22.40. Some crews from other squadrons reported several large explosions, one of particularly extensive proportions occurring at 22.45, from which smoke rose to 12,000 feet, and the city was well alight as the last of the bombers turned away to leave a glow in the sky visible for a hundred miles. The main town area north of the River Saar sustained massive damage and it was through this area that the railway lines passed and were severed. Local reports gave a figure of 5,882 houses destroyed with a further 1,140 seriously damaged and 344 fatalities, a modest figure in view of the level of destruction, and the likelihood is that the town's close proximity to the Siegfried Line had already prompted most of the residents to evacuate.

From this point until the end of the war, German towns and cities would fall victim to a rampant Bomber Command, and the opening rounds of a new Ruhr offensive began on the 6th with daylight attacks on the Ruhr-Benzin AG and Hydrierwerke-Scholven oil plants at Sterkrade-Holten and Scholven-Buer respectively by a combined 4 Group Halifax force of 254 aircraft supported by forty-six 8 Group Lancasters and twenty Mosquitos. Meanwhile, a 3, 6 and 8 Group force of 523 aircraft was assembled for an attack that night on Dortmund, 3 Group contributing 171 Lancasters, while the 248 Halifaxes and forty-five Lancasters provided by 6 Group would be 6 Group's largest single contribution of the war. 5 Group was also to be active, conducting what would prove to be the thirty-second and final raid of the war on the city of Bremen with a force of 237 Lancasters and seven Mosquitos. A signal to all stations from Bomber Command HQ on this day brought the news of a reduction in the length of a tour from thirty-five to thirty-three sorties, and this would be an unexpected bonus for some crews, who could spend the evening celebrating in the mess rather than exposing themselves to risk over Germany. However, this was not the final word on the length of a tour, which would take on the characteristics of a piece of elastic. Each of the twenty-six 90 Squadron Lancasters received a bomb load of a cookie and fourteen Nº 14 incendiary cluster bombs before departing Tuddenham between 16.33 and 17.04 with W/C Ogilvie and S/L Shepherd the senior pilots on duty. All reached the target to find clear weather conditions and well-placed red and green TIs, which were bombed by the Tuddenham brigade in concentrated fashion from 18,000 to a lofty 25,000 feet between 20.26 and 20.41 to produce explosions and many fires. The flak was less intense than expected, with shells seen to explode well below the level of the bombers, and night-fighters were few, and returning crews commented also on the fires still burning in Gelsenkirchen following the afternoon raid. Post-raid reconnaissance revealed heavy damage in industrial and residential districts and to transportation, and a relatively modest death toll of around two hundred people suggested that a large number of residents had evacuated the city.

Orders were received across the Command on the 7th to prepare for daylight attacks on the German frontier towns of Cleves (Kleve) and Emmerich prompted by the failure of Operation Market Garden, which, as a consequence, had left the Allied right flank exposed and vulnerable to a German counter-attack. Five miles apart and separated by the Rhine, both would face large forces, Cleves of 351 Halifaxes and Lancasters from 3, 4 and 8 Groups and Emmerich of 340 Lancasters and ten Mosquitos from 1, 3 and 8 Groups. 3 Group detailed eighty Lancasters for Cleves and seventy-five for Emmerich and it was for the former that 90 Squadron loaded each of its twenty-four Lancasters with eleven 1,000 and four 500-pounders before sending them on their way from Tuddenham between 11.20 and 11.42 with S/Ls Scott and Shepherd the senior pilots on duty. They flew in over The Hague and stirred the local flak batteries into action and a number of aircraft sustained damage, mostly superficial, from flak splinters, but all arrived in the target area to find favourable conditions, which they exploited to deliver their high explosive payloads in accordance with the Master Bomber's instructions from 9,000 to 14,000 feet between 14.04 and 14.10. Many explosions and fires were observed in central and northern districts until smoke concealed the ground from view, but it was clear that the town had undergone an ordeal. F/O Rouse and crew returned on two-and-half engines courtesy of flak and technical gremlins, while F/Sgt Turton and crew reported losing their starboard-outer engine before bombing and shedding height. The decision was taken to bomb the southern fringe of the town rather than risk being hit by bombs from above if they pressed on to the designated aiming point.

On the 9th, the fourteen crews that represented 90 Squadron's C Flight were, on paper at least, posted across the tarmac to form the nucleus of the reforming 186 Squadron, which had originally been reformed as a fight-bomber unit in April 1943 and had since lost its number. It would share Tuddenham for the next ten weeks under the command of W/C Giles, who, it will be recalled, had commanded 90 Squadron during the second half of 1943. The permanent station staff would remember him fondly, but such was the turnover of a front-line bomber squadron that few of the current aircrew would recognise him. The two squadrons would operate as one for the ensuing week-and-a-half while the freshman crews were brought up to speed and W/C Giles would put himself on the Order of Battle to banish any cobwebs acquired while flying a desk.

After Emmerich, 3 Group remained on stand-by to support ground forces but was not called upon and an entire week passed without operations. The 14th brought the opening salvoes of

Operation Hurricane, a terrifying demonstration to the enemy of the overwhelming superiority of the Allied air forces ranged against it. Bomber Command ordered a maximum effort from all but 5 Group to attack Duisburg, for which 1,013 Lancasters, Halifaxes and Mosquitos answered the call. The American 8th Air Force would also be in business on this day, targeting the Cologne area further south with 1,250 bombers escorted by 749 fighters. 3 Group briefed 196 crews, a record twenty-nine of them at Tuddenham, twenty-one of which received a bomb load of eleven 1,000 and four 500-pounders and the rest a cookie and fourteen Nº14 incendiary cluster bombs, before taking off between 06.10 and 06.46 with W/C Giles the senior pilot on duty. Not a single Tuddenham Lancaster turned back early and, in fact, only two from 3 Group dropped out before the Path Finder spearhead arrived over the city's western suburbs to find drifting cloud in layers at between 8,000 and 14,000 feet. This created challenges for the Master Bombers, who had five aiming points to control, not all of which could be identified, and instructions were issued to main force crews to bomb the built-up area generally. Some of the 3 Group crews observed the ground through gaps in the cloud, while others tried to use G-H, but found the release pulse to be weak. Many of the 90 Squadron crews picked out the distinctive Ruhrort docks complex, Germany's largest inland dock facility, while others pinpointed on the marshalling yards and carried out their attacks from 17,000 to 20,000 feet between 09.02 and 09.09. They contributed to a total of 4,500 tons of high-explosives and incendiaries that fell into the city to cause unimaginable destruction at a cost to the Command of thirteen Lancasters and a single Halifax.

That night, 1,005 aircraft were detailed to take part in a second raid on Duisburg, which would be conducted in two waves, two hours apart, and would press home the point about superiority. Such was the efficiency of the ground crews on all 3 Group stations that 193 Lancasters were ready at take-off time, twenty-eight of them at Tuddenham, all but one of which carried a bomb load of eleven 1,000 and four 500-pounders. W/C Giles and S/L Shepherd were the senior pilots on duty as take-off began at 22.18, and four minutes later, HK610 swung and left the runway in the hands of P/O Clayden, who was able to bring it to a halt without serious damage, and the crew's participation was scrubbed. It was not uncommon for such incidents to act as a harbinger of more serious events in the near future. Take-offs continued until 22.57 and again there were no early returns to Tuddenham, although a dozen other 3 Group crews did abandon their sorties. The first wave crews, including those from Tuddenham, picked up the target from some distance out by the glow of fires still burning from the morning raid, and found it to be under clear skies. Marking was superfluous but went ahead never-the-less, and red TIs provided a reference point at the designated aiming points as the 90 Squadron crews carried out their attacks from 18,000 to 23,000 feet between 01.28 and 01.35. The burning city stood out even more clearly for the second wave main force crews, who aimed their bombs at red and green TIs in accordance with the instructions of the Master Bomber, and the glow from the tortured city was still visible from the Dutch coast as the bombers reached the safety of the North Sea. This time five Lancasters and two Halifaxes failed to return and among the former was LM165, which disappeared without trace with the 186 Squadron crew of F/Sgt Cook RAAF. More than 4,000 tons of bombs fell into the city with greater concentration than earlier in the day and Duisburg ceased to exist as a functioning city. The commitment of 2,018 aircraft to Duisburg in under twenty-four hours was a massive achievement by the Command, and this figure did not include the 233 Lancasters and seven Mosquitos sent by 5 Group to Braunschweig while the evening raid was in progress. After surviving previous attempts to deliver a crushing blow, Braunschweig's heart was finally torn out as the old town was reduced to rubble.

There was no immediate respite from operations as preparations were put in hand on the 15th to attack Wilhelmshaven that night. Crews would have done their best to catch up on sleep as the work of the day went on around them, and some of those who had landed at dawn were up, briefed and fed in time to join others for an early evening take-off in an overall force of 506 aircraft drawn from all but 5 Group on what would turn out to be the last of fourteen major raids on this naval and ship-building port. 3 Group contributed seventy Lancasters to the main event, thirteen of them belonging to 90 Squadron, which departed Tuddenham between 17.26 and 17.47 with S/L Shepherd the senior pilot on duty and eleven 1,000 and three 500-pounders in each bomb bay. The skies were clear until the midpoint of the North-Sea crossing, when cloud gradually built-up to ten-tenths thin stuff with tops at around 2,000 feet. The ground markers could be seen, however, and their accuracy confirmed by aircraft equipped with H2S, but what may have been spoof green TIs were reported some five miles to the west and north-west of the target, and these attracted some bomb loads. The 90 Squadron crews bombed from 12,000 to 21,000 feet between 19.48 and 19.55, aiming at red and green TIs, fires and release-point flares, before all but one returned safely to report a scattered attack. Absent from debriefing was the crew of F/O Clayden, who had all perished when PD341 was brought down by naval flak to crash at 20.05 on open ground near Norden, a coastal region some forty miles west of the target.

3 Group was now ready to conduct daylight operations using G-H, a system based on the original Gee principle, which required bombers to fly to the target in a loose formation called a gaggle, and within that, were smaller sub-formations of three or four aircraft each, as designated by the squadron. The gaggle had an appointed leader and within each vic or box, there was a G-H leader, who carried the G-H equipment and was able to locate the aiming point by a radio signal and a beam arc, similar to that employed by Oboe. As the gaggle neared the target, formations tightened up, then as each G-H leader detected the trigger pulse and dropped his bombs, the two or three accompanying aircraft would release theirs also. The approach was similar to the system used by the Americans, but unlike that, G-H could be used at night. In order to make them stand out in a gaggle, the Lancasters of G-H leaders had their tailfins painted with clearly-identified twin yellow bands to enable those following to attach themselves.

It was necessary to carry out a large-scale trial of the method, for which the virtually virgin city of Bonn was selected on the 18th, so that assessment of the results would not be compromised by previous damage. 3 Group prepared a force of 128 Lancasters, of which fourteen were provided by 90 Squadron, whose crews had actually been briefed on the 17th and were close to take-off when a cancellation order came through. The same crews now departed Tuddenham between 08.12 and 08.22 with S/L Scott the senior pilot on duty and a cookie and fourteen N° 14 incendiary cluster bombs in each bomb bay. This operation marked the independence of 186 Squadron, which would operate in its own right for the first time. F/O Hooper and crew dropped out soon after take-off because of engine failure, and for the remainder it proved harder than expected to form up into the planned vics of three aircraft, each with a G-H leader, and some leaders found themselves alone, while others had four of five in their section. The meteorological brains had promised ten-tenths cloud over the target, but crews were greeted by three to five tenths cloud and a heavier than anticipated flak defence, which broke up the formations. An additional problem was a fading of the G-H release pulse, and some crews decided to bomb visually rather than wait for their leaders. Some 90 Squadron crews latched onto a G-H leader, while others bombed visually from 16,500 to 18,500 feet between 11.00 and 11.10. Those persevering with G-H produced good results, however, and the operation was surprisingly successful given the difficulties, which would be overcome in time with practice. The heart of the city was left devastated with seven hundred buildings destroyed and a further one thousand seriously damaged, and it was achieved for the loss of a single Lancaster.

When orders came through on 1, 3, 6 and 8 Group stations on the 19th for an all-Lancaster attack that night on Stuttgart, 3 Group detailed 176 aircraft, eighteen of them representing 90 Squadron. They were part of an overall force of 565 aircraft, which would form two waves separated by four-and-a-half hours with seven of the 90 Squadron crews assigned to the first wave and eleven to the second. The former took off between 17.17 and 17.23 with S/L Shepherd the senior pilot on duty and a cookie and six 1,000-pounders in each bomb bay and reached the target to find nine-tenths cloud and both sky and ground marking in progress. Most bombed on the "Wanganui" skymarkers from 18,000 to 19,000 feet between 20.23 and 20.29, but some picked up the glow of TIs through the cloud and aimed for these. They were well on their way home as the second-phase aircraft began to take to the Cambridgeshire skies between 21.49 and 22.08 led by F/L Reid as the senior pilot. Six of them carried a cookie and six 1,000-pounders each, while five supplemented their cookie with ten of the new deeper SBCs, each of which contained 150 x 4lb incendiaries. By the time they arrived over southern Germany, the cloud had increased, and bombing took place on skymarkers and the glow of fires burning from the earlier attack from 16,000 to 18,000 feet between 01.04 and 01.11. It was impossible to assess the outcome, but it was established later that central and eastern districts had sustained substantial damage, as had a number of outlying towns, and the important Bosch factory had been hit.

Five 90 Squadron Lancasters were detailed for mining duties in the Kattegat on the 21st, but the operation was cancelled at the last minute, but not before F/L Watkinson and crew had actually taken off and had to be recalled.

An operation to Essen planned for the 22nd was also cancelled and a G-H attack on Neuss substituted for the 3 Group element of one hundred Lancasters. A dozen 90 Squadron Lancasters each received a bomb load of a cookie and eleven SBCs each containing 150 x 4lb incendiaries and departed Tuddenham between 13.01 and 13.14 with F/L Spanhake the senior pilot on duty. Forming up again proved to be difficult, but all from 90 Squadron reached Neuss to find it completely concealed by cloud, which was negated by the efficiency of G-H, and the bombing took place from 16,000 to 19,000 feet between 15.54 and 16.02. Post-raid reconnaissance revealed the attack to have been accurate and concentrated and the operation was considered to be another success for the G-H system. The mining expedition to the Kattegat was rescheduled for later that evening, for which five 90 Squadron Lancasters departed Tuddenham between 16.13 and 16.17 with S/L Scott leading the way and six mines in each bomb bay. They were bound for the Silverthorn III garden, which they found under ten-tenths cloud and established their positions by H2S, pinpointing on the northern tip of Samsø Island and Ebeltoft on the mainland to the north. The vegetables were planted according to brief from 7,000 to 9,400 feet between 19.48 and 19.59 after timed runs of up to six minutes, during which some nineteen miles would have been covered, and all returned safely to describe good trips and a successful night's work.

The Essen raid was rescheduled for the 23rd, for which a record force of 1,055 aircraft was assembled and loaded with 4,538 tons of bombs, more than 90% of which was high explosive, and once again this massive effort would be achieved without the involvement of 5 Group. Of 561 Lancasters, 171 were provided by 3 Group and sixteen by 90 Squadron, which departed Tuddenham between 16.46 and 17.01 with W/C Ogilvie the senior pilot on duty and a cookie and twelve SBCs of 4lb incendiaries in each bomb bay. They climbed into scattered cloud on their way south to exit England over the Sussex coast at Beachy Head and set course for the French coast and a southerly approach to the target over heavy cloud. This would take them through the narrow corridor between Cologne and Mönchengladbach and up into the central Ruhr, and by the time that the target hove into view, the cloud had become ten-tenths up to 14,000 feet. The Path Finders had prepared a ground and skymarking plan to cover this precise eventuality, and once the Oboe TIs had been swallowed up by the cloud, red skymarker flares were released at 19.28 to be followed by greens three minutes later. Bombing by the 90 Squadron crews took place from 16,000 to 22,000 feet between 19.45 and 19.54 onto what was left of the built-up area, and although it proved impossible to observe the fall of the bombs, an intense glow on the cloud told its own story that there was still plenty of combustible material in the tortured city. Local reports confirmed the destruction of 607 buildings with a further eight hundred seriously damaged and a death toll of 667 people.

Not yet finished with Essen, the command dispatched a reduced force to it of 771 aircraft on the 25th, for which 3 Group detailed 170 Lancasters and 90 Squadron eighteen, each loaded with a cookie and a dozen SBCs of 4lb incendiaries. S/Ls Scott and Shepherd were the senior pilots on duty as they departed Tuddenham between 12.42 and 12.56, and after climbing out adopted a route that took them across Belgium to enter Germany near Aachen, from where they proceeded to the target in cloudy, but quite favourable weather conditions. They encountered ten-tenths cloud with tops at between 6,000 and 12,000 feet during the run-up to the target, but isolated breaks appeared, which allowed crews to assess the accuracy of the red and yellow TIs in relation to the Krupp complex or simply to bomb visually or on skymarkers. The master Bomber ordered the red TIs to be ignored in favour of the yellows, which appeared to be a little to the north of the aiming-point, before a massive explosion close by at 15.29 created a pall of smoke, which the Master Bomber was then able to employ as the focus for the rest of the bombing. The 90 Squadron crews delivered their payloads from 15,000 to 23,000 feet between 15.36 and 15.47 and contributed to a more concentrated attack than that achieved by the larger force thirty-six hours earlier. Post-raid reconnaissance and local sources revealed that 1,163 buildings had been destroyed and the Krupp steel works badly damaged, but most of the city's industry had been moved out, meaning that this one-time powerhouse of war production had ceased to be so.

Leverkusen, a city on the eastern bank of the Rhine north of Cologne, was posted as the target for a 3 Group G-H attack on the 26th, for which 104 Lancasters were made ready. It was home to the Bayer arm of the infamous I G Farben conglomerate that was massively supporting Germany's war effort as a major producer of synthetic oil and chemicals. Sixteen 90 Squadron Lancasters each received a bomb load of either a cookie and six 1,000-pounders or a cookie and thirteen SBCs of 4lb incendiaries before departing Tuddenham between 12.50 and 13.17 with S/L Scott the senior pilot on duty. The forming up procedure went well, as did the attack by the 90 Squadron element through ten-tenths cloud from 15,000 to 18,000 feet between 15.28 and 15.31. The release pulse was fixed upon the Bayer chemicals factory, and although it was not possible to assess the results, it was believed that the operation had been successful, and no aircraft had been lost.

An early briefing for 277 crews on the 28th prepared them for operations against five coastal batteries on the Island of Walcheren at the mouth of the Scheldt. Seventy-six Lancasters of 3 Group were assigned the three sites near Flushing (Vlissingen) on the south-western corner, and the eight belonging to 90 Squadron departed Tuddenham between 08.15 and 08.21 with S/L Shepherd the senior pilot on duty and bomb loads of either a cookie and six 1,000 and two 500-pounders or eleven 1,000 and four 500-pounders in the bomb bays. The skies were clear and positions established by a visual identification of the harbour and canal and the attacks were delivered from 7,000 to 8,000 feet between 10.01 and 10.04. The bombing appeared to be concentrated around the aiming point and an explosion was observed followed by black smoke. HK602 must have been hit by the accurate light flak as four parachutes were seen to deploy before the Lancaster hit the ground, but two crew members landed in the sea and were drowned, while two others fell among the bomb detonations, and sadly, none of the crew of F/O Higgins survived.

While this operation was in progress, other elements of the Command were preparing for a major Hurricane-style assault on Cologne involving 733 aircraft, eighty-four of the Lancasters provided by 3 Group. 90 Squadron loaded each of its eleven aircraft with a cookie and twelve N° 14 incendiary cluster bombs and sent them on their way from Tuddenham between 13.00 and 13.10 with F/Ls Reid, Rowell and Verroneau the senior pilots on duty. The operation was to be conducted in two phases, with one aiming-point in the district of Müllheim, to the north-east of the city centre, and the other in Zollstock to the south-west, both with major marshalling yards in the vicinity. The bomber stream encountered a weather front over the North Sea on their way to making landfall on the French coast in the Dunkerque region, and a dozen Halifaxes turned back as a result, it is believed, because of icing that affected engines and prevented them from climbing. The others pressed on to the target, where five to ten-tenths cloud prevailed, through which red TIs were glimpsed by some on the ground at aiming point G, which is believed to be the Müllheim district. The bombing was carried out visually or on red skymarkers from 18,000 to 20,000 feet from around 16.00 onwards and extensive fires were observed that remained visible for a hundred miles into the return journey. A large explosion was reported at 16.04 in the Zollstock district following a direct hit on a factory, and smoke was rising through 15,000 feet from Müllheim as the force retreated. The ORB provides no real clue as to which aiming point was attacked by the 90 Squadron element, as crews described a bend in the river and a Rhine bridge, features common to both. We know only that they attacked from 19,000 to 20,000 feet between 15.45 and 15.48 and that W/O Kluczny's PB196 was hit by flak at 20,000 feet during the bombing run and the mid-upper gunner sustained a head wound. F/O Wade and crew made reference to the area to the east of the river being well alight, which suggests that aiming point G was the squadron's designated target. Despite reservations about the quality of the bombing of aiming-point H, both aiming-points had been devastated, local reports confirming the destruction of 2,239 blocks of flats and fifteen industrial premises, along with many other buildings of a public nature. Severe damage had also been inflicted upon power stations, transportation and railway installations and river docks facilities.

1, 3, 4 and 8 Groups put together a force of 358 aircraft on the 29th to attack eleven German positions resisting the Allied advance across Walcheren. 3 Group detailed seventy-five Lancasters for a return to Flushing to attend to the three coastal batteries, 90 Squadron providing eight, each loaded with eleven 1,000 and four 500-pounders before departing Tuddenham between 09.28 and 09.43 with a bunch of pilots of flight lieutenant rank taking the lead. They encountered favourable weather conditions over the Scheldt estuary with large gaps in the cloud, and two of the sites were bombed with great accuracy, the 90 Squadron contingent attacking red and green TIs from a uniform 8,000 feet between 11.00 and 11.03 under the guidance of the Master Bomber. The markers at the third aiming point, near Westkapelle, to which the Kiwi crews were assigned, were not as well-placed, however, and attracted a proportion of the bombing, although some crews ignored the markers and bombed visually under the instructions of the Master Bomber.

The next G-H operation by 3 Group was mounted on the morning of the 30th against the Union Rheinische Braunkohlen-Kraftstoff A G oil refinery at Wesseling on the western bank of the Rhine to the south of Cologne. 102 Lancasters were prepared, of which a dozen represented 90 Squadron and departed Tuddenham between 09.00 and 09.18 with F/Ls Reid, Rowell and Watkinson the senior pilots on duty and a cookie and sixteen 500-pounders in each bomb bay. As they approached the target over a layer of ten-tenths cloud, some crews picked up a false release pulse, which was discovered later to have come from a new G-H station testing its equipment. Their bombs fell five miles short of the intended aiming point, but the others pushed on and carried out what was believed to be an accurate attack, those from 90 Squadron releasing their loads as those of the G-H leaders' fell away from 16,000 to 18,000 feet between 11.57 and 11.59. No assessment was possible, but returning crews were confident in the effectiveness of their work.

Later that evening, 90 Squadron made ready seven of its Lancasters as part of a 3 Group contribution of ninety-nine to an overall "Hurricane" force of 905 aircraft, the destination for which was Cologne, or that which remained standing in the Rhineland capital city. They departed Tuddenham between 17.55 and 18.04 with S/L Shepherd the senior pilot on duty and a cookie in each bomb bay, supplemented with either six 1,000 and six 500-pounders or twelve Nº 14 incendiary cluster bombs. They climbed away into ten-tenths cloud with a full moon shining brightly above to reveal the presence of the vast armada of bombers, and over the Channel the cloud tops reached 20,000 feet. They had lowered to 10,000 to 15,000 feet as the target drew near, and main force crews were greeted by red and white marker flares delivered by nine of the Oboe Mosquitos. They drifted in concentrated fashion into the cloud tops, and main force crews confirmed their accuracy by Gee and H2S before carrying out their attacks, those from 90 Squadron from 19,000 to 22,000 feet between 21.02 and 21.04. Fortunately, the Luftwaffe Nachtjagd failed to appear and missed a golden opportunity provided by the conditions to score heavily. Apart from the glow of fires lighting up the cloud, it was impossible to assess what was happening on the ground and the expectation at Bomber Command HQ was of a scattered attack with light damage. The reality, however, was destruction on a massive scale, particularly in the suburbs, where civilian housing suffered most, but railways and public utilities were also hit, plunging the tortured city into a deeper state of chaos. The operation was concluded without loss to further demonstrate the overwhelming superiority of Allied air power.

3 Group detailed 101 Lancasters on the 31st for a G-H raid on a Fischer-Tropsch process coal liquefaction oil plant located in the Welheim district of Bottrop, situated on the northern edge of the Ruhr, for which 90 Squadron made ready a dozen Lancasters. They departed Tuddenham between 11.55 and 12. 14 with pilots of flight lieutenant rank leading the way and a cookie and sixteen 500 pounders in each bomb bay. They flew out in vics of three behind a G-H leader, who were carrying flares, which were to be released with the bombs so that any crews not able to bomb with the leader could aim for them on a given heading. The operation seemed to progress according to plan in the face of an intense flak barrage, the 90 Squadron element bombing from 15,000 to 18,000 feet between 15.01 and 15.03. Only one Lancaster failed to make it home, and sadly that was 90 Squadron's PD269, which came down in the general target area taking the lives of F/L Ward RNZAF and his crew. F/L Ward was a highly experienced pilot who had completed at least thirty-three sorties, and his presence and that of his crew would be missed by the squadron and station communities.

Cologne's torment was not yet over, as a force of 493 aircraft was prepared for another attack on it that night, for which 3 Group detailed seventy-one Lancasters and 90 Squadron just three, which each received a bomb load of a cookie and six 1,000 and six 500-pounders. The crews of F/Sgt Turton, F/O Kaiser and W/O Kluczny departed Tuddenham between 18.15 and 18.20 and reached the Rhineland capital to be greeted by ten-tenths thick cloud with tops at 6,000 to 10,000 feet, by which time proceedings had begun with red and white flares delivered by Oboe Mosquitos at 20.56. These were backed up in what appeared to be concentrated fashion by greens from the Path Finder heavy marker element, and the main force crews established their positions by Gee and H2S-fix. The 90 Squadron trio attacked from 20,000 feet between 21.03 and 21.11 and observed the bombing to be concentrated around the markers as they sank slowly towards the cloud tops. Returning crews could only report on the glow of fires in the clouds and the lack of opposition and it was difficult for post-raid reconnaissance to determine how much additional damage had been caused, but it seems that the main weight of the attack had fallen into southern districts.

During the course of this very busy month the squadron participated in twenty-two operations, more than half of them by daylight, and dispatched a record 336 sorties for the loss of four Lancasters and crews.

November 1944

Operations began for 3 Group on the 2nd, with a G-H attack on the Rheinpreussen (Meerbeck) oil refinery at Moers/Homberg opposite Duisburg, the scene of an unhappy night for the group back in July. It was mounted to follow up on an unsuccessful attempt by 5 Group on the previous day, and that in itself was sufficient to produce a warm glow of satisfaction in the 3 Group briefing rooms. The fact that the much-vaunted 5 Group, highly successful as it was, and with the "glamour boys" of 617 Squadron grabbing all the headlines, had been shown to be fallible, and that 3 Group had been chosen to rectify its failure, was a matter of great pride. 184

Lancasters were detailed, drawn from all ten of the group's "squadrons of the line", with seventeen of them representing 90 Squadron, and the crews were further cheered by the news that two hundred Spitfires would shepherd them to and from the target. They departed Tuddenham between 11.07 and 11.19 with F/Ls Rowell, Spanhake and Verroneau the senior pilots on duty and a cookie and twelve M17 cluster bombs in each bomb bay. They were given a time-on-target of 14.00 and a forecast of scattered light cloud with minimal ground haze. The plan called for a bombing height of 20,000 feet and the usual G-H method to be employed, but not all aircraft were assigned to a G-H Leader, and these additional crews were instructed to bomb on "Wanganui" flares dropped by the leaders at the same time as their bombs. This last point suited all self-respecting bomb-aimers, who much preferred to bomb on their own equipment, rather than watch the bomb bays of their G-H leaders. The cloud in the target area turned out to be five-tenths as the attack began, the 90 Squadron crews delivering their payloads from 18,000 to 22,000 feet between 14.00 and 14.03, and although the bombing would be described by some returning crews from other squadrons as scattered, the Tuddenham crews were more positive and reported explosions in and around the oil plant and large fires and a thick column of black smoke as they turned away. Flak opposition was moderate to intense and five Lancasters failed to return, while many others bore the scars of battle.

That night 992 aircraft took off to attack Düsseldorf in the absence of a contribution from 3 Group, and those reaching the target destroyed or seriously damaged five thousand houses in predominantly northern districts, while reducing further the city's capacity to support the war effort.

The medium sized town of Solingen, situated on the south-eastern edge of the Ruhr, had built a reputation over centuries as the centre for high quality sword, knife and scissor manufacture, and it was probably its iron foundries that made it a target now, at a time when the Ruhr's major industrial centres had been reduced to rubble. It was posted on the 4th as the target for a G-H raid by 177 Lancasters of 3 Group, of which eighteen were made ready at Tuddenham and each loaded with a cookie and six 1,000 and six 500-pounders. They took off between 11.31 and 11.46 with no fewer than eight pilots of flight lieutenant rank leading the way and found seven to ten-tenths cloud in the target area, which allowed some crews a sight of the built-up area. The 90 Squadron crews attacked from 18,000 to 22,000 feet between 14.04 and 14.08 and the operation seemed to go well with little flak opposition, but four aircraft failed to return, which, in the absence of flak and fighters, perplexed the planners at 3 Group HQ. Curiously, three of the missing Lancasters belonged to 195 Squadron at Witchford, and a number of reports suggested that "friendly" bombs may have been responsible for their demise, the fact that two of these exploded with great force over the target seeming to support that conclusion. That night more than seven hundred aircraft from 1, 4, 6 and 8 Groups attacked Bochum, home among other war industry factories to the Bochumer Verein steelworks and destroyed or seriously damaged four thousand buildings. The Luftwaffe chose this night to make its presence felt, and twenty-three Halifaxes and five Lancasters failed to return.

The raid on Solingen was repeated on the following day at the hands of a 3 Group G-H force of 172 Lancasters, of which eighteen belonged to 90 Squadron, and this time the cookie in each bomb bay was supplemented with twelve Nº 14 incendiary cluster bombs. They departed Tuddenham between 09.46 and 10.00 with the recently posted-in S/L Crossley the senior pilot on duty for the first time, and all reached the target to encounter ten-tenths cloud and little opposition from the ground. The attack appeared to be concentrated and was described by returning crews as the best G-H performance yet, but this was based on the cohesion of the gaggle and individual G-H leader elements rather than an assessment of what was happening beneath the cloud. Local sources described a town reduced to ruins, with 1,300 houses destroyed along with eighteen industrial premises and sixteen hundred other buildings seriously damaged with up to eighteen hundred people killed. Just one Lancaster failed to return, and this XV Squadron aircraft was seen to be hit by falling bombs.

A force of 738 aircraft was assembled during the morning of the 6th to send against Gelsenkirchen, where the Nordstern synthetic oil plant was the specific aiming point. The raid became somewhat scattered, but more than five hundred aircraft had bombed the approximate area of the refinery before smoke obscured the ground. It was difficult to assess the outcome, but local reports suggested extensive damage to the town in general. 3 Group did not participate in this operation but was called into action later in the day to provide 128 Lancasters for a G-H raid on Koblenz, an old city nestling in the confluence of the Rivers Rhine and Mosel some forty miles south-east of Cologne. The force should have been larger but bombing-up problems at Methwold led to the cancellation of twenty-one aircraft. A cookie was winched into each of the eleven 90 Squadron Lancasters, to be supplemented with a variety of other ordnance including cluster bombs and SBCs of 4lb and 30lb incendiaries. They departed Tuddenham between 16.34 and 17.06 with S/L Scott the senior pilot on duty and climbed out into favourable conditions with excellent visibility, which persisted throughout the outward flight and enabled them to identify the target visually. The TIs that dropped with the G-H leaders' bombs were tightly bunched as they fell towards the built-up area, and the pattern of streets and waterways was plain to see in their light. In fact, only seventeen of an intended forty-five aircraft delivered TIs, but this was more than adequate and the 90 Squadron crews exploited the opportunity to carry out their attacks from 17,000 to 18,000 feet between 19.29 and 19.35. The operation was hugely destructive and left half of the town in ruins, with the glow from the extensive fires visible on the horizon for seventy miles into the return journey.

The second attack of the month on the Meerbeck oil refinery at Homberg was mounted on the 8th by a 3 Group G-H force of 136 Lancasters, a dozen of which were provided by 90 Squadron and each loaded with either eleven 1,000 and four 500-pounders or a cookie, cluster bombs and SBCs of incendiaries. They departed Tuddenham between 07.53 and 08.07 with five pilots of flight lieutenant rank leading the way and struggled in the early stages to form up into a cohesive gaggle in the cloudy conditions. Despite the challenges, all reached the target, where they released their payloads from 16,000 to 18,000 feet between 10.32 and 10.37, when a large gap in the clouds over the north-western corner of the Ruhr allowed them to confirm that their bombs were on the mark and that the site was burning fiercely and belching black smoke into the air. The flak was heavy and accurate, and some aircraft were hit, HK610 returning in the hands of F/O Grass and crew with extensive damage to its port wing and fuselage.

Crews were out of their beds early on the 11th as preparations were put in hand for an attack on the town of Heinsberg, which together with Düren and Jülich, stand in an arc north to east of Aachen, where American forces were about to break through. In the event, the operation was cancelled, and the ordeal facing the residents of these towns would ultimately be postponed for five days. However, as 122 crews were washed, fed and primed for action, they were called to briefing rooms to learn that a new target awaited them, the Klöckner Werke A G synthetic oil plant at Castrop-Rauxel in the north-eastern Ruhr, to which, as usual, they would be accompanied by a heavy fighter escort. The twelve 90 Squadron Lancasters each received a bomb load of a cookie and sixteen 500-pounders before departing Tuddenham between 07.55 and 08.10 with S/L Shepherd the senior pilot on duty, and all reached the target which lay under a blanket of cloud with tops at 8,000 to 9,000 feet. According to some crews, the G-H marker flares drifted with concentration into the cloud-tops and the bombing proceeded according to plan, while others claimed a degree of chaos as aircraft bombed on a variety of headings. The 90 squadron participants bombed from 17,000 to 22,000 feet between 11.04 and 11.08 and believed the attack to be effective, and their main concern was the heavy flak coming up at them from the Arnhem area on the way in, which inflicted damage to a number of aircraft.

That afternoon, the crews of F/L Spanhake and F/O Orr took off at 15.43 and 15.45 with six mines in each bomb bay destined for planting in the Onion garden off Horten in Oslo Fjord, where they would be joined by eight others from the group. They established their pinpoints visually on the harbour and Jelo island and confirmed them on H2S, before planting successfully from 10,000 feet at 19.47 and 19.50 and returning to land at Tain in Scotland after seven hours aloft.

After operations against a variety of intended targets were cancelled on the 13th, 14th and 15th, fifteen of the squadron's Lancasters was each loaded with a cookie and sixteen 500-pounders, while their crews attended briefing to learn of their part in a G-H raid by 177 Lancasters on the Hoesch-Benzin oil plant in the Wambel district of Dortmund at the eastern end of the Ruhr. No fewer than seven pilots of flight lieutenant rank took the lead as the 90 Squadron contingent lifted off the runway at Tuddenham and climbed out to head for the rendezvous point, where the forming-up procedure went well on this occasion, and at the target, the concentration of flares and bombing by the G-H leaders was described as very good. The 90 Squadron crews carried out their attacks from 17,000 to 21,000 feet between 15.39 and 15.45 in the face of intense flak in the early stages, but it diminished somewhat towards the end having been responsible for the loss of two Lancasters. Returning crews were unable to offer an assessment of the raid because of the ten-tenths cloud with tops at 10,000 feet, but it was believed to have been successful.

The previously mentioned postponed operations against the towns of Düren, Jülich and Heinsberg, which were standing in the way of an American advance in the area of Aachen, were rescheduled for the 16th, when the last-mentioned was assigned to a 3 Group G-H force of 182 Lancasters. 90 Squadron armourers winched a cookie, six 1,000 and six 500-pounders into each of sixteen Lancasters before they departed Tuddenham between 13.03 and 13.35 with W/C Ogilvie the senior pilot on duty. Their destination was the most northerly of the towns, situated no more than five miles from the Dutch frontier south-east of Roermond and was an exclusively 3 Group target, while Düren and Jülich were to face much larger forces from 1, 5 and 8 Groups and 4, 6 and 8 Groups respectively. The Master Bomber at Heinsberg was W/C Watkins DSO, DFC, DFM, the commanding officer of XV Squadron, who had completed more than fifty operations as a navigator, some of them with the Feltwell station commander at the time, the late G/C John "Speedy" Powell. As his Lancaster, piloted by F/L Sanders RNZAF approached the target it was shot down, and W/C Watkins alone of the eight occupants survived to fall into enemy hands, suggesting that the aircraft had broken up and thrown him clear with his parachute attached. The Deputy Master Bomber took over his duties and rescued the operation from failure after the G-H release co-ordinates were found to be inaccurate. The 90 Squadron crews attacked from 8,000 to 10,000 feet between 15.31 and 15.38 helping to all-but erase the town from the map, but fortunately, only 110 civilians were still resident in the town and half of these lost their lives. This was in contrast to more than three thousand fatalities at Düren, and no report was available from Jülich. In the event, the American advance was thwarted by wet ground and proceeded very slowly and with great difficulty.

On the 20th, sixteen 90 Squadron Lancasters were made ready to return to the Meerbeck oil plant at Homberg for the third time in the month as part of a 3 Group G-H force of 185 aircraft. The bomb bays were each filled with a cookie and sixteen 500-pounders before they departed Tuddenham between 12.42 and 12.55 with S/L Crossley the senior pilot on duty. The outward flight proved difficult for all crews because of the towering ice-bearing clouds with tops at 23,000 feet, and six crews turned back early probably because of severe icing. Some climbed to 25,000 feet in an attempt to break free of ice, while others found a clear lane at 20,000 feet and managed to formate on a number of G-H leaders and deliver their bombs from 19,000 to 22,000 feet between 15.12 and 15.20. Despite the efforts to keep on track, the operation was a failure at a cost of five Lancasters, three of them belonging to 75(NZ) Squadron at Mepal, for which this particular target already held bad memories, and it was clear that this target would require further attention.

There may have been a sharp intake of breath inside the Mepal briefing room on the following morning, when twenty-one crews were told of a return to Homberg that afternoon, while some twenty miles to the south-east fourteen 90 Squadron crews settled at their long tables to await the arrival of the station and squadron commanders and their entourage to inform them of their part in the plan for a G-H raid involving 159 Lancasters. Out on the dispersals their Lancasters were each receiving a bomb load of a cookie and sixteen 500-pounders, while three others were loaded with five mines each for delivery to the Onion garden in Oslo Fjord. The bombers took off first, between 12.20 and 12.53 and would be well on their way home before the mining trio got away. S/L Crossley was the senior pilot on duty as they climbed out and headed towards The Wash to form up, but on reaching Stoke Ferry on the way to King's Lynn his rear turret became unserviceable, forcing him and his crew to turn back. The others found clear conditions over the target, which enabled them to identify ground detail, but the problems on this occasion centred on the failure of G-H equipment and heavy, accurate flak, which upset the run of those leaders with functioning sets. The 90 Squadron crews delivered their hardware either on the fall of the leaders' bombs or on the accompanying TIs from 19,000 to 20,000 feet between 15.07 and 15.13 and observed bursts, explosions and fires within the plant and brown oily smoke emanating from it, but also described the attack as scattered. F/L Daniel and crew came home on three engines after losing the starboard-inner to flak over the target. Based on debriefing reports, 3 Group HQ judged this to be a not particularly effective attack, yet a Bomber Command report mentioned that a vast sheet of yellow flame had been witnessed, followed by black smoke rising to a great height, and it must be assumed from this that it was, therefore, a successful raid.

The mining trio consisting of the crews of F/Os MacLean and Floyd and F/L Myers departed Tuddenham between 15.52 and 15.55 and set course to the north-east for the long North Sea crossing to southern Norway, where they would be joined by three other 3 Group Lancasters. Clear skies and excellent visibility in the target area facilitated a visual identification of ground features including a lighthouse near Tonsberg, and the vegetables were planted according to brief from 10,000 feet between 19.39 and 19.54, before all returned safely after sorties of seven to eight hours duration.

A day away from the operational scene on the 22nd was followed on the 23rd by the briefing of a dozen 90 Squadron crews for an attack on the Nordstern synthetic oil plant at Gelsenkirchen. They were to be part of a 3 Group G-H force of 168 Lancasters and departed Tuddenham between 12.54 and 13.10 with F/Ls Hick, Myles and Spanhake the senior pilots on duty and a cookie and sixteen 500-pounders in each bomb bay. On the way out a 195 Squadron Lancasters was seen to catch fire and blow up before crashing in the sea off Walcheren. All from 90 Squadron reached the target area, where ten-tenths cloud was present with tops at 12,000 feet according to the 3 Group ORB, 8,000 feet as recorded by the 75(NZ) Squadron ORB and 15,000 to 20,000 feet if one believes the 90 Squadron crews! The G-H formations were good, the equipment worked well and the 90 Squadron participants mostly delivered their loads on the fall of the leaders' from 19,000 to 20,000 feet between 15.17 and 15.20, while any deflected by the intense flak barrage employed their navigational aids. Black smoke inside the cloud suggested a successful raid, although the outcome could not be accurately assessed.

On the 26th a G-H force of seventy-five Lancasters was assembled for a raid on marshalling yards at Fulda in central Germany as a test to ascertain the range of G-H signals. Each of 90 Squadron's twelve Lancasters was loaded with a cookie, two 1,000 and nine 500-pounders before departing Tuddenham between 07.50 and 08.15 with S/L Scott the senior pilot on duty. The target lay 160 miles due east of the German frontier south of Aachen and the G-H signal faded before it was reached, leaving the crews to persevere with the system and drop their bombs as the leaders' fell away into ten-tenths cloud from 20,000 to 21,000 feet between 11.07 and 11.09, trusting that their navigation had been accurate. All returned safely from an unopposed raid lasting some six hours, and had little to pass on at debriefing, leaving 3 Group HQ to conclude that the test had failed.

On the following day, 3 Group assembled a G-H force of 169 Lancasters to send against the Kalk-Nord marshalling yards situated on the eastern edge of Cologne, an operation for which 90 Squadron made ready sixteen Lancasters, loading each with a 4,000lb cookie and sixteen 500-pounders. They departed Tuddenham between 12.28 and 12.40 with F/Ls Daniel, Gray, Hick and Myles the senior pilots on duty, and all arrived at the target to be greeted by moderate, accurate flak, the 3 Group ORB complaining that the navigator at the tip of the spearhead seemed to lead the formation through most of the Ruhr defences on the way. Those following his leadership were believed to have overshot the yards by a quarter of a mile, while others chose a more direct route, and their bombs were concentrated within the yards with apparently good results. F/O Jones and crew were two minutes from bomb-release at 20,000 feet when their starboard-inner engine was hit by flak and shortly afterwards the navigator's table was damaged. After the bombs had been dropped at 20.07, they began to lose height and were hit again at 18,000 feet by the Bonn defences at 20.17, before turning to the west with petrol streaming from the ruptured tank and NN698 continuing to sink slowly. They traversed Belgium and had crossed the frontier into France when the fuel became exhausted, and on breaking cloud at 400 feet, narrowly missed trees, houses and a railway embankment, before crash-landing at speed at 16.05 in Allied-held territory near Valenciennes, writing off the Lancaster but not the crew, who walked away unscathed. The rest of the squadron, meanwhile, had carried out their attacks from 19,000 to 20,000 feet between 15.05 and 15.08 and reported strikes on the aiming point but also some under and overshooting.

During the night, seventy 6 Group aircraft landed on 3 Group stations on return from Neuss, the city that was to host yet another raid on the 28th by 145 Lancasters of 3 Group, for which 90 Squadron loaded fourteen Lancasters with a cookie, supplemented either with six 1,000 and six 500-pounders or SBCs of 4lb incendiaries, and one Lancaster with a single 8,000-pounder and three 1,000 and four 500-pounders. They departed Tuddenham between 02.21 and 02.34 with W/C Ogilvie the senior pilot on duty and formed up into a stream that included eight ABC Lancasters from 1 Group, while a second force of 270 Halifaxes of 4 Group and thirty-two Lancasters of 1 and 8 Groups accompanied by Obe Mosquitos headed at the same tome towards Essen to bomb the Krupp complex. The Two destinations were only twenty miles apart and this would lead to confusion as some crews ended up in the wrong stream. Neuss-bound gaggles reached the target area over ten-tenths cloud and the bombing was carried out on G-H "Wanganui" skymarkers, the 90 Squadron crews delivering their payloads from 19,000 to 20,000 feet between 05.33 and 05.45, before returning home for an early breakfast. An assessment was not possible, but local reports described modest damage predominantly in residential districts.

3 Group mobilized 120 Lancasters on the 30th, which were to be divided equally between two targets in the Ruhr, the coking plant at Bottrop-Welheim and a benzin plant at Osterfeld, a district of Oberhausen. 90 Squadron supported the latter with fifteen Lancasters, each of which received a bomb load of a cookie and sixteen 500-pounders before departing Tuddenham between 11.00 and 11.12 with a host of pilots of flight lieutenant rank leading the way. They reached the target area to find a blanket of ten-tenths cloud with tops at 8,000 to 10,000 feet and the 90 Squadron contingent carried out their attacks from 19,000 to 20,000 feet between 13.11 and 13.13 in what appeared to be an accurate and concentrated assault, for which the only evidence was smoke rising through the cloud.

During the course of the month the squadron took part in seventeen operations and dispatched 226 sorties for the loss of a single Lancaster, and this was the first month since becoming operational that no aircrew casualties had been recorded.

December 1944

December would follow a similar pattern to that of November, and it began for 3 Group on the 2nd with a G-H raid on the Zeche-Hansa benzol plant in the Huckarde district of Dortmund north-west of the city centre, for which a force of ninety-three Lancasters was assembled. Just four of them belonged to 90 Squadron, and each received a bomb load of a cookie, six 1,000 and four 500-pounders before departing Tuddenham in favourable weather conditions between 12.53 and 13.12 with S/L Scott RNZAF the senior pilot on duty. They flew out in bright sunshine above the thick cloud with tops at around 13,000 feet and found the ground in the target area to be obscured, but these were ideal conditions for a G-H attack, and for the first time, all G-H aircraft detailed to employ the system did so, which the 3 Group ORB described as "a fine achievement, from the manipulation by the crews to the servicing of the equipment by the radar tradesmen". The 90 Squadron crews attacked from 19,000 to 20,000 feet between 14.57 and 15.02 in the face of a moderate and erratic flak response and the operation appeared to be successful and concluded without casualties.

The main operation that night was carried out by five hundred aircraft of 1, 4, 6 and 8 Groups against the Ruhr town of Hagen, which was left in ruins with most of its factories put out of action for months. Among them was the Akkumulatoren Fabrik AG (AFA), which was producing accumulator batteries for the new type XXI U-Boots and was of vital importance to the war effort.

The Ruhr remained the focus of attention on the 4th, when Oberhausen was revealed at briefings as the target for a 160-strong 3 Group G-H attack, which was to be directed principally at the city centre, probably with the main railway station as the aiming point rather than the oil plants further north. The fact that this was an area raid was made evident by the predominance of high capacity "blockbuster" bombs being loaded into the bomb bays at some stations, like Mepal, where the rarely used 12,000-pounder and slightly more common 8,000-pounders were to be employed along with incendiaries. At Tuddenham, the fourteen 90 Squadron Lancasters each received a fairly standard load of a cookie supplemented with six 1,000 and six 500-pounders, and took to the air between 11.52 and 12.12 with S/L Scott the senior pilot on duty. The winds were lighter than forecast, and this caused the G-H leaders to fly at too great a speed for satisfactory formation-keeping, which elongated the stream by the time that the spearhead reached the target area to find the expected nine to ten-tenths cloud with tops at 10,000 feet. The 90 Squadron crews carried out their attacks from 19,000 to 20,000 feet between 14.06 and 14.08 and were among the 87% of crews bombing on their equipment as opposed to on marker flares. It was not possible to assess the results, but a local report mentioned 472 houses destroyed and a similar number seriously damaged.

That night, 5 Group attacked the southern city of Heilbronn, which had the misfortune to sit astride a north-south railway line and in an orgy of destruction lasting only a few minutes, 1,254 tons of bombs destroyed 82% of the built-up area and killed seven thousand people.

3 Group detailed ninety-four Lancasters on the 5th to attack the highly important marshalling yards at Hamm to the north-east of the Ruhr, and fifty-six others to attempt to destroy the Schwammenauel Dam at the confluence of the Roer (Rur) River and the Rur reservoir near the town of Heimbach in Germany's Eifel region close to the Belgian frontier. On the previous day a small force from 8 Group had attempted and failed to hit the nearby Urft Dam, and further attacks would be launched against it over the ensuing days by elements of 5 Group including 617 Squadron with Tallboy earthquake bombs, but the structure would remain intact, if a little scarred. The attacks were intended to prevent the Germans from strategically releasing water to hamper the advancing American ground forces downstream, which, in the event, is precisely what they were able to do. 90 Squadron loaded fourteen of its Lancasters with thirteen 1,000-pounders each and dispatched them from Tuddenham between 08.50 and 09.16 with F/Ls Croft

Griggs and Hooper the senior pilots on duty. They arrived in the target area to find ten-tenths cloud with tops at 12,000 feet, at which point the Master Bomber abandoned the operation for an undisclosed reason and sent them home with their bombs. Meanwhile, some 140 miles to the north-east, the attack on Hamm had been highly successful, and it would be established after the war that 140 acres, or 39% of its built-up area, had been laid waste in this raid alone.

A 1, 3 and 8 Group heavy force of 475 Lancasters was assembled on the 6th for an attack on the synthetic oil plant at Leuna near Merseburg, one of many refineries located in an arc from north to south to the west of Leipzig in eastern Germany. The I G Farben-owned plant was the second largest in Germany and was the one employed to develop the Bergius process of producing high grade petroleum from bituminous coal. 90 Squadron loaded nine 1,000-pounders into each of its twelve Lancasters, which were part of the 3 Group contribution of 123, and they departed Tuddenham between 16.55 and 17.06 with F/Ls Croft Griggs, Daniel, Gray and Verroneau the senior pilots on duty. The weather outbound was poor and caused a few early returns, although it was on finding the special navigation equipment missing that 90 Squadron's F/O Barry and crew turned back at Reading, while F/L Croft Griggs and crew made it as far as Vignacourt, between Abbeville and Amiens before their starboard-inner engine let them down. A ground marking (Newhaven) plan had been prepared, but the presence of ten-tenths cloud over the target with tops at 14,000 feet forced a change to "Wanganui" flares, which fell plentifully and continuously with good concentration throughout the raid. The 90 Squadron crews attacked from 20,000 to 24,000 feet between 20.49 and 20.59 and along with other returning crews reported the glow of fires beneath the cloud and a spirited flak barrage. Post-raid reconnaissance confirmed that the one thousand-mile round-trip had been worthwhile and had inflicted extensive damage upon the oil refinery.

A 3 Group G-H attack on the marshalling yards at Duisburg was briefed out to 163 crews on the 8th, fourteen of them from 90 Squadron at Tuddenham, where their Lancasters each received a bomb load of either a cookie and nine 1,000-pounders or thirteen 1,000-pounders, before taking to the air between 08.18 and 08.29 with F/Ls Croft Griggs, Gray, Hooper and Woods the senior pilots on duty. Their first task was to rendezvous with the rest of the gaggle, a process made highly challenging by the presence of cloud in thick layers up to 25,000 feet, which stretched all the way to the German frontier and prevented the stream from forming up into a G-H configuration. However, the navigation was so good, that on emerging from the cloud the aircraft were in close enough contact to be able to form up and were in cohesive formations by the time that the bombing by the 90 Squadron crews took place from 19,000 to 20,000 feet with the tops of the nine to ten-tenths cloud some eight thousand feet below them. The marker flares and the bombing were concentrated, and one 75(NZ) Squadron crew reported black smoke rising through the cloud-tops at 15,000 feet as they turned away. Icing was a problem on the way home, restricting the movement of control surfaces and freezing bomb doors to prevent some crews from jettisoning parts of bomb loads.

Orders came through to 3 Group stations on the morning of the 11th to prepared for an attack on the Osterfeld district of Oberhausen, where the marshalling yards would provide the aiming point for ninety-eight Lancasters, while fifty-two others targeted the coking plant. There is no indication concerning the destination for individual squadrons, but an intelligent guess might suggest that the 32 Base squadrons, which included Tuddenham, were bound for the marshalling yards and those from 33 Base the coking plant. Fourteen Lancasters were made ready at Tuddenham, and each loaded with eleven 1,000 and four 500-pounders, before taking off between 08.17 and 08.50 with F/Ls Gray and Verroneau the senior pilots on duty. Forming up and climbing to bombing height became a challenge because of cloud over the bases, and F/O Gillespie and crew were performing a wide circuit at 7,000 feet in cloud at 09.30, when another Lancaster, believed to by 90 Squadron's WP-T, crossed in front and forced them to take violent evasive action in the form of a dive to 4,000 feet, during which, another Lancaster is thought to have sliced off part of the port fin. The starboard-inner engine over-revved and the propeller had to be feathered at the same time as the special navigation equipment gave up the ghost, and with no sign of a formation to latch onto, it was decided to head for the jettison area to lighten the load for landing. The others set course over cloud that topped out at 15,000 feet and those reaching the central Ruhr found the cloud tops at 19,000 feet, which forced the attack to be delivered from higher than intended, the 90 Squadron crews bombing from 19,000 to 20,000 feet between 11.03 and 11.07. The G-H flares disappeared quickly into the cloud, which was most unhelpful, and this contributed to scattered bombing at both aiming points.

On the following day 3 Group detailed 140 Lancasters for a raid on Witten, a large mining town tucked in a pocket of the Ruhr south-west of Dortmund and south-east of Bochum. Thirteen Lancasters departed Tuddenham between 10.59 and 11.23 with F/Ls Hooper and Verroneau the senior pilots on duty and a cookie in each bomb bay supplemented with either fourteen 500-pounders or fourteen N°14 cluster bombs. On the run into the target the stream divided into two parts, a small bunch from 31 and 32 Bases (Stradishall, Chedburgh, Tuddenham and Methwold positioning itself about seven miles ahead of the main concentration. The bulk of the fighter escort remained with the rear section, but the fighter leader had the foresight to send one squadron ahead to cover the lead group, which was fortuitous, as the Luftwaffe was waiting for them over the Ruhr, having chosen this day to mount its largest effort since daylight bombing operations began in June. A strong force of BF109s managed to break up the forward section of bombers, shooting down, among others, four 195 Squadron Lancasters, and this led to a scattered start to the attack. However, on observing the events ahead, the main section tightened its formation, which helped to create very concentrated bombing and forty of the forty-six G-H leaders were able to use their equipment effectively. The 90 Squadron contingent arrived at the target to find nine to ten-tenths cloud topping out at 15,000 feet and attacked from 19,000 to 21,000 feet between 14.04 and 14.09, all but one employing either their own special navigation aids or the G-H leaders' bombs as a trigger, while one aimed at red flares with green stars. No assessment could be made through the cloud, but flak was described as moderate, and two aircraft sustained slight damage. The presence of enemy fighters was noted, but no combats with 90 Squadron aircraft took place.

S/L Crossley had been declared tour-expired and was posted away, it is believed to 31 Base, and his now headless crew was posted to XV Squadron at Mildenhall to pick up a new pilot and continue their tour.

F/O Grass and crew were called to briefing on the 14th to learn that they were to be 90 Squadron's only representative in a mining operation in the Kattegat involving ten 3 Group Lancasters. They departed Tuddenham at 15.17 and set course for Jutland's western coast and a final destination in the Baltic in the Silverthorn V garden off Sweden's Kullen Point. They arrived in the target area to encounter ten-tenths cloud with tops at 5,000 to 6,000 feet and planted six vegetables from 10,000 feet by H2S-fix before returning safely to land at Lossiemouth after a round-trip of a little over six hours.

The squadron dispatched thirteen Lancasters on the 15th as part of a 3 Group G-H force assigned to the marshalling yards at Siegen, situated fifty miles east of Cologne, but they were recalled after the fighter escort was unable to take-off in the prevailing weather conditions. The operation was rescheduled for the following day, when a force of 108 Lancasters was assembled, of which ten were provided by 90 Squadron, six of them loaded with a cookie and five 1,000 and five 500-pounders, three with a cookie and fourteen Nº14 cluster bombs and one with a 8,000-pounder supplemented with a single 1,000-pounder and five 500-pounders. They departed Tuddenham between 11.35 and 11.50 with S/L Scott the senior pilot on duty and set course for the North Sea crossing, encountering icing-bearing cloud as far as 06° East with tops at 20,000 feet, which led to sixteen early returns, none of them 90 Squadron aircraft. When the cloud began to break up at the fighter rendezvous point at 03° East, the bomber stream found itself to be about fifteen minutes ahead of schedule and orbited before forming up into a recognisable gaggle, which was maintained for the remainder of the outward flight. The target was covered by nine-tenths cloud, but the G-H flares were concentrated, and the bombing appeared to be accurate, while the USAAF 8th Air Force escort kept enemy fighters at arm's length. The 90 Squadron participants delivered their attacks from 16,500 to 19,500 feet between 15.00 and 15.02 and most of it hit Siegen and the neighbouring town of Weidenau but destroying many public buildings and houses rather than the railway yards.

It was on the 16th that the German counterattack began in the Ardennes in what became known as the Battle of the Bulge, when the inexperienced American units were taken completely by surprise as the German armoured divisions forced their way through the Allied lines in an attempt to recapture Brussels and the port of Antwerp. The German advance coincided with a spell of unfavourable weather conditions including low cloud, which would prevent the Allies from responding from the air. On the 17th, 186 Squadron moved out of Tuddenham to take up residence at Stradishall, leaving 90 Squadron officially to revert to a two-flight set-up. That night, while more than five hundred aircraft from 4, 6 and 8 Groups targeted Duisburg, a 1 Group main force took off to attack the city of Ulm, situated on the Danube to the south-east of Stuttgart and west of Augsburg in southern Germany. It was similar in nature to the recently-bombed Heilbronn, and as a result of the catastrophic raid there, the local Gauleiter had urged the women and children to evacuate the inner city urgently. Plans were put in place to begin evacuation on Monday the 18th, so that Advent could be observed on the Sunday, but something caused a change of plan and loudspeaker vans toured the city on Sunday urging the population to leave at once, which proved to be a fortuitous move. Unlike Heilbronn, Ulm contained industry, including the important Magirus-Deutz and Kässbohrer lorry factories, and there were also military barracks and depots. One square kilometre of the city became engulfed in flames, affecting in some way 82% of the built-up area and even though the evacuation saved many lives, seven hundred fatalities were recorded.

On the 19th a force of thirty-two 3 Group Lancasters from Methwold and Mildenhall was all that could be mustered for a G-H raid on the railway yards at Trier, after adverse weather conditions grounded the other stations. The target, a city located on the eastern bank of the

Rhine close to the Luxembourg frontier, was a possible gateway through which the enemy could bring reinforcements to the battle front, but it was the town rather than the railway yards that sustained substantial damage. A dozen other 3 Group Lancasters did manage to take off for mining duties in the Baltic, four of them departing Tuddenham between 15.40 and 15.47 bound, according to the ORB for Flensburg Bay, where there was no named garden. Now that the French U-Boot bases had been captured, the Kriegsmarine was forced to operate out of its Baltic ports and it was possibly to isolate the Flensburger Schiffsbau-Ges U-Boot construction yards, which had launched eight U-Boots between the 27th of March 1941 and the 22nd of November 1944, that this mining operation was mounted. However, a closer examination of the map references recorded by the crews reveals that the target area was actually the Sweet Pea garden in Mecklenburg Bay, where the crews of F/Os Barry, Buning, Orr and Wade arrived to find ten-tenths cloud with tops at 4,500 feet. They established a pinpoint by H2S-fix on Gedser Head at the southern tip of Denmark's Falster Island and planted five vegetables each into the briefed locations from 10,000 feet between 19.31 and 19.39, before returning to land at Lossiemouth after more than seven hours aloft.

W/C Ogilvie went on leave on the 20th, allowing S/L Scott to step temporarily into his shoes as acting squadron commander. F/L Buning and crew returned from Lossiemouth in poor visibility on the 21st and twice overshot the landing, before touching down at the third attempt only for the starboard undercarriage to collapse and write-off NG323 in the ensuing crash, happily without crew casualties. Trier was the target again on that day, when a 3 Group force of 145 Lancasters was made ready for a two-phase attack. Thirty-two aircraft, mostly from 31 Base, were unable to take-off in the prevailing weather conditions, leaving 113, including a dozen from 90 Squadron, to do the job. They departed Tuddenham between 12.34 and 12.47 with five pilots of flight lieutenant rank leading the way and a bomb load in each Lancaster of a cookie, ten 500 and six 250-pounders. On the way out over the sea, F/L Croft Griggs suffered a severe headache which affected his vision, and he was forced to turn back, leaving the others to reach the target to find it concealed beneath a layer of low cloud, which had not been forecast. Originally intended as a visual attack controlled by a Master Bomber and Deputy, it was changed to G-H at the last minute and the Tuddenham crews bombed either with their leaders or on their own equipment from 17,000 to 19,000 feet between 15.01 and 15.04. As the bombers turned away, a circle of thick, black smoke began to drift up through the cloud tops and the consensus among returning crews was of a concentrated and successful raid, although no genuine assessment was possible, and it was a local report that mentioned heavy casualties as a result of the second phase attack.

That night, other groups attacked railway targets at Cologne and Bonn while 5 Group attended to the I G Farben-owned Wintershall synthetic oil refinery at Politz near Stettin. Meanwhile at Tuddenham, F/L Reid was promoted to acting squadron leader rank on the 22nd to succeed S/L Crossley as A Flight commander. There was to be no rest for Trier, which was posted on the 23rd to host its third attack at the hands of 3 Group, this time involving a force of 153 Lancasters, among them seventeen representing 90 Squadron, whose crews had been briefed for this operation on the previous day and had been on stand-by waiting in vain for a break in the weather. They departed Tuddenham between 11.46 and 12.00 with S/L Scott as Master Bomber and a cookie in each bomb bay supplemented with either eight 500 and eight 250-pounders or ten 500 and six 250-pounders. They benefitted from the much-improved weather conditions as they formed up and headed south-eastwards to cross the enemy coast at Dunkerque, and it was shortly after doing so that F/O Sullivan's port-outer engine had to be shut down, depriving the rear turret of its power and forcing a return. The others ran the gauntlet of intense, predicted flak as they traversed the battle front after crossing the Luxembourg frontier into Germany, and it was here that F/O Floyd's HK664 was hit in the bomb bay and exploded with great force, spreading itself and its eight occupants far and wide to become the single Bomber Command casualty of the operation. The rest continued on to cover the short distance to the target, which they found beneath clear skies, and the planned visual attack took place under S/L Scott's excellent control. He cancelled the one errant TI, before calling in the main force, those from 90 Squadron delivering their payloads from 17,000 to 18,000 feet between 14.29 and 14.34 and observing the town to be enveloped in smoke and dust.

The target for an early-evening attack by 104 Lancasters of 3 Group's 31 and 32 Bases on the 24th was Hangelar airfield near Bonn, for which Tuddenham was not called into action, possibly because 3 Group stations had been shrouded in fog all day and not all could launch their aircraft. Thick fog reduced visibility to no more than a hundred yards on the 25th, ensuring that, once the day's planned operation had been cancelled during morning briefing, the final wartime Christmas could be celebrated in traditional style.

The weather had improved greatly by Boxing Day, finally allowing support for the Allied ground forces in the Ardennes as the German advance ran out of steam around St Vith in Belgium. 90 Squadron was not called into action but made ready fourteen Lancasters on the 27th for an attack on Cologne, which was then cancelled and a raid on the marshalling yards at nearby Rheydt substituted involving a force of two hundred Lancasters and eleven Mosquitos of 1, 3, 5 and 8 Groups. 3 Group was responsible for ninety-one of the Lancasters, those from Tuddenham taking off between 12.06 and 12.22 with S/L Reid the senior pilot on duty and each crew sitting on nine 1,000, four 500 and two 250-pounders. They joined up with the rest of the force for a visual attack controlled by a Master Bomber, which took place under clear skies and produced accurate and concentrated bombing, that by the 90 Squadron element from 19,000 to 21,000 feet between 14.58 and 15.00. Clouds of smoke were seen to rise over the target and post-raid reconnaissance revealed severe damage in the southern half of the yards and widespread destruction in the town to the east. Several crews reported the considerable danger posed by bombs cascading from aircraft above at 23,000 feet, in some cases forcing them into violent evasive action.

On the following day fifteen crews were briefed at Tuddenham for a raid on the Gremberg marshalling yards situated south-east of Cologne city centre. It was a 3 Group show involving 167 Lancasters, for which the 90 Squadron bomb bays were filled with a cookie, ten 500 and four 250-pounders before setting off between 12.28 and 12.39 with F/Ls Gray and Hooper the senior pilots on duty. They arrived in the target area to find favourable conditions, but the approach to bomb was beset with a great deal of jockeying for position as crews attempted to attach themselves to a G-H leader. Some aircraft were observed to be well above the main bunch, as high as 21,000 feet, and this put others in danger of being hit by falling bombs. There were complaints that some crews were releasing "window" in "brick" form without breaking the string holding the bundles together, while others found themselves boxed in by other aircraft and, unable to manoeuvre into a more favourable position, were forced to watch as bombs passed within feet of them. The 90 Squadron crews attacked from 19,000 to 20,000 feet between 15.05 and 15.07, and despite this organised chaos, the bombing was concentrated, and a mushroom of smoke was seen to rise through the low cloud to reach 9,000 feet as the force retreated.

The railway theme continued for 3 Group at Koblenz on the 29th, a main centre serving the Ardennes battle front with two sets of marshalling yards, for which a force of 167 Lancasters was assembled. The Mosel marshalling yards near the city centre had been attacked by elements of 1 and 8 Groups a week earlier and would now face 184 Halifaxes and Lancasters of 4 and 8 Groups, while the Lützel yards in a northern suburb would host eighty-five Lancasters. Thirteen 90 Squadron Lancasters were made ready and given a variety of bomb loads, three having a cookie, three 1,000, six 500 and four 250-pounders winched into their bomb bays, three others a 8,000-pounder with two 1,000, three 500 and two 250-pounders, while one was given a 12,000lb HC blockbuster. They departed Tuddenham between 12.13 and 12.35 with S/L Reid the senior pilot on duty and all reached the target area to find good visibility and the 4 Group attack in progress. The 3 Group attack began as planned at H+8 and the 90 Squadron crews bombed from 18,000 to 19,500 feet between 15.10 and 15.13 and mixed opinions were offered by returning crews as to the effectiveness of the raid, some describing it as scattered and inaccurate, while others reported concentrated bombing with explosions and black smoke. 3 Group leaned towards the former, blaming a poor G-H signal, clear skies allowing the flak gunners to be more accurate, and the tail-end of the 4 Group raid becoming mixed up with the lead aircraft from 3 Group. A local report spoke of the bombing completing the destruction begun by the Americans on the previous day and reported the railway to be blocked and the Koblenz-Lützel bridge to be out of action for the rest of the war.

The night of the 30th was devoted to mining and SOE operations as far as 3 Group was concerned, the former involving eleven Lancasters, four of them belonging to 90 Squadron, which departed Tuddenham between 16.45 and 16.48 bound for the Rosemary garden in the Heligoland Bight with F/L Williams RNZAF the senior pilot on duty. They were to employ "special equipment", which usually referred to H2S, and arrived in the target area under clear skies to plant five vegetables each from 6,000 to 7,000 feet between 18.59 and 19.03. Enemy night-fighters were spotted in the vicinity, and F/O Kaiser and crew were stalked by a Ju88 for ten minutes over the North Sea before it disappeared from view.

The final operation of the year was against the railway yards at Vohwinkel, situated on the south-eastern edge of the Ruhr between Düsseldorf and Wuppertal, for which 90 Squadron contributed fourteen Lancasters to a 3 Group G-H force of 155 aircraft. Each received a bomb load of a cookie supplemented with either ten 500 and six 250-pounders or three 1,000, six 500 and four 250-pounders, before departing Tuddenham between 11.49 and 12.22 with S/L Reid the senior pilot on duty. They had to pass through accurate heavy flak on the way to the target and found themselves driven on by a wind forty m.p.h faster than had been forecast, despite which all of the 90 Squadron participants arrived at the target to find up to six-tenths cloud with tops at around 6,000 feet. They carried out their attacks from 19,000 to 20,000 feet between 14.43 and 14.45, but F/O Harries and crew were thwarted by a complete hang-up and managed to jettison their cookie with difficulty and watched it detonate on a crossroads at Remscheid. On return to Tuddenham the crews reported a scattered attack, for which they blamed the wind and the operation cost just two Lancasters, both belonging to 218 (Gold Coast) Squadron and both victims of bombs from above.

During the course of the month the squadron took part in eighteen operations including the recall and dispatched 202 sorties for the loss of one Lancasters and crew. It had been another uncompromising year for the crews of 3 Group since its return to the forefront of operations with the advent of the Lancaster, and 90 Squadron had come through with flying colours, based on an excellent serviceability rate and remarkably low casualties. The end was in sight as the scent of victory wafted in from the Continent, but much remained to be done before the proud and tenacious enemy finally laid down his arms, and more crews would be sacrificed in the remaining months of the war.

January 1945

The year in which victory would finally be achieved brought no let-up in the pace of operations, although worthwhile targets were becoming increasingly difficult to find. The defences, while stretched beyond their limit to protect all corners of the Reich, were still capable of hitting back and many more crews would go down before the end finally came. The New Year began in hectic fashion as the Luftwaffe launched its ill-conceived and ultimately ill-fated Operation Bodenplatte (Baseplate) at first light on the 1st. Designed to catch Allied aircraft on the ground at the liberated airfields in France, Belgium and Holland, it succeeded only modestly and cost the enemy day fighter force 250 aircraft and around 150 pilots killed, wounded or captured, a setback from which it would never recover, while the Allies could make good their losses within hours from their enormous stockpiles.

3 Group's 1945 campaign began with a return to the railway yards at Vohwinkel on the 1st, for which 90 Squadron made ready fifteen Lancasters as part of an overall G-H force of 146. Each received a bomb load of a cookie, ten 500 and six 250-pounders, before departing Tuddenham between 15.55 and 16.11 with F/Ls Daniel, Gray, Kaiser and Williams the senior pilots on duty. Two crews failed to complete the outward flight, F/O Wakeham and crew's interest in proceedings ending with an engine issue when almost two hours out, while P/O Hanger and crew strayed off track and found themselves some forty miles south of where they were supposed to be with insufficient time to reach the target. They turned back and jettisoned their bomb load "live" on the German side of the frontier with Belgium near St-Vith. The others were able to pick out ground detail and identified the aiming point by red TIs confirmed by H2S, the 90 Squadron crews carrying out their attacks from 19,000 to 21,000 feet between 19.39 and 19.54. The bombing took place in the face of a strong wind, which had made it difficult to maintain formations, and appeared to be concentrated between two sets of red TIs. Returning crews reported a red glow, and the consensus was of a successful operation, which was confirmed by post-raid reconnaissance photographs. One of the consequences of Operation Bodenplatte was a bunch of itchy fingered American flak gunners in Belgium, who had been spooked by the morning's frenetic activity and now popped off at anything that flew within range, bringing down, it is believed, three 3 Group Lancasters.

More than nine hundred aircraft made their way to southern Germany on the 2nd, 514 of them Lancasters belonging to 1, 3, 6 and 8 Groups bound for Nuremberg, while 389 mostly Halifaxes from 4, 6 and 8 Groups were assigned to Ludwigshafen on the western bank of the Rhine opposite Mannheim. Fourteen Lancasters had departed Tuddenham between 15.30 and 15.40 with F/Ls Daniel, Kaiser and Williams the senior pilots on duty and a cookie and ten Nº14 cluster bombs in each bomb bay, and all reached the target under clear skies with a rising full moon to aid visibility. The Path Finders had prepared a ground marking plan employing red and green TIs, and the 90 Squadron crews, who were near the head of the stream, saw them ahead and were guided in by them to bomb from 16,000 to 18,000 feet between 19.30 and 19.39 in accordance with the instructions of the Master Bomber. The city centre sustained massive damage during the concentrated attack and residential districts in the north-east and the south were also devastated, a local report detailing 4,640 houses as destroyed and more than four hundred industrial buildings were also wrecked along with railway installations. Woods to the south of the city were also reported to be on fire, suggesting a degree of over or under-shooting. The death toll was also high, at 1,838, with others still missing at the time of the local report, and this was undoubtedly the most effective raid of the war on this great symbol of Nazism. Returning crews reported the glow of fires visible from 150 miles into the homeward flight and a very modest four Lancasters and three crews were lost over enemy territory.

On the 3rd, 3 Group put together a force of ninety-nine Lancasters, fifty to attack the Zeche-Hansa benzol plant in the Huckarde district to the west of Dortmund's centre, and forty-nine to target the Klöckner Werke A G refinery at Castrop-Rauxel, a short distance to the north-west. Eight crews were briefed at Tuddenham for the former, while each of their Lancasters was being loaded with a cookie and ten 500 and six 250-pounders, before taking off between 12.44 and 12.52 with S/Ls Reid and Scott the senior pilots on duty. Conditions for a G-H raid were perfect with ten-tenths cloud up to 12,000 feet, through which intense and accurate flak emerged to burst in the clear sky above. The 90 Squadron element was at the head of the main force and attacked at the opening of the raid from 20,000 to 21,000 feet between 15.30 and 15.32 based on "follow-the-leader" or H2S, but they were not able to assess what was happening beneath the cloud. S/L Scott and crew suffered a hang-up and eventually released the 500 and 250-pounders "live" on the western fringe of Dortmund and the cookie between Cologne and Mönchengladbach. A 622 Squadron Lancaster was seen to explode over the target, and this would be the only loss from the two operations. Returning crews offered mixed opinions as to the effectiveness of the raid, some complaining that the stream had been too spread out and the bombing not concentrated, while others reported black smoke rising through the clouds as they turned away.

The group's next target was the marshalling yards at Ludwigshafen, situated on the western bank of the Rhine opposite Mannheim, which required a deep penetration into southern Germany under a fighter escort on the 5th. 90 Squadron contributed fourteen Lancasters to the 160-strong 3 Group force, and they each received a bomb load of a cookie and ten 500 and four 250-pounders before departing Tuddenham between 11.29 and 11.40 with W/C Ogilvie the senior pilot on duty and undertaking what would prove to be his final sortie as squadron commander. P/O Wannop and crew turned back early because of a port-inner engine issue, leaving the others to arrive at the target and experience a weak G-H tracking pulse, which led to a poor bombing run, while the clear skies over the target allowed the flak gunners to draw a bead on the attackers and break up the stream. The 90 Squadron crews carried out their attacks visually, on flares or by "follow-the-leader" from 19,000 to 20,000 feet between 15.06 and

15.12 and were divided in their opinions of the outcome between a "good prang" and a scattered attack and a number of references were made to the raid leader disappearing off track and taking others with him. Enemy fighters turned up, but it was flak that accounted for 90 Squadron's HK603, which contained the eight-man crew of F/O Wakeham RAAF. He and five others were able to save themselves to fall into enemy hands, but the wireless operator and rear gunner lost their lives. W/C Ogilvie and crew were set upon by a BF109, at which the mid-upper gunner fired two ten-second bursts and claimed the enemy as probably destroyed. F/O Gilbert's PD433 was hit by flak, which put the rear turret out of action, but when a BF109 attacked from dead astern later, it was seen off by return fire from the mid-upper and rear turrets, the latter as the result of manual rather than powered operation of the guns. Post-raid reconnaissance confirmed that the railway yards had been hit, but the northern suburbs and outlying communities had also found themselves in the firing line and 535 houses and eighty-seven industrial building had been destroyed or seriously damaged.

The targets for the 6th were railway installations at Hanau, to the east of Frankfurt, and Neuss in the Ruhr, and the latter was to be a joint effort between 1 and 3 Groups, which provided thirty and 117 Lancasters respectively. The force was about to take-off when the operation was cancelled, only to be re-instated later in the day, by which time nine 90 Squadron Lancasters had each received a bomb load of a cookie and fourteen 500-pounders. They departed Tuddenham between 15.49 and 15.59 with S/L Scott the senior pilot on duty and all reached the target to find nine to ten-tenths thin, low cloud and G-H-laid TIs with additional skymarkers as a back-up. The attack became somewhat scattered, the 90 Squadron crews bombing from 19,000 to 19,500 feet between 18.45 and 18.51 and observing the glow of fires beneath the cloud, and it was left to post-raid reconnaissance to ascertain that the marshalling yards had been hit, but that most of the bombing had fallen into adjacent areas, where 1,749 houses, nineteen industrial and twenty public buildings were destroyed or seriously damaged.

While this operation was in progress, nine 3 Group Lancasters were sent to the eastern end of the Baltic, to the Bay of Danzig, to mine the waters of the Tangerine garden off Pillau, now known as Baltiysk in Russia, the gateway to the port of Königsberg, now Kaliningrad, which the Germans were using to supply the beleaguered eastern front. It was the most distant of Bomber Command's mining areas and required an outward flight of four-and-a-half hours, which began for the 90 Squadron crews of F/L Williams and F/O Barry with take-off from Tuddenham at 16.15. The target area was covered by nine to ten-tenths cloud with tops at 7,000 to 14,000 feet, and a pinpoint to the east of Danzig was established by H2S before a timed run of around forty miles culminated with the planting of four vegetables each from 15,000 and 15,500 feet at 20.45 and 20.59. They returned safely from successful and uneventful sorties after round-trips of up to nine hours and fifty minutes duration.

The final heavy raid of the war on Munich by Bomber Command was briefed out on the 7th to 645 Lancaster crews, of which ninety-six represented 3 Group. Of these, fourteen departed Tuddenham between 18.31 and 18.58 with F/Ls Buning, Daniel and Gray the senior pilots on duty and a cookie and nine N°14 incendiary cluster bombs in each bomb bay. It was a two-phase operation with a two-hour gap between waves, and the 3 Group participants formed part of the second wave. F/O Gillespie and crew turned back within ninety minutes because of an electrical issue, while the rest of the force pressed on across France to find thick ten-tenths cloud at 12,000 feet over the aiming point, which all-but obscured the TIs, while variable winds upset the timings. The 90 Squadron crews bombed on red skymarkers with green stars, the hint of red TIs or the glow of fires from the earlier raid from 18,500 to 20,000 feet between 22.22 and 22.40, but curiously, F/O Harries and crew saw no markers at all and orbited for seven minutes before giving up and taking their cookie home. A large mushroom explosion was observed by some, followed by a red glow and the horizon remained red for a hundred miles into the return flight. Many returning crews had nothing to report and it was left to post-raid reconnaissance to establish that severe damage had been inflicted upon central and industrial districts. This completed a busy first week of the year.

Sixteen crews were briefed at Tuddenham on the morning of the 11th in preparation for an attack on the marshalling yards in the Uerdingen district of Krefeld on the western edge of the Ruhr. They were part of a 3 Group G-H force of 152 Lancasters and took off between 11.26 and 11.53 with S/L Scott the senior pilot on duty and each crew sitting on a cookie, ten 500 and four 250-pounders. The target area was covered by ten-tenths cloud, much of it cirrus up to a height of 21,000 feet, and whether or not this was responsible for the general state of disorder on approach to the target is uncertain, but a 75(NZ) Squadron crew would complain on return of being cut up by a 622 Squadron Lancaster ten minutes from the aiming point, which almost caused a collision. This was by no means the first accusation of dangerous flying by a 622 Squadron crew, and others were unhappy that the briefed bombing height was ignored by some and put them in danger of being hit by falling bombs. The 90 Squadron crews appeared to be oblivious to the dramas and delivered their bomb loads from 20,000 to 20,500 feet between 15.12 and 15.17, and despite the difficulties, the main weight of the attack fell into the eastern districts containing the railway yards and enormous damage resulted.

3 Group was invited on the 13th to prepare a force of Lancasters to attack the railway yards at Saarbrücken and 158 answered the call, fifteen of them loaded at Tuddenham with a cookie, ten 500 and four 250-pounders before taking off between 11.52 and 12.03 with five pilots of flight lieutenant rank taking the lead. All reached the target on Germany's frontier with France to find good visibility but the usual range of cloud conditions from zero to nine-tenths, which did not inhibit the crews' ability to pick out ground detail, including the marshalling yards, and the G-H-laid blue smoke-puff markers proved to be very effective against the background of snow. The 90 Squadron crews employed either "follow-the-leader" or H2S to establish their positions and released their loads from 18,000 to 19,200 feet between 15.35 and 15.36. The flash of detonations and rising smoke were evidence of a concentrated and successful raid, and this was the consensus at debriefings, although an element of overshooting was observed. As a result of the doubt, a follow-up operation by 274 aircraft of 4, 6 and 8 Groups was scheduled for that night, while a 3 Group G-H force of 134 Lancasters returned on the following day in the absence of a 90 Squadron contribution. The latter operation took place in good visibility and was concluded successfully without loss.

On the 15th the squadron bade farewell to W/C Ogilvie at the end of his successful tour of duty as squadron commander, and while he went off to a staff job at Bomber Command HQ, thirty-two-year-old W/C Peter Dunham DFC arrived as his successor, having served in the rank of flight lieutenant with 218 (Gold Coast) Squadron in 1941/42. Two targets occupied the group on the 15th, both believed to be benzol plants, one in the coal-mining town of Erkenschwick near Recklinghausen on the north-eastern edge of the Ruhr and the other, the Robert Muser refinery at Langendreer, situated between Bochum and Dortmund some ten miles to the south. In fact, the factory in Erkenschwick was synthesising nitrogen from coal originally for use in the agricultural fertilizer industry, for which Fritz Haber had won the Nobel Prize for chemistry in 1911, but since the outbreak of war in the manufacture of explosives, and it was for this destination that 90 Squadron made ready fifteen Lancasters as part of a force of eighty-two, while sixty-three were assigned to the Dortmund target. The 90 Squadron contingent departed Tuddenham between 11.35 and 11.59 with pilots of flight lieutenant rank leading the way and each crew with a cookie, ten 500 and four 250-pounders beneath their feet, the G-H leaders also carrying six red flares with green stars. The two forces adopted a common route over Belgium, passing to the west and south of Brussels and Liege before swinging towards the north-east for a run across the southern Ruhr to the targets, which were hidden beneath ten-tenths cloud with tops at 6,000 feet. The 90 Squadron crews bombed with the G-H leaders or on flares or H2S from 20,000 to 20,500 feet between 15.01 and 15.06 and the blue and green smoke-puffs again proved to be effective, the blue ones more so than the greens as they remained visible for longer. Returning crews were unable to provide an assessment of the results at both targets, and it seems that no report was made available, but local sources confirmed that the nitrogen plant had been destroyed and the adjacent coal mines severely damaged.

Briefings took place on 3 Group stations on the 16th in preparation for an attack on the Nordstern oil refinery at Gelsenkirchen, which was subsequently cancelled. However, the crews were briefed again later, this time for a night attack on the Krupp Treibstoffwerke benzol plant at Wanne-Eickel, a little further to the north-east towards Herne, for which each of 90 Squadron's fifteen Lancasters was loaded with a cookie supplemented with ten 500 and four 250-pounders. They departed Tuddenham between 22.53 and 23.08 with W/C Dunham and S/L Gray the senior pilots on duty, the former displaying excellent leadership qualities by putting himself immediately on the order of battle, a move that would be appreciated and respected by all flying personnel. They joined up with the rest of the 138-strong G-H force and flew out over low cloud, which was ten-tenths over the target with tops at up to 8,000 feet, and bombing was carried out by four of the 90 Squadron crews on H2S and ten on skymarkers and the glow of red TIs and fires from 18,500 to 20,000 feet between 02.15 and 02.27. F/O Sullivan and crew were unable to let their bombs go because of a malfunction in the bomb-release system, and the wireless operator managed to drop the cookie manually somewhere near Wuppertal on the way home. There was never a chance of observing any results and a red glow observed beneath the clouds was the only indication that the bombing had found the mark, and no post-raid reconnaissance took place.

On the 20th, S/L Day arrived from 138 Squadron at Tempsford to assume command of C Flight and would be allowed time to settle in, while a dozen crews who had enjoyed a few days away from the operational scene were called to arms on the 22nd, when Duisburg was revealed to be the target for 286 Lancasters and sixteen Mosquitos from 1, 3 and 8 Groups. They departed Tuddenham between 16.57 and 17.09 with S/L Reid the senior pilot on duty and a bomb load each of a cookie, eight 500 and four 250-pounders, and lost the services of F/L Rist and crew during the climb-out after the ammunition feed to the rear turret ran amok and filled it with rounds. Shortly afterwards, F/O Cocks and crew abandoned their sortie when their radio equipment failed, leaving the others to reach the target to find clear conditions with moonlight, which enabled them to identify the Rhine and observe the TIs falling onto the aiming point. The 90 Squadron participants carried out their attacks from 20,000 to 20,800 feet between 20.00 and 20.06 and observed many explosions and fires in a compact area, and as they retreated to the west watched thick, black smoke climbing skywards. The raid was concluded successfully and almost totally unopposed and it was established later that five hundred bombs had hit the Thyssen steelworks, which the local authorities assumed to have been the specific target.

The Gremberg marshalling yards in the south-east of Cologne was offered as the target for 153 Lancasters of 3 Group on the 28th, and it was probably something of a relief to crews across the group, who had attended briefings almost daily since the last operation but had been left frustrated by cancellations. It is difficult to comprehend how men with the most dangerous jobs in the war became listless and agitated when deprived of the opportunity to put themselves at further risk, but after a long lay-off, cheers accompanied the prospect of going to war again. F/Ls Edmunds, Orr and Wade were the senior pilots on duty as the fourteen 90 Squadron Lancasters took to the air between 10.19 and 10.40, each with a cookie, ten 500 and four 250-pounders in the bomb bay, and headed out over cloud, which broke in the target area to leave clear skies and excellent visibility. The main problem was the formation of condensation trails, which made formation-keeping and the run-in to the target somewhat challenging, while isolated patches of cloud got in the way of the vertical view. Despite this, the 90 Squadron contingent mostly delivered their attacks from 19,000 to 20,500 feet between 14.12 and 14.15 based on the G-H leader system and in the face of a spirited flak defence, some of which reached an estimated 29,000 feet. F/O Cocks and crew suffered a complete hang-up and tried in vain every method imaginable to effect a release, and eventually persuaded the cookie and four 250 pounders to fall away safe. F/O Gillespie and crew returned on three engines after losing the starboard-inner to flak, and F/O Wannop and crew were forced to land at Juvincourt in France after all four engines were damaged and the starboard-outer failed altogether. They would spend four days waiting for the weather to allow them to return. An analysis of the raid confirmed that many bomb loads had hit the marshalling yards, which was half full of rolling stock, but revealed a degree of overshooting in the early stages.

A large raid on the Stuttgart area was mounted that night by more than six hundred aircraft from 1, 4, 6 and 8 Groups, which attacked specific targets two hours apart. The railway yards in the town of Kornwestheim to the north and Stuttgart's north-eastern suburb of Zuffenhausen, containing the Hirth aero-engine factory, were both hit, but many stray bombs fell into other northern districts of the city, where a Bosch plant sustained damage. This was the last major raid of the war on this much-bombed industrial city.

The group operated for the final time in the month on the 29th, when the marshalling yards at Uerdingen in Krefeld was posted as the target for the second time in the month. A force of 148 Lancasters was made ready, of which fourteen took off from Tuddenham between 10.24 and 10.49 with pilots of flight lieutenant rank at the forefront and a cookie, ten 500 and four 250-pounders in each bomb bay. The forming up process was accomplished without difficulty and was maintained all the way to the target, which was covered by eight to ten-tenths cloud with tops at 5,000 feet. Some crews from 75(NZ) Squadron reported problems with another squadron cutting across, disrupting the formation and raining down bombs from above, but the 90 Squadron crews described a good formation and no problems as they carried out their attacks from 19,500 to 21,000 feet between 13.56 and 13.57. Having been troubled in the past by wrongly forecast winds, a Master Windfinder system was tried out on this operation, and it proved to be effective, while the bombing appeared to be concentrated and a large white mushroom of smoke was seen to rise through the clouds as the bombers turned for home.

During the course of the month the squadron took part in fourteen operations and dispatched 177 sorties for the loss of a single Lancaster and crew. With the European war moving into the final phase and plans in the pipeline for a contribution by Bomber Command to the war in the Pacific, a new 3 Group G-H Training Flight was established at RAF Feltwell to train crews in the use of the new radar navigational aids. This replaced 3 Group's Lancaster Finishing School, which closed down at the end of January. The first G-H Course was held on the 22nd of January and from then until the end of the war, most 3 Group crews attended, spending five days at Feltwell, their logbooks displaying the requisite two G-H training flights of between ninety minutes and three hours duration in one of eight Lancasters with a "MU" coding.

February 1945

Weather conditions over the Continent would prove challenging for the bombers during the first week of the new month, which began operationally with a daylight 3 Group G-H raid on the general town area of Mönchengladbach on the 1st, an operation originally briefed out but cancelled on the previous day. A force of 160 Lancasters was made ready, of which fourteen were provided by 90 Squadron, and they departed Tuddenham between 13.22 and 13.32 with W/C Dunham the senior pilot on duty, each bomb bay containing a cookie and either fourteen cluster bombs or ten 500 and four 250-pounders. The bomber stream headed south to cross the Channel on a southerly approach to the western fringe of the Ruhr and all arrived at the target to find up to ten-tenths cloud with tops at 12,000 feet and little opposition. The 90 Squadron crews released their bombs on H2S, blue smoke-puff markers or simply followed the G-H leaders from 17,800 to 19,000 feet between 16.26 and 16.28, and on return there were mixed opinions concerning the effectiveness of the raid. The consensus was of a scattered attack, which was confirmed by post-raid photographs that suggested that the main weight of bombs had fallen to starboard of the railway yards.

The first and only attack of the war on Wiesbaden, a city situated twenty miles west of Frankfurt, was planned for the night of the 2/3rd and the job handed to 1, 3, 6 and 8 Groups, which put together a force of 495 Lancasters and a dozen Mosquitos. 3 Group's contribution amounted to 160 of the former with 90 Squadron responsible for fourteen of them, each of which received the standard cookie/500lb/250lb bomb load before departing Tuddenham between 20.34 and 21.03 with S/L Gray the senior pilot on duty and thirty-three-year-old W/C William Bannister, who was on detachment from 32 Base, undertaking his first operation, presumably to gain experience before being given a command of his own. It has been written repeatedly that he had been 90 Squadron's commanding officer since December, but this is untrue and he had no prior connection with the squadron until his detachment in late January 1945. He was an elite athlete, who had competed for Great Britain in the Berlin Olympic Games of 1936 and in RAF service was an armaments specialist, who had held his rank since March 1941 and had been on loan to the RCAF in Canada for eleven months up to February 1943. Thereafter, he commanded various training units until transferring to 3 Group for operational duties and, therefore, probably had no operational experience at all. Thirty-three minutes after leaving the ground and during the climb-out and forming up process, W/C Bannister's HK610 collided with PD336 containing the crew of F/O Harries, and fell away out of control to crash near Bury St Edmunds with fatal consequences for the eight occupants. PD336 been hit from the port quarter forward and was severely damaged and difficult to control with the port tailplane missing, the rear turret hanging off and Sgt Hudspeth trapped inside, slumped over his guns. The mid-upper gunner managed to extricate him, bring him forward and administer morphine, while F/O Harries headed for The Wash to dump the bombs, after which, in the absence of a functioning radio, a distress cartridge was fired during the final approach to Tuddenham and a landing carried out with a burst tail-wheel tyre.

While this drama was being enacted, the rest of the squadron reached the target area, which was covered by cloud with tops in places as high as 21,000 feet. Skymarkers were employed by the Path Finder element and some crews observed dummy flares deployed by the enemy that attracted an occasional bomb load. Most crews bombed on a Gee-fix, H2S or DR, those from 90 Squadron from 18,000 to 20,000 feet between 23.40 and 23.50, and apart from bomb flashes, it was impossible to assess what was happening on the ground. It was left to local sources to suggest an effective attack, mentioning the destruction of more than five hundred houses with a slightly lower number seriously damaged and a death toll of approximately a thousand people. The 3 Group ORB lamented a bad night for the group, which had also seen the loss of the newly appointed 149 Squadron commanding officer, W/C Kay DFC, and had lost a few sorties to the bogging down of aircraft prior to take-off.

A dozen crews were briefed at Tuddenham on the 3rd and learned that they were to be part of a 149-strong 3 Group G-H attack on the Zeche-Hansa benzol plant situated in the Huckarde district of Dortmund to the north-west of the city centre. Each Lancaster received the standard bomb load before taking off between 16.10 and 16.22 with pilots of flight lieutenant rank leading the way and all arrived in the target area to find clear conditions and searchlight activity for the first time in months. Flak was also quite intense at the outset, though diminishing quickly, giving rise to the speculation that ammunition must be in short supply, but not before LM157 had been hit when two minutes short of the target and the starboard-outer engine set on fire. The damage was not terminal, and F/L Sullivan RAAF and crew carried on to deliver their payload with the rest of the squadron from 18,000 to 20,000 feet between 19.30 and 19.48. At debriefings the marking and bombing were reported to be accurate, even though one set of TIs had clearly overshot the aiming point, and one particularly large explosion had been observed at around 19.38, followed by a huge flash at 19.45 and fires taking hold as they turned away. Enemy night-fighters made their presence felt but no combats were reported by 90 Squadron crews. Post-raid reconnaissance revealed that the operation had not been successful, after the main weight of bombs had fallen into areas north and north-west of the aiming point. Among four missing Lancasters was 90 Squadron's PA158, which crashed somewhere in the Ruhr region with no survivors from the experienced crew of F/L Buning, whose parents lived in The Hague.

Having been repaired, LM157 was taken on an air-test by F/L Sullivan and crew and crash-landed at 15.20 near Newmarket after suffering engine failure and was destroyed by fire. Of the nine men on board, only the rear gunner, Sgt Mathias lost his life, although a number of others sustained injuries.

Eleven Lancasters were detailed at Tuddenham on the 7th to take part in a 3 Group G-H raid on the Krupp Treibstoffwerke synthetic oil plant at Wanne-Eickel involving a hundred aircraft, but as one of the heavy mobile G-H stations was out of position, and a light mobile pulse was all that was available to operate at considerable range, it was decided to scrub the 33 Base contribution altogether and reduce the size of the force to fifty. The 90 Squadron Lancasters each received the standard bomb load and took to the air between 11.52 and 12.02 with W/C Dunham the senior pilot on duty, only for three to turn back early, the crews of F/O Barton and F/L Wade after running into icing conditions over Belgium which affected engine performance, while F/Sgt Edgecombe lost a number of flying instruments. On arrival in the target area, their squadron colleagues delivered their attacks from 19,000 to 23,000 feet between 15.17 and 15.29, but around 25% of the force failed to bomb because of the difficult weather conditions and the results were inconclusive. That evening heavy raids were carried out on the frontier towns of Goch and Cleves (Kleve) ahead of the advancing British XXX Corps, and involved aircraft from 1, 4, 6 and 8 Groups.

Briefings took place on 3 Group stations on the morning of the 8th for an operation against an oil refinery at Lützkendorf, a location which no longer appears on a map and is now known as Mücheln or Krumpa and was one of the many such sites close to Leipzig. The site actually contained a small Wintershall refinery, a Bergius hydrogenation plant and a Fischer-Tropsch processing plant, but it is believed that the first-mentioned was the specific target for this operation. However, the raid was cancelled during the afternoon and replaced by one against the Hohenbudberg railway yards at Krefeld, a city perched on the western edge of the Ruhr south-west of Duisburg and north-west of Düsseldorf, for which 90 Squadron made ready eight Lancasters as part of a G-H force of 151. It was well into the early hours of the 9th before the raid was launched, departure from Tuddenham taking place between 03.30 and 03.49 with no fewer than eight pilots of flight lieutenant rank leading the way. They formed into a gaggle as they headed south, passing over Reading at altitudes ranging from 7,000 to 15,000 feet, and all reached the target to find eight-tenths cloud with tops at 10,000 feet, little flak, but effective searchlights. The 90 Squadron crews delivered their standard bomb loads from 18,500 to 20,000 feet on red TIs or an H2S-fix between 06.23 and 06.34 and returned with divided opinions as to the effectiveness of the attack, some believing it to have been concentrated after observing the glow of TIs through the cloud, but no accurate assessment could be made while the attack was ongoing. Post-raid reconnaissance revealed eventually that the bombing had fallen to the north-west of the aiming point and that no new damage could be detected.

No further major operations were undertaken for five days until the first round of the Churchill-inspired Operation Thunderclap series against Germany's eastern cities took place, which was devised partly to act in support of the advancing Russian ground forces and also as a demonstration to Stalin of RAF air power, should he turn against the Allies after the war. The historic and culturally significant city of Dresden was selected to open the offensive in another two-phase affair, with a 5 Group force of 246 Lancasters and nine Mosquitos leading the way, to be followed three hours later by 529 Lancasters of 1, 3, 6 and 8 Groups. It had proved to be a successful tactic thus far, with the 5 Group low-level marking system and main force attacks providing a beacon for the second force, and should it be required on this night, 8 Group would provide any necessary marking for phase two from high level. This would become the most controversial Bomber Command operation of the war and would define Bomber Command's entire war effort, unjustly blighting the reputation of ACM Sir Arthur Harris and calling into question the legitimacy of the part played by every member of aircrew throughout the conflict.

The briefing at Tuddenham that evening included a contribution from the squadron's bombing leader, who presented reconnaissance photos of the railway marshalling yards nominated as their aiming point. 90 Squadron's twelve Lancasters each received a bomb load consisting of a cookie and five cluster bombs containing 750 bomblets each, and they departed Tuddenham between 21.33 and 21.51 with S/L Reid the senior pilot on duty as part of a 3 Group contingent of 162 Lancasters. The 5 Group first phase attack delivered eight hundred tons of bombs through a thin layer of cloud after the aiming point had been marked from low-level by Mosquitos of 627 Squadron. This opening phase of the operation was moderately successful and created fires that were concentrated south of the River Elbe between the marshalling yards and the second phase aiming point. They had three hours to develop and become a beacon visible from a hundred miles away, and as the second force approached the target area, the cloud dispersed to leave clear skies. The existing fires provided the anticipated reference for the Path Finder element and although the bombing was a little scattered at first, the Master Bomber soon corrected it and the remainder of the 1,800 tons of bombs carried by this force fell in great concentration. The 90 Squadron crews carried out their attacks from 18,000 to 20,000 feet between 01.34 and 01.44 and contributed to a firestorm of terrifying proportions along the lines of that experienced in parts of Hamburg in July 1943. It devoured large parts of the city, the population of which had been swollen by an influx of refugees from the eastern front, and returning crews expressed confidence in the success of the operation, reporting the glow of fires to remain visible on the horizon for a hundred miles into the return flight.

A few hours later, a daylight raid by 311 American B17s delivered a further 771 tons of bombs, intended ostensibly for the railway yards, and some of the escort fighters descended to rooftop height to strafe open spaces and traffic on the roads around the city with the express purpose of increasing the level of chaos. There is a mistaken belief in Dresden even today, that the RAF was responsible for the strafing, but Bomber Command did not employ escort fighters on night operations. Initial propaganda-inspired reports from the Office of the Propaganda Minister, Joseph Göbbels, falsely claimed a death toll of 250,000 people to paint the hapless city and its residents as a victim of terror bombing, but an accurate figure of twenty-five thousand has been settled upon since.

The destruction of Dresden has been used in Germany and also by some elements in this country as a weapon with which to condemn Bomber Command and Harris and label them as war criminals. Curiously, no similar accusations have been levelled at the Americans. It should also be understood that Harris had no interest in attacking Dresden and had to be nagged by Chief-of-the-Air-Staff Portal to fulfil Churchill's wishes. Dresden was Germany's seventh largest city and its largest predominantly intact built-up area, which, according to American sources, contained more than a hundred factories and fifty thousand workers contributing to the war effort. It was also an important railway hub, to the extent that the marshalling yards had been attacked twice in late 1944 by the USAAF. The aircrew simply did the job asked of them and the attack on Dresden was no different from any other on a city. The death toll at Hamburg was much higher, and yet there has been no similar outcry. The legacy of this operation served to deny Harris and the men under his Command their due recognition for the massive part they played in the ultimate victory, and only in recent times has a monument been erected in Green Park in London and a campaign clasp awarded, sadly, far too late for the majority. Churchill, with his eyes set on a peacetime election, betrayed Harris and the Command in a typical politically motivated U-turn, in which he accused Harris of bombing solely for the purpose of inflicting terror. In the post-war honours, Harris was the only commander in the field to be omitted and was vilified for the rest of his life.

The following night brought round two of Operation Thunderclap, when Chemnitz was posted as the target for 717 Lancasters and Halifaxes of 1, 3, 4, 6 and 8 Groups, which would be divided into two waves separated by three-and-a-half hours. 5 Group would also be in the area with 224 Lancasters and eight Mosquitos to target an oil refinery in the small town of Rositz, situated twenty-five miles due south of Leipzig and thirty miles north-west of Chemnitz. Located about thirty miles west-south-west of Dresden, the city produced military hardware and was home to the Astra-Werke A G oil refinery, which was supplied with labour from the nearby Flossenburg female forced labour camp. Ten Lancasters were fuelled up at Tuddenham for the long round-trip and loaded with a cookie each and five cluster bombs, before taking off between 20.08 and 20.26 with S/L Gray the senior pilot on duty. They set course for the Belgian coast and F/L Rist and crew had penetrated as far as southern Luxembourg before engine issues persuaded them to turn back, one of thirteen from 3 Group to abandon their sorties, leaving the rest to fly out in clear skies until about fifty miles from the target, when they encountered two thin layers of ten-tenths stratus cloud with tops at 10,000 and 18,000 feet. The Path Finder blind illuminators opened the attack at 20.52, but as the cloud precluded identification of the aiming-point, the Master Bomber called for skymarking from 20.59 onwards. Salvoes of green/red flares were released by seven aircraft but proved to be scattered over a wide area with no point of concentration, however, with nothing else to aim at, the Master Bomber instructed crews to bomb on DR or navigational aids (H2S), and some managed to aim at the brief glow of flares as they fell through the upper layer of cloud. The 90 Squadron crews delivered their attacks from 18,000 to 20,000 feet between 00.32 and 00.36 and on return many admitted to a suspicion that the raid had been scattered and ineffective. This was confirmed by post-raid reconnaissance, which revealed that many parts of the city had been hit, while the majority of bombs had fallen into open country.

The town of Wesel, which nestles on the east bank of the Rhine, north of Duisburg, found itself directly in the path of the advancing Canadian 1st Army, and a series of raids over the ensuing days would see it effectively wiped off the map. The first one was mounted on the 16th by a 3 Group force of one hundred Lancasters with a single Path Finder Mosquito to provide the initial markers by Oboe. 90 Squadron made ready five Lancasters, which departed Tuddenham between 12.58 and 13.01 with F/L Wade the senior pilot on duty and the standard cookie, ten 500 and four 250-pounders in each bomb bay. The intention of the attack was to hit all road and railway communications to prevent enemy reinforcements from passing through, and clear skies aided the bombers to find the mark and put most of the bombs in the right area. The 90 Squadron crews attacked on H2S or G-H leaders from 18,500 to 20,000 feet between 15.56 and 16.00 before smoke and dust obscured the ground towards the end of the attack. All aircraft returned home safely and at debriefings their crews reported that the town and the railway installations had been smothered by bomb bursts.

Elements of 4, 6 and 8 Groups returned on the following day, when thick cloud was present, and the Master Bomber called a halt to proceedings after just a handful of aircraft had bombed. Similar conditions prevailed on the 18th, when 3 Group sent 160 Lancasters back to the town to carry out a G-H raid, to which cloud offered no impediment. 90 Squadron dispatched twelve Lancasters between 12.02 and 12.09 with pilots of flight lieutenant rank leading the way and all reached the target to find ten-tenths cloud with tops at 10,000 feet. G-H worked well and the 90 Squadron participants released their standard bomb loads from 17,500 to 19,000 feet between 15.22 and 15.28, before attending debriefing to offer no assessment of the outcome, although confidence was high that a successful raid had taken place.

The final attack of the series took place on the 19th, for which the squadron made ready ten Lancasters in a 3 Group force of 168 and sent them on their way from Tuddenham between 13.24 and 13.31 with W/C Dunham the senior pilot on duty and captaining F/L Reid's crew. At the target they encountered seven-tenths cloud, through which they were able to identify the river and the town, and as W/C Dunham and crew bore down on the aiming point as a G-H leader with bomb doors open, a flak shell detonated the bomb load and PD336, the Lancaster involved in the collision with HK610 on the 2nd, disintegrated, spreading itself far and wide, obviously with no survivors, and the following gaggle was forced to fly through the debris to deliver the bombs accurately into what remained of the built-up area and the railway yards to the east. This was the operations only casualty, and it left 90 Squadron with a vacancy for a commanding officer, which would not be filled from within.

The pace of operations did not slacken, and a dozen crews attended briefing at Tuddenham on the 20th to learn that the southern half of Dortmund was to be their target that night as part of a 3 Group contingent of 111 Lancasters in a heavy force of 514 of the type drawn from 1, 3, 6 and 8 Groups. They took off between 21.35 and 22.11 with no fewer than eight pilots of flight lieutenant rank leading the way and a cookie and cluster bombs beneath the feet of each crew. The target was covered by nine to ten-tenths thin cloud with tops at around 6,000 feet, through which the TIs on the ground were visible to some, while the 90 Squadron participants mostly bombed on red skymarkers with green stars from 18,500 to 21,000 feet between 01.13 and 01.18. Returning crews reported some scattered bombing, but generally a successful attack which left fires burning, and such was the degree of chaos in the city that no local report was prepared. This was the last major night raid on Dortmund, but its ordeal was not yet over.

The group divided its resources on the 22nd between the Hydrierwerke-Scholven synthetic oil refinery in the Buer district in the north-west of Gelsenkirchen and the extensive marshalling yards at Osterfeld in nearby Oberhausen, dispatching eighty-six Lancasters from 31 and 32 Bases to the former and eighty-two from 33 Base to the latter. Ten of the eleven 90 Squadron Lancasters at Tuddenham were loaded with a cookie, ten 500 and four 250-pounders, while F/L Rist and crew would be sitting on twelve 500-pounders and a single 250-pounder in addition to a cookie, and all took off between 12.55 and 13.02 bound for Gelsenkirchen, again with flight lieutenant-ranked senior pilots on duty. F/O Hart and crew turned back early after the starboard-inner propeller feathered itself, while the remainder arrived over the central Ruhr to find largely clear skies and the expected industrial haze. They bombed on H2S or "follow-the-leader" from 20,000 to 21,000 feet between 15.58 and 16.01 and a large explosion was witnessed at 15.57. Both operations were deemed to have been successful, and the Gelsenkirchen raid was filmed by the Photographic Unit from a 463 Squadron RAAF Lancaster.

The pressure on the enemy's oil industry was maintained on the 23rd, when 3 Group sent 133 Lancasters back to Gelsenkirchen to carry out a G-H raid on the Alma Pluto benzol plant, 90 Squadron providing eleven Lancasters, each loaded with a cookie, ten 500 and four 250-pounders. F/Ls Barry and Rist were the senior pilots on duty as they departed Tuddenham between 11.18 and 11.30 and found a layer of ten-tenths cloud over the target with tops as high as 24,000 feet, horizontal visibility of between five hundred and a thousand yards and vertical visibility down to two hundred yards at times. These conditions made it difficult to maintain the formation for the bombing run, despite which, the 90 Squadron crews delivered their attacks from 19,500 to 21,000 feet between 15.00 and 15.03 either on H2S or "follow-the-leader". It was impossible to assess the outcome, but the consensus was of a concentrated marking and bombing performance.

In an indication of the destructive power of the Command, on the night of the 23/24th a force of 360 aircraft from 1, 6 and 8 Groups delivered 1,825 tons of bombs from 8,000 feet onto the southern city of Pforzheim in a twenty-two-minute orgy of destruction that created a firestorm and left 17,000 fatalities in its wake. This was the third highest death toll to result from a single attack on a German city after Hamburg (40,000) and Dresden (25,000). It was during this operation that the final Victoria Cross was earned by a member of RAF Bomber Command. It went posthumously to the Master Bomber from 582 Squadron, Captain Ed Swales SAAF, who continued to control the attack in a Lancaster severely damaged by a night-fighter, before sacrificing his life to allow his crew the opportunity to save themselves.

The group's participation in a raid on the Chemwerke Steinkohle oil refinery at Bergkamen in the Ruhr was cancelled on the 24th, but the operation went ahead anyway with a predominantly Halifax main force provided by 4 and 6 Groups. In the event, most of the bombs fell onto the adjacent town of Kamen and other nearby communities, necessitating a further attack, for which a 3 Group G-H force of 153 Lancasters was made ready on the 25th. Thirteen Lancasters departed Tuddenham between 09.45 and 09.54 with five pilots of flight lieutenant rank leading the way, and a cookie, ten 500 and four 250-pounders in each bomb bay. All reached the target to find it hidden beneath layers of thin stratus cloud with tops at around 8,000 feet, but a few gaps provided brief glimpses of the ground. The blue smoke-puff markers appeared to be concentrated as the 90 Squadron contingent carried out their attacks from 19,500 to 21,000 feet between 12.48 and 12.50 and observed orange flashes followed initially by orange smoke, before large amounts of white and then thick, black smoke was seen rising through 6,000 feet. F/Sgt Clarine and crew experienced a complete hang-up but managed to release the cookie manually a minute after passing the planned release point and the rest of the bomb load a further minute later. At debriefings crews reported that as they left the target area, they could see that the bombing had been concentrated on one side of the aiming point, and they also commented on the hostility of the flak while over enemy territory, particularly on the way home.

W/C Scott became the new commanding officer on the 26th, not the S/L A R Scott RNZAF, who had served the squadron so well as a flight commander, but W/C Eric G Scott, who had begun his operational career on Wellingtons with 115 Squadron back in 1940, and he would see the squadron through to the end of hostilities. Whether or not he arrived at Tuddenham in time to sit in on the morning briefing is uncertain and unlikely, but those attending learned that 149 Lancasters of 3 Group were to conduct a G-H attack on the Hoesch-Benzin benzol plant in the Wambel district of Dortmund, and that 90 Squadron would be responsible for a dozen of them. Each was loaded with a cookie and twelve 500-pounders before taking off between 10.45 and 11.16 with S/L Gray the senior pilot on duty, and all arrived at their destination to find the target to be covered by ten-tenths low cloud with tops in places up to 10,000 feet, and there was also a strong wind, which dispersed the skymarkers very quickly. G-H worked well and the 90 Squadron crews fulfilled their briefs from 18,500 to 21,000 feet between 14.02 and 14.05, most following the leader, while two bombed on their own H2S and returning crews believed the attack to have been concentrated.

Briefings took place on 3 Group stations on the 27th for a return to the Alma Pluto benzol plant at Gelsenkirchen, for which a force of 149 Lancasters was assembled, nine of them provided by 90 Squadron and loaded with a cookie and twelve 500-pounders. They departed Tuddenham between 11.30 and 11.35 with F/Ls Daniel, Ross and Williams the senior pilots on duty and all reached the target area to encounter ten-tenths thick cloud with tops up to 8,000 feet, through which they bombed on H2S or G-H leaders from 19,500 to 21,500 feet between 14.30 and 14.31. The cloud concealed the results of their efforts and flak claimed one Lancaster from 186 Squadron, which was seen to go down during the bombing run.

Gelsenkirchen was the destination again on the 28th, this time for a 3 Group G-H force of 156 Lancasters targeting the Nordstern synthetic oil refinery, among them a dozen representing 90 Squadron, which departed Tuddenham between 09.03 and 09.10 with F/Ls Aldhouse, Barton, Daniel and Orr the senior pilots on duty and a bomb load each of a cookie and twelve 500-pounders. They all reached the target area to find the expected blanket of thick cloud topping out at 8,000 feet and bombing began ahead of the planned 12.00 H-Hour, which was somewhat fortuitous, as G-H station 114 became unserviceable between 12.04 and 12.09 and could not send out a pulse. The 90 Squadron crews attacked from 20,300 to 21,000 feet between 12.00 and 12.01, before the malfunction occurred, and although no assessment was possible, signs of black smoke emerging through the cloud tops as they turned away suggested that the operation had been accurate.

During the course of the month the squadron undertook eighteen operations and dispatched 202 sorties for the loss of two Lancasters, two crews and a rear gunner.

March 1945

March was to be a massively demanding month for the Command as it attempted to eradicate the last pockets of enemy war-production, particularly oil, and cut all remaining communications by road and rail. The weather over Germany remained as it had been, and ten-tenths cloud greeted the 151 Lancasters of 3 Group as they headed for the Chemwerke-Steinkohle oil refinery at Bergkamen on the 1st. Fourteen 90 Squadron aircraft had departed

Tuddenham between 11.55 and 12.07 with W/C Scott the senior pilot on duty and a cookie and twelve 500-pounders in each bomb bay. The lead squadron seemed to overshoot the final turning point after failing to pick up the tracking pulse and orbited to converge on the main stream from a variety of angles, which had the effect of breaking up the formation and compromising some bombing runs. Others fared better and the 90 Squadron crews were among those in a cohesive formation bombing through ten-tenths cloud at 9,000 feet either on the G-H leaders or their own H2S from 18,700 to 20,500 feet between 15.03 and 15.05. At debriefings, crews commented on the paucity of the defences and plentiful and concentrated blue smoke-puff markers, but suspected that the bombing had been scattered and that the target had probably escaped serious damage. Meanwhile, the main operation on this day was the final heavy raid of the war on Mannheim, which was already a broken city after being bombed dozens of times. Its neighbour across the Rhine, Ludwigshafen, also sustained severe damage in the attack, as did outlying communities.

The final raid of the war on Cologne, which now lay on the front line, was mounted on the following day in two phases, the first in the morning involving a force of 703 aircraft and the second in the afternoon by 155 Lancasters from 3 Group. The cloud that had sat over western Germany for weeks had finally cleared by the time that the main raid took place, and further massive damage was inflicted on what was left of the city's built-up area. As this force landed, thirteen Lancasters departed Tuddenham between 13.02 and 13.10 with W/C Scott and S/L Gray the senior pilots on duty and fourteen 500-pounders supplementing the cookie in each bomb bay. F/L Daniel and crew were some twenty miles inland from Berck-sur-Mer when an engine issue ended their interest in proceedings, leaving the others to press on and this time have to negotiate troublesome flak in the Mönchengladbach area. It was soon afterwards that the G-H releasing station in England failed and aircraft lost access to the pulse, which prompted four 90 squadron crews and eleven others to jettison their cookies live east of the Rhine and south-east of the target and turn back. The rest arrived over Cologne over five-tenths cloud and orbited, waiting for the G-H leaders to drop their bombs, and it seems that the remaining 90 Squadron aircraft were the only ones to carry out an attack, from 19,500 to 21,000 feet between 16.07 and 16.12, while most others brought their full bomb loads back as instructed by the Master Bomber. They were frustrated when they learned that the operation was classed as abortive (DNC) and would not count towards the completion of a tour, despite the fact that they had flown over the target and had faced the dangers. Four days later this once-proud city and capital of the Rhineland fell to American forces.

The cloud had returned to German skies by the time that the Krupp-Treibstoffwerke synthetic oil refinery at Wanne-Eickel and the nearby marshalling yards were posted as the targets for a 3 Group G-H force of 128 Lancasters on the 4th. The fourteen provided by 90 Squadron each received a bomb load of a cookie and fourteen 500-pounders before departing Tuddenham between 09.40 and 09.49 with F/Ls Barton, Daniel and Rist the senior pilots on duty. During the sea crossing the lead squadron made an unplanned course change to starboard, and shortly after crossing the Belgian coast at Knokke, F/O Liddle and crew turned back because of an engine issue. When sone fifteen minutes flying time from the target, the lead squadron altered course again, this time to port, but the 90 Squadron lead navigator was convinced that he was on the correct course and maintained it, separating the squadron from the main element. This caused the 90 Squadron contingent to arrive at the target a few minutes in advance of the rest of the force, which meant that they had to face the full fury of the considerable predicted heavy flak that came up through the ten-tenths cloud at 16,000 feet below them and two Lancasters sustained damage. The formation remained compact as the bombing took place from 19,500 to 20,500 feet between 12.18 and 12.29 under the umbrella of an escort that kept enemy fighters at bay, and behind them the main element bombed on G-H leaders and blue smoke-puff markers. All indications were that the operation had been successful, but no assessment of the outcome had been possible.

Twelve Lancasters took off from Tuddenham between 10.41 and 11.13 on the 5th led by F/Ls Barry, Barton, Daniel and Rist and set course to form up at 8,000 feet with the rest of the 170-strong 3 Group G-H force bound for the Consolidated benzol plant in the Schalke district of Gelsenkirchen. They found the target to be under ten-tenths thin cloud with tops ranging from 11,000 to 21,000 feet, and the 90 Squadron crews bombed from 20,000 to 21,500 feet between 14.07 and 14.09, half on G-H leaders and half on H2S and red smoke-puff markers. Flak was less intense than on the previous day and one 90 Squadron Lancaster was hit, but the demise of a 149 Squadron Lancaster was witnessed by many crews and six parachutes were reported to have deployed. The attack appeared to be concentrated, but no results could be ascertained.

That night, Operation Thunderclap set off to return to Chemnitz with 760 aircraft drawn from 1, 4, 6 and 8 Groups and nine 6 Group aircraft crashed close to home after climbing into severe icing conditions. Those reaching the target left central and southern districts engulfed in flames and lost twenty-two of their number in the process.

The I G Farben-owned Wintershall synthetic oil refinery at Salzbergen, situated in the flat Münsterland region of Germany close to the Dutch border north of the Ruhr, was the oldest oil plant in Germany having been founded in 1860. 119 Lancasters of 3 Group were made ready on the 6th to carry out a G-H attack upon it, and the ten participants from Tuddenham took off between 08.31 and 08.45 with W/C Scott the senior pilot on duty and each crew sitting on a cookie and twelve 500-pounders. Conditions were again ideal for a G-H attack, with ten-tenths cloud topping out at between 9,000 and 12,000 feet, which allowed for a good and tight formation. The 90 Squadron participants bombed from 19,000 to 20,000 feet between 12.12 and 12.14, six on G-H leaders and four on H2S, and the attack appeared to be concentrated around the aiming point, a fact confirmed by the sight of black smoke billowing up through the clouds.

Later in the day, 3 Group detailed two forces, one of thirty-eight Lancasters and the other of forty-nine, to carry out attacks on Wesel to follow up on another by 8 Group Mosquitos earlier in the day. It was believed that many German troops and vehicles were holed up in the ruins of the town as they retreated to the east and needed to be flushed out, while the town's bridges across the Rhine were the only ones still intact north of Cologne. 90 Squadron briefed the crews of F/Ls Barton and Rist and F/Os Cocks and Souster for the early attack and sent them on their way from Tuddenham between 18.10 and 18.14 with a cookie and fourteen 500-pounders in each bomb bay. They arrived at the target to find ten-tenths cloud with tops at 15,000 feet and bombed on H2S from 17,000 feet between 21.03 and 21.13, before returning safely to offer their impressions. They were tucked up in bed by the time that the second element departed Tuddenham between 02.39 and 02.45 led by four pilots of flight lieutenant rank, all of which arrived in the target area to find ten-tenths thin stratus cloud. F/O Hart and crew were unable to bomb as their H2S failed at the critical moment, but the remaining five 90 Squadron participants delivered their payloads from 18,000 feet between 05.30 and 05.39 and observed concentrated bomb flashes through the cloud.

A force of 526 aircraft from 1, 3, 6 and 8 Groups was assembled on the 7th and their crews briefed for the first attack of the war on Dessau, situated some two hundred miles east of the Ruhr and a hundred miles south-west of Berlin. The city had been home to the famous Bauhaus architectural school until the Nazis shut it down, but remained a major centre of learning and probably attracted the bombers because it was a virgin target at a time when few other cities remained intact. 3 Group put up 124 Lancasters, of which just four belonged to 90 Squadron, and they departed Tuddenham between 17.12 and 17.16 bearing aloft the crews of F/L Harries, F/O Gillespie and F/Sgts Edgecombe and Kattner, each of them with a cookie and seven N°14 cluster bombs beneath their feet. An engine issue forced the Edgecombe crew to return early, leaving the three remaining crews to find the target area almost completely concealed by haze and a layer of thin cloud, in the face of which the Master Bomber instructed crews to bomb on the skymarkers. However, it was standard practice for the Path Finders to prepare for both sky and ground-marking, and two of the 90 Squadron crews were able to see red and green TIs, while the third focused on red skymarkers with green stars. They carried out their attacks from 19,500 to 21,000 feet between 22.00 and 22.12, and with an abundance of markers to aim at and barely any defence from the ground, accurate and concentrated bombing left many fires burning across the city and by morning most of it lay in ruins, to be rebuilt postwar with the typical eastern bloc featureless concrete architecture. It proved to be an expensive night for the Command and cost eighteen Lancasters mostly to night-fighters, but 3 Group was the least afflicted with just two failures to return.

An hour after the above element had taken off from Tuddenham, the crews of F/O Ballard and F/L Daniel and F/O Ballard took to the air at 18.26 and 18.28 respectively to join three others from 32 and 33 Bases for mining duties in the Melon garden in Eckernförde Bay, an inlet in the Baltic north of Kiel. They were greeted in the target area by five-tenths cloud, but the ground was visible throughout and pinpoints acquired on a promontory, from which a timed run took them to the release point, where each planted five vegetables from 15,000 feet at 21.55 and 22.07. The Daniels crew was caught briefly in searchlights, but otherwise the six-hour round trip for the 90 Squadron pair was uneventful.

As Germany's control of Europe shrank, so the need to supply resistance organisations diminished also, and it was decided to remove 138 Squadron from SOE duties and convert it to Lancasters for a new role as a 3 Group "squadron of the line". Its new home would be Tuddenham, where it would share the facilities with 90 Squadron, and the advance party arrived on the 9th to begin to prepare offices, accommodation and see to all of the other requirements necessary to send a squadron to war.

3 Group remained at home on the 8th, when elements from other groups attacked Hamburg and Kassel, but 159 Lancasters were made ready on the 9th to target two Emscher-Lippe benzol plants in the town of Datteln, situated on the north-eastern edge of the Ruhr. They were divided 78/81 between aiming points A and B, north and south, and 90 Squadron provided fourteen

aircraft, which departed Tuddenham between 10.37 and 10.47 with pilots of flight lieutenant rank leading the way and a cookie and fourteen 500-pounders in each bomb bay. They encountered ten-tenths cloud at the target but no opposition and the bombing at aiming point B was described in the 3 Group ORB as "excellent", while that at aiming point A was scattered. It is not specified which attack involved the 90 Squadron element, we know only that they carried out their attacks from 20,000 to 21,000 feet between 13.56 and 13.57, nine on G-H leaders and four on H2S. At debriefings, crews reported observing blue smoke-puffs, a good formation at bomb-release time, and a simultaneous dropping of bombs in a well-co-ordinated G-H attack, followed by a mushroom of smoke rising through the cloud tops as they turned away. Post-raid reconnaissance confirmed the effectiveness of the attack on aiming point B, and also revealed that the nearby Dortmund-Ems Canal, a vital component in the enemy's communications network, had been breached and rendered 100% unnavigable, presumably by stray bombs. Absent from debriefing was the eight-man crew of F/L Aldhous in PA254, which was the only failure to return from the operation and had been brought down by flak. It is believed that F/L Aldhous was on the last operation of his tour, and only the rear gunner survived after baling out over Allied territory.

Twenty-four hours later 155 Lancasters from 3 Group retraced the steps of the previous day, to within ten miles of Datteln, to target the Hydrierwerke-Scholven synthetic oil refinery in Gelsenkirchen. Fourteen 90 Squadron crews made the trip, departing Tuddenham between 12.26 and 12.37 with F/Ls Barry, Barton, Gillespie and Harries the senior pilots on duty, and each crew sitting on a cookie and fourteen 500-pounders. F/Sgt Kattner had to feather the starboard-outer engine during the climb-out and headed directly for the jettison area, while the others joined the formation to approach the target in tight formation above ten-tenths cloud at 10,000 feet and bomb together from 19,000 to 20,500 feet between 15.30 and 15.31 in another example of a well-co-ordinated G-H attack. An assessment was impossible, but the accuracy and effectiveness of the bombing was confirmed when the post-raid reconnaissance photos were developed and posted.

A new record was set on the following morning, when 1,079 aircraft took off to deliver the final raid of the war on Essen, 3 Group contributing 143 Lancasters, of which ten represented 90 Squadron. They departed Tuddenham between 11.30 and 12.00 with W/C Scott the senior pilot on duty and lost the services of F/L Daniel and crew to an engine issue, probably at the enemy coast, as the cookie was jettisoned over the midpoint of the Channel at 15.20 on the way home. The others reached the target to find it covered by ten-tenths cloud with tops at 6,000 feet, which required the Path Finder element to employ skymarkers in the form of blue and later red smoke puffs, and the first of these went down at 14.59 to be backed up throughout the course of the raid. A 75(NZ) Squadron wireless operator reported that "the sky was filled with kites from horizon to horizon", and it must have been an awe-inspiring sight, not only for the crews, but also for those on the ground in liberated territories as the giant armada passed overhead to pound the hated enemy homeland. The Path Finders provided the marking for the main force, while 3 Group employed G-H, and the 90 Squadron formation was tight, which allowed for concentrated bombing from 19,000 to 20,500 feet between 15.35 and 15.36. The clouds were seen to take on a brown tinge as the attack developed, before black smoke was observed by some to billow through the tops. It was impossible to assess what was happening on the ground, but the 4,661 tons of bombs delivered in this attack left the city paralyzed and nine hundred people dead.

The record set on the 11th lasted barely twenty-four hours and was exceeded on the 12th when a force of 1,108 aircraft took off to deliver the final heavy raid of the war on the Ruhr city of Dortmund. A dozen Lancasters departed Tuddenham between 12.58 and 13.07 with F/Ls Reece and Ross the senior pilots on duty and the usual cookie/500-pounder bomb load, and they were part of a 3 Group contribution to the operation of 159 aircraft. They arrived over the Ruhr to find it still under a blanket of ten-tenths cloud with tops at 6,000 feet, conditions for which the Path Finders had prepared a skymarking plan based on green and blue smoke puffs. The first Oboe-aimed greens appeared at 16.26 to be followed a minute later by blues from the blind primary markers, and the Master Bomber directed the main force crews to aim for the blues. It was not long before brown smoke was climbing through the clouds to 8,000 feet from the northern end of the city, and crews also reported a ring of smoke encircling the entire area so dense, that it remained visible for 120 miles into the return flight. The 3 Group attack was delivered on the same lines as the previous day, on G-H after approaching in tight formation with F/L Reece and F/O Elliott the G-H leaders. In the event, eight of the 90 Squadron crews bombed on H2S, three on the G-H leaders and one on green smoke-puffs, and together they contributed to a new record of 4,851 tons of bombs dropped on central and southern districts, which ended all further war production. The loss of just two Lancasters spoke volumes about the enemy's inability to defend itself.

It was back to the Ruhr again for 3 Group on the 14th, to target coking plants at Datteln and Hattingen with forces respectively of eighty and eighty-nine Lancasters. It is possible that the latter, located just south of Bochum, was the giant Heinrichshütte steelworks with blast-furnaces that dominated Hattingen, rather than a coking plant, but this is speculation. Thirteen crews were briefed at Tuddenham, while out on the dispersals the armourers loaded each of their Lancasters with a cookie and twelve 500-pounders before sending them on their way between 13.24 and 13.34 with F/Ls Barton and Whyte the senior pilots on duty. They joined up with the others as they headed for the sea crossing, and according to the 3 Group ORB, were greeted by clear skies, which created problems for the Datteln element in particular as it came under accurate fire from flak batteries that broke up the formation. In contrast, the 90 Squadron ORB describes ten-tenths cloud with tops at 10,000 feet over Hattingen but also a heavy flak response, in spite of which a tight formation was maintained throughout and a concentrated attack delivered, eight of the 90 Squadron element bombing on G-H leaders and five on H2S from 19,000 to 19,900 feet between 16.43 and 16.45. Flak damage was widespread, but only one Lancaster failed to return and 90 Squadron came through unscathed.

3 Group was handed two targets on the 17th, the coking plant attached to the Gneisenau colliery at Oespel on the outskirts of Dortmund and the Auguste Viktoria benzol plant at Marl/Hüls, situated on the north-eastern edge of the Ruhr north-west of Recklinghausen. Fourteen Lancasters departed Tuddenham between 11.30 and 11.39 and set course for the former with S/L Gray the senior pilot on duty and a cookie and fourteen 500-pounders in each bomb bay. There was ten-tenths cloud at 12,000 feet in the target area and thin stratus up to 21,000 feet, which, along with the forming of condensation trails, created visibility problems and made it difficult for aircraft to maintain close contact with each other. The 90 Squadron crews bombed

from 19,500 to 21,000 feet between 15.01 and 15.03, ten on the G-H leaders, S/L Gray and F/O Gilbert, and four on H2S, and although no results were observed, the consensus was of an effective raid, as was that at Hüls.

The oil offensive continued on the 18th, when 3 Group was again handed two assignments for which it detailed fifty Lancasters each. The targets were the coking ovens and benzol plants at Hattingen and Bruchstrasse, the latter a north-western district of Duisburg, situated barely a mile from the Homberg oil refinery that had caused some 3 Group squadrons so much pain in the previous summer. One feature of this operation, in which 90 Squadron did not take part, was a special flight from 514 squadron equipped with the new G-H/H2S Mk III, which was not employed on this occasion for marking but to check that the system was working.

On the 19th 3 Group detailed seventy-nine Lancasters to attack the Consolidated coking plant in the Schalke district of Gelsenkirchen, for which 90 Squadron made ready fourteen of its Lancasters and loaded each with a cookie and fourteen 500-pounders. They departed Tuddenham between 12.43 and 12.53 with F/Ls Barton, Harries, Reece and Ross the senior pilots on duty and attempted to take their place in the formation behind 31 Base and 149 Squadron but lost them at the English coast and found themselves alone and in the lead. After crossing the Belgian coast they orbited over Brussels, at which point F/O Leach and crew turned back because of the failure of the rear turret. They orbited again at Aachen until the rest of the formation caught up, but 90 Squadron remained at the head of the force with F/L Reece and F/O Liddle the G-H leaders as the 90 Squadron element arrived at the target under clear skies and in the face of accurate flak. The ground was clearly visible when the bombing took place from 17,500 to 19,500 feet between 16.13 and 16.16, seven releasing their loads on the G-H leaders, five on H2S and one visually on railway track and most witnessed a large explosion at 16.16. As F/O Paine and crew began their bombing run they were hit by flak, which wounded the rear gunner, and immediately after bombing were hit again, this time in the nose, severely wounding the bomb-aimer. A third hit wounded the flight engineer, damaged an engine and set the aircraft on fire and F/O Paine would have ordered the crew to abandon ship at that point, had the bomb-aimer not been lying across the escape hatch and another crew member's parachute not been damaged. With a windmilling port-outer propeller, two engines on fire and no prospect of getting home, they set course for Juvincourt for a crash-landing, and as they passed through heavy flak over Düsseldorf a third engine caught fire persuading F/O Paine to throw the Lancaster into a dive in an attempt to extinguish the flames. It was clear that the end was nigh and HK608 was crash-landed at 16.44 in Allied-controlled territory about four miles from the centre of Mönchengladbach without further casualties and this would prove to be the final 90 Squadron aircraft to be lost on operations during the war.

90 Squadron was not involved when ninety-nine 3 Group Lancasters were assembled on the on the 20th for an attack on the important marshalling yards at Hamm, which promised to be a hot one because of its importance to the enemy's communications system. They arrived at their destination to find six to seven-tenths cloud with tops at 10,000 feet and perhaps less flak than might have been expected and no enemy fighters. The lead squadron deviated from track, causing the formation to scatter and creating confusion as it tried to get back together, but some semblance of order was regained and the bombing achieved a degree of concentration. The target could be seen through gaps in the cloud, and it appeared that the main weight of bombing

fell to the south-east of the aiming point, although some bomb bursts were observed to be within the boundary of the yards.

With the war so close to the end and the enemy's defensive capabilities so depleted, it must have seemed that the days of multiple losses for individual squadrons were firmly in the past, but events on the 21st brought a stark reminder that it wasn't over until it was over. Fourteen 90 Squadron crews attended briefing to learn that they were part of a 3 Group G-H force of 160 Lancasters assigned to deal with marshalling yards and a nearby railway viaduct in Münster, a city located in the flat agricultural land to the north of the Ruhr. They departed Tuddenham between 09.31 and 10.11 with F/L Barry the senior pilot on duty and the usual payload on board each Lancaster, but did not know that the G-H co-ordinates had been reversed inadvertently, and this would lead to some of those assigned to the viaduct attacking the marshalling yards instead. They arrived in the target area under clear skies and in good visibility to face a moderate amount of very accurate flak, and the first indication that all was not proceeding according to plan was when a section of the force overshot and had to turn back and run across the target from the wrong direction, exposing it to aircraft bombing from higher altitudes and causing it to break up just before bombing. The 90 Squadron element was not affected and bombed from 17,800 to 19,000 feet between 13.10 and 13.12, ten on the G-H leaders, F/L Barry and F/O Cocks, and four on H2S and noted in a slightly "Goldilocks" moment that someone else, namely 33 Base, had been "eating their porridge", in other words, bombing their aiming point. A reasonable concentration was achieved, but three Lancasters were seen to go down in the target area, and all belonged to 75(NZ) Squadron.

The frontier town of Bocholt, located some dozen or so miles north of the ruin that was once Wesel, was posted as the target for a 3 Group G-H force of one hundred Lancasters on the 22nd, presumably to cut communications and prevent retreating German forces from bringing up reinforcements. At the same time, some 110 miles away to the east-north-east, 220 Lancasters of 1, 6 and 8 Groups would be laying waste to the culturally significant city of Hildesheim, destroying 70% of its built-up area and killing more than sixteen hundred people. 90 Squadron loaded all eleven participating Lancasters with a cookie and twelve deep SBCs each containing 150 x 4lb incendiaries and sent them on their way from Tuddenham between 10.45 and 11.06 with F/Ls Barton, Jansen and Reece the senior pilots on duty. The skies over the Münsterland region were clear, but haze from a smoke screen protecting the American 21st Army Group drifted across the target area and the head of the bomber stream appeared to undershoot. The 90 Squadron crews carried out their attacks from 16,500 to 17,500 feet between 14.04 and 14.06 on the G-H leaders, H2S or visual reference, and the town was soon ablaze and sending black and brown smoke rising through 10,000 feet.

It was decided that Wesel required further softening-up before the Allied crossing of the Rhine preceded the capture of the town, and 3 Group was invited to send a force of eighty Lancasters to flush out any remaining enemy units. Seven 90 Squadron crews were briefed and departed Tuddenham between 14.20 and 14.24 with F/Ls Barry, Harries and Reece the senior pilots present, and each Lancaster carrying eleven 1,000 and three 500-pounders. The skies over the target were clear, the aiming point was identified visually, and all aircraft bombed together on G-H, those representing 90 Squadron from 18,300 to 18,500 feet between 17.33 and 17.35. Results were as planned and that night 5 Group carried out the final raid on the unfortunate pile of rubble once known as Wesel, and on the following morning the British 2nd Army crossed the Rhine to take the town with just thirty-six casualties, finding some of their German prisoners to be so traumatized that they could not be interrogated for forty-eight hours. A message of congratulations was received at Bomber Command HQ from General Montgomery and his American counterpart, General Dempsey. After the war, local authorities claimed that Wesel had been the most completely bombed town of its size in Germany, boasting just 3% of its built-up area still standing.

Thereafter, the Group was rested for a few days, before returning to the fray with another G-H raid on the 27th, this time against two targets, a benzol plant at Altenbögge, a site located north-east of Königsborn, which itself lies on the northern outskirts of Unna, a satellite town of Dortmund, and a coking plant at Sachsen, a suburb in the north of Hamm. 3 Group detailed 150 Lancasters and it must be assumed that they were divided roughly equally between the two locations. 90 Squadron made ready thirteen of its Lancasters, loading each with a cookie and fourteen 500-pounders destined for the Altenbögge site, and dispatched them from Tuddenham between 10.30 and 10.38 with F/Ls Barry, Barton and Jansen the senior pilots on duty. They found ten-tenths cloud in the target area with tops at various heights from 7,000 to 14,000 feet and held a tight formation as they bombed with concentration and precision from 18,500 to 20,000 feet between 13.54 and 13.55, ten on the G-H leaders, F/L Barry and F/O Elliott, and four on H2S. No results could be seen, but thick, black smoke rose through the cloud tops at both locations and the crews went home happy with their day's work.

The final operation of a hectic month was posted on the 29th, when the Tuddenham briefing was attended by eleven crews, who learned that they were part of a 3 Group G-H force of 130 Lancasters to attack the Hermann Göring benzol plant at Hallendorf, a suburb of Salzgitter, a satellite town to the south-west of Braunschweig that was dominated by the massive Hermann Göring steelworks. The group was bolstered by the operational debut on Lancasters of 138 Squadron with three crews, who departed Tuddenham at the same time as those from 90 Squadron between 12.27 and 12.37, each carrying a cookie and nine 500-pounders. F/Ls Barry, Harrison and Whyte were the senior pilots on duty as they climbed out and headed for the North Sea and eventually the Dutch coast, on the way losing the services of F/L Harrison and crew to an engine issue. Those reaching the target found it to be covered by cloud with tops at 19,000 feet and thin cloud and contrails above to 23,000 feet, which reduced visibility to five hundred yards and made formation-keeping a challenge. This operation marked the introduction of G-H/H2S Mk III as a marking device, but the tracking pulse was found by some to be intermittent and back-up blue smoke-puff markers quickly disappeared into the cloud, all of which probably caused the bombing to be scattered. The 90 Squadron crews delivered their payloads from 19,500 to 22,500 feet between 16.43 and 16.50, mostly on the G-H leaders, F/L Barry and F/O Souster, and were unable to assess the outcome, most believing that the bombing had been scattered and had fallen to the north of the target.

Thus ended the penultimate month of the bombing war, which had been busy in the extreme, and had involved the squadron in twenty-one operations, which generated 226 sorties for the loss of two Lancasters and one crew.

April 1945

In contrast to the hectic schedule during March, operations in early April would be sparse, and it was not until the 4th that the first crews were called to briefing at Tuddenham to learn that their target was the I G Farben-owned oil refinery at Leuna (Merseburg) near Leipzig, for which a 3, 6 and 8 Group heavy force of 327 Lancasters was prepared. This was just one of three major operations against Germany's oil industry on this day, the others involving 327 Halifaxes and Lancasters of 4, 6 and 8 Groups at Harburg/Hamburg and 258 Lancasters of 5 Group at Lützkendorf-Mücheln, also located near Leipzig. The thirteen 90 Squadron Lancasters each received a bomb load of a cookie and seven 500-pounders and took off between 18.30 and 18.56 with S/L Gray the senior pilot on duty. They all made it safely into German airspace to pass close to the town of Nordhausen and nearby barrack complex some forty miles short of the target, which had been attacked earlier in the day by 5 Group and on the previous day by 1 and 8 Groups. This created a bunch of jittery flak batteries, which fired at the formation and caused severe damage to at least one Lancaster. Those reaching the target found a layer of low cloud with tops up to 5,000 feet, through which the Path Finder red TIs were barely visible and the red skymarkers with green stars of little help. The 90 Squadron crews carried out their attacks from 17,500 to 20,000 feet between 22.35 and 22.58 aiming at whatever ground or skymarkers provided the best reference and were aware that the bombing was scattered and probably inaccurate. On return F/O Francis and crew reported attacking Magdeburg, some fifty miles north of Leuna, at the same time that the others were over the designated target and claimed that they had also bombed on red skymarkers with green stars.

The above-mentioned site located four miles north-north-west of the town of Nordhausen was believed to be a military barracks but was actually the only visible part of a highly secret underground manufacturing facility under the Kohnstein Hill. The site had been developed originally by the BASF Company to mine gypsum between 1917 and 1934 and consisted of two large parallel tunnels, which had been left abandoned until the destruction of Peenemünde in August 1943 prompted their resurrection. Smaller tunnels were cut to form a horizontal ladder effect linking the two main tunnels, and the site was turned over to the Mittelwerk GmbH (Gesellschaft mit beschrenkter Haftung, or Limited Company) for the manufacture of V-2 rockets and other secret projects. The "barracks" were part of the Mittelwerk-Dora forced workers camp, where inmates existed under the most horrendous conditions and brutal treatment, while they were starved, worked to death or simply murdered by an increasingly desperate regime seeking to change the course of the war.

3 Group remained off the order of battle for the next four days, and missed, therefore, the final heavy raid of the war on Hamburg's shipyard district, which was delivered by over four hundred aircraft from 4, 6 and 8 Groups on the night of the 8/9th. A force of 591 aircraft was assembled from 1, 3 and 8 Groups on the 9th for a two-pronged attack on the harbour district of Kiel, where the Germania Werft, Deutsche Werke and Howaldtswerke shipyards were located. This was a big night for 3 Group, which put up a record 241 Lancasters, of which fourteen belonged to 90 Squadron and departed Tuddenham between 19.24 and 19.53 with W/C Scott the senior pilot on duty and a cookie and twelve 500-pounders in each bomb bay. At the same time, seven other Lancasters took off for mining duties in the Forget-me-not garden on the approaches to Kiel, where they would be joined by eleven others from the group. The bombers reached the target

to find ground haze but clear skies, and a Master Bomber was on hand to assess the Path Finder marking and direct the main force bombing, the 90 Squadron contingent delivering their payloads from 19,500 to 20,000 feet between 22.30 and 22.42 and contributing to the extensive damage inflicted upon the Deutsche Werke U-Boot yards. Nearby, the Deutschland class "pocket" battleship, Admiral Scheer, sank and the cruisers Emden and Admiral Hipper were damaged, and the other shipyards were also hit along with adjacent residential districts, a success achieved for the modest cost to the Command of three Lancasters and their crews.

Meanwhile, six of 90 Squadron's gardeners were establishing their positions in the southern Baltic, while F/L Reece and crew were contending with the failure of their H2S and eventually abandoned their sortie and brought their mines home. The others planted their five or six vegetables each from 12,000 feet between 22.39 and 22.52 after conducting timed runs from coastal pinpoints and returned safely from an uneventful night's work.

The next time the squadron appeared on the order of battle it was for a return to Kiel on the 13th, for which fourteen Lancasters were made ready as part of a 3 Group element of 199 in an overall 3, 6 and 8 Group heavy force of 377 Lancasters and 105 Halifaxes. They departed Tuddenham between 20.25 and 20.40 with six pilots of flight lieutenant rank leading the way and a cookie and twelve 500-pounders in each bomb bay. They had been preceded into the air between 20.05 and 20.13 by the crews of P/Os Edgecombe and Proome and F/O Elliott, who were bound for mining duties in the Pumpkin garden in Samsø Belt, an area of the Baltic between Samsø Island and the north-western corner of Sjælland Island, the latter the location on its eastern seaboard of Copenhagen. The bombers reached the target to find ten-tenths thin stratus cloud with tops up to 5,000 feet, and Path Finder ground marking in progress under the guidance of a Master Bomber. The 90 Squadron crews released their bombs mostly on cascading red and green TIs from 16,500 to 19,500 feet between 23.24 and 23.40 and observed the glow of fires, which later became the aiming point, and two large explosions were witnessed, one of them resulting from a hit on an ammunition dump at the northern end of the harbour district. Generally, however, the bombing was scattered and focused largely on the suburb of Elmschenhagen two miles from the harbour. Meanwhile, the gardeners established their pinpoints on Sejerø Island and completed timed runs on a westerly course to plant their vegetables in the briefed locations from 12,000 feet between 23.28 and 23.36.

Harris's heavy bombers had left Berlin in peace for more than a year when orders came through on the 14th for an attack that night on Potsdam, situated some fifteen miles south-west from the centre of the German capital. This would be the first incursion into the Berlin defence zone for the heavy brigade since March 1944 and would prove to be the last major raid of the war on a German city. A force of five hundred Lancasters from 1, 3 and 8 Groups was assembled, a figure that included a 3 Group contribution of 198 Lancasters, fifteen of them representing 90 Squadron. Ten received a bomb load of a cookie and seven 500-pounders and five a single 8,000-pounder, before departing Tuddenham between 17.57 and 18.12 with pilots of flight lieutenant rank taking the lead. They found clear skies over north-eastern Germany and good visibility, which helped them to pick out the lakes on approach to the target. The Path Finders were responsible for the marking and a Master Bomber for keeping the raid on track, and he ordered crews to aim for bunches of red and green TIs, which were right on the aiming point in the city centre, the site of military barracks and railway facilities. The 90 Squadron contingent carried out their attacks from 19,000 to 20,000 feet between 22.46 and 22.55 in the face of moderate flak that was bursting below bombing height, but searchlights were numerous and effective and there was some evidence of night-fighter activity. Many extensive fires were observed, and a large explosion witnessed at 22.53, and it was clear that the raid was causing much damage and even spilled over into northern and eastern districts of Berlin itself. Casualties were extremely high, and although no official figure was forthcoming, it is believed to have reached five thousand fatalities.

The 18th brought a massive assault on the Island of Heligoland, situated in the North Sea some thirty miles out from the west coast of Schleswig-Holstein. It had been a fortress throughout the war, with a seaplane base, an airfield, U-Boot bunkers and coastal batteries and contained an air-raid shelter with an extensive tunnel system. It had attracted British attention during the early war years, but interest waned, although the waters around it in the Rosemary garden had been mined constantly. With the end of the war in sight and the Kriegsmarine running out of safe havens for its U-Boots and other craft, the island began to take on a greater significance. A force of 969 aircraft was assembled, of which 254 were provided by 3 Group, nineteen of them belonging to 90 Squadron, each of which received a bomb load of ten 1,000 and four 500-pounders and departed Tuddenham between 10.08 and 10.45 with W/C Scott the senior pilot on duty. When they arrived in the target area, which lay under clear skies, only the northern tip and western fringe of the island could be identified because the rest was concealed beneath smoke and dust as the surface of the island was reduced to, what in reconnaissance photographs, would resemble a cratered moonscape. The 3 Group crews bombed on the instructions of the Master Bomber, those from 90 Squadron from 18,000 to 19,500 feet between 13.02 and 13.04, and although some bombs were seen to fall into the sea, the majority hit the island, killing 285 people, most of them members of the flak crews and naval support staff.

The island's ordeal was not over, however, as thirty-six Lancasters of 9 and 617 Squadrons followed up on the 19th with Tallboy and Grand Slam earthquake bombs, and after being hit by 7,000 tons of bombs, the island was rendered uninhabitable and abandoned.

3 Group detailed a small G-H force of forty-nine Lancasters on the 19th to send deep into southern Germany, in fact to the foothills of the Alps to attack the Pasing marshalling yards located to the west of Munich city centre. 90 Squadron loaded five of its Lancasters with four 1,000 and ten 500-pounders and dispatched them from Tuddenham between 08.05 and 08.13 with F/L Whyte the senior pilot on duty and lost the services of F/O Wannop and crew to port-inner engine failure during the climb-out. The others pressed on to arrive in the target area over up to six-tenths cloud, and they relied on their H2S sets to establish their positions for bombing from 19,200 to 19,500 feet between 12.02 and 12.03. Bombs were seen to burst in the built-up area and on the marshalling yards and all returned safely from what appeared to be a concentrated and successful unopposed attack.

Seven 90 Squadron crew filed into the briefing room at Tuddenham on the 20th to learn of their part in a G-H raid by a hundred 3 Group Lancasters on petrol and oil-storage tanks in Regensburg, a medieval city deep in south-eastern Germany, which was home to an oil refinery and formerly a Messerschmitt aircraft factory producing BF109s. In actual fact, what had been the Bayerische Flugzeugwerke in Augsburg became Messerschmitt A G in 1938 and relocated to Haunstetten, some forty miles north-east of Augsburg and twenty-five miles west of Regensburg. A new housing settlement sprang up to accommodate the huge increase in the work force, which would reach a peak of 18,000 in 1944, 47% of which were either foreigners or slaves drafted in from satellite camps of Dachau. However, as far as the RAF and USAAF were concerned, for operational purposes the factory was referred to as located in Regensburg. The 90 Squadron element took off between 09.53 and 09.58 for the long round-trip with S/L Reid the senior pilot on duty and three 1,000 and ten 500-pounders in each bomb bay. S/L Reid and F/L Harrison were the G-H leaders as they flew out under clear skies that held all the way to the target, where the visibility was excellent and allowed crews to identify the river, the docks and the aiming point visually. The force approached from the north and the G-H system worked well for some, although the 90 Squadron element bombed on H2S from 17,000 to 19,500 feet between 13.59 and 14.00, and there was a degree of under and overshooting by some squadrons. The aiming point was plastered and a crew on the right-hand edge of the formation claimed a direct hit on a railway bridge in what was the final raid of the current series against Germany's oil industry and was completed for the loss to flak of a single 622 Squadron Lancaster.

3 Group provided 195 Lancasters in a combined force of 767 aircraft detailed on the 22nd to attack the south-eastern suburbs of Bremen ahead of the approaching British XXX Corps. 90 Squadron contributed fourteen Lancasters, which departed Tuddenham between 15.03 and 15.12 with F/Ls Harrison, Ross and Whyte the senior pilots on duty and a cookie and fourteen 500-pounders in each bomb bay. They approached the target on a south-easterly heading, passing over Wilhelmshaven at 17,500 feet at 18.30, and were greeted by seven-tenths cloud and accurate flak, although the 3 Group account states up to nine-tenths cloud with tops as high as 9,000 feet. The crews of F/L Harrison and F/O Hart lost the tracking pulse and opted to withhold their bombs, while the remainder released theirs on the G-H leader or their own H2S from 18,000 to 20,000 feet between 18.32 and 18.33, observing most of the hardware to fall within the built-up area, despite a little under and overshooting. W/C Mac Baigent of 75(NZ) Squadron wrote in his diary: "One of the pilots at the rear of the squadron said it was an unforgettable sight. Twenty-one Lancasters in tight formation, all with bomb doors open, cruising steadily up to Bremen, flak puffs all round, bombs poised, waiting for the leading aircraft to give the bombing signal. As our 12,000lb 'cookie' fell away a further twenty bomb loads of about 11,000 pounds each started their journey to the Bremen docks. The noise when the whole load landed must have been terrific." In fact, only 195 aircraft had bombed by the time that the Master Bomber called a halt to proceedings after dust and smoke obscured the aiming point and the whole 1 and 4 Group forces took their bombs home. The operation was successful, and the city would become the first German port to fall into Allied hands five days later. What was not known at the time, was that when F/L Whyte and crew landed at Tuddenham at 20.50, they would be the last from 90 Squadron to do so on return from an offensive operational sortie.

The bombing war for the other groups continued through the 25th, when elements of 1, 5 and 8 Groups targeted the Berghof and SS barracks at Hitler's Eaglesnest retreat at Berchtesgaden in the Bavarian mountains in the morning and elements of 4, 6 and 8 Groups attacked coastal batteries on the Frisian Island of Wangerooge in the afternoon. That night, 5 Group went to Tonsberg in southern Norway to deal with an oil refinery, and then it was all over, and the bomber fleet was turned over to a humanitarian role, first Operation Manna, to bring food to the starving Dutch people still under occupation, and Operation Exodus, the repatriation of prisoners of war from the Continent. 90 Squadron participated in Operation Manna on the afternoon of the 30th of April when sending fourteen Lancasters to deliver three packs of foodstuffs each to the Rotterdam area and followed this up at The Hague on the 1st, 4th, 7th and 8th of May, completing a total of forty-four sorties. The war and Operation Manna ended on the 8th, and on the following day 90 Squadron undertook its first seven sorties in support of Operation Exodus, each Lancaster collecting seventeen former prisoners of war from Juvincourt and delivering them to Dunsfold. Operation Exodus would continue through the summer months until all former PoWs were back home.

90 Squadron served Bomber Command with distinction during its two operational periods, despite being hampered at times by aircraft which were not up to the tasks asked of them. Once equipped with the Lancaster, however, it was able to assume its rightful place at the forefront of operations and contributed to the successful rebirth of 3 Group during the final year of the war. Unlike many other units, 90 Squadron was not disbanded after the war and continued to serve in different guises.

Farnborough and the Ju88

On the afternoon of the 24'th September 1943 the Appleby crew in BK784 WP-P made the short hop to the RAF research centre at Farnborough. As one of the most experienced surviving Stirling crew's at this time they had been selected to participate in test flights with one of the RAF's most secret possessions – a JU88 Night Fighter equipped with the latest German airborne radar.

In May a Ju88 R1 nightfighter had landed at Dyce airfield, Aberdeen, under the strangest of circumstances. The aircrafts crew had defected, bringing with them the latest in German radar technology. As the Ju88 flew across the North Sea crew radioed their base saying they had engine trouble and then gradually flew below radar level to disappear from the German radar and dropped life rafts into the sea to make believe they had ditched. Indeed, these life rafts were seen by German Search and Rescue and the Ju88 assumed lost. By this time it had been escorted into Dyce with a Spitfire escort.

It is still not clear whether the crew were long term agents of British Intelligence or had decided to do this this independently[1]. What is clear is that this was a great coup for the RAF. The acquisition of this Ju88 remained an important secret as the details of its radar were analysed by the research establishment at Farnborough.

All three German aircrew were given fake IDs and continued to work with British Intelligence in the UK. It is significant to note that they retained these new IDs after the end of the war until their deaths many decades later – the last to pass away being in 2002.

Over the next week they did five short flights whilst the Ju88, now bearing RAF roundels, flew above and around them. The longest of these flights was only 1h 15m and in the log books they were entered as "EXPERIMENTAL FLIGHT" with no other details given. According to Len Howell they were testing "Boozer" – an early radar detection device that was supposed to warn the crew if they were being tracked by German airborne radar.

F/Sgt Jock Guyan recalled how the JU 88 would be flying a few hundred feet behind the Stirling and a few hundred feet above the JU 88 was a Spitfire, presumably to ensure no eager RAF flight chanced upon the JU 88. Despite all the secrecy around the JU 88 Jock managed to take a photograph of the night fighter parked up next to the Stirling from the Stirling cockpit – presumably the authorities would not have been impressed if they knew (see page 95). Forty years later Jock had another photograph when he was re-united with this very aircraft in the RAF Museum at Hendon. The aircraft is now at IWM Cosford.

After this peaceful interlude they made the short, 30 minute, flight back to Wratting Common on the 1'st of October.
Upon return to the Squadron the whole crew found that they were being screened with immediate effect. - that they were being screened early because it had been a tough tour so far

---

[1] See http://aircrewremembered.com/schmid-herbert-defection.html for a modern analysis of this action

and the heavy squadron casualties were bad for moral, so it was good to see a crew successfully leave the Squadron. However, it is extremely unlikely that the decision was that sentimental (as borne out by Jock having to make up the numbers on his second tour) especially as such experienced crews were thin on the ground.

It was of the utmost importance that the fact the RAF was in possession of the latest German radar technology remained secret. It is more likely that it was decided that the risk could not be taken of any members of the crew surviving a shoot down and becoming a POW as the standard routine for Bomber Command survivors was that when captured they spent two weeks under interrogation before being sent to the POW camp. It is certain that some detail of their time with the Ju88 would have emerged in those circumstances. This seems to be backed up by the fact that as far as we can tell none of the crew went back on Operations for at least 12 months rather than the regular period of 6 months.

Details submitted by Andrew Guyan.

A Miscellany of 90 Squadron Photographs

Sgt Blackwood original rear gunner in Dennis Field Crew.

Tom Foreman, the very tall rear gunner in Sid Gay's crew.

Roll of Honour

Sgt	Brian Alfred	ABRAHAM	22.06.43.
Sgt	George Chirrey	ADAM	04.02.43.
F/Sgt	David	ADAMS	31.10.44.
F/L	Bernard Joseph	ALDHOUS	09.03.45.
Sgt	Robert	ALLAN	08.09.41.
F/O	Alexander	ALLAN	13.06.44.
P/O	John Guy	ALLEN	31.10.44.
Sgt	Edward Charles	ALLISON	23.12.44.
F/O	Henry Edward	ALLMAN	30.08.44.
F/Sgt	Sidney	AMBROSE	16.08.41.
F/Sgt	Leslie Edward	AMOS	23.04.44.
F/Sgt	Billie Albert	ANDERSON	28.08.43.
F/Sgt	John Alfred	ANDERTON	10.06.44.
Sgt	Albert Stanley	ANDREWS	22.06.43.
Sgt	Leslie Arthur	ANDREWS	15.10.44.
P/O	Joseph	ARMSTRONG	10.03.44.
Sgt	Ernest Arthur	ARNOLD	20.02.43.
Sgt	Ronald Leonard	ASTON	23.05.44.
Sgt	Eric Raymond	ATKINSON	30.08.44.
F/Sgt	Francis Frederick	AUSTERBERRY	29.10.44.
Sgt	Basil Albert	BACON	13.05.43.
Sgt	Denis Reginald	BAILEY	19.11.43.
W/C	William Geoffrey	BANNISTER	02.02.45.
Sgt	Josiah Trevor	BARBER	08.08.44.
Sgt	Clarence	BARROTT	21.04.43.
Sgt	Derek Alfred	BASSETT	21.07.44.
Sgt	Gordon George	BATTEN	09.11.43.
F/Sgt	Stanley	BAXTER	06.02.43.
Sgt	Oliver	BEARD	04.07.43.
Sgt	Robert Henry	BEATTIE	08.09.41.
F/Sgt	Wiliam Henry Taylor	BEATTIE	10.05.44.
Sgt	William Christie	BECK	30.05.43.
Sgt	William	BELL	03.10.43.
Sgt	Ernest Edward	BEMROSE	03.02.45.
Sgt	James Edward	BENNETT	19.02.45.
F/O	Harold Francis Sargent	BEST	21.07.44.
Sgt	William Hughes	BEVAN	26.02.43.
Sgt	John Frederick	BICKLEY	12.10.43.

Rank	Name	Surname	Date
F/O	William	BIRDSALL	23.09.43.
Sgt	James Walter	BISCOE	12.11.43.
F/O	Stanley Buckland Stewart	BISHOP	03.02.45.
Sgt	Horace Philip	BLACK	22.06.41.
Sgt	James Lawson	BLACKWOOD	02.12.43.
F/O	David Edward	BLAIN	18.11.43.
W/OII	Richard Barnett	BLAKE	15.04.43.
Sgt	John Lewis	BLOXHAM	01.09.43.
F/O	Charles Stewart	BOGLE	13.08.44.
F/Sgt	Leslie Arthur	BOLT	10.03.44.
Sgt	John Henry	BONE	15.03.44.
F/O	Hugo Hysert	BORCHARDT	21.07.44.
F/Sgt	Colin Baxter	BOWLING	13.04.44.
F/Sgt	James Ferguson	BOWMAN	26.07.43.
Sgt	James Henry Raymond	BOWTELL	01.09.44.
F/Sgt	Norman Collis	BOYD	23.12.44.
Sgt	James Riby	BOYES	27.04.43.
Sgt	Joseph Edward	BOZEAT	19.02.45.
F/Sgt	Reginald Gilbert	BRADLEY	28.07.41.
Sgt	Eric	BRADSHAW	22.06.43.
Sgt	Gordon Charles Arthur	BRADSHAW	23.09.43.
Sgt	John Olav	BRADSHAW	14.07.43
Sgt	Derek Malcolm	BRANDRICK	09.05.44.
Sgt	James	BRASON	23.05.43.
Sgt	Edward Raymond	BRAY	09.05.44.
F/Sgt	Hubert Charles Gerard	BROOK	28.07.41.
Sgt	Edward George	BROOKE	30.05.43.
F/O	Alexander Campbell	BROOKS	08.08.44.
Sgt	Leonard Stuart	BROOMFIELD	05.05.43.
F/O	Donald Arthur	BROWN	18.11.43.
F/Sgt	Hugh McBeath	BROWN	21.07.44.
F/O	James Edward	BROWN	16.09.44.
Sgt	John George	BROWN	03.02.45.
Sgt	John	BROWN	08.09.41.
Sgt	William	BRUCE	15.03.44.
Sgt	Robert George Frederick	BRYANT	28.02.43.
Sgt	William Harry	BRYANT	26.05.43.
F/O	James Stenhouse	BRYDON	16.02.43.
Sgt	Noel	BUCKBY	15.10.44.
F/L	Johannes Jacobus	BUNING	03.02.45.
P/O	Thomas Alfred	BURNETT	11.06.44.

Rank	Name	Surname	Date
Sgt	William Alexander	BURNETT	28.06.44.
Sgt	Hugh Faringdon	BURRETT	01.09.43.
Sgt	Harold William	BURTON	05.05.43.
Sgt	Spencer Christopher John	BUTCHER	21.07.44.
Sgt	Thomas Alfred George	BUTT	15.02.43.
W/O	James William	BUTTERWORTH	21.07.44.
Sgt	Arthur John	BUXTON	13.05.43.
Sgt	Thomas David Stoddart	CAIRNS	08.08.44.
Sgt	William Denmark	CAIRNS	10.06.44.
P/O	Martin Philip	CALLAWAY	01.09.43.
F/Sgt	Lawrence Gordon	CALMAN	28.10.44.
F/Sgt	Ronald Sutton	CAMIER	13.08.44.
Sgt	Archibald Thomas Wilson	CAMPBELL	18.08.43.
Sgt	Colin Desmond Harry	CAMPBELL	26.06.43.
P/O	Sydney	CAMPBELL	31.10.44.
F/Sgt	William Wright	CAMPBELL	13.04.44.
P/O	Ernest	CANDY	14.07.43.
Sgt	Stanley Richard	CANN	15.02.43.
Sgt	Cornelius Charles	CANNON	21.07.44.
F/O	Howard Francs John	CARLTON	19.02.45.
Sgt	Harold	CARTWRIGHT	01.09.43.
F/Sgt	Hugh Desmond	CAWSON	25.06.44.
Sgt	Alfred	CHADWICK	21.04.43.
Sgt	Jeffrey James	CHIDWICK	02.02.45.
F/O	Alexander Anthony	CHRISTIE	23.12.44.
Sgt	James Frederick	CHRISTON	06.02.43.
Sgt	Charles Henry Arthur	CLARK	28.09.43.
F/O	Frank Arthur	CLAYDEN	15.10.44.
Sgt	Leonard	CLIFTON	31.07.43.
Sgt	Frederick William	CLINCH	23.12.44.
Sgt	Eric Royston	COCKER	13.06.44.
Sgt	Ronald Francis	COCKING	27.04.43.
Sgt	George Edward	COLLINS	15.03.44.
F/Sgt	Basil Edgar	COLUMBUS	13.09.44.
F/O	Patrick Hector	CONROY	26.07.43.
Sgt	Thomas Alfred	CONSTABLE	20.02.43.
F/O	Alec Victor Ibbetson	COOK	26.06.43.
F/Sgt	John	COOLING	15.10.44.
F/L	Cyril Ernest	COOMBS	14.07.43.
Sgt	Alan Norman	COOPER	25.06.43.
Sgt	Maurice Charles	COTTERELL	23.03.40.

Rank	Name	Surname	Date
Sgt	Peter Barnard	CORBETT	08.09.41.
Sgt	Edward	COULDWELL	15.02.43.
F/Sgt	James Ross	COURT	26.08.44.
P/O	James Boyd	COURTNEY	05.03.43.
F/Sgt	Bernard	COWARD	28.10.44.
P/O	Frederick Allan	CRESSWELL	19.02.44.
P/O	Sydney Nelson	CROSS	21.04.43.
Sgt	Cyril Leslie	CRUTTENDEN	21.04.43.
F/Sgt	Gordon Edwin	DALTON	03.10.43.
F/O	Pennell Stilis	DALTON	28.09.43.
Sgt	Cecil Geoffrey Nigel	DARLOW	31.10.44.
Sgt	Edward Francis	DAVANY	09.11.43.
F/Sgt	Allan Edward Dearlove	DAVEY	26.02.44.
Sgt	Douglas William Henry	DAVEY	30.08.44.
Sgt	John Charles	DAVIDSON	26.06.43.
Sgt	David John	DAVIES	22.06.43.
F/L	Francis James	DAVIES	07.03.41.
Sgt	Digby Gwilym St. John	DAVIES	09.10.43.
F/O	Ronald Jack	DAVIS	05.05.43.
Sgt	William Gorden	DAWSON	14.07.43.
F/Sgt	Nelson John	De La HAYE	25.06.44.
Sgt	Yves	De MEILLAC	03.10.43.
Sgt	Alfred William	DENBY	28.10.44.
Sgt	John Edward William	DICKINSON	21.07.44.
Sgt	Jeremiah Francis	DINEEN	21.07.44.
F/O	Henry Alington	DISBROWE	26.07.43.
Sgt	Cyril William	DIXON	25.06.43.
F/Sgt	Alexander	DOBSON	27.08.44.
Sgt	Norman James John	DOBSON	23.04.44.
Sgt	Vincent	DOOLEY	29.01.44.
Sgt	Edwin	DRAPER	02.12.43.
S/L	Joseph	DUGDALE	26.07.43.
F/Sgt	Thomas Douglas	DUGGAN	13.04.44.
W/C	Peter Francis	DUNHAM	19.02.45.
Sgt	Reginald Herbert	DUNSTAN	21.04.43.
Sgt	John Henry	DYER	26.02.43.
Sgt	Frederick William	EALDEN	26.06.43.
W/OII	Michael George King	EAST	26.05.43.
F/Sgt	John David	EATON	26.02.44.
F/Sgt	Alfred Henry	EDWARDS	03.02.45.
Sgt	Albert Victor	EDWARDS	13.05.43.

Rank	First Names	Surname	Date
Sgt	Terry	EDWARDS	20.10.43.
Sgt	Patrick Joseph	EGAN	04.02.43.
Sgt	Harry George	EGGBEER	23.05.44.
F/Sgt	Edward Laverne	EITEL	29.07.44.
Sgt	Edward William	EKE	13.05.43.
Sgt	George Cornelius	ELLARD	13.08.44.
F/O	Albert Clark	ELLIOTT	13.06.44.
P/O	Reginald Frederick	ELLIOTT	21.04.43.
F/Sgt	John Reginald	ENNOR	23.12.44.
F/O	Kenneth Trevor	ESCOURT	30.05.43.
Sgt	Arthur Henry	ESTCOURTE	15.03.44.
F/Sgt	David Geoffrey	EVANS	26.07.43.
Sgt	Norman Louis	FAUVEL	21.04.43.
Sgt	Charles Henry	FENTON	04.07.43.
Sgt	Clifford Richard	FENWICK	23.06.43.
Sgt	Robert Jeffrey	FERRANS	28.06.44.
P/O	Myron	FETCHISON	29.07.44.
Sgt	Robert Hamilton	FINLAYSON	26.08.44.
Sgt	Stanley George	FISHER	20.02.43.
Sgt	Jack Herbert	FLACK	02.12.43.
Sgt	Edward John	FLAHERTY	21.07.44.
F/Sgt	John Stuart Selby	FLEMING	19.11.43.
F/O	Herbert George	FLOYD	23.12.44.
F/O	William Alexander	FOWLIE	05.03.43.
P/O	Charles	FOY	09.03.45
Sgt	Lyle Albert	FRANCE	06.02.43.
W/O	John Carr	FRANCIS	10.06.44.
Sgt	Robert	FREELAND	04.07.43.
S/L	Max Ingram	FREEMAN	28.09.43.
F/L	Cyril Vincent	FRENCH	05.03.44.
F/L	Leonard Arthur	FRENCH	08.08.44.
Sgt	Robert Cooper	FROST	20.02.43.
Sgt	Roy Warren Melvin	FULFORD	26.08.44.
Sgt	Arthur Ronald	FULLER	03.10.43.
P/O	Frederick George	GARDINER	13.04.44.
Sgt	John Campbell	GARDNER	25.06.43.
F/Sgt	George James	GARWOOD	22.06.41
Sgt	Cedric Brian	GAZZARD	23.09.43.
P/O	Joseph Isador	GEDAK	13.05.43.
Sgt	Alfred Charles Dempsey	GENT	12.09.44.
W/OI	Robert William	GIBSON	23.12.44.

Sgt	Cyril Stanley	GILBERT	13.08.44.
Sgt	Leslie Mathers	GILL	16.09.44.
Sgt	David	GILLIS	22.06.43.
P/O	Andrew Patrick	GILMOUR	04.07.43.
Sgt	Stanley	GLAISTER	23.04.44.
Sgt	Mervyn John Frederick Poole	GODDARD	03.02.45.
Sgt	Martin	GOLDRICK	20.02.43.
F/O	Francis Edward	GOOD	26.08.44.
Sgt	Stanley Francis	GOULD	15.04.43.
Sgt	Newell	GRAHAM	23.06.43.
Sgt	Robert	GRAHAM	28.08.43.
Sgt	John Edwin	GRAY	06.09.43.
P/O	William Leslie	GRAY	31.07.43.
F/O	Roy	GREAVES	09.10.43.
Sgt	Charles	GREEN	13.05.43.
Sgt	Clarence Charles	GREENAWAY	06.02.43.
P/O	John Douglas	GREENWOOD	29.01.44.
Sgt	Leslie Mayberry	GRIFFITHS	09.11.43.
Sgt	John Fraser McKenzie	GUNN	22.09.43.
F/O	John Vernon	GUSTOFSON	30.05.43.
F/Sgt	William Trevor	GUY	03.10.43.
Sgt	Arthur Cooper	HAIGH	18.02.40.
Sgt	Leslie	HAININ	29.04.43.
Sgt	Albert Ernest	HALL	30.08.44.
Sgt	Thomas Edwin	HALL	21.04.43.
W/O	William Derek Taylor	HALSTEAD	27.08.44.
Sgt	Reginald	HAMMOND	23.06.43.
Sgt	Samuel	HAMMOND	15.04.43.
F/O	John	HAMPTON	19.11.43
Sgt	Ronald Jesse	HARBOUR	18.02.40.
Sgt	Kenneth Lovell	HARDING	29.01.44.
Sgt	Robert Edward	HARDINGHAM	27.04.43.
Sgt	Aubrey Charles	HARRIS	25.06.43.
F/Sgt	Leo Frederick	HARRIS	06.09.43.
Sgt	William Gothwaite	HARRIS	06.02.43.
F/Sgt	Edward Arthur	HARRISON	13.04.44.
P/O	Frank Gordon	HART	08.09.41.
F/O	Norman John Patrick	HARTNEY	16.02.43.
F/Sgt	Richard James Travers	HAWKES	28.06.44.
F/O	John Charles Michael	HAWLEY	22.06.41.
Sgt	George Alfred	HAYES	09.10.43.

Rank	First Names	Surname	Date
Sgt	Francis Ernest	HAYMAN	22.09.43.
Sgt	Colin	HAYNES	23.09.43.
Sgt	Herbert William	HAZELL	13.09.44.
F/Sgt	Donald George	HEADLAND	28.10.44.
Sgt	William	HEAHER	23.04.44.
F/Sgt	Leonard William	HEASON	18.11.43.
P/O	Gerald Frederick	HEATHCOTE-PEIRSON	29.04.43.
F/Sgt	William Andrew	HEBDEN	31.07.43.
F/Sgt	Gordon	HENDERSON	25.06.43.
Sgt	Robert	HENDERSON	28.07.41.
Sgt	Thomas Raymond	HEWITT	15.03.44.
P/O	Leslie William	HIGGINS	09.05.44.
F/O	Robert Josephus Constable	HIGGINS	28.10.44.
Sgt	Donald Colin	HILL	06.09.43.
P/O	George Robert	HILTON	12.10.43.
F/Sgt	Hugh Donald	HILTS	29.07.44.
Sgt	Robert	HINDMARCH	28.08.43.
Sgt	John Charles	HINDS	13.08.44.
Sgt	Arthur Vivian Derrick	HINES	26.02.43.
W/OII	William Joseph	HOAR	28.09.43.
Sgt	Douglas Edward John	HOBBS	23.09.43.
Sgt	Desmond Frank Augustus	HOBBS	26.07.43.
P/O	Frederick Jame	HOGAN	08.09.41.
Sgt	John Stanley	HOLDCROFT	26.08.44.
Sgt	Douglas Leon	HOLLAMBY	18.11.43.
Sgt	Gordon Reginald	HOLLAND	29.01.44.
Sgt	Eric Howeth	HOLMES	26.02.43.
Sgt	Alec	HOLT	20.02.43.
Sgt	Walter George	HONEY	08.09.41.
P/O	William John	HOPE	26.08.44.
Sgt	Jpseph Kenneth	HORN	28.06.44.
Sgt	Kenneth George	HORNE	29.04.43.
Sgt	Douglas William	HOWARD	06.02.43.
Sgt	Joseph	HOWARTH	23.09.43.
Sgt	Kenneth Brian	HOWELL	15.10.44.
F/Sgt	John	HUDSON	23.09.43.
Sgt	Cecil William	HUGHES	30.05.43.
F/Sgt	Gordon Henry	HUGHES	23.09.43.
F/L	John Bernard William	HUMPHERSON	22.06.41
Sgt	Leonard Joseph	HUMPHREY	28.02.43.
Sgt	Harry Richard Stuart	HUNNISETT	21.07.44.

Rank	Name	Surname	Date
W/OII	Joseph Wilfred Jean Paul	HUOT	29.07.44.
F/Sgt	Nathan Merrill	HURLBUT	13.09.44.
Sgt	Frederick Joseph	HUXEN	10.03.44.
Sgt	Dennis James	INGRAM	29.07.44.
F/Sgt	Harold Elburn	ISLES	09.05.44.
Sgt	Cyril Douglas	JAMES	08.09.41.
Sgt	Douglas Anthony	JAMES	23.09.43.
F/Sgt	Joseph Davis Stephen	JAMES	10.06.44.
Sgt	Stanley	JAMES	13.05.43.
Sgt	John	JEFFERSON	13.04.44.
Sgt	Gordon Clarence	JEFFREYS	24.08.43.
Sgt	Leslie Howard	JENKINS	04.02.43.
Sgt	Lionel Fairfax Furner	JOHNS	30.05.43.
F/O	Harry	JOHNSON	16.09.44.
Sgt	George Arthur Francis	JOHNSTON	30.05.43.
Sgt	Robert Alexander	JOHNSTON	20.02.43.
F/Sgt	Howell Idris	JONES	09.11.43.
Sgt	Percy William	JONES	13.08.44.
Sgt	Ronald Lloyd	JONES	24.08.43.
F/Sgt	Wallace Edgar	JONES	20.10.43.
F/L	Lawrence	JOSEPH	10.05.44.
Sgt	John	KAY	05.05.43.
Sgt	Derek Henry	KEALEY	31.07.43.
F/Sgt	John William	KEALY	03.10.43.
F/Sgt	James Hamilton	KEELEY	26.07.43.
F/Sgt	Alfred George Alexander	KEENOR	25.06.44.
F/O	Francis Henry Ross	KEMP	05.01 45.
Sgt	Harold Moore	KENNARD	20.02.43.
Sgt	James	KENNEDY	15.02.43.
Sgt	Stanley Thomas	KETTLETY	09.10.43.
Sgt	Denzil Charles	KIBBLE	13.06.44.
F/Sgt	Maurice	KIEFF	26.08.44.
S/L	Terence Sydney Raymond	KING	10.03.44.
Sgt	Guy	KIPLING	23.06.43.
F/L	Abraham Lionel	KIRSCH	13.09.44.
F/L	Robert Langley	KNOWLES	20.02.43.
Sgt	James Readdie	LAING	24.08.43.
Sgt	Gerald	LAMB	15.10.44.
Sgt	Arthur John	LANE	22.09.43.
F/Sgt	William	LANE	21.07.44.
F/Sgt	Lawrence	LANGLEY	12.10.43.

F/O	Derek Cunningham	LAW	12.09.44.
Sgt	John Downing	LAW	22.09.43.
Sgt	Robert Ronald	LAW	22.06.43.
Sgt	George Witham	LAWSON	23.06.43.
F/O	Jack	LEADBEATER	30.08.44.
Sgt	Michael John	LEAHY	16.08.41.
Sgt	Victor Gorge	LEAK	27.04.43.
F/O	Edward (Teddy)	LEAR	28.02.43.
Sgt	Peter John	LEATHER	27.08.44.
Sgt	William Trevor	LEATHLEY	21.04.43.
Sgt	Eric Kenneth	LEEVES	03.10.43.
S/L	Henry Philip	LEE-WARNER	26.08.44.
Sgt	Arthur Fredrick Robert	LEONARD	04.07.43.
Sgt	Mervyn	LEONARD	21.04.43.
F/O	Robert William John	LETTERS	30.05.43.
Sgt	Hyman	LEVINE	25.06.43.
Sgt	Arthur Moseley	LIMBRICK	20.02.43.
F/Sgt	Keith Roland	LINDENBERG	29.01.44.
Sgt	John Desmond	LINDREA	21.04.43.
Sgt	Albert Eric	LLOYD	24.08.43.
Sgt	Charles Alexander	LONG	14.07.43.
Sgt	Leslie Wilfred	LONGMAN	03.10.43.
Sgt	Kenneth William	LONGMORE	24.08.43.
W/OII	Leslie Allen Ralph	LOWE	13.04.44.
F/Sgt	Morley Percival	LOYST	09.11.43.
Sgt	Donald Frederick	LUXFORD	02.02.45.
P/O	George Douglas	MACDOUGALL	04.02.43.
Sgt	Charles Dale	McKELVIE	21.04.43.
F/O	Ian Fraser	MACKENZIE	27.04.43.
Sgt	Leslie Thomas	MACSWAYNE	20.10.43.
Sgt	Claud Gordon Humphrey	MACTAVISH	04.02.43.
Sgt	George Derrick	MAIR	01.09.43.
P/O	William Gordon	MAIR	30.08.44.
P/O	Wilfred Roy	MAJOR	26.02.43.
Sgt	John	MANNING	23.12.44.
Sgt	Arthur Forster	MARSHALL	21.07.44.
Sgt	Norman	MARSHALL	29.04.43.
F/O	Alan	MARTIN	26.08.44.
F/Sgt	Kenneth Andrew	MARTIN	12.09.44.
Sgt	John Lawrence	MATHIAS	06.02.45.
S/L	Alexander	MATHIESON	08.09.41.

Rank	Name	Surname	Date
P/O	Edward Thomas	MATON	13.05.43.
Sgt	Thomas Granville	MATTHEWS	13.05.43.
P/O	Clifford Leigh	MAUNDER	21.04.43.
Sgt	Frederick Charles	MAXWELL	05.05.43.
S/L	Robert Seayears	MAY	29.04.43.
F/Sgt	Hilton Henry	McATEER	12.09.44.
F/Sgt	Robert Browning	McCORMACK	13.08.44.
Sgt	Phillip Joseph	McCRORY	23.05.44.
ACII	William	McEWAN	18.02.40.
F/Sgt	Ian Malcolm James	MCGARVIN	18.12.42.
Sgt	Alexander Patrick	MCGINLEY	04.07.43.
F/O	Frank	MCGLONE	21.07.44.
Sgt	William	MCGUIRE	04.07.43.
F/L	Frederick Charles	MCKENZIE	26.06.43.
F/Sgt	Charles	MCKERNS	21.04.43.
P/O	Joseph Arthur	MCKIM	21.07.44.
F/Sgt	Donald Harvey	MCKITTERICK	03.10.43.
F/O	Richard Edwardes	MacLAREN	13.09.44.
Sgt	Andrew	MCLAUGHLIN	03.10.43.
F/O	Alexander George	McLEAN	31.10.44.
P/O	James Archibald Dunlop	McLEAN	18.02.40.
F/Sgt	Hugh Cole	MACMILLAN	06.09.43.
P/O	Patrick Colin	MCNAIR	23.06.43.
F/Sgt	David William	MEIKLE	12.10.43.
F/O	Robert Bruce	MEIKLEJOHN	22.06.43.
F/Sgt	Stanley	MELLORS	25.06.44.
Sgt	Hugh	MERRILL	08.09.41.
F/O	Thomas	METCALFE	19.02.45.
Sgt	Vernon Ivor	MICHAEL	05.01.45.
F/Sgt	Francis John	MILES	26.02.43.
Sgt	John Ashworth	MILLER	30.08.44.
Sgt	Thomas Richard	MILLER	07.10.43.
Sgt	Andrew Aitken	MILLIGAN	29.04.44.
Sgt	William Andrew Gardner	MILNE	12.09.44.
F/O	Clifford	MITCHELL	09.11.43.
Sgt	Angus McKay	MOLLISON	05.03.43.
P/O	William Greenhalgh	MONK	29.04.43.
Sgt	Alan	MOORE	02.02.45.
W/OII	George Wallace	MOORE	22.09.43.
F/Sgt	Wesley	MOREY	13.05.43.
Sgt	William Alfred	MORGAN	22.09.43.

Rank	Name	Surname	Date
Sgt	William Norman	MORGAN	21.07.44.
Sgt	George	MORRALL	20.02.43.
F/Sgt	Malcolm Lionel Brian	MORRISON	04.07.43.
P/O	John Donald	MORTON	29.07.44.
F/Sgt	William Cuthbert	MORTON	16.02.43.
F/Sgt	Ronald Charles Andrew	MUIR	28.07.41.
Sgt	Dennis Andrew Frederick	MUNDY	11.06.44.
Sgt	Harold	MUNNERY	21.04.43.
Sgt	Desmond Norman	MURPHY	10.03.44.
Sgt	Hugh	MURRAY	04.07.43.
Sgt	William	MURRAY	13.05.43.
Sgt	Francis	MYERS	13.08.44.
Sgt	Robert Brotherstone	NASH	10.05.44.
Sgt	Reginald Percy	NAYLOR	21.07.44.
Sgt	Basil Leonard	NEAL	21.04.43.
Sgt	Harold	NEEDLE	16.08.41
Sgt	Herbert Ernest	NEWMAN	26.08.44.
F/L	John Verdun	NEWTON	14.01.44.
P/O	Harry Samuel	NICKLESS	03.02.45.
Sgt	William Noble	NISBET	25.06.43.
W/O	Denis John	NIXON	02.12.43.
Sgt	Harry	NOAR	15.04.43.
P/O	Edward Albert	NORTON	30.05.43.
Sgt	Frederick John	NOYES	12.09.44.
F/O	Cornelius Frederick	O'CONNELL	26.05.43.
Sgt	George Louvain	ODGERS	06.09.43.
Sgt	Edwin Marley	OFFEN	21.04.43.
Sgt	David Elwyn	OWEN	28.08.43.
Sgt	Frederick Gordon	OWEN	26.08.44.
Sgt	Stanley	OWEN	13.05.43.
Sgt	Cecil Arthur	PAGE	11.06.44.
F/Sgt	Leslie Alfred	PAGE	19.02.45.
P/O	Charles Dixon	PALMER	09.03.45.
Sgt	Robert John	PALMER	15.04.43.
Sgt	Cyril George	PARR	20.02.43.
Sgt	Edward Lionel	PARRISH	26.02.44.
F/O	Frederick Arthur	PARTON	04.02.43.
F/O	John Charles	PATON	09.03.45.
Sgt	Ronald	PAYTON	22.09.43.
Sgt	Bernard	PEARCE	23.05.44.
P/O	Trevor Anthony	PEELER	16.10.39.

Rank	Name	Surname	Date
Sgt	William John	PENHALIGON	10.05.44.
P/O	Anthony Lambert	PERRETT	12.09.44.
P/O	Herbert Norman	PETERS	22.06.43.
F/Sgt	Leo	PETERSEN	25.06.43.
Sgt	George	PETTINGER	26.02.43.
W/O	Charles	PHILLIPS	28.08.43.
F/Sgt	Ralph Clifford George	PHILLIPS	12.09.44.
Sgt	Jack	PICTON	23.06.43.
F/L	Robert Charles	PLATT	04.07.43.
F/Sgt	Charles Leslie	POLLARD	15.10.44.
Sgt	William John	POLLARD	12.10.43.
Sgt	Kenneth William	POLLITT	20.10.43.
W/OII	Ernest Sinclair	POLLON	26.05.43.
Sgt	William Charles	POMFRET	29.07.44.
Sgt	James Thomas	POOLEY	05.05.43.
Sgt	John Smith	PORTER	23.06.43.
Sgt	Eric Bradley	POTTER	14.07.43.
F/Sgt	James Leeman	POULTER	26.05.43.
Sgt	Dennis Howitt	POWELL	20.02.43.
Sgt	James Henry	POWELL	11.04.44.
Sgt	Stephen	POWER	09.03.45.
F/L	Antony Seton Wombwell	PRIOLEAU	21.04.43.
Sgt	Philip Stanley	PUGH	28.07.41.
Sgt	Cecil Joseph	PURCELL	24.08.43.
F/Sgt	Leonard Sidney	QUELCH	13.04.44.
F/Sgt	Clarke Edward	QUICKFALL	02.12.43.
Sgt	John Francis	QUICKFALL	24.08 43.
Sgt	William Halkett	RAMSAY	15.03.44.
Sgt	Eric	RAMSBOTTOM	15.10.44.
Sgt	Henry	RANDALL	27.08.44.
Sgt	Ronald	RAVEN	30.05.43.
Sgt	Dennis Kenneth	RAY	23.04.44.
Sgt	Cyril	REDDELL	04.07.43.
Sgt	Basil Horace	REEVE	29.04.43.
F/Sgt	Alexander Millson	REID	31.07.43.
Sgt	Reginald James	RENTON	06.09.43.
Sgt	Kenneth Christopher	RICHARDS	26.08.44.
Sgt	John Wilson	RICHARDSON	19.11.43.
Sgt	Peter Harry	RICHARDSON	21.07.44.
F/O	Frederick Charles	RILEY	08.08.44.
W/O	Edward Charles	ROBERTS	25.06.44.

Rank	Name	Surname	Date
Sgt	Donald Hubert	ROBINSON	13.05.43.
S/L	David Alan Hope	ROBSON	22.06.41
F/Sgt	James Allan	ROBSON	23.06.43.
F/Sgt	Alan	RODD	10.06.44.
F/L	Robert Young	RODGER	09.11.43.
W/OII	Joseph Jean Paul Adrien	RODRIGUE	26.02.44.
F/O	David Albert Alton	ROMANS	08.09.41.
Sgt	Ronald Vivian Steven	ROOKE	28.02.43.
F/O	George Frederick	ROSE	12.09.44.
W/OII	Willard Kennedy	ROSENBERRY	16.02.43.
F/L	Philip John	ROSSINGTON	21.07.44.
Sgt	Gordon	ROYSTON	29.01.44.
Sgt	Ronald George	RUNYARD	10.05.44.
Sgt	Edward John	RYAN	08.08.44.
F/Sgt	Charles Little	SAUNDERCOCK	26.05.43.
Sgt	Cyril Thomas	SAYER	28.06.44.
Sgt	Derrick Balcombe	SAYER	20.02.43.
Sgt	Frederick George	SCARR	28.08.43.
Sgt	Max	SCHEDDLE	04.07.43.
F/Sgt	Lester Charles	SCHMIDT	03.10.43.
P/O	Albert Bloomer	SCHOLEY	20.02.43.
Sgt	John Patrick	SEDDON	29.01.44.
F/Sgt	Victor James	SHARP	28.09.43.
Sgt	Leslie	SHARPEN	23.05.44.
Sgt	Edwin Arthur	SHAW	15.04.43.
Sgt	Royce Selwyn	SHAW	13.05.43.
Sgt	Donald Brian	SHEEHAN	23.04.44.
Sgt	Ernest francis	SHERWIN	10.06.44.
Sgt	Norman	SHIELD	21.04.43.
F/O	Lloyd Elmer	SIBBALD	24.08.43.
Sgt	Alec	SIMMONS	15.02.43.
P/o	Arthur Vernon	SIMMONS	26.08.44.
Sgt	John William	SIMPSON	21.07.44.
P/O	Ross McCulloch	SIMPSON	18.11.43.
F/Sgt	Stuart Edward	SIMPSON	19.11.43.
F/Sgt	Herbert David Platten	SLEATH	08.09.41.
Sgt	Alfred Burford	SLEEP	30.08.44.
F/Sgt	Roy Victor Edward	SLOWLEY	12.09.44.
P/O	Albert Richard George	SMALL	31.07.43.
Sgt	Eric John	SMALLDON	16.09.44
F/Sgt	Alan	SMEE	09.03.45.

Rank	Name	Surname	Date
Sgt	Douglas James	SMITH	28.06.44.
F/Sgt	Frederick William	SMITH	03.10.43.
P/O	Geoffrey Charles	SMITH	04.07.43.
F/Sgt	Lees	SMITH	09.11.43.
F/L	Leonard Anthony	SMITH	19.11.43.
Sgt	Roy	SMITH	28.07.41.
W/O	Sidney Walter	SMITH	06.09.43.
F/Sgt	Walter Perry	SMITH	28.06.44.
Sgt	Ronald Edward	SNELLING	27.08.44.
P/O	Jack William	SNOOK	19.11.43.
P/O	Ronald	SOUTH	09.03.45.
P/O	Vernon Enright	SPAIN	28.02.43.
F/Sgt	Harold Omond	SPENCE	20.10.43.
F/Sgt	Ervine Eugene	SPENCER	20.10.43.
F/Sgt	Joseph Vernon	SPRING	15.03.44.
F/O	Richard Edmund	STAINBANK	12.09.44.
Sgt	Clifford	STAPLETON	12.09.44.
F/Sgt	John Minorgan	STEEL	25.06.43.
Sgt	Harry Ernest	STEELE	02.12.43.
P/O	Gerald	STEPHENS	04.02.43.
W/OII	Lloyd Martin	STORMER	24.08.43.
Sgt	Dennis	STOWE	21.04.43.
Sgt	Paul Gilbert	STRAKER	23.09.43.
W/OII	George Edward	STRINGER	26.02.44.
Sgt	Douglas Charles	SULLIVAN	03.10.43.
F/L	David Hugh	SUMSION	30.08.44.
F/O	Paul Douglas	SWALLOW	14.07.43.
Sgt	Robert	SWAN	02.02.45.
Sgt	Sandom	SWEET	05.05.43.
F/Sgt	Eric Whitton	SYKES	18.11.43.
ACII	Harold Ernest	SYMONDS	07.05.44.
P/O	Lionel William	TABOR	15.02.43.
Sgt	Lancelot	TAGG	21.04.43.
Sgt	Kenneth Gordon	TAYLOR	03.10.43.
Sgt	Patrick James	TAYLOR	25.06.43.
Sgt	William Arthur	TAYLOR	25.06.43.
Sgt	Harry	TAYLORSON	25.06.43.
F/Sgt	Walter Henry	TEEDE	25.06.43.
F/Sgt	Kenneth	TEMPEST	27.08.44.
F/L	George Atherton	THATCHER	10.06.44.
Sgt	Benjamin James	THOMAS	23.09.43.

F/O	David Selwyn	THOMAS	16.09.44.
Sgt	Alan	THOMPSON	23.06.43.
Sgt	Patrick John	THOMPSON	12.09.44.
Sgt	Bernard	THORPE	09.10.43.
W/O	Glyn Anthony	TIMLIN	12.11.43.
P/O	Cyril James	TODD	28.06.44.
Sgt	Alan St. John	TOLLITT.	25.06.44.
Sgt	Harry Peer	TOMLINSON	08.08.44.
F/O	Paul William	TOOLEY	16.09.44.
Sgt	Walter Eric	TOPPING	13.04.44.
F/Sgt	Jack	TOWERS	29.04.44.
W/OII	John	TRAIN	02.02.45.
Sgt	Edward George	TRUMAN	23.09.43.
F/Sgt	John Martin	TURACHEK	30.08.44.
Sgt	Joseph	TURNER	31.10.44.
Sgt	Leopold	URRY	13.05.43.
F/Sgt	Owen Neville	USSHER	18.11.43.
Sgt	Kenneth William	VALENTINE	15.02.43.
Sgt	Richard	WADSWORTH	26.05.43.
Sgt	Arnold	WALKER	23.04.44.
Sgt	David Alexander Robertson	WALKER	28.10.44.
F/Sgt	Kenneth Charles	WALKER	13.06.44.
P/O	Philip Alsop	WALKER	27.04.43.
Sgt	Charles Peter	WALLER	11.04.44.
F/O	Albert Baulcombe	WALLIS	31.07.43.
Sgt	William Edward	WALTER	26.06.43
F/L	John	WARD	31.10.44.
Sgt	William Alexander Fernie	WATSON	13.04.44.
F/Sgt	Victor Alfred	WEAVER	24.08.43.
Sgt	George Leonard	WEBB	02.02.45.
Sgt	Frank Alan	WELLS	30.05.43.
Sgt	Wilfred	WHALLEY	23.05.44.
Sgt	Reginald	WHITFORD	12.10.43.
Sgt	Ronald Gordon	WHITMARSH	02.12.43.
F/Sgt	Eric Charles	WHITTALL	27.08.44.
Sgt	Roy	WHITTINGTON	16.09.44.
F/Sgt	John	WHYTE	23.05.44.
Sgt	John Charles	WIGGIN	08.08.44.
Sgt	Robert	WILKIN	08.09.41.
F/Sgt	Victor Lawrence	WILKINSON	13.09.44.
Sgt	Herbert Francis	WILLCOCKS	13.04.44.

F/Sgt	Gordon Deane	WILLIAMS	21.07.44.
F/L	Henry Arthur Wellington	WILLIAMS	02.02.45.
Sgt	Richard Thompson	WILLIAMS	04.02.43.
F/Sgt	William Frederick	WILLIAMS	10.03.44.
Sgt	Robert	WILLIS	08.09.41.
Sgt	Thomas James	WILLS	22.06.41.
Sgt	David Millar	WILLMOTT	13.06.44.
Sgt	Ernest	WILSON	26.06.43.
P/O	Hugh	WILSON	26.08.44.
Sgt	Joseph	WILSON	27.04.43.
Sgt	Robert	WILSON	09.11.43.
F/Sgt	Stanley Alan	WILSON	13.04.44.
P/O	Ronald John	WINCHESTER	13.09.44.
ACII	Kenneth Charles	WINTERTON	23.03.40.
Sgt	Frederick George John	WOOD	12.09.44.
F/Sgt	John	WOOD	06.02.43.
Sgt	Herbert Henry	WOODING	25.06.44
Sgt	Frank Ernest	WORSLEY	01.09.43.
F/O	Arnold Edwin	WYTON	09.10.43.
Sgt	George Arthur	YATES	20.10.43.
F/L	Keith Riley	YATES	09.10.43.
F/O	William Hector John	YEO	24.08.43.
P/O	Gordon William	YOUNG	26.05.43.
Sgt	Norman Albert	YOUNG	26.07.43.

90 Squadron

Motto Celer (Swift) **Codes** WP/XY

Stations

WATTON	07.05.41. to 15.05.41.
BODNEY (Detachment)	12.05.41. to 15.05.41.
WEST RAYNHAM	15.05.41. to 28.06.41.
GREAT MASSINGHAM (Detachment)	15.05.41. to 28.06.41.
POLEBROOK	28.06.41. to 14.02.42.
BOTTESFORD	07.11.42. to 29.12.42.
RIDGEWELL	29.12.42. to 31.05.43.
WRATTING COMMON (formerly West Wickham)	31.05.43. to 13.10.43.
TUDDENHAM	13.10.43. to 31.05.46.

Commanding Officers

WING COMMANDER J MACDOUGALL	07.05.41. to 26.07.41.
WING COMMANDER P F WEBSTER	26.07.41. to 21.11.41.
WING COMMANDER J G W SWAIN	21.11.41. to 12.02.42.
WING COMMANDER J C CLAYDON	07.11.42. to 07.06.43.
WING COMMANDER J H GILES	07.06.43. to 12.43.
WING COMMANDER G T WYNNE-POWELL	12.43. to 09.01.44.
WING COMMANDER F M MILLIGAN	09.01.44. to 24.06.44.
WING COMMANDER A J OGILVIE	24.06.44. to 15.01.45.
WING COMMANDER P F DUNHAM	15.01.45. to 19.02.45.
WING COMMANDER E G SCOTT	26.02.45. to 10.45.

Aircraft

B17C FORTRESS I	05.41. to 02.42.
STIRLING I	12.41. to 05.43.
STIRLING III	02.43. to 06.44.
LANCASTER I/III	05.44. to 12.47

Operational Record

OPERATIONS	SORTIES	AIRCRAFT LOSSES	% LOSSES
412	4613	86	1.9

CATEGORY OF OPERATIONS

BOMBING/SOE	MINING
293	119

2 GROUP

OPERATIONS	SORTIES	AIRCRAFT LOSSES	% LOSSES
20	52	3	5.6

3 GROUP

OPERATIONS	SORTIES	AIRCRAFT LOSSES	% LOSSES
392	4561	83	1.8

CATEGORY OF OPERATIONS

BOMBING/SOE	MINING
273	119

3 GROUP STIRLINGS

OPERATIONS	SORTIES	AIRCRAFT LOSSES	% LOSSES
211	1937	58	3.0

CATEGORY OF OPERATIONS

BOMBING/SOE	MINING
111	100

3 GROUP LANCASTERS

OPERATIONS	SORTIES	AIRCRAFT LOSSES	% LOSSES
181	2624	25	1.0

CATEGORY OF OPERATIONS

BOMBING	MINING
162	19

Aircraft Histories

B17C FORTRESS From May 1941 to February 1942.

AN518 WP-B	To 220 Squadron.
AN519 WP-H	To Aeroplane and Armament Experimental Establishment.
AN520	To 220 Squadron.
AN521	To 220 Squadron.
AN522	Broke up in the air over Yorkshire during air-test 22.6.41.
AN523 WP-D	Crash-landed at Roborough, Plymouth on return from Brest 16.8.41.
AN525 WP-D	FTR Oslo Norway 8.9.41.
AN526 WP-G	Became ground instruction machine October 1942.
AN527	To 220 Squadron.
AN528	Destroyed by fire on the ground at Polebrook 3.7.41.
AN529 WP-C	To Middle East.
AN530 WP-F	To 220 Squadron.
AN531	To 220 Squadron.
AN532 WP-J	To 220 Squadron.
AN533 WP-N	FTR Oslo Norway 8.9.41.
AN534	Broke up in the air over Northamptonshire while on air-test 28.7.41.
AN535 WP-O	Crash-landed at Kinloss on return from Oslo Norway 8.9.41.
AN536 WP-M	To 220 Squadron.
AN537	To 220 Squadron.

STIRLING. From December 1942 to June 1944.

R9198	From 214 (Federated Malay Staes) Squadron. To 1665 Conversion Unit.
R9256 WP-G	To 1651 Conversion Unit.
R9271 WP-Q	From 149 (East India) Squadron. FTR Essen 5/6.3.43.
R9276 WP-G	From 149 (East India) Squadron. FTR Wilhelmshaven 19/20.2.43.
R9306 WP-J	From 7 Squadron via 7 Squadron Conversion Flight. Crashed in Dorset on return from Lorient 16.2.43.
R9349 WP-U	From 218 (Gold Coast) Squadron. FTR St-Nazaire 28.2/1.3.43.
W7510	From 149 (East India) Squadron. To 1657 Conversion Unit.
W7575	From 214 (Federated Malay Staes) Squadron. To 1657 Conversion Unit.
W7623	From Controller of Research and Development. To 1665 Conversion Unit.
W7627 WP-A/E	From 214 (Federated Malay states) Squadron. Crashed on take-off from Ridgewell while training 18.3.43.
BF324 WP-H	From 214 (Federated Malay States) Squadron. To 1657 Conversion Unit.
BF346 WP-G	From 218 (Gold Coast) Squadron. FTR from mining sortie 28/29.4.43.
BF376	From XV Squadron. To 1657 Conversion Unit.
BF383 WP-T	FTR Duisburg 26/27.4.43.

BF404 WP-A	From 218 (Gold Coast) Squadron. To 214 (Federated Malay States) Squadron.
BF407 WP-S	To 1657 Conversion Unit.
BF409 WP-R	Crashed on landing at Ridgewell while training 5.4.43.
BF410 WP-E	FTR Nuremberg 25/26.2.43.
BF414 WP-F/R	Crashed on landing at Ridgewell while training 19.5.43.
BF415 WP-S	FTR Hamburg 3/4.2.43.
BF435 WP-X	From XV Squadron. To 1657 Conversion Unit.
BF438 WP-D	FTR Cologne 14/15.2.43.
BF442 WP-K	FTR Rostock 20/21.4.43.
BF449 WP-J	Crashed on landing at Ridgewell following early return from mining sortie 9.3.43.
BF454 WP-W	Crashed on take-off from Ridgewell while training 13.4.43.
BF460	To XV Squadron.
BF462 WP-P	FTR Stuttgart 14/15.4.43.
BF463 WP-Q	FTR Rostock 20/21.4.43.
BF464 WP-E	To 570 Squadron.
BF466	To 214 (Federated Malay States) Squadron.
BF471 WP-L	Crash-landed near Manston on return from Frankfurt 11.4.43.
BF473 WP-D	From 218 (Gold Coast) Squadron. To 75(NZ) Squadron.
BF503	From 149 (East India) Squadron. To 620 Squadron.
BF504 WP-F	Crashed on landing at West Wickham (Wratting Common) on return from Cologne 4.7.43.
BF508 WP-S	FTR Rostock 20/21.4.43.
BF521	To XV Squadron.
BF523 WP-G	FTR Duisburg 12/13.5.43.
BF524 WP-N/U	FTR from Special Operations Executive (SOE) sortie to France 8/9.5.44.
BF526 WP-R/G	From 7 Squadron. To 1651 Conversion Unit.
BF527 WP-K	To 1657 Conversion Unit.
BF529	To 196 Squadron.
BF532 WP-W	From 7 Squadron. To 1657 Conversion Unit.
BF566 WP-T/G	FTR Hanover 22/23.9.43.
BF574 WP-F	From 214 (Federated Malay States) Squadron. To 1660 Conversion Unit.
BK598 WP-N	From 149 (East India) Squadron. To 1657 Conversion Unit.
BK625 WP-D	Crash-landed at Ridgewell while training 29.12.42.
BK626 WP-C/W	Crash-landed at Shipdham on return from air-sea rescue sortie 25.5.43.
BK627 WP-F/P	FTR Wilhelmshaven 19/20.2.43.
BK628 WP-G	FTR Wuppertal 24/25.6.43.
BK644 WP-T	FTR from mining sortie 5/6.2.43.
BK655 XY-X	FTR Bremen 8/9.10.43.
BK661 WP-O	FTR Duisburg 12/13.5.43.
BK665 WP-V/D	From 149 (East India) Squadron. FTR Mülheim 22/23.6.43.
BK693 WP-A	To 214 (Federated Malay States) Squadron and back. Crashed on landing at Stradishall on return from Hamburg 28.7.43.

BK718	WP-M	FTR Cologne 3/4.7.43.
BK723	WP-D	From 7 Squadron. FTR Kassel 3/4.10.43.
BK725	WP-M	FTR Mannheim 16/17.4.43.
BK775	WP-H	FTR Remscheid 30/31.7.43.
BK779	WP-L	From 7 Squadron. FTR Berlin 23/24.8.43.
BK780	WP-L	Crashed on landing at Ridgewell while training 25.4.43.
BK781	WP-E/O	To 149 (East India) Squadron.
BK784	WP-P/O/M	Crashed in Cambridgeshire soon after take-off for a mining sortie 23.5.44.
BK804	WP-J	FTR Mülheim 22/23.6.43.
BK811	WP-V	To 1653 Conversion Unit.
BK813	WP-O	FTR Wuppertal 24/25.6.43.
BK814	WP-T	FTR Dortmund 4/5.5.43.
BK816	WP-B	From 199 Squadron. To 149 (East India) Squadron.
EE871	WP-Q	From 214 (Federated Malay States) Squadron. FTR Berlin 31.8/1.9.43.
EE873	WP-D	FTR Aachen 13/14.7.43.
EE887	WP-T	FTR Krefeld 21/22.6.43.
EE889		To 190 Squadron.
EE896	WP-J/O	To 1653 Conversion Unit.
EE900	WP-Y	To 190 Squadron.
EE901	XY-U	From 214 (Federated Malay States) Squadron. FTR Kassel 3/4.10.43.
EE904	WP-S	FTR Essen 25/26.7.43.
EE916	WP-F	Crashed on take-off from West Wickham (Wratting Common) when bound for Hamburg 29.7.43.
EE939		To 1651 Conversion Unit.
EE951	WP-B	Crashed on take-off from Wratting Common (formerly West Wickham) for air-test 3.9.43.
EE952	WP-F	Crashed near Cambridge on return from Hannover 28.9.43.
EE974	WP-M	From XV Squadron. Abandoned over Suffolk on return from SOE sortie to France 28/29.4.44.
EF129	WP-Q	FTR Mannheim 5/6.9.43.
EF147	WP-J	FTR from SOE sortie to France 5/6.3.44.
EF159	WP-B	From 620 Squadron. FTR Laon 22/23.4.44.
EF162	WP-K	FTR from SOE sortie to France 12/13.4.44.
EF179	WP-V	Ditched off Cromer on return from a mining sortie 8.10.43.
EF182	WP-V/M	To 1651 Conversion Unit.
EF183	WP-Z	From XV Squadron. To 1657 Conversion Unit.
EF188	WP-Z	To 149 (East India) Squadron.
EF191	WP-H	FTR from mining sortie 1/2.12.43.
EF193	WP-Q	To 149 (East India) Squadron.
EF196	WP-L	To 1651 Conversion Unit.
EF198	WP-F/H	Crashed in Suffolk on return from mining sortie 25/26.2.44.
EF251	WP-P	From 75(NZ) Squadron. To 1653 Conversion Unit.
EF254	XY-Q	From 75(NZ) Squadron. FTR from SOE sortie to France 9/10.5.44.
EF294	WP-B	FTR from SOE sortie to France 2/3.6.44.
EF302		To 1651 Conversion Unit.

EF328	Crash-landed at Ridgewell after early return from mining sortie 8/9.3.43.
EF334 WP-U	To 1657 Conversion Unit.
EF336	To 149 (East India) Squadron.
EF346 WP-G	From 218 (Gold Coast) Squadron. To 1665 Conversion Unit.
EF349 WP-Y	From 218 (Gold Coast) Squadron. FTR Wuppertal 29/30.5.43.
EF397 WP-K	Crashed near Stradishall on return from Wuppertal 30.5.43.
EF426 WP-S/W	Crashed while landing at Wratting Common during air-test 12.10.43.
EF431 WP-X	To 149 (East India) Squadron.
EF439 WP-C/H	FTR Nuremberg 27/28.8.43.
EF441 WP-G	To 1653 Conversion Unit.
EF443 XY-M	FTR from mining sortie 28/29.1.44.
EF446 WP-O	To 570 Squadron.
EF458 XY-Y	From 75(NZ) Squadron. FTR Mannheim 23/24.9.43.
EF459	From XV Squadron. To 199 Squadron.
EF497 WP-L	Crashed in Oxfordshire during air-test 20.10.43.
EF509 XY-X	FTR from SOE sortie to France 9/10.5.44.
EF510	To 1654 Conversion Unit.
EF511 WP-C	Crashed near Bury-St-Edmonds on return from mining sortie 26.11.43.
EH876 WP-J	FTR Düsseldorf 25/26.5.43.
EH900 WP-Y	FTR Gelsenkirchen 25/26.6.43.
EH906 XY-T	FTR from SOE sortie to France 4/5.3.44.
EH907 WP-O	FTR Cologne 3/4.7.43.
EH908 WP-R/U	Crashed in Suffolk while training 12.11.43.
EH937 WP-S	FTR Berlin 23/24.8.43.
EH939 WP-P	From 75(NZ) Squadron. To 1653 Conversion Unit.
EH944 WP-A	Crash-landed at Lakenheath on return from Hannover 23.9.43.
EH947 XY-S	From 75(NZ) Squadron. Crashed in Suffolk on return from SOE sortie 10/11.4.44.
EH958 WP-O	To 1660 Conversion Unit.
EH982 WP-Y	To 218 (Gold Coast) Squadron.
EH989 WP-N/P	Crashed in Northamptonshire after collision with an OTU Wellington on return from Amiens 15/16.3.44.
EH996 WP-H	FTR Mannheim 18/19.11.43.
EJ115 WP-K	From 199 Squadron. To 149 (East India) Squadron.
EJ122 WP-E	To 149 (East India) Squadron.
LJ460 WP-E/XY-U	FTR from SOE sortie to France 10/11.4.44.
LJ470 WP-C	To 1332CU.
LJ477 WP-L	From 214 (Federated Malay States) Squadron. To 149 (East India) Squadron.
LJ483 XY-V	From 1657 Conversion Unit. FTR from SOE sortie to France 12/13.4.44.
LJ506 WP-F	To 218 (Gold Coast) Squadron.
LJ509 WP-F	From 214 (Federated Malay States) Squadron. FTR from SOE sortie to France 10/11.3.44.
LJ579 WP-O	To Empire Central Flying School.

LJ581	To 1654 Conversion Unit.
LJ625	To 218 (Gold Coast) Squadron.
LK379 WP-F	FTR Mannheim 18/19.11.43.
LK380 WP-Y XY-Y	Crashed near Mildenhall after collision with a Hurricane while training 9.11.43.
LK383 WP-W	To 149 (East India) Squadron.
LK392 WP-A	To 149 (East India) Squadron.
LK516 WP-J	From 149 (East India) Squadron. To 1651 Conversion Unit.
LK568	From 149 (East India) Squadron. To 218 (Gold Coast) Squadron.
LK569	To 1651 Conversion Unit.
LK570	To 1651 Conversion Unit.
LK571	To 1653 Conversion Unit.
MZ262 WP-K	Crashed in Suffolk when bound for Hannover 22.9.43.

LANCASTER. **From May 1944.**

L7532	From 3 Lancaster Finishing School. No operations. To 1656 Conversion Unit.
R5514	From 3 Lancaster Finishing School.
R5631	From 3 Lancaster Finishing School. Became ground instruction machine.
R5692	From 75(NZ) Squadron. To 3 Lancaster Finishing School.
R5845	From 3 Lancaster Finishing School. To 1656 Conversion Unit.
W4885	From 15 Squadron via 5 Lancaster Finishing School.
W4980 WP-R	From 15 Squadron via 3 Lancaster Finishing School. To 1661 Conversion Unit.
HK602 WP-E/X	FTR Walcheren 29.10.44.
HK603 WP-E/D	FTR Ludwigshafen 5.1.45.
HK604 WP-G	FTR Kiel 26/27.8.44.
HK605 WP-A	FTR Frankfurt 12/13.9.44.
HK606 WP-Y XY-V	To 186 Squadron.
HK607 WP-Y	To 1654 Conversion Unit.
HK608 WP-G/P	Force-landed in Allied territory on return from Gelsenkirchen 19.3.45.
HK609 WP-F	To 10 Maintenance Unit.
HK610 WP-Z	Collided with PD336 (90 Squadron) and crashed near Bury-St-Edmonds when bound for Wiesbaden 2.2.45.
HK611	To 10 Maintenance Unit.
HK613 WP-Y XY-Y	To 186 Squadron.
HK622	From 15 Squadron. To 186 Squadron.
HK625	From 15 Squadron. To 10 Maintenance Unit.
HK664 WP-V	FTR Trier 23.12.44.
HK685	
HK692	To 186 Squadron.
HK694	To 186 Squadron.

HK696	To 115 Squadron.
LM110	To 15 Squadron.
LM111 WP-C/G	FTR Mare de Magne 7/8.8.44.
LM128 WP-Y	Crashed in Suffolk on return from Stettin 29/30.8.44.
LM157 WP-C	Crash-landed near Newmarket during an air-test 6.2.45.
LM158 WP-P	FTR Gelsenkirchen 12/13.6.44.
LM159 WP-H	
LM160 XY-W	To 186 Squadron.
LM164 WP-V XY-V	FTR Mare de Magne 7/8.8.44.
LM165 WP-T	FTR Duisburg 14/15.10.44.
LM169 WP-R^2	FTR Moerdyk 16/17.9.44.
LM179 WP-M	FTR Rimeux 24/25.6.44.
LM183 WP-L	FTR Homberg 20/21.7.44.
LM184 WP-K	FTR Stettin 29/30.8.44.
LM185 WP-D	FTR Homberg 20/21.7.44.
LM187	To 218 (Gold Coast) Squadron.
LM188 WP-S XY-S	To 186 Squadron.
LM189 WP-U	FTR Homberg 20/21.7.44.
LM280 WP-F	
LM575	To 15 Squadron.
LM576	To 15 Squadron.
LM588 WP-W/F	FTR Rüsselsheim 25/26.8.44.
LM615 WP-B	To 1653 Conversion Unit.
LM617 WP-X XY-X	Completed 58 operations.
LM618 WP-U XY-U	To 186 Squadron.
LM692 XY-R	From 149 (East India) Squadron. To 186 Squadron
ME802 WP-S	FTR Rüsselsheim 25/26.8.44.
ME838 WP-D	FTR from mining sortie 11/12.9.44.
ME852 WP-Q	FTR Brunswick 12/13.8.44.
ME860	To 218 (Gold Coast) Squadron.
ME862	To 625 Squadron.
ND387	From 7 Squadron. Shot down by intruder near Woolfox Lodge on return from a mining sortie 4.3.45.
NE145 WP-K/D	Shot down by an intruder over Suffolk on return from Biennais 27/28.6.44.
NE149 WP-A	FTR Dreux 10/11.6.44.
NE177 WP-H	FTR Dreux 10/11.6.44.
NE178	To 1651 Conversion Unit.
NF987 XY-R	
NG137 XY-D	
NG138 WP-C/U	
NG140	

NG146		
NG148	XY-B	
NG149	XY-D	
NG175		To 186 Squadron.
NG176	XY-H	To 186 Squadron.
NG306	WP-B	
NG323	WP-G	Crashed on landing at Tuddenham while in transit from Lossiemouth 21.12.44.
NG408		From Telecommunications Flying Unit.
NG465		From Signals Intelligence Unit.
NG467		From Signals Intelligence Unit.
NN698	WP-U XY-A	FTR Cologne (crash-landed in France) 27.11.44.
NN720	XY-K	
NN753		
NN761	WP-V	From 115 Squadron.
NN762	WP-V/Y	From 115 Squadron.
NN783	WP-E	
PA158	WP-S	FTR Dortmund 3/4.2.45.
PA159	WP-V	To 1651 Conversion Unit.
PA167	WP-K	
PA193		
PA239	WP-S	
PA252		
PA253	WP-B/Z	
PA254	WP-C/A	FTR Datteln 9.3.45.
PB193	WP-N	FTR Frankfurt 12/13.9.44.
PB196	WP-A	To 195 Squadron.
PB198	WP-M	FTR Stuttgart 28/29.7.44.
PB204	WP-R	To 1653 Conversion Unit.
PB488		From 149 (East India) Squadron. To 186 Squadron.
PD269	WP-Q	FTR Bottrop 31.10.44.
PD336	WP-P	Collided with HK610 (90 Squadron) over Suffolk when bound for Wiesbaden 2.2.45. and landed safely. FTR Wesel 19.2.45.
PD341	WP-P	FTR Wilhelmshaven 15/16.10.44.
PD400		From 115 Squadron.
PD402	WP-G	From 115 Squadron.
PD430	WP-A	
PD433	WP-P/R	
PP679		To 138 Squadron.
PP680	WP-D	
PP682	WP-J	
RF184	WP-C	From 15 Squadron.
RF185	WP-T	From 15 Squadron.
SW267		To 186 Squadron.
SW272		To 186 Squadron.

SW275   To 186 Squadron.

HEAVIEST SINGLE LOSS.

20/21.04.43. Rostock.   3 Stirlings FTR.
22/23.09.43. Hannover.   1 Stirling FTR 2 crashed.
20/21.07.44. Homberg.   3 Lancasters FTR.

www.ingramcontent.com/pod-product-compliance
Lightning Source LLC
Chambersburg PA
CBHW080423230426
43662CB00015B/2199